KEEPING CANADA RUNNING

McGill-Queen's/Brian Mulroney Institute of Government Studies in Leadership, Public Policy, and Governance

Series editor: Donald E. Abelson

Titles in this series address critical issues facing Canada at home and abroad and the efforts policymakers at all levels of government have made to address a host of complex and multifaceted policy concerns. Books in this series receive financial support from the Brian Mulroney Institute of Government at St Francis Xavier University; in keeping with the institute's mandate, these studies explore how leaders involved in key policy initiatives arrived at their decisions and what lessons can be learned. Combining rigorous academic analysis with thoughtful recommendations, this series compels readers to think more critically about how and why elected officials make certain policy choices, and how, in concert with other stakeholders, they can better navigate an increasingly complicated and crowded marketplace of ideas.

Keeping Canada Running

Infrastructure and the Future of Governance in a Pandemic World

G. BRUCE DOERN, CHRISTOPHER STONEY,
AND ROBERT HILTON

McGill-Queen's University Press
Montreal & Kingston • London • Chicago

© McGill-Queen's University Press 2021

ISBN 978-0-2280-0656-5 (cloth)
ISBN 978-0-2280-0657-2 (paper)
ISBN 978-0-2280-0724-1 (ePDF)
ISBN 978-0-2280-0725-8 (ePUB)

Legal deposit third quarter 2021
Bibliothèque nationale du Québec

Printed in Canada on acid-free paper that is 100% ancient forest free
(100% post-consumer recycled), processed chlorine free

We acknowledge the support of the Canada Council for the Arts.

Nous remercions le Conseil des arts du Canada de son soutien.

Library and Archives Canada Cataloguing in Publication

Title: Keeping Canada running: infrastructure and the future of governance
in a pandemic world / G. Bruce Doern, Christopher Stoney, and Robert
Hilton.

Names: Doern, G. Bruce, author. | Stoney, Christopher, author. | Hilton,
Robert (Lecturer in public policy), author.

Series: McGill-Queen's/Brian Mulroney Institute of Government studies
in leadership, public policy, and governance; 3.

Description: Series statement: McGill-Queen's/Brian Mulroney Institute
of Government studies in leadership, public policy, and governance; 3 |
Includes bibliographical references and index.

Identifiers: Canadiana (print) 20210214333 | Canadiana (ebook)
20210214465 | ISBN 9780228006565 (cloth) | ISBN 9780228006572
(paper) | ISBN 9780228007241 (ePDF) | ISBN 9780228007258 (ePUB)

Subjects: LCSH: Infrastructure (Economics)—Government policy—Canada.

Classification: LCC HC120.C3 D64 2021 | DDC 363.0971—dc23

This book was typeset by Marquis Interscript in 10.5/13 Sabon.

Contents

Figures and Tables

Preface

This book is the product of the authors' work on infrastructure policy and governance in Canada and internationally over the last five decades. During this extensive period of teaching, reading, discussion, research, and interviews, we owe numerous debts of thanks, gratitude, and learning to many individuals and to many agencies and institutions involved directly and indirectly with the story of Canadian infrastructure policy, governance, and democracy.

We are also grateful to many infrastructure policy academics and practitioners from across Canada and internationally. We have drawn on their scholarly research which we cite and debate throughout the book. In particular, we would like to thank colleagues such as Michael Prince and John Coleman, whose research, ideas, or comments on drafts of the book manuscript chapters have informed and strengthened this book. We also thank the two scholars who were the peer reviewers asked by McGill-Queen's University Press to review our research.

A continuing intellectual and personal set of thanks are owed to colleagues and staff at our home academic and research institutions, the School of Public Policy and Administration at Carleton University in Ottawa and the Politics Department, University of Exeter in the UK. We also owe a debt of special thanks to Joan Doern for her computer and editing expertise.

G. Bruce Doern, Christopher Stoney,
and Robert Hilton

Abbreviations

ACOA	Atlantic Canada Opportunities Agency
ACST	Advisory Council on Science and Technology
AECL	Atomic Energy of Canada Ltd
AER	Alberta Energy Regulator
AEUB	Alberta Energy and Utilities Board
AFP	alternative financing and procurement
AG	Auditor General
AHSTF	Alberta Heritage Savings Trust Fund
BCF	Building Canada Fund
BDC	Business Development Canada
BIRS	Banff International Research Station
BRT	Bus Rapid Transit
CANARIE	Canadian Network for the Advancement of Research, Industry and Education
CANCEA	Canadian Centre for Economic Analysis
CC	Compute Canada
CCA	Canadian Construction Association
CCGS	Canadian Coast Guard ship
CCOHS	Canadian Centre for Occupational Health and Safety
CCPPP	Canadian Council for Public-Private Partnerships
CCS	carbon capture and storage
CDL	Creative Destruction Lab
CDP	Community Development Partnership
CEI	critical energy infrastructure
CEPA	Canadian Energy Pipeline Association
CER	Canada Energy Regulator

CESD	Commissioner of the Environment and Sustainable Development
CETA	Canada-EU Trade Agreement
CFI	Canada Foundation for Innovation
CFIB	Canadian Federation of Independent Business
CFM	Canadian Federation of Municipalities
CFMM	Canadian Federation of Mayors and Municipalities
CIB	Canada Infrastructure Bank
CIHR	Canadian Institutes of Health Research
CIRC	Canadian Infrastructure Report Card
CIWP	Canada Infrastructure Works Program
CLS	Canadian Light Source
CMA	Census Metropolitan Area
CMHC	Canada Mortgage and Housing Corporation
CN	Canadian National Railway
CNRS	Canadian Nuclear Safety Commission
CPC	Canadian Polar Commission
CPP	Canadian Pension Plan
CPPIB	Canada Pension Plan Investment Board
CPR	Canadian Pacific Railway
CRA	Canada Revenue Agency
CSIF	Canada Strategic Infrastructure Fund
CTA	Canadian Transportation Agency
CTF	Canadian Taxpayers Federation
DIAND	Department of Indian Affairs and Northern Development.
DRI	digital research infrastructure
DRIE	Department of Regional Industrial Expansion
EAP	Economic Action Plan
ECE	Economic Commission of Europe
EEP	Energy East Pipeline
ERDA	Economic and Regional Development Agreement
EU	European Union
FCM	Federation of Canadian Municipalities
GATT	General Agreement on Tariffs and Trade
GDA	General Development Agreement
GDP	Gross Domestic Product
GDPR	General Data Protection Regulation
GGH	Greater Golden Horseshoe region
GHG	greenhouse gases

GIF	Green Infrastructure Fund
GLSLS	Great Lakes St Lawrence Seaway Study
GMF	Green Municipal Fund
GST	Goods and Services Tax
GTA	Greater Toronto Area
GTF	Gas Tax Fund
HBC	Hudson's Bay Company
HQM	Highly Qualified Manpower
HST	Harmonized Sales Tax
ICIP	Investing in Canada Infrastructure Plan
ICP	Infrastructure Canada Program
ICSP	Integrated Community Sustainability Plan
IDA	Investment Dealers Association of Canada
IIP	Immigrant Investor Program
IIROC	Investment Industry Regulatory Organization of Canada
ING	Intense Neutron Generator
IRAP	Industrial Research Assistance Program
ISDS	Investor-State Dispute Settlement Mechanism
ISP	Infrastructure Stimulus Plan
IT	information technology
KOA	Knowledge and Outreach Awareness
KPMG	Klynveld Peat Marwick Goerdeler
MFN	Most Favoured Nation
MIC	Major Infrastructure Component
MMA	Montreal, Marine & Atlantic Railway.
MPMO	Major Projects Management Office
MRIF	Municipal Rural Infrastructure Fund
MRF	major research facilities
MSUA	Ministry of State for Urban Affairs
NABST	National Advisory Board on Science and Technology
NAFTA	North American Free Trade Agreement
NATO	North Atlantic Treaty Organization
NCE	Networks of Centres of Excellence
NDP	New Democratic Party
NEB	National Energy Board
NGO	non-governmental organization
NGTL	NOVA Gas Transmission Ltd
NIMBY	not in my backyard
NRC	National Research Council of Canada

NRCan	Natural Resources Canada
NRTEE	National Roundtable on the Environment and Economy
OECD	Organization for Economic Cooperation and Development
OH&S	Occupational Health and Safety
OMERS	Ontario Employees Retirement System
ONC	Ocean Networks Canada
OPEC	Organization of Petroleum Exporting Countries
OSFI	Office of the Superintendent of Financial Institutions
OTA	Office of Technology Assessment
OTN	Ocean Tracking Network
P3	Public Private Partnership
PCO	Privy Council Office
PPP Canada	Public Private Partnerships Canada
PTF	Public Transit Fund
ROI	return on investment
SEC	Securities and Exchange Commission
SHC	Saskatchewan Housing Corporation
SLSDC	Saint Lawrence Seaway Development Corporation
SLSMC	Saint Lawrence Seaway Management Corporation
SME	small-medium enterprise
SNOLAB	Sudbury Neutrino Observatory Laboratory
SRO	self-regulatory organization
STI	science, technology, and innovation
TBS	Treasury Board Secretariat
TDG	Transportation of Dangerous Goods Directorate
TPP	Trans-Pacific Partnership
TRIPS	Trade-Related Intellectual Property
UCP	United Conservative Party
UDA	Urban Development Agreement
USMDA	United States Missile Defence Agency
VfM	value for money
VIDO	Vaccine and Infectious Disease Organization – International Vaccine Centre
WCS	Western Canada Select
WDBA	Windsor-Detroit Bridge Authority
WHMIS	Workplace Hazardous Materials Information System
WHO	World Health Organization
WTI	West Texas Intermediate
WTO	World Trade Order

KEEPING CANADA RUNNING

Introduction and Analytical Framework

This book provides an in-depth academic analysis of six Canadian infrastructure policy and governance regimes and eras covering over five decades and spanning numerous Liberal and Conservative federal governments. Based on this analysis, and on the identification of key themes and trends, it also explores future challenges and opportunities for infrastructure funding and governance. This includes the potentially devastating health and economic impacts of the 2020 pandemic, with major implications for investment in public and private infrastructure including schools, hospitals and medical infrastructure, senior care, airlines, hotels, and universities, in addition to the vast numbers of social, sports, recreational, and cultural institutions affected. As the book demonstrates, governments increasingly respond to economic crises with short- and medium-term spending on infrastructure projects designed to stimulate the economy and advance political and policy objectives such as green, urban, Northern, and First Nations agendas. The transformational nature of the pandemic crisis makes it harder to imagine the type of infrastructure that will be required in a post-COVID-19 world; governments may need to offer a different type of response to effectively identify and address future infrastructure needs and priorities.

Though we intend this book mainly for academics and students interested in the developments, strengths, and weaknesses of Canadian infrastructure policy and governance, we have also kept in mind readers who are governmental, business, and professional infrastructure policy and governance practitioners. In addition, the book is intended to be accessible to interested citizens and social-interest-group participants who benefit from, or may be disadvantaged or in some cases harmed by, infrastructure policy and governance developments, delays, and shortfalls. The overall goal of the book is to chart and make sense of the complex nature of Canadian infrastructure policy, funding, and governance in order to enable readers to better understand the importance and impact of infrastructure investment, and to inform and improve policy decisions at each level of government.

FIVE RESEARCH QUESTIONS

1 How has infrastructure policy emerged on the policy and governance agenda?
2 Is there a credible definition and understanding of what infrastructure is and the implementation challenges and risks that it engenders in a federal multi-level system of policy, governance, and democracy?
3 Is corruption a growing or declining feature of infrastructure policy, governance, and democracy in Canada, and to what extent has there been change with respect to how it is defined, policed, and regulated?
4 Is the funding of infrastructure characterized by the imperatives of distributive retail politics or are other viable funding models present or emerging?
5 What are the main challenges for Canada's infrastructure policy and governance following the pandemic and over the next decade to twenty-year period?

The book examines and explains how and why Canadian infrastructure needs, policy aims, governance, and programs have evolved over the last fifty years, covering the Justin Trudeau, Harper, Chrétien-Martin, Mulroney, and Pierre Trudeau eras. Earlier periods are also discussed as needed. Although the book's initial focus is on the federal role in infrastructure, it also examines the provincial and city-municipal roles and perspectives in chapter 2 as well as in later regime chapters.

While our initial starting definition of infrastructure in chapter 1 relates to public and private assets and their life cycles, any recent or earlier literature, including public agency and interest group reports, shows the diverse yet understandable range of definitions and discourse involved (Allan, Gordon, Hanniman, Juneau, and Young 2018; McNally, Ferreira, and Gordon 2018; Statistics Canada 2017c;

Conference Board of Canada 2017; Emery 2018; Canadian Infrastructure Report Card 2016; 2012; Breen 2015; Infrastructure Canada 2015c; Canada West Foundation 2013; Doern, Maslove, and Prince 2013; Gaudreault and Lemire 2003; Auld 1985). These include: the built environment, basic physical and organizational asset structures and facilities, critical infrastructure, capital projects, capital budgets, construction, public works, procurement, sustainable infrastructure, city and municipal infrastructure, housing stock, rural infrastructure, border infrastructure, platforms, ports, mega-projects, supply chains and related logistics, information and internet infrastructure, and tangible capital stock. They also extend to notions of environmental capital, natural capital, and land and landscapes.

This definitional range emerges in the overall analysis of both the foundational literature in chapter 1 and multi-level federalism and infrastructure in chapter 2, and is further extended in our analysis of the six infrastructure policy and governance regimes in chapters 4 to 9. Indeed, it will be quickly evident that there are literally hundreds of types and descriptors of infrastructure in the full regime analysis. These include infrastructure in relation to Indigenous populations and inequities, including the Wet'suwet'en and other Indigenous peoples seeking justice and support federally and across and within Canada's provinces and the North. Concerns of the Wet'suwet'en include missing and murdered Indigenous women across Canada in addition to Indigenous youth, impacted as they are by pipelines (Bracken and Cecco 2020). Benjoe (2020) argues as an activist woman and parent that "Canada's history with Indigenous people is cruel and unfair" (1). First Nations overall have also been active and concerned as they seek funding to clean up oil and gas wells in Western Canada (Bakx 2020). In exploring these issues and concerns we examine Canadians in several locations in the context of different types of infrastructure both in the North and in cities and communities in several of our six regime chapters.

An initial useful analytical example of some of these infrastructure types and complexities at the local government level is found in the above-mentioned *Canada Infrastructure Report Card* (2016) study, where the sector assets and asset management types and realms cover: potable water, waste water, stormwater, roads and bridges, buildings, sport and recreation facilities, and public transit (43–140). Its glossary of features also includes linear assets, non-linear assets, reinvestment rate and target investment rate, and replacement value (143).

FOUR KEY INITIAL DEFINITIONAL REALMS

Infrastructure policy refers to formal statements of infrastructure policy goals and values expressed in laws; in Throne Speeches and Budget Speeches as primary agenda-setting processes and events; in government reports and studies; in regulations, guidelines, codes, and standards; in tax and spending measures; in speeches that are a form of political exhortation; and in departmental websites with language and discourse that, in the internet and social media age, are often easily embellished and restructured for partisan and political communication purposes.

Governance is a concept that emerged in the practice and literature on politics, policy, and public administration over the past thirty years (Aucoin 1997; 2008). It can be understood simply as an effort to recognize analytically, comparatively, and more explicitly that governing Canada involves more than government, more than the state, and more than public policy as pronounced and implemented by the state and its bureaucracies (Pal 2014). It implies the state fostering more explicit public-private efforts to improve the content, quality, and complex implementation of policy and the delivery of services (Harmes 2019). For our purposes of infrastructure governance analysis, it means the need to map and understand the nature of varied infrastructure business and social interest groups, labour unions, and lobby organizations. But it is also a test of the continued need, in many instances, for key features of public-sector financial management (Elgie 2020; Graham 2019) and for strong state-led capacities (Dyer 2020; Bell and Hindmoor 2009). In Canada the broad manifestations of governance have also been present in varied forms at the level of provincial governments and policy systems involving diverse urban and local governments (Hale 2017; Atkinson et al. 2013). In Alberta, for example, in the current pandemic context, Premier Jason Kenney announced that his government would spend "10 billion on projects that will immediately create jobs, including health care facilities, pipelines, schools, drug treatment centres and more," and cast the plan "as the largest infrastructure build in Alberta history" (Anderson 2020, 2).

Markets are systems of voluntary commercial exchange between businesses (and other suppliers and sellers of products and services) and consumers (including businesses as consumers). Such exchange is based on the features, performance, price, quality, and reliability of the products and services available, and the terms and time frames on which the exchange takes place (Hale 2017). In a field such as infrastructure policy (and in other policy fields as well), the notion of consumers is usually not the simple one of a hypothesized "average" consumer (Doern 2006). This is especially the case regarding infrastructure development, asset life cycles, and replacement features in diverse spatial settings. All markets are governed by varied and complex economic and social laws, rules, and norms including property rights, corporate law, contract and insurance law, corruption and its avoidance and policing, bankruptcy law, competition law, and consumer safety and environmental laws and practices, in addition to international and internal liberalized trade policies and agreements. In most important ways, markets could not exist or function at a basic level without the state. The role of business corporations also needs to be understood as involving their inherent role as limited liability entities and the roles of their shareholders, main owners, and senior executives in situations of economic success, as well as their paths of failure and dysfunction, where bankruptcy can be a frequently deployed political-economic weapon of choice (McIntosh 2019).

Democracy we define broadly to include all the main values, criteria, and arenas at play in the Canadian political system. These include: elected, representative, cabinet-based parliamentary democracy; federalism, including provincial and urban democracy; interest-group pluralism; civil society; and the tools and practices of direct democracy including internet-based social networks (Lalancette, Raynauld, and Crandall 2019; Hale 2017; Kitchen and Slack 2016; Pal 2014; Savoie 2013; Bickerton and Gagnon 2009; Williams 2009; Rainie and Wellman 2012). All of these involve various types of engagement and consultation, but they also involve exclusion by design or neglect, and they can involve corrupt practices by government, businesses, and social interests.

OUR TWO-PART ANALYTICAL FRAMEWORK

We deploy a two-part analytical framework (see table 0.1).

a) Infrastructure Policy and Governance *Regimes* defined as interacting systems of public-private asset values, policies, laws, rules, processes, and institutions, some more vertical and sectoral in their basic nature and others more framework-based and horizontal in nature, and with different asset life cycles. These regimes compel us to look across multiple forms of delegated governance and democracy, ranging from federal departments in the context of parliamentary government to arm's-length agencies, complex public-private arrangements, networks, and foundations. Our focus initially is federal, but crucially we also explore infrastructure policy and governance at the provincial level and extend our analysis to include cities and urban areas as well as infrastructure challenges faced in the North. Consequently, we also examine multi-level infrastructure policy and governance and complex multi-asset life cycles and risks. We then examine six infrastructure policy and governance regimes (see further discussion below).

b) Three functioning and interacting *Elements* of infrastructure policy and governance that help propel and explain infrastructure policy change or inertia within and across the six regimes:

- *Ideas, Discourse, and Agendas* (e.g. as assets; as types of "capital"; as "investment" spending; as private assets and their depreciation/replacement provisions; as private-public dependence; as debates over valued means and valued ends).
- *Power Structures, Democracy, and Governance* (e.g. ministerial-parliamentary; federal-provincial-municipal; business, unions, NGOs, and consumer-related interests; federalist; pluralist; spatial/regional; direct democracy).
- *Temporal Realities, Cycles, Conflicts, and Technology* (e.g. electoral and business cycles; disasters or crises; life cycles; generational or intergenerational demographic changes; annual versus multi-year budgeting; infrastructure banks; pension-plan investment time-lines; technology, as defined and changing fixed and mobile spatial assets in our current internet and social media age).

Policy and Governance Regimes

Policy and governance *regimes* are the first feature of our analytical framework. Regimes are complex, integrated realms of policy ideas, institutions, interests, instruments, and rules (Doern, Auld, and Stoney 2015). The six infrastructure policy and governance regimes we map and examine empirically are listed above in table o.1.

Table 0.1
Analyzing Canadian infrastructure policy

Context	Analytical framework	Six infrastructure policy and governance regimes
Conceptual foundations (chapter 1, drawn from literature and analysis on) • Infrastructure policy ideas, paradigms, and discourse • Infrastructure governance, power, and democracy • Infrastructure technology and complexities Canadian infrastructure policy in Canadian multi-level federalism (chapter 2) Canada–US and international infrastructure policy and institutions (chapter 3)	Infrastructure policy regimes • As interacting systems of ideas, values, policies, laws, rules, processes, and institutions • As vertical and horizontal in direction and scope • With economic and social intent and intended, unintended, or ill-considered social and economic asset life-cycle impacts Regime elements • Policy ideas, discourses, and agendas • Power structures, democracy, and governance • Temporal realities, cycles, conflicts, and technologies	Change and inertia in the regimes for: • Business infrastructure (chapter 4) • Infrastructure financing (chapter 5) • Transport infrastructure (chapter 6) • Housing infrastructure (chapter 7) • Energy-environment-resources pipelines (chapter 8) • Science, technology, and innovation (chapter 9)

The notion of a *regime* is often used interchangeably with terms such as "jurisdiction," for example in the federal, provincial, urban, or international constitutional jurisdiction, or as a "system" or "domain," such as in analyses of risk domains or of individual policy areas such as the food safety or the drug approval systems (Hood, Rothstein, and Baldwin 2001; Harris and Milkis 1989). We map and examine regimes within infrastructure as relatively complex policy and governance spheres, levels, and temporal periods where different policy, taxation, spending, regulation-making, and compliance challenges are faced, debated, reframed, or ignored.

Wherever there is political-economic debate, academic discourse, or institutional politics, there are bound to be agreements and disagreements about the precise boundaries of what we refer to as regimes. Indeed, boundary issues and overlaps are often a key feature driving the analysis of regime challenges, debates, and outcomes. Some of the regimes we discuss in this book have been present and recognized in the academic analysis of infrastructure for long periods while others are more recent in their coverage (but certainly not brand new). Numerous pressures, ideas, technologies, logistics, risks, corruption, and changing institutional forms are present in the overall regime structure and mix. We refer to these developments in our literature review in chapter 1 and elsewhere in the book.

Policy Regime Elements

Elements are the second needed feature of our analytical framework. They refer to basic important analytical features that help us understand and explain some of the basic causes of both infrastructure policy *change* and *inertia*, as well as providing insights into the overall socio-economic content of this policy and governance field. The three main elements we discuss and then analyze summarily at the end of each regime chapter are infrastructure:

• policy ideas, discourse, and agendas;
• power structures, democracy, and governance; and
• temporal realities, cycles, conflicts, and technology.

Each of the three elements poses different challenges about qualitative and quantitative evidence and the time periods being covered.

The mixes of dominant and contending policy ideas, discourses, and agendas are found in the historical advocacy and adoption of policy. They are still relevant, and show up in the changing content of laws, Speeches from the Throne, budget speeches, and ministerial speeches and talking points. Ideas and preferred discourse are also revealed in opposition political party, interest-group, think-tank, and academic papers and sound-bite discourse developed by the electronic media, bloggers, and social networks.

Our six regimes deal with entrenched and shifting systems of economic and social power. Within the state, power can grow, fluctuate, or wane based on minority versus majority government situations and on the styles and performance of ministers and prime ministers. Business corporations, firms, and industry associations also figure prominently in our assessment of power, largely *private* economic power. Both Canadian and foreign infrastructure businesses and interests are important in this field, but they are also complex to map. Private economic power works partly in tandem with Infrastructure Canada. Provincial infrastructure ministries are typically, as we see in chapter 1, combined transport *and* infrastructure ministries, with a core transport mandate paired with an infrastructure mandate regarding the entire set of provincial ministerial departments. But economic power also works with the federal Department of Finance as well as with Innovation, Science and Economic Development Canada, and, in addition, certain other line ministries such as Public Services and Procurement Canada, Natural Resources Canada, or special operating agencies with industry-specific mandates and capacity. Indeed, overall there are well over forty federal departments and agencies with infrastructure roles. Consumer and environmental interests exercise social power and influence, albeit arguably not on as sustained or influential a basis as business does; but their influence is crucially focused on safety and security, and diverse conceptions of the public interest. All these actors are networked with each other, whether consciously or intentionally or not.

Varied and changing kinds of temporal realities and conflicts and technology underpin the structure and dynamics of the different regimes. Time and temporal realities interact or collide with technologies and related policy advocacy. These realities range from temporal decision processes, cycles, and realities, including intermittent crises, risks, or disasters, including disaster recovery planning; annual or multi-year business, political, or electoral cycles; and long-term, structural, life-cycle, generational, or intergenerational demographic changes.

As previewed in table o.2, across the full six regime analyses, we examine seventeen *infrastructure policy and governance histories*, some related in different ways as well to longer-term future policy and governance challenges.

We draw empirically on reports and studies of Canadian and international infrastructure policy and governance by academics, think tanks, government, and business, complemented by our own infrastructure and related research in the disciplines of policy, politics, and governance, and economics and business. This work is complemented by a large number of interviews conducted by the authors with infrastructure policy officials and players.

The historical content of the empirical chapters mainly cover a forty-to-fifty-year period, but some sections go back even further if needed. We proceed sometimes in chronological order, but often we necessarily move back and forth among the five prime ministerial eras, and in a multi-level Canadian federalism-cities context, to show the complex interplay of ideas, power, and temporal realities and conflict and technology.

OUR SEVEN MAIN ARGUMENTS

Throughout the analysis we advance seven main arguments that contribute to answering the book's five research questions set out earlier, as brought together in our conclusions in chapter 10. These seven arguments are that:

1 Infrastructure policy has not ranked highly in federal agenda-setting Throne Speeches and Budget Speeches over the past fifty years as a whole. It has rarely been a standalone issue and discourse because it is typically embedded in and/or combined with numerous other socio-economic policy fields and buried amid literally dozens of unmanageable and even unknowable funding programs.
2 Credible definitions and understandings of infrastructure are emerging, but in a world of complex policy fields and traditional and fast-changing social media agendas and descriptive discourse, the politics of infrastructure discourse will always shift in unexpected directions and ways.

Table 0.2
Infrastructure policy and governance histories in the six regimes

Infrastructure policy	Policy and governance histories and governance regimes
The business infrastructure policy and governance regime (chapter 4)	• Businesses and evolving core self-funding and banking system-funded infrastructure, 1960s to present • SMES and startup businesses and infrastructure, 1970 to present • Public-private partnerships (P3s) infrastructure, early 1990s to present
The infrastructure financing regime (chapter 5)	• Managing and paying for municipal public assets, 1930s to 2003 • Financing through public-private partnerships, 1980 to 2019 • Canada infrastructure bank: indemnification, loans, and other inducements, 1930s to 1980s, 2017 to present
The transport infrastructure policy and governance regime (chapter 6)	• Transportation infrastructure in freight-rail and trade-related supply chains, 1990s to present • Transport infrastructure in Canada's many norths, 1970 to present • Transit infrastructure in cities, early 1990s to present
The housing infrastructure policy and governance regime (chapter 7)	• Federal mortgage and housing policy and the Canada Mortgage and Housing Corporation (CMHC), 1940s to present • Provincial and city housing and social housing infrastructure, 1970s to present • Globalization of housing: foreign ownership/investment impacts and Airbnb technology and market impacts, 1980s to present
The energy-environment-resources pipelines infrastructure policy and governance regime (chapter 8)	• Energy, environment, resource policy, and institutional nexus dynamics, 1970s to present • Pipeline battles and survival for competing/colliding and threatened major pipelines, 1980s to present
The science, technology, and innovation (STI) infrastructure policy and governance regime (chapter 9)	• Formative Big Science Projects Policy and Governance, 1960s to 1980s • The Canada Foundation for Innovation as an STI infrastructure foundation, 1997 to present • The internet: from permissionless innovation STI infrastructure to regulated infrastructure media and threat to democracy, 1990s to present

3 Canada, at all levels of government, needs to develop actual *capital budgets* so that funding captures and involves asset life cycles, is actually costed as a true investment activity, and is therefore funded in ways different from current normal operational public budgeting.

4 Most infrastructure is now built and fostered at the urban/city level of government because that is where 70 per cent of Canadians live and work. Cities, however, have the weakest and most inadequate revenue sources, centred only or mainly on property tax sources. Federal-provincial-municipal tax systems need major reform to give cities access to income tax revenue sources for some kinds of infrastructure repair in particular.

5 Some other funding models for infrastructure funding are emerging, such as infrastructure banks, but these at present also seem too often to be simply timely reforms that can be announced. They tend not to be linked to the current role of the existing banking system in infrastructure funding and lending, nor to how reforms may play out in global banking and pension fund investment institutions.

6 The regulation of infrastructure is not normally or easily captured by existing regulatory theory or governance practice. Indeed "rule-making" about infrastructure is far more likely to be carried out under tax and spending rules and rule-makers rather than via regulatory oversight institutions per se. Infrastructure decisions often involve corruption, both financially and regarding failures of democracy.

7 Other long-term related policy and governance needs for infrastructure also depend on a greater understanding of what kind of core expertise is needed to cope with and anticipate policy and governance in diverse infrastructure and related technological fields. These include expertise in logistics, national and international supply chains, and information-centred big data usefulness and abuses. Better underlying mappings are also needed of what the infrastructure socio-economic interest group structure is and how it is seeking to change how government works in Canadian multi-level federalism. The COVID-19 pandemic has illustrated the importance of each of these components of (critical) infrastructure, policy and governance and revealed many vulnerabilities and gaps that exist in current infrastructure raising serious questions about how to optimize future investment.

Part I of the book examines Canadian infrastructure policy conceptually and in a historical context. Chapter 1 examines key parts of the foundational literature. Chapter 2 maps and analyzes infrastructure policy and governance approaches in Canadian multi-level federalism involving: the federal government; the provinces and territories; and cities and municipal government. Chapter 3 looks at Canada-US and other international infrastructure policies, developments, institutions, and pressures. Several examples are traced, including: Canada-US infrastructure relations overall, including Trump-era America-first agendas; the St Lawrence Seaway and related water shipping infrastructure; border, bridge, and port infrastructure; and infrastructure policy influences via international bodies such as the OECD, the World Bank, the European Union, and the United Nations. But the international dynamics and power features also include the role of China as a global power.

Part II provides our extensive empirical analysis of the six key infrastructure policy and governance regimes, including their basic historical features and the manner in which the three regime elements help us to understand change and inertia. Our conclusions and main final arguments follow in chapter 10 as answers to the five overall research questions posed.

PART ONE

Conceptual Foundations
and Historical Context

1

Conceptual Foundations

INTRODUCTION

The conceptual foundational literature on which we draw is historical and contemporary as well as Canadian and comparative. It emerges from a variety of social science and natural science disciplines and fields including political science, macro- and microeconomics, public finance and fiscal policy, logistics, business, risk management, public policy, science and technology studies, urban policy, sociology, geography, governance, and public administration. It also draws on governmental and other studies on infrastructure policy and governance and other closely related policy fields. Chapters 2 and 3 and the infrastructure regime analysis in part II of the book draw on an additional subset of Canadian and international infrastructure policy and governance-relevant literature.

Our presentation on the foundational theoretical and applied literature on infrastructure policy is organized into three central streams: infrastructure policy ideas and discourse; infrastructure governance, power, and democracy; and infrastructure technology and complexities. We explore each stream, highlighting key literature themes and authors, and commenting on ways in which they are linked and overlap, as well as how they can be used both in our analytical framework and in the discussion of our central themes throughout the book.

IDEAS AND DSCOURSE

Our survey of ideas and discourse about infrastructure policy is centred in both academic literature and also socio-economic statements of infrastructure policy ideas and purposes, both at the federal level and at the provincial and city, municipal, and local levels of jurisdiction and policy expression. The *idea of explicit capital budgets* for government has emerged because public-sector budgeting does not make viable accounting distinctions between capital versus operational spending the way that private companies do. Auld (1985) strongly made the case for real capital budgets, showing that public assets and related capital items are not costed or shown with annual depreciation allowances over their useful life. Instead, they are often shown as a once-only disbursement. While Auld recognized that there clearly are difficulties in measuring public assets and in assigning depreciation and replacement capital costs, he also argued that there can be little doubt that the basic method then (and currently) used significantly distorts not only the way deficits and surpluses are debated politically and economically, but also the way basic decisions may be viewed in government (Clark 2018; Hanniman 2018; Doern, Maslove, and Prince 2013). Some decisions and kinds of spending may not be treated or analyzed as actual investment decisions even if they are rhetorically referred to as "investment."

Capital budgets have been discussed and advocated for financing local government in Canada and the US (Champagne and Beaudry 2018; Hanniman 2018; Kitchen 2004; Boasson et al. 2012; Mintz and Smart 2006). Hanniman (2018) raises issues about how it might be better if local governments did not themselves borrow, but rather found ways to centralize such budgeting, possibly via the federal government but with a high sense of caution about what kinds of options make sense. Kitchen (2004) noted earlier that capital expenditures in local government "tend to be lumpy. Large expenditures in one year may preclude similar expenditures in subsequent years with little, if any consistent trend or pattern" (3). Related basic concerns influence the Boasson et al. (2012) analysis of US municipal and capital budgeting decisions and cause them to advocate the application of "modern portfolio theory" as used in the private sector. Thus they advocate that "local projects should not be evaluated in isolation of each other. Rather they should be evaluated collectively as a portfolio of investments so as to ensure that the overall welfare is maximized for the community" (58).

More broadly, and with an implied focus on national governments, Mintz and Smart (2006) examined "incentives for public investment under fiscal rules" related to deficit financing. They argued that the "current budgetary approach to limit deficits to a fixed portion of

Gross Domestic Product (GDP) or to balance budgets could undermine political incentives to invest in public capital with long-run returns since politicians concerned about electoral prospects would favour expenditures providing immediate benefits to their voters" (2). They examine whether capital budgets centred on longer temporal periods should only be governed by deficit limits, or if there are forms of capital funding that have their own valid and accepted basis.

Interestingly, in fiscally conservative Alberta there has been historical experimentation with long-term bond financing of assets as initiatives of the long-dominant governing Social Credit Party in Alberta, a political party that was very suspicious and critical of normal "credit" by Eastern Canadian-dominated banks (Asach 1999; Hesketh 1997). Alberta has also experimented, in the Peter Lougheed Conservative era, with long-term financing via the Alberta Heritage Savings Trust Fund (AHSTF) funded by fast-growing oil revenues (Maslove, Prince, and Doern 1986; Warrack 1982).

Conceptions of *capital*, and the discourse of investments and of long asset-based time periods in budgetary politics, extend well beyond physical capital. The term encompasses ideas of human capital, social capital, and natural or environmental capital. Each of these have entered governmental thinking to some extent, both because of the role of academic and think-tank analysis and advocacy, and also from within the federal government's relevant departments and agencies. In each realm of these extended conceptions of capital, there is support for the underlying ideas, but there are also definitional ambiguities, complexities, and problems of acceptance especially vis-à-vis measurement. It is often difficult, moreover, to detect whether such research and analysis is traceable in concrete spending and tax decisions or program innovation and structure.

Human capital, for instance, includes "the nutrition and stimuli received in the early years of life, formal education, and skills and knowledge acquired by work experience and knowledge" (Riddell 2008, 2). Investments in such capital (public and private) positively relate to future growth in GDP (Gu and Wong 2010) as well as to social benefits such as increased civic participation. There are, however, many choices regarding what investments to make at the margin in terms of the greatest social and economic return. Among these choices are greater investments in early childhood education.

Social capital is, according to one definition, "the ways in which one's social relationships provide access to needed information, resources and supports" (Policy Research Initiative 2006). In the 2004 to 2006 period, the federal government commissioned cross-governmental research and held consultations on this arguably even more difficult concept of capital. In its effort to use social capital as a lens for understanding the health of a community or civil society, this initiative found the concept difficult to operationalize for public policy and budgetary development, in part because of problems and also differences when it was seen thematically across areas such as poverty reduction, healthy aging, community crime prevention, and the settlement of new immigrants to Canada (Policy Research Initiative 2006, 2).

Natural capital is defined by one environmental NGO as "the sum of all of the resources and free services provided by nature" and thus it is normally "unaccounted for in traditional economics" (Pembina Institute 2011, 1). The climate change debate and negotiations and the advocacy of sustainable development as a policy paradigm are quintessentially about such kinds of capital, and so are various overall concepts of resource stewardship. Federal environmental advisory bodies such as NRTEE tied concepts of natural capital to much earlier notions of nature conservation (National Roundtable on the Environment and Economy 2003). NRTEE identified many barriers regarding the adoption of a natural capital concept, including a failure to integrate the true costs and benefits of nature in federal decision-making. Among its recommendations was the need for spatial concepts such as "conservation planning for whole landscapes" (NRTEE 2003, 43).

Also related to natural capital is the expressed idea of *landscape as infrastructure*. Belanger (2009, 179) makes the argument that the "conventional meaning of modern infrastructure" needs to be changed by "amplifying the biophysical landscape that it has historically suppressed, and to reformulate landscape as a sophisticated instrumental system of essential resources, services, and agents that generate and support urban economies." The analysis builds from North American sites where "real or perceived environmental hazards dot the landscape," including brownfield sites, and shows the "paradoxical, sometimes toxic relationship between pre-industrial landscape conditions and modern industrial systems" (179). Like many ideas about infrastructure it shifts the discourse to capture complex phenomena.

Political capital as an operative linked further idea has been suggested and examined by Hilton (2007) with respect to the politics of "need" regarding the federal government government's municipal infrastructure programs. It joins a series of related ideas and discourse that includes *pork-barrel projects, slicing pork,* and *"retail" politics* in the context of stimulus budgets that include infrastructure funds (Pal 2011; Bennett 2012; Dutil and Park 2012; Doern 2015). Ultimately, these are related to different political eras where the distributive public budgeting strategies of governments were applied and analyzed, including spending via grants and subsidies, and via regional programs and agencies, with subsidies later becoming much less available when free trade agreements made them illegal or subject to complex dispute settlement processes.

Infrastructure spending/investment discourse fits easily into conceptions of the temporal presence of *political business cycles* (Schultz 1995; Drazen 2000), an idea and theory that provides a broader tactical view of the political economy of budgeting. At its heart, this idea refers to the efforts and practices of elected governments to create economic growth, especially just before and during elections, to garner voter support and electoral success. It can also suggest the way that governments might adopt more conservative economic policies after elections or between elections to demonstrate economic managerial competence. The political-voter calculus is said to include the art of offering program and project announceables and funds to the crucial swing voter in the swing riding or seat. Political business cycle behaviour finds some favour in the conventional observation that voters at election time are somehow being bribed with their own money.

The discourse of infrastructure as a *platform* has been present historically. We introduce it here initially, but we will see it again in the final section of this chapter when it is tied in complex ways to technological change and especially digital, internet-centred and social production systems, which are in turn cast also as platforms and semi-platforms of the modern age (see further detail in chapter 9). Our initial historical notions of platforms are best captured with examples. Baldwin and Woodword (2009) cite an Oxford English Dictionary sixteenth-century definition of a platform used "to denote a raised level surface on which people can stand and, usually a discrete structure intended for a particular activity or operation" (19). Baldwin and Woodword for their own purposes define a platform "as a set of stable components that supports variety and evolvability in a system by constraining the linkages among other components" (19).

It is not difficult to find practical examples, both old and still current. Thus the platforms of railway stations are not only where trains stop to let off and pick up passengers, but are also used by others dropping off and picking up goods, or dropping off and waiting for travelling friends or family. The platform is typically not owned by the train company, but rather is governed by local governments. Platforms also exist in the operations of variously owned educational, cultural, community, and sporting organizations.

A useful but little-known Canadian operational platform example is Ridley Terminals Inc., whose work and governance has been audited by the Auditor General of Canada (2018). It is "a marine terminal at Prince Rupert, British Columbia, offering year-round services of loading and off-loading bulk commodities such as coal and petroleum coke" (1). The company is a "federal Crown corporation established in 1981 under the Canada Business Corporations Act ... and its main customers are coal mines and refineries in northern British Columbia, Alberta and Saskatchewan." Of interest is the fact that the Crown Corporation does not receive funding from Parliament. For some time, Transport Canada has raised concerns about the company board's oversight role and the department's future scrutiny of its obligations (1–2). It is worth citing this particular platform example because in our later regime chapters we will see that it is by no means the only Crown Corporation where it is not self-evident what its "Crown" status means, or how public versus private governance or joint governance interact.

We leave until later in the technology section of this chapter (and again, we also come back to this in other regime chapters such as chapter 9) the discussion of technology-driven platforms, including disruptive ones, where we look at the rapid order of the emergence of such entities as eBay, Microsoft Windows, Google, Facebook, Uber, Airbnb, Amazon, etc., and their governance and the nature of the debates about who should be, or is capable of, regulating or monitoring and taxing them.

The discourse of *mega-projects* and later *major projects* emerged in Canada in 1981 in the final Pierre Trudeau government and flowed from a Major Projects Task Force (1981) report on *Major Capital Projects in Canada until 2000*. It identified $440 billion of potential projects (primarily energy-related) that were being considered for investment. The government's intention was "to provide the owners of these projects with 'one-stop-shopping' both regionally and in Ottawa" (Doern 1982, 18), but this implied two contradictory dilemmas: one was the question of "Canadian versus regional criteria for determining economic benefits ... and the second [was] the overall conflict between the economic efficiency of the particular mega-project itself and the larger social, economic and political impacts it [had]" (18). In addition, there were limits regarding the use of the procurement instrument in governing the process. Canada-US issues and contradictions were also pivotal, given that many planned projects were by US firms.

During the Harper era, strategies for major projects, in particular major resource projects, were centred in the 2007 creation of the Major Projects Management Office (MPMO) (Canada 2017). Anchored by a new Cabinet Directive on Improving the Performance of the Regulatory System for Major Resource Projects, the MPMO is based in Natural Resources Canada. The pro–natural resource and energy development agenda of the Harper government was centred on speedier more efficient regulatory approvals, often by weakening environmental assessments (Doern, Auld, and Stoney 2015). In chapter 9 we also examine major projects regarding the Science, Technology, and Innovation (STI) regime, traceable to World War II and the post-war era but also to more recent periods.

In the Justin Trudeau era (see more in chapter 8) new legislation has created two new entities, the Canadian Energy Regulator to replace the National Energy Board, and the Impact Assessment Agency of Canada to conduct and coordinate the impact assessments for designated projects and to replace the Canadian Environmental Assessment Agency. Environment is no longer part of the title of the new agency since the key to the Impact Assessment Agency is to cover health, social and economic issues as well (Canada 2018a; Canada 2018b; Duke 2018; Canadian Environmental Law Association 2018).

Also important to mention in the context of major project discourse is the central role of *procurement in "major Crown projects,"* as relating to recent changes to policies on the management of projects as a feature of the mandate of Public Works and Government Services Canada (Canada 2017b), both overall and with respect to certain kinds of procurement decisions and approaches (Spence 2014; Plamondon 2010; Allen 2007; 2006; Neima and Stoney 2006). The ideas at play here are complex regarding obtaining *value for money*, and in Canada and internationally they include the presence of political *patronage* and *regional growth* strategies as well as the impact of corruption and the need to *avoid corruption* (Locatelli et al. 2017). Federal policy relates to projects whose estimated cost will exceed $100 million and which the Treasury Board would assess as *high risk*

(Canada 2017b, 2). Under such projects "no one department can act solely from its legislative point of view to the exclusion of the other participants" (2). A procurement example of this kind is the "National Shipbuilding Model" for government procurement as analyzed by Spence (2014). But other procurement battles have also related to delays under both the Harper Conservatives and the Justin Trudeau Liberals on decisions to replace aging military aircraft. In May 2018 criticisms emerged regarding the Justin Trudeau government and its $500 million contract with IBM, a foreign vendor, without Shared Services Canada seeking bids (Beeby 2018).

Enthusiasm regarding a potential revival of mega-projects also emerged with the late 2018 announcement that a new $40 billion liquefied natural gas (LNG) project had been approved to be built in northern BC (Schmunk 2018; Morgan 2018; Bundale 2018). This LNG Canada project "will see a pipeline carrying natural gas from Dawson Creek in northeastern B.C. to a new processing plant on the coast in Kitimat. There, the gas would be liquefied for overseas export" (Schmunk 2018, 1–2). Funded by five major global companies, the project was announced as having already received initial approval by the federal NEB, Fisheries and Oceans Canada, BC Hydro, and also twenty-five First Nations. Prime Minister Trudeau and BC Premier John Horgan were present at the launch. Analysis by Morgan (2018) also picked up the mega-project theme of "first of many," but also showed how the project was criticized on environmental grounds by the BC Green Party as part of the coalition supporting Horgan's NDP government. We will pick up on the LNG project's complexity in chapter 8 when we discuss the pipelines regime in more detail. But the LNG mega-project announcement also garnered some support in Nova Scotia for two of its long-dormant projects, Bear Head and Goldboro. Nova Scotia spokespersons were enthusiastically cautious about the larger notions of mega-project revival excitement (Bundale 2018).

Major issues of, and concerns about, corruption are also never far from the surface. For example, they were pivotal in the Charbonneau Commission created in Quebec in 2011 on the Awarding and Management of Public Contracts in the Construction Industry, but have proceeded with continuing lags and sluggishness in actions and findings in the period since (Shingler and McKenna 2016; Dalton 2015). Caron (2018) shows that Quebec is the only province whose Treasury Board Secretariat is responsible for infrastructure planning rather than an infrastructure department per se.

Nimbyism (not in my backyard) is also an idea and analytical realm of some importance to some of the politics and economics of location and place regarding infrastructure (Fast 2014). It relates to all kinds of urban transport policy and politics, for instance airports (Dourado 2016), and is present in urban and federal-provincial-city and municipal policy regarding housing, such as developing and promoting affordable housing where and when it is needed in cities (Mathieu 2018). As published analyses of nimbyism show, most citizens both support it and oppose it at the same time, depending on the nature of their personal interests (Innovative Research Group 2013; Devine-Wright 2009). That makes it exasperatingly complex. In this book, "backyard" can be cast spatially in infrastructure in Canada's north as the "high Arctic" north, the "territorial government" north, and the "southern north" defined as the northern parts of each province. An economic analysis by Bone (2018) looked at the link between "demographic characteristic and anti-development sentiments" (1) as a "way to measure the amount of NIMBYism in a community." The study analyzed the Ontario Municipal Board (OMB) regarding its decisions and approaches on cases that have been appealed to the board, and also looked at the causal effect of replacing the OMB with a proposed new Local Planning Repeal Tribunal (10–11).

In British Columbia, analysis by Cattaneo (2018) focuses initially on the federally owned Port of Vancouver, which faces concerted opposition from the group Against Port Expansion in the Fraser Estuary BC, which charges that "various mega projects ... put the Fraser at risk" (2). Cattaneo then goes on to cite opposition to projects from pipelines to liquefied natural gas terminals, and railways to airports. The Kinder Morgan Trans Mountain pipeline from Alberta (again, see chapter 8 for our analysis of pipelines) is also highlighted. The nimbyism imperative is not hard to see if one resides in Vancouver. Whether looking out from a ten-story residence or walking down the coastal beach, the existing ten or so large stranded container ships are evident. It is not hard to imagine in nimby terms what it would look like post–Kinder Morgan when the number of container ships, ever larger in size, reaches thirty or more in number.

Free trade, neo-liberalism, and the regulation of international trade as general and infrastructure impact ideas are important both conceptually and in relation to deregulation and regulation debates and intertwined realities. Not surprisingly, free trade involves reduced intervention by government to gain sustained access to foreign and regional markets (Cameron 1988; Doern and Tomlin 1991; Mendoza, Low, and Kotschwar 1999; Cameron and Tomlin 2000). This also involves neo-liberalism and globalization as free trade and related ideas were advocated, acted upon, and opposed within and among countries. But from the outset, Canadian trade authorities and agencies also knew they had to deal with the *regulation* of international trade (Trebilcock and House 1995; Trebilcock 2011; Trebilcock et al. 2013). These included trade authorities involved with the GATT/ WTO, NAFTA, and the European Union. These trade authorities had to deal with rule-making regarding: dispute settlement; exchange rates and balance of payments; tariffs and the Most Favoured Nation Principle (MFN); health and safety regulation and standards; anti-dumping regulations; subsidies and countervailing duties; safeguard regimes; trade in agriculture; trade in services; trade-related intellectual property (TRIPS); trade and investment; trade and environment; trade and labour rights; trade and competition policy; and the international movement of people. Within Canada the issues of opening up the internal trade system emerged, leading to an initial Canadian Agreement on Internal Trade cast as free trade-federalism (Doern and MacDonald 1999) and revised and reformed in different (often slow) ways in the last two decades. Trade within Canada was also bound up in the diverse features and policy fields functioning in and across Canada's system of multi-level governance. Thus, the impetus for trade liberalization has been strong over the past forty years, but it is still embedded within rules.

However, Brexit in the UK and the Donald Trump "America First" agenda have produced new uncertainties and deep international disputes that neither a belated Brexit agreement nor the election of President Biden appears sufficient to resolve, especially in the midst of a pandemic and with "vaccine nationalism" further fuelling tensions in international relations. Some of the Trump-era "America First" trade policy dynamics and Canadian responses and tactical politics especially need to be highlighted, keeping in mind that trade rules may or may not be explicit about infrastructure impacts (Gertz 2018; Irwin 2018; Moscrop 2018; McGregor 2018; Donnan 2018; Georges 2017; Swanson 2018; *Economist* 2018d; Monbiot 2018). They include the complexity of dealing with possible reform of the World Trade Organization (WTO) when the US and China are overt threats to each other. America First rhetoric by President Trump had been intended to invoke the notion that Americans had been unfairly treated in various trade agreements, resulting in job losses; but there was also a sense in Trump's discourse and tactics that one could not have *mutual* winners from trade. We trace this analytically in four chronological steps. First, we look at early developments, focused on negotiations to change NAFTA. Second, US tariffs against Canada and planned Canadian retaliatory tariffs in May 2018 led to the traumatic G7 summit in Quebec in early June 2018, and to Trump's belligerence regarding all six of the other G7 members and his personal attack against Canada and Prime Minister Justin Trudeau. Third, we consider the announcement and content of the USMCA as the new replacement NAFTA; and fourth and finally, we look at how trade is being transformed by digital technology as pivotal infrastructure – not only West-East trade but also global "South-South" trade, including the pivotal role of China.

Trump's initial target was NAFTA, and so he launched a process of renegotiating NAFTA with Canada and Mexico, backed by the threat of ending the agreement and/or requiring a five-year sunset clause. George Monbiot, who dislikes Trump intensely, argues that Trump is right about NAFTA and says "the people of North America did not explicitly consent to NAFTA. They were never asked to vote on the deal and its bipartisan support ensured there was little scope for dissent" (2018, 2). The Trump belligerence against Mexico, centred on building a wall along the border, also made the purely trade issues difficult for Mexico and Canada. Indeed, in 2018 Trump tweeted that he would rather have nothing but bilateral trade agreements because he did not like multi-country negotiations/agreements. Different parts of infrastructure also became a part of the tactical politics and economics, including the auto industry regarding changing its "rules of origin" features (*Economist* 2018d) and jet aircraft manufacturer Bombardier. On the car industry, a key US demand was to rewrite NAFTA's rules about cars, and especially about NAFTA's rules of origin, where any changes would redefine what counts as a North American car. The Bombardier element of the Trump-era dynamics involved the US Commerce Department imposing a steep 300 per cent duty on imported Canadian jets. Boeing had sought the trade penalty regarding Bombardier's new C Series aircraft. But in January 2018 another US agency, the United States International Trade Commission, unanimously struck down the 300 per cent duty (Swanson 2018). Meanwhile,

Justin Trudeau's government was also adopting the strategy of visiting and lobbying in several US states where there had been demonstrable joint success in mutual trade and job gains (Georges 2017).

It is crucial to stress, however, that a growing number of countries had been signing regional or bilateral trade agreements, including Canada, which now has bilateral trade and investment agreements with more than fifty other countries. Virtually all of the agreements have implications for infrastructure in one form or another, and more continue to emerge; for example, the Canada-EU Trade Agreement (CETA) signed in 2014 was eventually approved by EU member states. The Trans-Pacific Partnership Free Trade Agreement (TPP) opposed by the US Trump Administration is now still proceeding to a likely successful conclusion. If nothing else, every new agreement will alter trade patterns, which will *always* affect (a) supply and demand for aspects of infrastructure; (b) the pattern of trade routes and supply chains by which goods move from producer to consumer; (c) competition among nations to attract those trade routes into their countries because of the prosperity it tends to bring; and (d) competition among marine, air, and land carrier infrastructure to haul the goods, which in turn usually dictates the kind of infrastructure (for example, depth of harbours and throughput capacity of container ports) that a country must offer if carriers are not to go else where and serve other markets, and take the vigorous trade routes with them. A larger "trade and" agenda has also emerged as a prominent feature of the expanding liberalized trade regime. This refers to the broadening content of agreements, which usually include "trade and" services such as procurement, investment, and intellectual property, each a complex policy field.

These "trade and" agreements have tested (and often stirred) the policy and regulatory waters in such realms as competition policy as well. These issues were partly resolved in the overall Uruguay Round of WTO agreement through separate related agreements on these subjects, with links to WTO institutions. Many of these changes arguably were the product of US power and aggressive unilateralism – or, in short, raw hegemonic American political and economic power (Ostry 1997; Sell 1998).

US tariffs against Canada and planned Canadian retaliatory tariffs were announced in late May 2018. Trump imposed 25 per cent steel tariffs and 10 per cent aluminum tariffs on Canada, Mexico and the EU. Citing an official national security rationale against long-time allies was, not surprisingly, taken as an insult in Canada's immediate reply. The Trudeau Liberal government responded with a retaliatory list of tariffs on over a hundred US products that would take effect on 1 July 2018 (Canada Day). The list included a 25 per cent tariff on industrial steel and small increases on aluminum items, but also a small 10 per cent tariff on selected consumer products from maple syrup to ketchup and toilet paper: overall, a total of about $16.6 billion worth of goods. The list was "designed to exert maximum political pressure on Congress with an eye on particular districts and individuals of both parties" (Dale, Campion-Smith, and Maccharles 2018, 2). Any NAFTA replacement agreement would have to be approved by Congress in the complex politics and economics of the Senate and the House of Representatives.

The early June 2018 Quebec G7 Summit, hosted by Canada and chaired by Justin Trudeau, witnessed Trump's aggressive opposition to all six of the other G7 members, which had all been hit by the new Trump tariffs with the same security rationale. While this was Trump's America First strategy operating full throttle, Nobel economist Paul Krugman (2018) anchored his *New York Times* article "Debacle in Quebec" by arguing that Trump "didn't put America first; Russia first would be a better description … because Trump started with a call for readmitting Russia to the group, which makes no sense at all" (1–2). Overall, Krugman used the word "disaster" to describe the G7 meeting, in that it "could herald the beginning of a trade war, maybe even the collapse of the Western alliance. At the very least, it will damage America's reputation as a reliable ally for decades to come" (1). For Canada, the meetings also ended with further direct personal attacks on Trudeau by Trump and some of his cronies. One of the immediate political impacts was that the Canadian Parliament, across party lines, rallied to defend Trudeau (Bilefsky and Porter 2018), as did other key provincial premiers and former Conservative and Liberal prime ministers. As a 2019 federal election moved closer, this would be the basis for Trudeau's overall strategy to retain power for a second term as prime minister, but as the 2019 federal election minority government result showed and is showing, it was by no means a guaranteed success.

There is little doubt, however, that Canada could face serious impacts from a devastating trade war, "one which Canada, as a middling economic power, would likely lose" (Cecco 2018, 2). Cecco cites a C.D. Howe Institute study arguing that "tariffs will cause significant economic pain in both countries: Canada could lose as many as

6000 jobs and a 0.33% GDP reduction, whereas the US would lose 22,700 jobs, but only a 0.02% disruption to the GDP" (quoted in Cecco 2018, 2). Canadian historian Margaret MacMillan (2018) defended the historic value of Canada-US friendship as allies and neighbours and the value of the world's longest undefended border. Her concern, as others have also expressed, is that "Trump himself seems far more comfortable with authoritarian regimes such as Russia, the Philippines or Saudi Arabia than he does with older friends such as Britain, France or Germany. The G7 was a useful meeting place for like-minded nations. It is probably done for. What next? NATO? the IMF? World Bank? World Trade Organization?" (3).

The third stage is centred on the content of and reactions to the announcement on 1 October 2018 of the USMCA agreement as the new NAFTA. President Trump announced the agreement as a personal triumph for himself and the US. An assessment from the Brookings Institute in Washington (Gertz 2018) led with a view that "overall, the changes from the old NAFTA are mostly cosmetic" and that the "three parties are going to end up with a new trade deal that looks remarkably similar to the old NAFTA. The main structure of the deal is largely intact" (1). Gertz saw the biggest changes as "higher rules-of-origin requirements for the auto sector, marginally greater access to the Canadian dairy market, and a scale back of the investor-state dispute settlement (ISDS) rules" (1). But he also noted Trump's fixation on the new brand name "USMCA," a "terrible, unpronounceable name" (1) compared to NAFTA. A *New York Times* analysis by Irwin (2018) described the USMCA as a feature of a Trump strategy where he and his trade officials have been "beating up on traditional allies, including Canada" to soften them up "to extract moderate concessions favourable to American interests," but more crucially, to later eventually get them to be allies against China and to "isolate China and compel major changes to Chinese business and trade practices" (2). But he also suggests that it is not at all clear whether the US will be able to call on a "coalition of the willing" or a "coalition of the coerced" (4).

Canadian reactions such as that by Moscrop (2018) noted the way the Trudeau Liberals characterized the new agreement as a "modernizing" one but also saw it as evidence of Canada as a weak player dealing with a global power now in full America First mode. An initial analysis by McGregor (2018) focused on the impacts of the USMCA on the content rules for auto manufacturing in Canada as producing a "safe landing zone" but also warned that "continental auto trade will be less free than ever" (2).

By the end of January 2020, the USMCA politics was centred on the signing ceremony by President Trump on the White House South Lawn, at which "the NAFTA nightmare" was declared ended and the USMCA presented as a "colossal victory" for the United States (Martin 2020, 1). Neither Prime Minister Trudeau, nor Deputy Prime Minister Chrystia Freeland, who previously as Foreign Minister had led the Canadian USMCA negotiations, was present. The US Democrats were scarcely present at the event even as Trump was simultaneously in the midst of possible impeachment proceedings.

A fourth feature of recent and future trade policy centres on how trade is also being transformed by digital technology as pivotal infrastructure. Lund and Tyson (2018) highlight three transformational changes already well underway. They show that "the movement of data is already surpassing traditional physical trade as the connective tissue in the global economy" (132). Second, they show the imperatives of the "rise of the rest" (133), by which they mean China, as well as how the geography of globalization is changing "within" the developing world in that "more than half of all international trade in goods involves at least one developing country and the trade in goods between developing countries – so-called South-South trade – grew from seven percent of the global total in 2000 to 18 percent in 2016" (134). This has implications for the nature of supply chains and augurs further "the coming disruption" (135) that will impact on dynamics related to immigration and migrants, changing rules of competition – including those around patents – and concerns about cybersecurity and decisions about where companies decide to locate their factories in this larger North-South and South-South context and set of choices (136–7). By early 2020 but with key signs earlier, the Chinese company Huawei was being aggressive in its efforts to develop, in other key Western countries, its 5G network technology (Sengupta 2020, 2). This kind of global technology capitalism involved practical concerns that the company was also at the heart of Chinese national security practices.

Critical infrastructure as a policy idea has emerged rapidly, including ideas concerning disaster recovery planning (Graham 2011; Wrobel and Wrobel 2009). So too have key notions of *strategic infrastructure* (World Economic Forum 2015). While the crafting of this policy discourse is increasingly 'normal' because of underlying features where infrastructure is seen as critical or strategic to given communities and modern supply chains, the ideas and discourse gained traction following the US 9/11 disaster resulting from international terrorism (Motef 2015). Lewis (2015) reviews US policies centred on the strategies of the Department of Homeland Security and other US departments and agencies engaged in "defending a networked nation." Canada also sought to develop action plans for critical infrastructure centred around the work of Public Safety Canada particularly regarding Canada-US border infrastructure (Hale 2012). Public Safety Canada (2014) plans were also aimed at developing "critical infrastructure resilience efforts across Canada." The relationship between critical infrastructure ideas and natural disasters is also important. Disasters such as the 2016 Fort McMurray wildfire, the June 2013 southern Alberta floods, the 2003 Northeastern US-Canada electric power blackout, and the ice storms of 1998 that saw dozens of electricity pylons pummelled and lying on the ground across Quebec and Ontario all drew massive media coverage and concern and yielded major follow-up studies and strategies to avoid (hopefully) any repetition in the future. At present, the above-mentioned 2016 Fort McMurray disaster in northern Alberta, which saw more than 80,000 people forced to flee, is still in the slow painful stages of rebuilding, with only "20 per cent of homes" in 2018 having been rebuilt, as insurance claims are processed and construction actually occurs (Griwkowsky 2018).

An important historical example of critical infrastructure that more than succeeded for future generations is the so-called "Duff's Ditch" story (Lambert 2009). Following the disastrous Winnipeg flood of 1950, Duff Roblin, then the leader of the Manitoba Conservatives, spearheaded the idea of creating what became the 47-kilometre-long Red River Floodway. He was criticized royally for this "folly," but when he became premier, he saw to it that the floodway was built (it took six years to build) to divert river water around Winnipeg. At the time only the Panama Canal was a bigger "earth moving project." The investment has since "paid off many times over" (7), especially in 1997 when a massive flood did not impact Winnipeg because of the floodway, but swamped areas in the south, including the city of Grand Forks, North Dakota, that had no such infrastructure protection. To date, the floodway has been put into operation around Winnipeg more than twenty times, justifying the initial investment several times over.

Housing as "infrastructure" is in one sense a curiously expressed idea. A UK article (Fearn 2014, 1) was titled "If Housing Were Seen as Infrastructure There Would Be a Lot More of It." This hypothesis was offered in part because infrastructure funding was seen by many as being inherently more about economic matters, whereas housing was seen as being social in nature. Most scholars of housing, Canadian and international, know that housing is quintessentially infrastructure and is about buildings that people live in and pay for via mortgage financing, or that they rent, and that it is socio-economic in nature. So the term "infrastructure" is seemingly not expressly needed in policy and political discourse, but analysis shows the intricacies of how it does emerge and has to emerge.

As Prince (1995) stressed in a review of Canadian housing policy, a "house is far more than a roof over one's head" and "it serves numerous other functions in modern society," such as being a "tool for economic development and ... an environmental good" (721). Canadian social housing has been a particular focus historically, some of it bound up in the forces and reforms that led to the establishment of the Central Mortgage and Housing Corporation (CMHC), which, from the mid-1960s on, helped create a series of housing programs centred mainly on housing finance and mortgage insurance (Rose 1980). The CMHC legacy included the fact that in the 2008–14 global crisis period, Canada's housing market was in far superior shape to that of the US. Suttor (2016) traces social housing ideas through six periods of program development but overall more recently sees a period of devolution and retrenchment in the 1990s and modest re-engagement in the 2000s (chapters 6 and 7).

We examine the housing infrastructure regime in chapter 7. Recently, further ideas and discourse have emerged in relation to rental housing, new versus old housing stock, housing for inner cities versus the suburbs, housing for young people who cannot find any housing at reasonable costs, and soaring house prices. Some of these last are related to foreign investment in housing in big, fast-growing Canadian cities such as Vancouver and Toronto, as well as to technological impacts, including the emergence of Airbnb in the "gig economy" and the short-term rental market in many global cities, including Canadian cities.

The *supply chain* as a conceptual and practical idea emerged in the early 1980s. It captures the idea of a system of companies, organizations, logistics, information, and expertise involved in moving and

transforming resources, products, and services and delivering them
to end-customers and users domestically and internationally, often in
the context of liberalized trade and trade agreements (Baldwin 2012;
Council of Supply Chain Management Professionals 2015; Wieland
and Handfield 2013).

In practical situations the supply chain is also a de facto "demand
and supply" chain in market terms and thus involves multiple infrastructures including ports, transport, storage facilities and the like
functioning as networked public-private institutions and players.
Supply chain ideas have grown in importance and have driven transport and regulatory policy (Coleman 2015; Prentice 2012). National
and international food regulation is also seen increasingly as having
to deal with intricate supply chains that go in complex and often
circuitous ways from "farm gate to plate" (Doern and Prince 2012).
The notion of logistics is also combined conceptually with supply
chains (Christopher 2016). In the institutional and professional context, the Logistics Institute was formed in Canada in 1990. It defines
logistics as "the art and science of managing and controlling the
flow of goods, energy, information, and other resources from the source
of production to the marketplace. More than 750,000 Canadian
workers are employed in the logistics field, making it the second to
third largest employment sector in Canada. Many logisticians work
in supply management, executive management, consulting, transportation, traffic, customs, distribution, manufacturing, purchasing, and
warehousing. They work in small, medium and large companies"
(Logistics Institute 2016, 1). "Almost overnight," the Institute says,
"the responsibility of logistics grew from simply getting the product
out the door to the science of controlling the optimal flow of goods,
energy, and information through purchasing, planning and transportation management" (1).

An analysis in the *Economist* (2018b) critiques "global logistics"
and relates it to more complex supply chains and growing digitaliza-
tion. It refers initially to the highly computerized Munich Maersk
entering the transport marine shipping market in 2017, and says that
"sailing her 214,000 tonnes from port to port takes a crew of just
28. Loading and unloading the 20,000 containers she carries only
needs the supervision of one crew member" (18). The analysis then
goes on in some detail to show how slow many other merchant and
other transport networks and supply chains are because they inherently have business strategies and experience built around the value

to them of complexity and of being "adrift in a sea of paper" (18). The analysis also cites examples of data on "cascading costs" by sector, including infrastructure, execution in road, rail, sea, and air transport, but also encompassing postal delivery and courier, express, and parcel services, as well as services and advisory regarding forwarding and contract logistics (19).

Nation-building and *province-building* as changing and variously expressed and grouped ideas have been pivotal as infrastructure drivers, initially in the transportation policy field. Prime Minister Sir John A. Macdonald saw the building of the Canadian Pacific Railway (CPR) as the physical linchpin for connecting Canada as a nation. A related later version of nation-building was forged under Prime Minister Sir Wilfred Laurier with the formation of Canadian National Railways (CN) (Murray 2011; Gwyn 2011). It was also part of the policy package that became the *Crow's Nest Pass Agreement* in the 1890s, which combined federal subsidies to CPR with freight-rate guarantees to meet the needs and concerns of farmers and settlers in an era of strong prairie populism (Laycock 1990; Cruikshank 1991; Darling 1980) who were angry about the CPR's power and asymmetrical pricing practices.

In the context of province-building, each province's history is centred on the building of transport links within its territorial boundaries, including trails, roads, river systems, canals, and, as new modes developed, air transport. These often include north-south connections, small remote airfields, and airports. Eight of the ten provinces have *infrastructure* combined with *transportation* in the ministry title. Infrastructure is itself therefore a mandate policy idea, but this raises the question of how the ideas and priorities might be brought forward and judged, given that in most such ministries, the infrastructure elements relate to the provincial government's entire infrastructure purview and not just to transport infrastructure (Doern, Coleman, and Prentice 2019, chap. 1).

Social ideas in infrastructure and related policy fields have a long trajectory of changing and overlapping discourse, including the *public interest* in the context of *social regulation*; ideas and aspirations about the *social license*; and *corporate social responsibility* (Doern 2015). Safety goals have been a part of this larger story and in many ways were given renewed emphasis in the 1960s. Concepts of "the public interest" and of social regulation were then (and still are) closely entwined. Public interest as a concept and process has been of major relevance for decades (Pal and Maxwell 2003). It involves the role of values and interests beyond private market interests – and, moreover, even beyond the interests of the state as represented by elected governments. The notion that governments, their officials, and private firms have to act in the public interest emerged most sharply in democratic societies in concert with the concept of social regulation.

Social regulation has long been differentiated from economic regulation (Prince 1999). The latter refers to rules governing entry into and exit from markets; and it covers competition law and policy and corporate law, which centre on how companies are born and incorporated as limited-liability entities, as well as how they die or disappear under bankruptcy law and policy (Doern, Prince, and Schultz 2014, chap. 7). Social regulation was born at the same time as the formal emergence of the consumer movement. It was primarily concerned with notions of consumer safety, consumer protection, and the fairness of markets (Schultz 2000; Sparrow 2000). Only later did environmental issues come under the ambit of social regulation, for example the requirement for formal environmental assessment of projects proposed or planned by private interests and government (Doern, Auld, and Stoney 2015).

GOVERNANCE, POWER, AND DEMOCRACY

Federal Prime Ministerial Power
in Cabinet Government and Parliament

Policy governance and power as exercised over all policies, including infrastructure policy, are centred in Canada in the prime minister, Cabinet, and Parliament, with Canada's nominal infrastructure minister being, at first glance, but one voice in a Cabinet currently consisting of 37 ministers, and but one MP in a 338-member House of Commons.

The structure of Cabinet power resides under increasing amounts and forms of prime ministerial oversight and control. This has been true for some time but especially since the late 1990s under the Chrétien-Martin and even more so the Harper governments from 2006 to 2015 (Savoie 2013; 2010; Doern, Prince, and Maslove 2013). In significant ways, prime ministers act as de facto infrastructure policy ministers, through various actions that support, discourage, or sideline considerations of infrastructure in national and international agendas. Closely aligned in this portfolio and power equation is the minister of Finance, who exerts varying degrees of control vis-à-vis macroeconomic fiscal, economic, and budgetary policy (see more below).

While executive governance is our primary focus, the House of Commons as the elected house of representative democracy is also a part of the story (Aucoin, Jarvis, and Turnbull 2011; Fletcher and Blais 2012; Malloy 2004). Opposition parties and their infrastructure agendas (or lack thereof) will be examined in later chapters, as will the roles of parliamentary committees and parliamentary watchdog agencies. At present those committees include mainly the Standing Committee on Transport, Infrastructure and Communities, and other subject-matter committees where infrastructure issues bubble up, for example in Energy pertaining to oil and gas pipelines, and in some social and social policy contexts and fields, such as those concerned with housing. Also important here are accountability reports by the Auditor General of Canada and by the Commissioner of the Environment and Sustainable Development (CESD).

Infrastructure Canada, Other Infrastructure Ministers, and Inter-Ministerial Coordination and Power

Infrastructure Canada is the lead federal department and ministry (see chapter 2 for further detailed analysis of the multi-level federalism infrastructure story). Other ministers with partial infrastructure mandates include Transport Canada, which was first established in 1936; the Treasury Board Secretariat (TBS); Public Works and Government Services Canada; Indigenous Peoples and Northern Affairs; the CMHC; and the regional agencies. As Hilton (2007) shows, the original Canada Infrastructure Works Program was housed in the TBS, itself a central agency with budgetary and managerial oversight tasks, and then was transferred to the Privy Council Office (PCO), another central agency, and then to Industry Canada.

The dynamics of inter-ministerial jurisdictional and political power are to be expected in Cabinet government, given that few issues are ever confined to a single minister's scope of interest or authority. And they are in turn impacted by dictates and interventions from prime ministers and Finance ministers as well as other Cabinet executive central agencies (Pal 2014; Savoie 2015; Doern and Phidd 1992). The dynamics can often play out behind the scenes and occur via bilateral and multilateral meetings, discussions, and ministerial leaks to the media, and include political threats and counter-threats.

One interesting development in inter-ministerial dynamics with the Justin Trudeau Liberal government, elected in October 2015, was the publication of *ministerial mandate letters* from the prime minister to each minister. These were said to be operational for the four-year life of the government (Tang 2015). The letter for the minister of Infrastructure and Communities said that they, "in concert with Transport Canada and others, will have the lead, and in consultation with provincial and territorial governments, as well as municipalities, develop and implement an Infrastructure Strategy which will see significant investments made to improve public transit infrastructure and green infrastructure" (Prime Minister of Canada 2015, 2). The minister of Infrastructure and Communities will also "have the lead, on the delivery of the newly focussed *Building Canada Fund* which will make greater investments in Canada's roads, bridges, transportation corridors, ports, and border gateways, helping Canada's manufacturers get their goods to market" (2). Some of the threads and dynamics of inter-ministerial cabinet government are important, for good and for ill – historically as well as at present. They also emerge in the regime chapters in part II of this book.

In practical terms, however, it is also true that all cabinet ministers have infrastructure concerns and responsibilities in that they function in one or more departmental buildings and also regional offices of superior, good or below average quality and efficacy. They also depend on communications infrastructure ranging from websites to social media communication, both linked to demands for privacy and information provision, but also to growing fears for cyber-security.

Macro-Economic and Fiscal Policy

Ultimately the ideas about capital budgets for infrastructure discussed earlier have to find their place among even larger and more crucial ideas and theories about macroeconomic and fiscal policy. These have been centred in conjoined debates about Keynesian demand management and later structural fundamentalism or micro-economic growth theory and policy (Doern, Maslove, and Prince 2013; Phillips and Castle 2013; Atkinson et al. 2013). In the period from the 1980s to the present, macro policy has been directed primarily to addressing long-term structural issues and has been much less short-term cyclically oriented as governments have explicitly become less confident about their ability to smooth out fluctuations in the economy. Yet the earlier Keynesian era of active stabilization policy fundamentally altered citizens' expectations of government, creating political pressures that have forced government responses, thereby setting up a tension between long-term structural goals and short-term stabilization goals, and also between cyclical and structural "deficits." These could and easily do translate in infrastructure terms to life-cycle deficits as well. In addition, and crucially, Clark (2018) analyzes the Justin Trudeau government's decision to finance infrastructure via deficits, which received electoral support because of adverse austerity impacts in Canada (and globally), but Clark also raises immediate issues of solving these impacts in federal-provincial and city governmental fiscal agenda and infrastructure terms.

Analyses of the above kinds also show that macro fiscal budgets also reflect an amalgam of the government's core values and goals, such as its basic views of the nature and extent of state intervention in the economy and in society and the need to address the constraints and pressures of international markets and economic and political conditions, as well as unforeseen domestic developments and controversies. At times the government's core values emerge quite clearly; at times the larger market and national and international political imperatives drive the fiscal agenda. Versions of these ideas are also present at the provincial government level where, as at the federal level, choices also have to comply with "fiscal rules" defined as "all the rules and regulations that govern how budgets are drafted, approved, and implemented. More narrowly they refer to deliberate restrictions on the possible outcomes of budget making" (Atkinson et al. 2013, 64).

The notion of "structural fundamentalism" captured the importance of "getting the fundamentals right" so that the Canadian economy was well placed to do as well as possible under varying economic circumstances (Doern, Maslove, and Prince 2013, chap. 3). The fundamentals were twofold: the fundamentals of the public purse, such as budgetary deficits; and the structural fundamentals of the economy, such as the taxation, investment, and regulatory regime and environment. While there have been short and specific revivals of Keynesianism, the structural fundamentalism paradigm still basically reigns in Canada, and thus the notion and practicality of infrastructure capital budgets as ideas must find their space in these larger policy dynamics and systems of power.

The Provinces and Their Combined
Infrastructure "and" Transport Ministries

All the provinces have had transportation ministries from the time of their entry into Confederation. This was even before the first nominal federal "transportation" ministry was formed in 1936. At the turn of the millennium, twenty years ago, most provincial transport departments bore the "transport" nomenclature. But now the vast majority are called "transport and infrastructure" ministries, either in that order or even the reverse (Doern, Coleman, and Prentice 2019, chap. 1). Infrastructure nomenclature and mandates reflected the overall emergence of infrastructure as its own policy field both federally and provincially and, perhaps especially, in patterns and sources of federal-provincial and federal-urban funding, as we discuss further below and in later regime chapters.

Provincial transport-infrastructure governance must therefore find its own ministerial and inter-ministerial bargains and balances, precisely because it has political duties across the whole government for all infrastructure and not just for transport interests and projects per se. In funding terms, they function like miniature treasury boards or budget offices. Provincial transport governance also involves periodic reviews and review processes. But ultimately, infrastructure and its governance in concert with transportation is a challenge and a puzzle because it is a conjoined and complex part of the federal-provincial-cities-communities governance space. Moreover, the intermixing of the two (transportation and infrastructure) implies that policy-making does not differentiate between static infrastructure and infrastructure that consists of the movement of aircraft, vehicles, and ships and – especially – the intelligence and strategies by which these movements are choreographed and executed to provide services for individual Canadians and the economy (see chapter 6).

Business and Corporate Power

Claims about democratic governance in any policy field, including infrastructure policy, have to contend with at least five arenas and kinds of democracy and various notions of democratic deficits, imperfections, and power (Lenard and Simeon 2013; Doern and Prince 2012; Dryzek and Dunleavy 2009; Pal 2014). They were defined briefly in our book's Introduction as: 1) *representative democracy*,

2) *federalized democracy*, 3) *interest group pluralism*, 4) *civil society democracy*, and 5) *direct democracy*.

Business and corporate power are invested partly in interest-group pluralism, but typically they are discussed in terms of the more-privileged advantages of corporations in Canadian and international capitalist economic systems. Infrastructure lobbies and power systems concentrate their attention on federal and provincial infrastructure ministries, but they also have good access to other ministries and centres of cabinet power – the prime minister, and ministers of finance, industry, agriculture, natural resources, communications, and procurement, to name only a few.

To the best of our knowledge there is no systematic or complete analytical literature on Canadian infrastructure business and corporate power as exercised by individual infrastructure corporations or interest groups and associations. There are accounts, as noted above, of corporate power and influence of individual firms such as CPR and CN in rail transport and related infrastructure, both when they were initially publically owned and then after and at present as privatized corporations. Related configurations have also occurred regarding electricity restructuring (Dewees 2005).

With regard to infrastructure interest groups and associations in the role of lobbyists and players, in addition to think tanks, our research indicates a complex initial listing of about forty entities which regularly research infrastructure issues and lobby governments at all three levels of Canadian federalism. These include the:

- Canadian Construction Association;
- Canadian Public Works Association;
- Canadian Society for Civil Engineering;
- Federation of Canadian Municipalities (which we discuss below as a key initial set of lobby groups);
- Canadian Water and Waste Association;
- Global Infrastructure Investor Association;
- Canadian Gas Association;
- Canada West Foundation;
- C.D. Howe Institute;
- Fraser Institute;
- PPP Canada;
- Canadian Chamber of Commerce;
- Canadian Ship-Owners Association;

- Business Council of Canada (formerly the Council of Chief Executives);
- Canadian Trucking Alliance;
- Association of Canadian Port Authorities;
- Canadian Association for Business and Economics;
- Canadian Home Builders Association;
- Insurance Bureau of Canada;
- Canadian Life and Health Insurance Association;
- Freight Management Association;
- Air Transport Association;
- Building Industry and Land Development Association;
- Ontario and Canadian Home Builders' Association;
- Mining Association of Canada;
- Railway Association of Canada;
- Information Technology Association of Canada;
- Canadian Centre for Emergency Preparedness;
- Western Canada Road Builders and Heavy Construction Association;
- Downtowns Canada;
- Residential and Civic Construction Alliance of Canada;
- Canadian Council of Public Private Partnerships;
- Canadian Institute of Planners;
- Ontario Teachers Pension Plan;
- Ontario Advisory Council on Government Assets;
- Canadian Airports Council; and
- Logistics Institute.

Many others also emerge in our regime chapters.

The first four listed above are the four founding organizations of the Canadian Infrastructure Report Card (CIRC) cited in our Introduction. They collectively form the CIRC's Project Steering Committee. But even here, fourteen other entities beyond the core four were involved as Report Card Advisory Board members for the 2016 report, including the Association of Consulting Engineering Companies, the Canadian Association of Municipal Administrators, and the Canadian Urban Transit Association. We have already emphasized in our book's Introduction the importance of the Canadian Infrastructure Report Card 2016 and its task of "informing the future." The role of municipal administrators warrants separate mention, given the way in which it ensured that smaller municipalities were given emphasis in the report, including in the report's glossary of terms. The latter drew attention to "small municipalities with populations under 30,000; medium municipalities 30,000 to 99,999; and large municipalities greater than 100,000" (143). It also differentiated between "upper-tier municipalities" formed by two or more lower-tier municipalities; "lower-tier municipalities, when there is another level of municipal government such as a county or region in providing services to residents"; and "single-tier municipalities" that "do not form part of an upper-tier municipality and have responsibilities for all local services to their residents" (144). This kind of differentiation is understandable in many ways and we offer examples in later chapters of how small municipalities often have to recalibrate for survival. This may require them to think through what kind of possible local tourism infrastructure they need to attract people and businesses to the region, in addition to the needs of citizens already living in their municipality.

The above categorization of larger city municipalities also stands in stark contrast to the focus below, and in other regime chapters, on very big high-growth cities such as Toronto, Vancouver, and Calgary, which are the real impetus for the fact that over seventy per cent of Canadians now live in cities.

We cannot, of course, analyze all of the interest group entities highlighted in this initial list. What can be said at this stage is that this interest-group structure is complex and stretches across multiple infrastructure asset types and realms such as potable water, wastewater, storm water, roads and bridges, buildings, sport and recreational facilities, and public transit as highlighted and analyzed, as an example, in the Canadian Infrastructure Report Card 2016.

Infrastructure Banks, Banking, and Public-Private Partnership (P3) Governance

This is a fast-changing, complex, and experimental governance realm. The current aspect receiving analytical attention is the Trudeau Liberal government's Canada Infrastructure Bank (CIB) as proposed by its Advisory Council on Economic Growth; this is central to its planned deficit fiscal policy borrowing for the medium term and for long-term growth (Hanniman 2018; Demers and Demers 2016). Nevertheless, criticisms centre still on the notion that Canada "is an infrastructure laggard in a world where these investments matter more and more"

(Public Policy Forum 2016). The CIB is seen (see related regime analysis in chapters 4 and 5) as a key part of the solution because it is centred on more public-private leveraged systems of finance, but its overall efficacy in addressing Canada's infrastructure gap remains a source of contention and debate.

Proposed new infrastructure banks, however, cannot really be thought through and assessed until one compares them and locates them in relation to, for example, *regular banks* (see chapter 4), which fund infrastructure all the time via normal corporate finance or "on-balance sheet finance." They typically do so to fund "lower value projects" (World Bank Group 2017), but frequently also handle high volumes of these kinds of infrastructure loans. Moreover, new types of infrastructure financing instruments and incentives are being mapped and critiqued nationally and internationally (OECD 2015).

The OECD's study begins with the observation that infrastructure "financing can present particular challenges owing to the nature of infrastructure assets," including: "capital intensity and longevity; economies of scale and externalities; heterogeneity, complexity and presence of a large number of parties; and opaqueness" (8). Overall, the report argues that the "potentially large information asymmetries that may exist in infrastructure, along with the long term nature of infrastructure investment, may lead parties to deviate ex post from ex ante decisions, a risk which among others may impede private financing" (8). Consequently, risks and risk perceptions are a constant but always changing presence. As the global economy came out of the 2008 to 2014 international banking and fiscal crisis, new banking rules were also "steering banks away from long-term loans" (*Economist* 2014, 1).

Public finances thus always involve complex issues of trust in the funding of programs that are unambiguously long-term in nature. A significant success story in budgetary trust and innovation was the establishment in 1998 of the Canada Pension Plan Investment Board (CPPIB) (Prince 2003). Created as a Crown Corporation by the Chrétien government and participating provincial governments, its mandate was to invest CPP savings in capital markets. Concerns had arisen in the mid-1990s about the sustainability of the CPP, which was taxpayer-funded on a pay-as-you-go basis. Provincial governments under the old system also had full access to CPP funds at preferential interest rates. These Canadian reforms were seen as successful in their own ways and along with related changes in Australia, the two countries were cast together as exceptions to the larger US, Asian, and

European overall systems – this in a decade when major experiments were underway, each with risks and dilemmas to solve, driven by the complex political and economic parties and interests involved (Inderst and Della Croce 2013; Darryl et al. 2011).

Capital and infrastructure financing and governance also come out in the context of the emergence of public-private partnerships (PPPs or P3s) in more formal terms (Newman 2017). These projects for roads, schools, and other infrastructure involve complex and long-term contracts in which the private sector puts up some or all of the capital costs and then governments lease the facilities. Intricate notions of risk and liability if things go wrong are also a part of these long-term deals (P3 Canada 2016; Caselli, Vecchi, and Corbett 2015; Bordeleau 2012). (See further regime discussion in chapters 4 and 5).

Canada "currently has 245 public-private partnerships (P3s) with the largest and one of the more unique being Bruce Nuclear Generating Facility" (Bruce Power and the Canadian Council for Public-Private Partnerships 2017, 2). Formed in 2001, Bruce Power describes itself as "Canada's only private sector nuclear generator. It is the world's largest operating 8-unit nuclear facility and is located in rural southwestern Ontario. The company is a Canadian-owned Partnership of Ontario Municipal Employees Retirement System (OMERS), Trans-Canada Corporation, the Power Workers Union and the Society of Energy Professionals" (Bruce Power 2016, 2). The company also stresses that it has signed a "long term agreement with the Province of Ontario that will see Units 3–8 refurbished over the next two decades, extending the life of the site to 2064" (2). It is also regulated by the federal Canadian Nuclear Safety Commission (CNRS) and states that it has supported "Ontario's climate change goals by staying off coal" (2). Thus, it does show its formal and important P3 governance and financing features, but its de facto "partners" also include the Ontario government and the CNRS. The overall Bruce Power story certainly includes the private investment of billions of dollars and planned billions more (Bruce Power and Canadian Council for Public-Private Partnerships 2017, 14–15), but it also is anchored legally on the reality that the "site is leased from the Province of Ontario under a long-term lease where all of the assets remain publically owned" (5). Bruce Power's investment in the units includes all refurbishment and maintenance costs (16–17).

Space clearly does not allow any coverage here of the other 244 public-private partnerships said to exist, let alone other de facto quasi-partnerships that exist in any number of policy fields with infrastructure content, or the numbers that are likely to form around the work of the Canada Infrastructure Bank and existing pension funds, nationally and internationally. Suffice to say they are likely to garner criticism from authors and analysts depending on their values and relative level of support for the public sector versus private business, and also depending on whether one can follow the complex cause and effect trails and roadblocks inherent in (and intended to be in) P3s, in addition to the specific policy field in which they are experimenting with the public interest (Whiteside 2015a; 2015b; Siemiatycki 2018; 2016; 2012). Similar to the Bruce Power example cited above, one can also see, for instance, the electricity utility Hydro One (formerly Ontario Hydro) now engaged in a controversial takeover of Avista, a large US utility (Wells 2018).

Regulatory Governance and Infrastructure

Regulatory theory and practice in Canada and elsewhere is frequently entwined with infrastructure either as an object of regulation or as a mentioned or unmentioned, but nevertheless present, feature in combination with diverse related regulatory challenges. The areas of regulation (federal and provincial) include competition policy, environmental law, international and internal trade, health and safety, deregulation, the avoidance of regulatory capture by key interests/ businesses, and the issue of regulatory complexity.

It may be tempting to argue that the era of economic deregulation continues in the Canadian economy, but this has not been strictly true for the past twenty years in Canada, nor in many other countries (Doern, Prince, and Schultz 2014). Some scholars have cast this era as one with a strong element of "regulatory capitalism." The concept emerged both conceptually and empirically (Braithwaite 2008; 2005; Levi-Faur 2005). It consists of the involvement of large numbers of companies in setting and enforcing rules over the behaviour of their respective industry sectors and the players within them. Enforcement usually consists of applying marketplace tools, such as granting or withholding influential certifications, as just one of many examples. It reflects the fact that regulation is growing markedly, not so much by rules and their enforcement by governments alone, but increasingly as a system of co-regulation that involves governments and businesses, and non-governmental interests and networks as well (OECD/Korean

Development Institute 2017; Doern 2017; Grabosky 2012). The distributed (and often unruly) nature of this co-regulation does not mean it is any less authoritative than government rule-making and enforcement alone. And it provides a wider range of tools for dealing with complex situations, including those that governments acting alone as regulators often have difficulty discovering or using. But these complexities and practices also involve an intricate understanding of what one author referred to as the linked importance of "motivation, agency and public policy" (LeGrande 2004).

Important analytical insights are found in a variety of critical literature (comparative and Canadian) that extends back to the efforts and failures regarding banking and financial regulation, to earlier neoliberal contexts, and in the practice of "liberal authoritarianism" (Massey 2018) as witnessed in the recent debacle regarding Carillion's UK- and Canadian-based firms. Carillion in the UK had built up a business model that built roads and hospitals, provided defense accommodation, and constructed other kinds of infrastructure. It became the UK's second largest construction firm, had 20,000 employees, and managed 450 government contracts. Numerous dubious business practices led to the bankruptcy of the firm early in 2018. The UK National Audit Office had shown earlier in 2016 that the UK "government spent about £225 billion on private and voluntary providers – almost 30 per cent of all government expenditure" (Jones 2018). Recent UK parliamentary reports blasted Carillion executives and directors, the government, auditors, and regulators (Davies 2018). There was an immediate Canadian connection via Carillion Canada, whose infrastructure business included hospital construction and maintenance and road-clearing. Carillion Canada was given immediate court-ordered creditor protection in Canada involving its four corporate entities (CBC News 2018).

The reference to auditors above is a further intricate part of the changing middle worlds of public-private governance overall and vis-à-vis infrastructure. Auditors as a profession imbued with duties to foster accountability were missing in the Carillion case, as was apparent earlier in the global banking crisis – in part because auditors as a business, indeed a big business, were themselves limited liability corporations dominated by the four big auditors: KPMG, Deloitte, Ernst & Young, and PricewaterhouseCoopers (PwC). As Brooks (2018) argues compellingly, they "audit 97% of US public companies and all of the UK's top 100 corporations ... and (they) are the only players large enough to check the numbers for these multinational organizations, and thus enjoy effective cartel status" (3). In Brooks's view they "are free to make profit without fearing serious consequences of their abuses, whether it is the exploitation of tax laws, slanted consultancy advice or overlooking financial crime" (3). These kinds of views about accountancy cast as "accountants, auditors, and credit-rating agencies" had been examined regarding the banking crisis and depression in the post-2006 period (Davies 2010, 109–30).

Greater attention has also been given conceptually to the role of "regulatory intermediaries" (Abbott, Levi-Faur, and Snidal 2017) to sharpen the need for an explicit view of regulation as a "three-party system in which intermediaries provide assistance to regulators and/ or the targets of regulation, drawing on their own capacities, authority, and legitimacy" (1). Regulatory intermediaries "range from profit making firms such as inspection companies and credit rating agencies, to NGOs such as human rights advocacy groups, to trans governmental networks of regulatory agencies" (2). While the above analysis includes a wide variety of regulatory intermediary realms, one analysis is centred on the regulatory governance of *buildings* infrastructure explicitly (van der Heijden 2017) and focuses on both the "brighter and darker sides of intermediation." Other chapters also deal with infrastructure content (but often without calling it that) in the context of other complex fields, including food safety and pharmaceuticals.

The issue of particular kinds of intermediaries has also been usefully explored regarding the role of agents of Parliament and legislatures in Canada at the federal, provincial, and territorial levels (Public Policy Forum 2018a). The research indicates that about 88 agents currently operate (31–2). They have "wide independence to critique the work of government from elections to finances and ethics to privacy but have few powers of enforcement if they see wrongdoing" (1). The report recommends several ways of sharpening their role so that parliamentary and legislatorial roles and power are made more explicit. Among the recommendations are that "legislators should set a high mark for creating new agents" and that "the creation of new agents should be the purview of Parliament and legislatures and not the executive. A majority of elected officials in at least two official parties should agree to the establishment of a new agent" (1). But even in their current operational state, it is impossible regarding infrastructure analysis not to have many of these bodies as part of the overall politics, policy, and governance, as several of our regime chapters will show.

A different but also interesting Canadian intermediary institution is the Investment Industry Regulatory Organization of Canada (2018a). IIROC is the "national self-regulatory organization which oversees all investment dealers and trading activity on debt and equity marketplaces in Canada." IIROC "writes rules that set high regulatory and investment industry standards ... screens all investment advisors employed by IIROC-regulated firms ... conducts financial compliance reviews and sets minimum capital requirements to ensure firms have enough capital for the specific nature and volume of their business" (1). IIROC "was established as a non-profit corporation through the consolidation of the Investment Dealers Association of Canada (IDA) and Market Regulation Services Inc. (RS)." Securities legislation (mainly provincial) requires investment dealers to apply and be accepted for membership with a self-regulatory organization (SRO) if they wish to operate in Canada. Prior to the early 1990s, membership in an SRO was voluntary, but it is now compulsory. IIROC reviews investor complaints and overall has significant power over penalties that can be imposed, including fines "up to a maximum of $1 million per contravention or an amount equal to three times the profit made, or loss avoided, due to the contravention" (4). For our purposes on policy and governance in and around infrastructure, the intermediary institutional elements can be seen in key features such as rules regarding standards, the sufficiency of capital, business conduct compliance reviews, and so on. IIROC's stated "vision" is to "demonstrate how our self-regulatory model serves the public interest" (2). Significantly, though IIROC is a national body, it is ultimately anchored in provincial legislation.

A review of fifty years of Canadian regulation by Doern, Prince, and Schultz (2014) demonstrated that recent history can be characterized by the growth of rules and unruliness. When it comes to systems of governance, unruliness consists of a growing inability on the part of governments to make effective rules and to enforce them. Regulation also extends well beyond statutes and delegated law. It also includes codes, guidelines, and standards, both domestic and international. It involves ever more complex relations and ambiguity in the regulatory governance system, including between and among *ends and means* (74–96).

A recent book on the European Union is cast as the "art of regulation" and focuses on competition in Europe and argues for greater wariness about the power of the wealthy (Koenig and von Wendland 2017). It argues that increasingly the EU market regulatory measures have been "introduced in pursuit of economic justice and welfare" but the need is also for regulation "that can prevent the abuse of dominance, in particular the abuse of public capital by the state" (1). Public capital referred to the fact that it was EU governments themselves that were building and paying for infrastructure across EU member borders. The analysis includes the dynamics of supporting infrastructure. Critical analysis has also emerged in research on *outsourcing the law* (Westerman 2018). As a legal scholar and judge, Westerman's review argues, in her examination of a philosophical perspective on regulation, that overall it is a system of "all ends and no means" (chap. 1, p. 1). Key components of her analysis explore the world "between compliance and performance," "commissioned self-regulation," and the "outsourcing of democracy" (chap. 3–5).

As infrastructure policy and spending emerged more strongly, particularly in the context of the current federal Liberal government's strong infrastructure focus and plans for an infrastructure bank, several studies by the C.D. Howe Institute have brought out more concretely the links between infrastructure and regulatory strategy in specific policy/funding infrastructure situations (Dachis 2017; Robins 2017; Found 2016). Among the Dachis study recommendations is that governments, "where necessary, create independent regulatory bodies to oversee infrastructure assets that ensure their owners, either government-owned corporations or institutional investors, act in the public interest ahead of private profit, and for long-term sustainability" (Dachis 2017, 1). The study by Robins focuses on Canada's airports and seeks to change Canada's airport ownership governance structure from "non-profit, non-share capital airport authorities, with the federal government owning and leasing land to airport authorities" (Robins 2017, 1), to one that requires selling off equity to allow for an "improved airport experience for services at airports" (1). The new model would also involve a complementary regulatory system as other studies have pointed out (Doern, Coleman, and Prentice 2019, chap. 7).

A further regulatory analysis centres on government procurement regulation (Georgopoulos, Hoekman, and Mavroidis 2017) in which several countries and realms of procurement regulation are examined. A chapter by Lalonde (2017, 300–18) reviews recent Canadian practices on the implementation of international agreements by Canada. These include Canada's CETA agreement with the EU, and a focus on deficiencies in Canada, namely public procurement practices as compared to the obligations embedded in the agreements, and basic standards of transparency and fairness in procurement. Lalonde also calls for improvements in the collection and public dissemination of procurement-related data, and raises issues about how these have affected the treatment of foreign bidders in the procurement process. Specific international procurement practices have also been analyzed regarding Canadian military-defence procurement in the Trudeau Liberals' "Strong, Secure and Engaged" document as a twenty-year funding model (Perry 2018).

Infrastructure Policy Agenda-Setting

Among the most complex and interesting elements of policy and governance dynamics is that of infrastructure policy agenda setting. We examine this later in several regime chapters, but first it needs to be seen in the context of broader conceptual theories of agenda setting. They are built around the complex interactions between politicians and policy-makers, the media, and the public. They arise from the issue-attention cycle by which all the different players – voters, citizens, the mass media, and governments themselves – engage in framing and reframing problems and opportunities (Eisler, Russell, and Jones 2014; Wolfe, Jones, and Baumgartner 2013; Howlett 1998; Kingdon 1993). But the dynamic nature of the system and the collective inability of people to sustain focus and interest on most (or perhaps any) issues also leads to "punctuated equilibria," a phenomenon in which most policy stays stable for long periods, while, in a punctuated fashion, some policies change quickly and dramatically (Baumgartner and Jones 1993; Jones and Baumgartner 2012; 2005). We address these kinds of agenda-setting dynamics and puzzles later, regarding Throne Speech and Budget Speech content and dynamics around infrastructure spending and discourse, in addition to examining how public-private partnerships are formed and reformed, many steps removed from central budgeting and political agenda-setting occasions.

INFRASTRUCTURE TECHNOLOGY ASSESSMENT, PLATFORMS, NETWORKS, AND COMPLEXITIES

This is the third stream of foundational literature. It is based on technology-driven or -enabled developments in infrastructure interacting with policy and institutional efforts to assess technology policy and related science developments, as well as the pace and legitimacy of such efforts; we label it "infrastructure technology assessment" and tie it to the presence and nature of platforms and networks, and to complexities and theories of complexity.

Technology Assessment

We begin with the evolving research on technology assessment, including its role in the evaluation of transformative and disruptive technologies. Formal calls for better technology-assessment institutions and processes emerged after World War II, when the accelerating pace of development of new technologies suggested that society and politics needed to assess them, their benefits, and their potential adverse impacts – *before* they emerged in the form of new products and production processes (Nordman 2004). Several high-profile cases arose in the late 1960s and early 1970s, for example, over the benefits and challenges of supersonic passenger aircraft. The United States established the Congressional Office of Technology Assessment (OTA) in 1972. It published numerous technology assessments but was abolished in 1995 in the wake of a Republican victory in the midterm elections in 1994 (Mooney 2005; Nye 2006). Its demise was due less to its usefulness and relevance from a public policy standpoint, than to sharp partisan politics by a (conservative-dominated) Congress that was portrayed as "anti-science" as well as being opposed to government intervention of the kind implied in technology-assessment processes initiated and sponsored by government. As we have seen earlier in this chapter, the early years of the US Trump era have been chaotically disruptive (Swanson 2018; *Economist* 2018; Monbiot 2018; see more in chapter 3).

Canada has never made as formal an effort to undertake prospective technological assessments as a matter of overall ongoing public policy; nevertheless, it has tried in its own way to build such capacity, including the input of science and scientists, for example via the establishment of the Science Council of Canada and also of later S&T advisory bodies such as the National Advisory Board on Science and Technology (NABST) and the Advisory Council on Science and Technology (ACST) (Doern and Kinder 2007). A major part of this science advice component has centred on and led to claims of government "muzzling" and political interference in science (Chung 2018; Office of the Science Advisor 2018; Doern, Castle, and Phillips 2016, 37–40; O'Hara and Dufour 2014).

Canada has also had to assess and regulate new "cutting-edge" infrastructure technologies, such as: nuclear power (International Atomic Energy Agency 2016; Doern and Morrison 2009; Bratt 2006); carbon capture and storage (Meadowcroft and Hellin 2010); genomics (Castle and Rise 2009); internet advancement via the early SchoolNet program (Tumin 2000) and the strategy labelled the Information Highway (Doern 1996); and social media (Doern, Castle, and Phillips 2016). In each of these the focus is on the technology but the analysis refers variously to relevant infrastructure and platforms, often without labelling them as such. Technology-assessment institutions and issues also continue to be examined through international bodies, for instance the International Association for Technology Assessment and Forecast Institutions and various university institutes. As we shall see in chapter 3, Canada also has ongoing links to, and awareness of, US and international global technology-infrastructure dynamics and policy advocacy.

The notion of transformative and disruptive technologies tends to define those periods of time and development in which economies and societies are remade by changes in foundational technology. This idea is closely linked to Schumpeter's earlier influential concept of "creative destruction" (Schumpeter 1954; 1934). The concept of disruptive technologies has found its way into analytical use, including for describing and characterizing intertwined technologies such as digital technology, nanotechnology, and the neurosciences, and even for smaller kinds of disruption that create new industries and products based on information and data (Zussman 2014). The latter are embodied in online businesses, which can grow with astonishing speed and quickly become an existential threat to established players in the industry (*Economist* 2014a). Uber as a technology company has had massive impacts on transportation even though it is not a transportation company per se. It has also impacted other urban infrastructures, including mass public transportation and changing key notions about the future of urban life in an era of app-driven technology and driverless cars. In a different way Amazon, via technology and its massive storage and distribution platform infrastructure, has fostered online shopping and changed business models everywhere (*Economist* 2017). That said, it also plans to invest in new bricks-and-mortar stores in key markets (Wingfield 2017), and to use drones as a further delivery technology.

Industry Canada under the Harper Conservatives described disruptive technologies as a key presence in the Canadian economy in both positive and negative senses, and in an unavoidable sense as well (Industry Canada 2014). They are certainly also a part of the Trudeau Liberals' agenda with respect to that party's innovation policies regarding start-up companies, and also its initial infrastructure focus (Doern and Stoney 2016). Disruption comes from the internet, information and communications technology, biotechnology, and nano-technologies, all of which have links to other sectoral technologies, products, and processes in a wide range of industries and social realms (Mazzucato 2013). Many or most such analyses look not just to the future, but to historical developments in terms of strategies of social resistance and how they change the technologies' trajectories and shapes (Bauer 2015).

Phillips (2007) stresses the inherent complexity, multi-stakeholder shared relations, and competing nature of the models of governance of contemporary transformative technology. He also shows the highly linked stages of innovation. Not surprisingly, these have involved wide-ranging debates about particular products and processes and the extent to which individuals and groups are actually or potentially harmed by such technologically centred and rapidly changing features (O'Doherty and Einsiedel 2013). The upshot of all this is that the development of frameworks and practices in technology assessment for public-policy applications is struggling to keep up with the accelerating pace and unruly nature of technological innovation. This includes technologies that are impacting infrastructure platforms in all kinds of ways.

Platforms

We have already discussed platforms in an initial historical context. Here our discussion is technology-centred and focuses initially on the World Wide Web, and then on the period since the late 1990s as later internet-linked technologies emerged cumulatively in rapid fashion. These technologies include Google, Facebook, Twitter, Microsoft, social production media, and Amazon, in addition to firms already mentioned such as Uber and Airbnb and others that feature later in our regime chapter analyses. *The Economist* (2018c) analyzes this overall history in its account of stages and views about how to "fix" the internet. One of its broader conclusions is that "to understand the internet's recent history, it helps to keep in mind that, like most digital systems, it is designed in layers" (6) and therefore "there is no single solution for decentralising the internet" (12).

An earlier analysis by Gawer (2009) built on the emergence of Microsoft Windows and Google, in which she observed that such "platforms invite us to examine carefully the intimate interactions between technology and business and in particular between the structure of technology and the modalities of interaction" (4). Herriman (2018) as a knowledgeable *New York Times* technology journalist focuses on eBay, a tech firm that went public in 1998. He argues that eBay "is a platform that connects buyers and sellers. It does not itself sell goods: it lists and sorts and processes, providing shelves for its users' inventory and aisles for their prospective customers. It mediates as little as possible, and it takes a cut" (1).

Herriman goes on to argue one should look at eBay to see what ails the modern internet. Citing work by Andrei Hagiu, Herriman also stresses that eBay "was among the first true *mega platforms* – the sort that establishes itself as something like online infrastructure" (2). When he links it later to Facebook, he shows the differences with eBay because Facebook is "a giant, multisided marketplace for buying and selling, in which the largest party – the users – doesn't do the buying or the selling. A social network's profitable transactions involve everyone but the users" (4). Hagiu has focused on the "nature of strategic decisions for multisided platforms" (Hagiu 2014) and also on such examples as Uber, regarding the situations that Uber faced (Hagiu 2015) regarding the "dividing line between independent contractors and contractors and employees" (2) in numerous cities and jurisdictions locally, nationally, and internationally.

Facebook has also been cast as a platform whose key difference is the degree to which its CEO, Mark Zuckerberg, controls the company. He is, as Naughton (2018) argues, the CEO of a "public company but it is in fact his fiefdom, as a casual inspection of the company's SEC filings confirms. They show that his ownership of the controlling shares means that he can do anything he likes, including selling the company shares against the wishes of all the other shareholders combined" (1). Facebook's and Zuckerberg's other activities were linked to Russia and Cambridge Analytica in a British select committee report (Cadwalladr 2018) that called for diligent internet regulation. Because of targeted political advertising, it included the need for a "new category of tech company to be formulated which tightens tech companies' liabilities and which is not necessarily either a 'platform' or 'publisher'" (2). We return to these and other fast moving and complex tech platforms, semi-platforms, choices, and change patterns later in our six domain chapters, chapters 4 to 9.

Networks

The notion of networks has received conceptual and analytical attention for some time. Initially, in political and policy analysis, some authors cast networks as a particular feature of broader arrays in a world of "policy communities" (Coleman and Skogstad 1990). They were conceived as an analytical category that went beyond traditional interest or lobby groups to embrace broader non-governmental organizations (NGOs). Later analyses broadened the concept of networks to encompass various kinds of scientific expertise and the roles of universities (Howlett and Ramesh 2003; Montpetit 2009). In economics and related fields, however, networks are being analyzed in a much broader context, often by contrasting them with markets and hierarchies as basic modes of social and economic organization (Agranoff 2007; Thompson et al. 1991).

Hierarchies are associated with bureaucracy, especially traditional Weberian state bureaucracy. They are systems of top-down, superior-subordinate political and administrative relations accompanied by formal rules, with many forms of civil service bureaucracies whose role is to support representative cabinet-parliamentary and other systems of democratic government (Aucoin 1997). Markets are organized on the basis of "voluntary" means of exchange involving money, commerce, and the making of profits, but with the state providing and enforcing key rules and protections for property rights and transactions. Networks differ from both of the above: they are forms of organization characterized by non-hierarchical and voluntary relations based on trust, and commonality of shared interests and values, where profit is not necessarily a defining characteristic (Agranoff 2007; Thompson et al. 1991). But hierarchies, markets, and networks are being increasingly combined by the players within them in very complex and creative ways.

Some attributes of networks as an institutional concept are expressed in terms of constructing *partnerships* as already discussed above. They can be truly voluntary in nature, but more often they take on the form of policy-induced or policy-required and contractual (or quasi-contractual) partnerships between or among public- and private-sector entities and interest groups. In this context, networks are similar to, or criss-cross with, supply chains and logistic functions. They also often acquire some of the characteristics inherent in markets or hierarchies, too (Kinder 2010), and they are a key part of theories of regulatory capitalism where, as we have seen above, co-regulation of diverse kinds is involved.

Complexity

Complexity is endemic to technology assessment, platforms, and networks. Theories of complexity per se have been developed and used within the natural sciences and engineering for decades. Some of this has crossed over into work that tries to characterize systems of society and social innovation, where it has become a part of public policy theory in the twenty-first century. Authors such as Geyer and Rihani (2012) and Morcol (2012) advocate more use of complexity theory based on their view that too many policy-makers and policy scholars treat policy and governance systems as being orderly, predictable, and controllable when in reality they are anything but. Complexity notions have also been needed, as Pal (2014) argues, in matters of policy and decision-making because of the need to model chaos in the face of accidents, floods, terrorism, crises, and infrastructure protection. Norberg and Cumming (2012) also use the idea of complexity to analyze sustainable development in a variety of policy fields; and Walby (2007) uses it to examine the nature of what she describes in social policy terms as "multiple intersecting social inequalities."

Indeed, concepts of complexity are a part of the literature on public policy and governance even when complexity theory is not centrally or overtly used. In his analysis of the internet, Naughton (2012) describes complexity as the "new reality," arguing that complexity is not easy to unpack and hence is hard to understand or predict (162–3). He also points out that the challenging "architecture" of complexity was initially raised by Nobel economist Herbert Simon (1962) well before the rise of the internet. This extends to innovation policy (economic and social) and the behaviour of network-based clusters, which embody or display most or all of the features of networks, clusters, and issues surrounding innovation policy. They are, therefore, complex whether anyone has a theory of complexity about them or not.

For example, complexity is rampant and explicit in emerging views about robotics, artificial intelligence (AI), and related forms of automation (Arntz, Gregory, and Zierahn 2016; International Federation of Robotics 2016). In a burgeoning literature, it is interesting for our purposes that robotics and automation are rarely described as infrastructure platforms, though they easily could be. Not surprisingly, the focus is on the impacts of robotics on jobs and the nature of work and paid employment (Dunlop 2016a; 2017; Acemoglu and Restrepo 2017; Cain Miller 2017). Dunlop makes the case for why, as a result of robotics, "the future is jobless" in the sense that jobs replaced by robotics are "gone and aren't coming back" (Dunlop 2017, 1). Robotics also cause job losses and depress wages, but on the more positive side Dunlop argues that humans "are going to have the edge over robots where work demands creativity" and that "creative industries will grow and the ability to work with ambiguity, diversity and empathy will be valued" (1). The Acemglu and Restrepo (2017) study of US job data from 1990 to 2007 showed that the addition of each robot into manufacturing industries resulted in the loss of 6.2 human jobs on average. Naughton (2018b, 2) strongly cautions against assumptions regarding the inevitability of AI, likening some of its supporters' and analysts' approaches to "magical thinking," and arguing that "there seems to be an inverse correlation between the intensity of people's convictions about AI and their actual knowledge of the technology" (see further analysis in chapter 9 on the STI regime).

Complexity in a digital world is also revealed in Canada, in a study and process by the Public Policy Forum (2018a) that reported on a summit discussion and the need for an Ontario "digital inclusion" process and for provincial experts "to share knowledge and identify key policy and research opportunities" (1). The report opens with the legitimate view that "our lives take place online, from how we engage with our communities, to how we apply for government services, to how we launch small businesses" (2). It then went on to say that "not everyone enjoys the myriad economic, social, health, educational and cultural benefits from digital technologies" and there are many digital divides "which are related to income, geography, literacy, comfort, culture, demographics and more" (2). Discussion highlighted the inclusion dynamics and needs regarding "older Canadians and the digital divide," "public sector legal information," and "advancing women leaders in technology" (7, 8). But still other different domains emerge in the discussions and report, including "democracy and civic engagement" and "art, creative industries and media" (18–19). Similar kinds of digital focus and complex fast-moving dynamics are highlighted in a further Public Policy Forum (2018c) study on "the next level border" and making technology "work for border policy," including the need to coordinate with the US and to deal with privacy matters.

The analysis of robots, AI and automation in Canada is also emerging (Johal, Thirgood, Urban, Alwani, and Dubrovinsky 2018; Lambe 2016). The Johal et al. study by the Mowat Centre links disruptive technology and the sharing economy to robotics and examines as well, with a focus on Ontario, how the resultant changing nature of work will impact on the tax base and the government's ability to generate revenue. A Ryerson University study by Lambe (2016) concluded that "nearly 42 per cent of the employed Canadian labour force is at high risk of being affected by automation over the next 20 years" (8). It also identified the top five high-risk occupations as: retail salespersons; administrative assistants; food counter attendants and kitchen helpers; cashiers; and transport truck drivers (12).

3D printing is often cited as one of the related automation disruptive technology platforms of the last decade, with examples of many specific kinds (Campbell, Williams, Ivanova, and Garrett 2011). A recent example is found in the Dutch housing industry where early stage plans are underway now to build "the world's first 3D-printed housing estate" (Boffey 2018). The "3D printer being used is essentially a huge robotic arm with a nozzle that squirts out a specially formulated cement" (1). In the foreseeable future "people will be able to design their own homes to suit them and then print them out" (1).

Overall there is growing evidence in many advanced economies that a high percentage of new jobs are part-time. Analysis also points to the fact that dominant tech firms such as Google and Facebook have relatively small full-time employee numbers compared to, say, earlier dominant industries such as auto companies in the 1960s and 1970s.

One can also take note of the nature and impact of *air conditioning* as a technology (and platform). This has a very long and changing history globally, regionally, nationally, and also seasonally in cities regarding building construction (Moore 2018). It has featured in the way shopping malls, office blocks, museums, homes, and overall building services are designed, including their heating, cooling, and ventilating systems. Many of these are also tied to the linked use of and habits concerning air-conditioned vehicles.

A final example of complex developments is centred on work by geologists on the Geographies of Technology (Warf 2017). It examines twenty-seven different technologies, "highlighting how they influence the structure and spatiality of society" (1). The technologies are grouped into six main categories: computational, communications, transportation, energy, manufacturing, and life sciences. The analytical focus is on technology but in fact in the detailed analysis infrastructures loom large, both definitionally and illustratively.

CONCLUSIONS

Drawn from three relevant streams of literature, we have set out the conceptual foundations underpinning our analysis of infrastructure policy and governance in Canada. These foundations, Canadian and comparative in nature, and drawing on diverse research disciplines and sources, have also informed the development of our analytical framework. The place of infrastructure per se needs detective work of different kinds in each of the three streams. Regarding ideas and discourse, we have seen shifts when infrastructure is cast variously as assets, projects, procurement, platforms, and various kinds of capital, but also in the categories of public versus private infrastructure.

We also have seen diverse notions of regulatory governance with complexities in how means and ends are treated or obscured or variously outsourced or delegated in the name of different notions of democracy. Regarding governance, power and, democracy, we have seen how infrastructure has to be captured and discovered, sometimes with difficulty, in core systems of prime ministerial and cabinet government, macro-economic and fiscal policy, Canadian federalism and multi-level governance, and in changing forms of regulation. Regarding technology assessment and networks, the complexities of infrastructure have been drawn out, but only initially, given the ongoing and exponential nature of change within society. We draw upon these foundational features again in our six regime chapters, along with other literature sources more specifically relevant to understanding change and inertia in each regime, including changes and challenges posed by the dynamics of the 2020 pandemic.

2

Overview of Infrastructure Policy and Governance in Canadian Multi-Level Federalism

INTRODUCTION

In this chapter we set out the constitutional context within which the federal government operates and the significant challenges this poses for the coherent multi-level governance of Canadian cities, including the challenges and implications for infrastructure funding. This is crucial because, although some of the raw data has been laid out briefly in chapter 1 and in the book's Introduction, this does not come close to telling the multi-level federalism story. This chapter accordingly has a two-part structure: 1) the realities and evolution of multi-level federalism; and 2) six periods of federal-municipal infrastructure funding. In different ways, both provide a needed broad and basic overview of who does what with respect to infrastructure responsibilities and maintenance, which levels of government but also which private-sector organizations invest in infrastructure, and their respective motivations and obligations to do so. This includes analysis of some of the key institutions and stakeholders that have influenced, led, and funded infrastructure policy within Canada over many decades. Although it is beyond the scope of this chapter to catalogue the myriad provincial and municipal initiatives, we do draw on examples, particularly those involving the federal government in multi-level initiatives. For example, the new programs currently being rolled out in response to the COVID-19 pandemic provide a timely reminder of the underlying tensions and challenges of inter-governmental infrastructure. The historical trends identified in this chapter are intended to provide a broader context within which to examine and assess current and past policies and to provide a platform for chapter 5, which examines in more detail the financing of infrastructure.

THE REALITIES AND EVOLUTION
OF MULTI-LEVEL FEDERALISM

Constitutionally, cities are the responsibility of the provinces in Canada, but the federal role in funding infrastructure is crucial because of the disproportionate amount of taxation revenues it raises (47 per cent) compared to the provinces (44 per cent) and municipalities (9 per cent). Municipalities own and maintain the majority of urban infrastructure across Canada; this makes them highly dependent upon other levels of government for infrastructure funding, requiring them to compete with other priorities for funds. While much of the provincial tax take is directed towards spiralling health and education budgets, municipalities have in the main been restricted to property taxes as a means of financing infrastructure renewal and repair. A highly transparent source of local taxation, property taxes are nonetheless not directly linked to usage, income, or economic growth, and have failed to keep pace with rapid urban growth and the corresponding need for greater infrastructure investment.

Historically the federal government's engagement with cities and urban infrastructure has ebbed and flowed as a result of changing ideology, economic and fiscal cycles, and politics and relations that are intergovernmental in many ways. Consequently, despite considerable rhetoric from the federal government and some notable examples of policy innovation, Canada has struggled to develop and sustain a coherent and credible framework to engage effectively with cities in pursuit of sustainable funding for urban infrastructure. These factors have led municipalities to experience a growing and severe shortfall between the amount needed to build and maintain infrastructure and the funds available. Commonly referred to as the "infrastructure gap," estimates ranging from $150 billion to $1 trillion illustrate both the potential magnitude of the problem and the difficulty of estimating it accurately (Lammam and MacIntyre 2017). The staggering scale of such estimates, allied to public perceptions and concerns about the state and safety of Canada's "crumbling" urban infrastructure, have firmly established infrastructure investment as a persistent policy challenge facing all orders of Canadian government. This is reinforced by respected international bodies (the WHO and OECD, for example), Canadian think tanks such as the Conference Board, and academics and consultants disseminating research and evidence demonstrating the urgent need for greater investment in public and innovative policies to fund it.

The importance of infrastructure for economic productivity, employment, health, safety, and quality of life has also helped to establish infrastructure financing as a defining political issue in modern elections (Ratner 1983; Aschauer 1988; 1990; Doern, Auld, and Stoney 2015). While municipal leaders and the Federation of Canadian Muncipalities (FCM) have become increasingly vocal and organized in campaigning for more funding, the federal and provincial governments have become equally skilled at exploiting funding initiatives for partisan advantage. The federal Liberals' 2004 "New Deal for Cities" and the Harper Conservatives' 2008 "Economic Action Plan" demonstrated the political importance of infrastructure spending as well as the potential to brand spending in pursuit of partisan advantage (see more below).

To develop these points further and provide some further context for the rest of the book, this chapter explores the constraints imposed by a complex multi-level governance framework, the dynamics this creates, and the challenges they present for developing a coordinated and "strategic" approach to infrastructure policy and investment in Canada.

WHO IS RESPONSIBLE FOR INFRASTRUCTURE?

Each level of government owns some infrastructure assets and has ultimate responsibility for the operation and maintenance of that infrastructure. In this section we provide some further detail of ownership as well as some of the trends over recent decades. Because the costs of infrastructure projects are often shared between the levels of government, the picture becomes increasingly blurred; we illustrate this before considering the implications for governance and policy. For example (see table 2.1), research covering the 1961–2002 period reveals that the content of Canada's stock of public infrastructure ownership remained consistent, with, municipally, local highways and roads constituting around 45 per cent, sewage treatment 12 per cent, and sanitary sewers 17 per cent; provincially, highways and roads accounted for 69 per cent, bridges 10 per cent, sewage treatment 4 per cent, and sanitary sewers 5 per cent; and federally highways and roads averaged 19 per cent, trunk and distribution lines 9 per cent, docks, wharves, piers, and terminals 13 per cent, sewage treatment 7 per cent, and sanitary sewers 12 per cent (Harchaoui, Tarkhani, and Warren 2004).

From this list of 'fixed' public infrastructure it is clear that ownership and responsibility for maintenance of highways, roads, bridges, sewage, and several other critical infrastructures are common to each

Table 2.1
Public infrastructure stock

Government	Local	Provincial	Federal
PUBLIC INFRASTRUCTURE STOCK	Highways and roads	Highways and roads	Highways and roads
	Sewage treatment	Bridges	Trunk and distribution mains
	Sanitary sewers	Sewage treatment	Docks, wharves, piers, and terminals
	Bridges	Sanitary sewers	Sewage treatment
	Canals and waterways	Canals and waterways	Sanitary sewers
	Outdoor recreational	Reservoirs	Runways
	Waste disposal facilities	Outdoor recreational	Railtrack
	Irrigation facilities	Irrigation facilities	Bridges
			Electric power construction
			Communication towers
			Other communication
			Canals and waterways
			Reservoirs
			Outdoor recreational
			Irrigation facilities

Source: Harchaoui, Tarkhani, and Warren 2004.

level of government. While this complicates matters, it is to be expected in a federal system, especially one as vast as Canada. As a rule of thumb, municipalities are largely responsible for urban infrastructure, provincial governments for infrastructure in the hinterland and between provincial centres, while the federal government has constitutional powers over inter-provincial infrastructure that is on a national scale (e.g. the Trans-Canada Highway) or inter-provincial projects (e.g. bridges that connect provinces with other provinces or internationally to the US).

However, over the same period, responsibility between the levels of government changed significantly. In 1961 the local-provincial share was 75 per cent; by 2002 this had risen to over 90 per cent. More specifically, in 2002 the local share of the public infrastructure stock had risen from 30 to 50 per cent, provincial had declined from 45 to 42 per cent, while the federal share had fallen from 25 to 7 per cent. This reflects the degree to which much of the economic growth over this period has been urban growth and development and less around hinterland resource development, but also demonstrates the trend towards downloading, whereby the federal and provincial governments have tended to devolve responsibility for infrastructure and services to municipalities. By 2004 municipal governments not only owned more infrastructure than the federal or provincial governments respectively but also about the same as both combined (Hemery 2017; Harchaoui et al. 2004).

However, these numbers do not tell the whole story. As indicated, most roads, bridges, and sewers usually fall under the municipal list of assets to build, renew, and maintain; but municipalities are also responsible for urban transit systems, which are often not captured in definitions and measures of 'fixed' capital stock. This would obviously include roads, bridges, rail track, etc., but does not capture mobile assets such as buses and trains that provide actual services and are also important determinants of economic growth. It also excludes massive public investments in light rail and other rapid transit systems that many Canadian cities now own, operate, and maintain at the municipal level.

Lammam and MacIntyre (2017) also assessed public infrastructure in Canada but included transit in the measure of core infrastructure and extended the analysis to 2013. They found the same trends identified by Harchaoui et al. (see figure 2.1, reproduced from the above-cited 2017 report). It displays the share of core public infrastructure

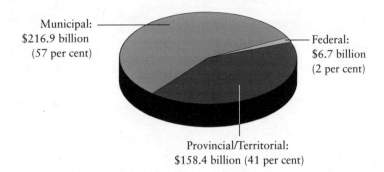

Municipal:
$216.9 billion
(57 per cent)

Federal:
$6.7 billion
(2 per cent)

Provincial/Territorial:
$158.4 billion (41 per cent)

Figure 2.1 Share of core public infrastructure* stock by level of government, 2013

* Core public infrastructure includes roads, bridges, transit, water, wastewater, culture and recreation, and sports infrastructure.

(roads, bridges, transit, water, wastewater, culture and recreation, and sports infrastructure) owned by each level of government in 2013. According to the report, the total stock of core public infrastructure in 2013 was $382 billion. Of that amount, the federal government owned only $6.7 billion, or 1.8 per cent.

It shows that municipalities collectively owned more than half of the core public infrastructure stock (56.8 per cent) and the remainder was owned by provincial and territorial governments (41.4 per cent).

IMPACTS OF A GROWING FISCAL IMBALANCE ON LOCAL INFRASTRUCTURE

To appreciate fully the scale of the challenge posed by this increasing reliance on municipal government to build and maintain infrastructure, it is important to reinforce our discussion in chapter 1 that municipal governments are the least well fiscally equipped to raise funds. Municipal governments rely heavily on property taxes that, while a dependable source of revenue, do not capture economic growth and rising income levels effectively, nor do they reflect the usage of public infrastructure such as roads, water, and sewage pipes, or services such as refuse disposal and waste treatment. Not only has this helped to widen the infrastructure gap but, in the absence of proper pricing for infrastructure, has been a major factor contributing to urban sprawl in Canada's cities which has in turn fuelled the need for new infrastructure in burgeoning exurban communities.

In addition to the financial challenges, municipal governments are also highly parochial, focusing on their local communities and interests. Unlike provincial and federal governments they are not well placed or empowered to coordinate regional or national priorities. Section 92 of the *Constitution Act* (1867) sets out the exclusive powers of provincial legislatures in sixteen areas, with section 92 (8) giving the legislature of each province total responsibility for making laws relating to that province's municipal institutions. Local governments are not recognized under the Constitution as a separate order of government and, often referred to as "creatures" of the provinces, are legally subordinate to them and dependent on provincial legislation for defining the parameters of their authority.

The asymmetry in power produced by the Constitution has become increasingly anachronistic over the last century as Canada's landscape and demographic profile have become increasingly urban, settling new immigrants in cities and drawing rural Canadians from the land. As the need for urban infrastructure has grown rapidly over this time, the pressure for all levels of government to increase their investment has increased. However, this has proven difficult to sustain given the constitutional barriers to federal involvement, the rising demands on provincial governments for spending in healthcare and education, and a series of economic downturns, crises, and budgetary deficits that have undermined sustained infrastructure investment. Consequently, as Mackenzie (2013, 12) suggests, it would be difficult to design a context more likely to produce a shortfall in public capital investment than the current one:

We have an evolving federation in which responsibilities for public capital have been shifting steadily from the federal government (with the most robust and flexible revenue system) to local level[s] of government (with the least flexible revenue system). We have a political atmosphere that is hostile to the deficit financing that commonly provides the funding for capital investment and to the taxation that is required to cover the carrying costs. Adding to the squeeze is the irresistible temptation faced by senior governments to export their fiscal problems by cutting transfer payments.

The constitutional and fiscal imbalance of Canada's multi-level governance framework has continued to impede municipal governments' ability to address the rising infrastructure gap. In particular, their heavy reliance on property taxes has been ensured by federal and provincial decisions and legislation. For example, municipal governments did historically possess the capacity to raise local revenues through income taxes, but this was suspended by the federal government in its efforts to finance the costs of the Second World War. Despite being much more suitable taxes for infrastructure funding, given their close association with economic growth, income-taxing powers were never returned to the municipalities following the war. At the provincial level, attempts to introduce user fees in some cities have been thwarted by provincial governments, concerned no doubt about the political fallout, despite their ability to reduce traffic congestion (Kitchen and Slack 2016).

For example, in 2016, Toronto's municipal government led by Mayor John Tory recognized the need to replace or repair the aging Gardiner Expressway – a key segment of city-managed roadway that bisects the downtown core. Its advanced state of disrepair and costly maintenance had led city councillors to explore new means of generating adequate funding. In December 2016, Toronto city council voted in favour of a plan to enact road tolls on both the Gardiner Expressway and Don Valley Parkway. The resulting revenue (almost $200 million) would be used to fund repairs to these roadways as well as building public transit infrastructure (Fraser 2016).

Despite council's support for the policy, Toronto could not enact the tolls under its own authority, since this requires the consent of the province. Tory expressed frustration at having to seek the province's approval, and this was compounded in January 2017 when the road tolls were refused. Although the province stated that it would provide additional funding to the city, this would only have been a fraction of the money that could have been generated through tolls (Benzie 2017). Moreover, provincial grants would not have the desired effect of 'pricing' public infrastructure and reducing congestion, and further would obfuscate the lines of public accountability between those politicians raising taxes and those responsible for spending.

Taken together, these factors illustrate the extent to which responsibility for infrastructure has shifted to the level of government that has the least fiscal capacity, constitutional powers, or regional/national perspective. This is counter-intuitive given the strategic importance of infrastructure for issues of crucial national importance, including productivity but also trade, competitiveness, employment, security, safety, mobility, health, and social well-being. It is also ironic but also crucial that this shift has occurred at a time when the pressures and demands on infrastructure have increased primarily because of *global* shifts such as urbanization, immigration, climate change, security threats, technological innovation, and other factors that are beyond municipalities' control. Given their limited autonomy and fiscal powers, municipalities lack the capacity to adequately address challenges of this scale and magnitude at the local level.

Although the federal and provincial governments have looked to assist municipalities in addressing the demands for infrastructure, they have preferred to transfer funds rather than devolve powers and fiscal tools, and have, for the most part, been reluctant to give up tax room. As a consequence, municipalities have become increasingly dependent on transfers to help fund local infrastructure. Although this financial support has provided crucial assistance, it has also generated significant problems with respect to accountability, policy rationale, program coordination, project completion, and politically motivated spending. The Ford government's announcement in December 2019 that it was cancelling $1 billion in provincial funding for the second phase of Hamilton's light rail system effectively killed the project, and provided a stark example of the mercurial nature of intergovernmental funding and the difficulty reliance upon it poses for municipal planners.

THE FEDERAL ROLE: WHY, WHEN, AND HOW MUCH?

As noted earlier, the federal role in urban matters, including infrastructure, has been heavily constrained and defined by the Constitution, and, as Berdahl (2004) showed, these limitations have been hugely significant in restricting a multi-level approach to urban sustainability with Canadian cities. Nevertheless, this did not stop Lithwick (1970) thirty-plus years earlier criticizing the federal government for avoiding an urban role: "The federal government has used theconstitution as an excuse to abstain from playing a responsible urban role, despite overwhelming evidence that it is the principal actor in the urban political reality" (57). Lithwick's comment reveals the basic paradox at the heart of federal-municipal relations in Canada: though the federal government is given no formal powers over local government, almost everything it does and spends has a direct or indirect impact on municipalities, and on larger cities in particular.

Federal government involvement in municipal and urban affairs carries several risks. Not least of these is the political wrath of the provinces, which guard their powers with fervour. As a result, federal interventions and spending in cities and communities have tended to be mercurial and unstable. The absence of constitutional authority also makes it difficult for the federal government to enforce conditions on provincial and municipal funding. Consequently, when other levels of government spend federal money, it becomes increasingly difficult to have federal coordination, evaluation, and accountability for results. The federal government also runs the risk that credit for investing in cities will be shared by provincial and municipal governments while its own role and contribution will go unrecognized by the electorate; hence the increasingly elaborate federal branding of infrastructure spending.

Despite the significant disincentives and constitutional limits, there is a significant history of federal involvement in urban affairs (Stoney and Graham 2009; Tindal and Tindal 2004). The primary reason for this is that federal governments are acutely aware of the significant opportunities to develop a stronger policy handle and maximize political capital by investing in urban programs and projects. Issues such as declining competitiveness, urban sprawl, the environment, crime, and so on may have urban epicentres, but the political fallout from them is national, and this has helped to galvanize arguments for a more collaborative and consistent multi-level approach (Doern, Auld, and Stoney 2015).

Because of the many challenges, federal involvement in urban and municipal affairs is not a linear progression; it ebbs and flows over time in response to a number of contingent factors and policy entry points. Wolfe (2003), for example, suggests that the concept of a national urban policy has emerged over the course of the twentieth century, particularly at times of urban crises in areas such as poverty, housing, and infrastructure. Connected to this role, federal spending in Canadian cities and communities can be seen as part of the national government's role in redistributing resources from more prosperous parts of Canada to relatively less well-off provinces, cities, and regions.

Two other factors also help to determine the degree of federal involvement in municipal affairs. The first is related to the finances of the federal government and the amount of money it has to spend on urban issues and programs. The second is the state of relations between federal and provincial levels of government, and, more specifically, the political climate with regard to federal powers and the

Constitution. The greater the tension and conflict between the two levels of government, politically and ideologically, the less likely and able the federal government is to become directly involved in urban and municipal affairs. Stoney and Graham (2009) concluded that the nature and extent of federal-municipal machinery can be closely collated with the dynamics of constitutional politics and, in particular, the cycle of conflict and cooperation that characterizes different "eras" in federal-provincial relations.

Young (2003) has argued that other contingent factors also play a part in driving and shaping federal-municipal governance and investment. He highlights the nature of the municipality, the policy field, the position and policy capacity of the federal government, and the role of the province in mediating the relationship as important factors. For example, Prime Minister Paul Martin's personal interest in urban issues was clearly a factor in driving the New Deal for cities and other tripartite initiatives across Canada. As Dunn (2005) states, "[i]n 2003 the urban file was not as central to the federal vision, in part because the cities' champion Martin had been banished from cabinet ... The years 2004 and 2005 saw the rebirth of the urban file with the advent of Martin as Prime Minister" (59). Although the federal role in urban affairs lessened during the Harper Conservative years, and was largely confined to infrastructure stimulus funding, it has grown again with the advent of the Trudeau Liberals and is likely to accelerate rapidly in the face of the pandemic and the subsequent health and economic fallout.

We now look at these and other periods more closely and identify patterns and eras of federal intervention. In so doing, we aim to highlight the changing and often conflicting rationales dominating federal funding and policies, in addition to the type of infrastructure priorities targeted and the programs used.

SIX PERIODS IN FEDERAL-MUNICIPAL INFRASTRUCTURE FINANCING

1 Infrastructure as Nation-Building: Post–World War I to 1960s

During this period, infrastructure was regarded principally as a key component of nation-building, particularly with respect to transportation such as rail and highways, but also energy, communication, water, ports, navigation, and eventually airports, which were all crucial to

settlement patterns across Canada. Although nation-building, immigration, and settlement have remained important drivers for federal
involvement in national and interprovincial infrastructure projects,
municipal infrastructure became increasingly important as urban
centres grew rapidly.

In the decades after World War I, the federal government occasionally provided municipal governments with financial assistance that
took the form of loans and grants for a variety of local public works
projects. Ottawa's financial assistance was intended to be short-term
rather than ongoing, targeting economic and social problems resulting
from high unemployment, housing shortages, urban decay, and environmental degradation.

The federal government had very little institutional capacity for
coordinating and delivering funding for municipal infrastructure
during this period, and programs and loans were provided mostly on
an ad-hoc basis. There was little attempt to promote or enhance the
federal role in providing municipal infrastructure, and little to distin-
guish Liberal from Conservative policies on local infrastructure spending. After a post-World War II boom in investment, infrastructure
began to wane as a percentage of GDP, as all governments faced
increasing fiscal pressures and service demands, particularly in housing and social services such as education and health.

2 The Federal Government as Municipal Banker: the Rise of "Keynesianism" and "Environmentalism," 1960s–70s

The 1960s saw rapid urban growth and expansion, particularly in
Canada's major cities, with car ownership fuelling and enabling
sprawling suburbs and longer distances for commuters seeking space
as well as newer and more affordable housing. In response to the need
for infrastructure investment to keep pace with urban expansion, the
federal government acted very much like a bank, augmenting the
financial resources available to provincial and municipal governments
(Hilton 2006; Hilton and Stoney 2009b). Federal participation was
temporary and arm's-length, limited to creating programs that provided either loans (requiring repayment), unconditional transfers of
funds (grants), or conditional payments (contributions using the
federal spending power that provided a share of costs matched by
the municipal and provincial governments).

During this period, the role and scope of the federal government had begun to expand, and included *Keynesian*-inspired stimulus programs and funding that allowed and enabled local governments and the provinces to undertake infrastructure projects that were intended to create jobs and kick-start the economy. For example, federal funding through the Sewer Treatment Program (1961–74) provided $979 million in loans and $131 million in grants to local governments to address the shortage of serviced land, which was a major impediment to expanding residential construction. The Municipal Winter Works Incentive (1958–68) provided $267 million to boost employment by supporting 50 per cent of direct payroll costs in municipalities. The *Municipal Development and Loan Act* established a $400 million fund during 1963–66 to stimulate employment by providing loans to local government that encouraged them to accelerate and expand their capital works. Programs such as these were designed to provide municipalities with temporary injections of cash, most of which were repayable loans.

The oil shocks of the early 1970s and the resulting global recession and 'stagflation' continued to dominate federal spending decisions. However, the growing reliance on oil and privately owned automobiles was also fuelling concerns and growing activism concerning expansion and the impact this was having on Canadian cities and the quality of life for many millions who resided in and around sprawling city-regions such as Toronto, Montreal, and Vancouver. In 1961 Jane Jacobs had published *The Death and Life of Great American Cities* criticizing the urban renewal projects of the 1950s that had prioritized the motor car and "destroyed communities," fuelling popular debate around city planning, public transit, and infrastructure. In Canada, public resistance in Toronto to the Spadina expressway became a focal point of what would eventually grow into the "new urbanism" movement.

Broader environmental concerns were also emerging internationally as urban sprawl and the resulting pollution became seen as a key contributor to acid rain and poor air quality. In 1979, Canada, the US, and thirty-two European countries signed the Economic Commission of Europe (ECE) Convention on Long-Range Transboundary Air Pollution. The Convention is a mechanism to deal with and manage "regional" transboundary air pollutants such as sulphur, nitrogen oxides, and volatile organic compounds, and air issues such as acid rain and ground-level ozone. Under pressure to take further measures, the Canadian government created the Department of the Environment in 1971 and the Ministry of State for Urban Affairs (1971–79), both of which signalled a growing awareness of urban issues and their significance for the environment.

The official mandate of the MSUA – to effect a beneficial federal government influence on the process of urbanization, integrate the federal government's urban policies with its other policies, and foster cooperative relationships on urban affairs with the provinces and municipalities – amounted to a clear and ambitious attempt to enable and institutionalize a multi-level governance approach. Although both organizations struggled to make an immediate policy impact during the 1970s, with the MSUA finally disbanded after only eight years, they did influence thinking about the consequences of infrastructure decisions for urban development and the resulting environmental impacts that would eventually lead to calls for 'green' infrastructure and more sustainable growth.

This period of institutionalized multi-level governance also produced a series of tri-level meetings and conferences aimed at integrating federal, provincial, and municipal responses to urban issues. The first tri-level meeting, in Winnipeg in April 1971, helped to set up a national tri-level conference. A second national tri-level conference, held in Edmonton in October 1973, addressed the management of growth, housing and land-use strategy, transportation, and public financing, and explored a possible three-way approach to managing growth. A third national tri-level conference, to discuss task force findings, was scheduled for the autumn of 1976 in Montebello, Quebec. However, faced with growing demands by the Federation of Canadian Municipalities (FCM) for constitutional recognition for municipal government, the event was eventually cancelled when provincial ministers of urban and municipal affairs announced they wouldn't be attending, and no further national tri-level conferences were held.

Following a merger in 1976, the Canadian Federation of Mayors and Municipalities had been renamed the Federation of Canadian Municipalities, marking another important realignment in the municipal landscape. The FCM quickly established itself as a highly effective institution, lobbying federal and provincial governments for increased, predictable investment in municipal infrastructure, and played an increasingly prominent role in advancing a progressive and sustainable environmental agenda for Canadian cities and communities. Eventually the FCM would receive federal funding directly to pursue these aims, providing a useful conduit through which to flow federal funds to municipalities in a partnership that continues today.

Responding to demands for predictable funding and a cleaner environment, the government introduced federal fuel taxes in the mid-1970s with a view to increasing and maintaining federal investment in municipal infrastructure over the long term. On 23 June 1975, John Turner – then federal minister of Finance – announced to the House of Commons that the government was introducing "a special excise tax on gasoline for personal use" (Department of Finance 1975, 35). The rate was set at ten cents per gallon and was expected to generate $350 million for the federal treasury during the first year. Together with increases in domestic oil prices, the measures introduced in Budget 1975 were intended to "encourage motorists to make their driving habits more efficient in terms of saving gasoline ... [and] encourage the use of public transportation, thereby helping to relieve the growing congestion in our cities" (35). Based on the cost-benefit principle of "user pays," fuel taxes were seen as a significant policy choice as they aimed to capture the often hidden "price" of road infrastructure and discourage fuel consumption while diverting funds into public transit infrastructure.

Despite the new taxes and a greater focus on urban and environmental challenges, the infrastructure gap would continue to grow, as demands for public infrastructure from an expanding private sector, as well as from individual citizens, increased rapidly during this period (Harchaoui et al. 2004).

3 Constitutional Wars: From National to Regional and Local Agreements, 1979–93

Growing provincial unrest, particularly in Quebec, signalled a period of constitutional wrangling that would threaten to separate the confederation, and severely limited the opportunity for the federal government to "interfere" in municipal affairs other than through arm's-length funding for infrastructure projects. Along with the demise of the MSUA, the cancellation of the tri-level conferences appeared to symbolize the end of an era defined by attempts to build a more comprehensive multi-level governance framework. As the climate of "cooperative" federalism gave way to "contested" federalism, federal-municipal relations began to take on a more regional dimension. National agreements and initiatives were quickly replaced by more opportunistic trilateral arrangements geared to specific cities and regions on a seemingly ad-hoc basis. For example, Urban Development Agreement collaborations (UDAs), pioneered in Winnipeg and later in Vancouver, brought together the problem-solving resources of different levels of government, the community and business sectors in an integrated strategy for community-driven revitalization. The best-known example during this period was the Winnipeg Core Area Initiative (1981–86) that brought the governments of Canada, Manitoba, and Winnipeg together as equal partners to focus on physical and socio-economic challenges in Winnipeg's downtown and inner core and neighbourhoods. With an investment of $96 million ($32 million each), the initiative established a decision-making policy committee with multi-level representation to target poverty and the deterioration in infrastructure.

By the early 1980s, General Development Agreements (GDAs) were being replaced with new agreements labelled Economic and Regional Development Agreements (ERDAS), and, in January 1982, the federal government created the Ministry of State for Economic and Regional Development and the Department of Regional Industrial Expansion (DRIE). Two significant regional organizations, the Federal Economic Development Initiative of Northern Ontario and the Atlantic Canada Opportunities Agency (ACOA), emerged as means for targeting infrastructure and other programs promoting economic stimulation and competitiveness.

With the federal emphasis on greater regional visibility and responsiveness, Ottawa dispatched bureaucrats across the country to gauge needs and establish a local presence. This was facilitated in 1982 through the creation of Regional Councils for Senior Federal Officials and the deployment of Federal Economic Development Coordinators. It was supported by increased emphasis on and funding for Community Development Partnerships (CDPs). These were intended to increase grassroots involvement in federal policy-making and delivery by helping to develop local capacity and understanding. Emphasis was on replacing centralized, homogenized policy responses with ones that were community-sensitive and innovative – what later would be described as a place-based approach.

4 A New Deal for Cities and Communities: From Federal Banker to Partner in "Green" Infrastructure and Economic Growth, 1993–2006

With the election of the Chrétien Liberal government in 1993, a new era in federal funding for municipal governments began. Despite the daunting $42 billion deficit in the federal treasury, a severe drop in federal revenues and increased spending on employment insurance benefits caused by a severe recession, the Liberals sought to stimulate a recovering economy by adjusting monetary and fiscal policies, which included new federal spending through a new infrastructure program. The Canada Infrastructure Works Program (CIWP) – with initial funding of $2 billion that was subsequently increased by an additional $400 million – was intended originally as a short-term means of stimulating the economy through job creation in the construction industry, much like programs from previous decades. However, the CIWP, which ran over two phases during 1994–99, morphed into something quite different. It called for a "partnership" among the three levels of government to jointly deal with a variety of public policy needs that could be addressed through investment in local infrastructure. The federal government would now provide its own "share" of the costs of municipal infrastructure projects, up to a maximum of one-third.

The Liberals' election platform in 1993 had outlined four objectives for a tripartite "shared cost, two-year $6 billion infrastructure program, to upgrade transportation and local services." The new program was intended to help create employment rapidly over a two-year period, build infrastructure that "support[ed] economic growth," develop infrastructure that "enhance[d] community liveability," and demonstrate to the public that the federal government could work cooperatively with other levels of government (Liberal Party of Canada 1993). While spending to help spur job creation remained the main driver behind the policy, there was a much more significant and enduring legacy of the CIWP: it established the concept of a 'tripartite shared cost' for municipal infrastructure that has helped to shape arguments calling for a realignment of the fiscal framework for the nation (Hilton 2006; Hilton and Stoney 2009b).

Following the CIWP, the federal government launched a series of other 'partnership' infrastructure programs, notably the Canada Infrastructure Program ($2.05 billion), the Municipal-Rural Infrastructure Fund ($1.2 billion), and the Canada Strategic Infrastructure Fund ($6 billion). While the first two were "bottom-up," requiring local governments to apply for matched funding from their province and the federal government, the third appeared more susceptible to politically motivated spending. Unlike previous infrastructure programs, there was no application and vetting process for the CSIF (nor for another program, the Border Infrastructure Fund). As Hilton observed, "Rather than basing (federal funding) decisions on public policy interests, the selection process became very much enmeshed in politics" (2006, 91).

The CSIF's design facilitated politically motivated spending, and this attribute was reinforced by the significant amounts of discretionary federal 'investment' in infrastructure projects: the federal share of costs involved tens and, in some cases, hundreds of millions of dollars. As well, the allowed maximum federal funding had now risen significantly, to 50 per cent of eligible project costs. Since spending in these programs was discretionary, there was considerable latitude both in choosing recipients and in the amount of funding they received.

The policy rationale underlying federal infrastructure programming also evolved. Projects receiving funding were intended to have a positive impact, improving the economy, the quality of life in communities, and the environment. A myriad of similarly vague objectives for each program served to justify federal funding, providing the narrative for press releases and speeches announcing federal funding for local infrastructure projects. Even very small infrastructure projects were heralded by federal politicians for their contribution to "improving national, provincial and local economic competitiveness," "supporting long-term economic growth," "improving economic opportunities," "improving the quality of life," and "promoting improved environmental quality" (Hilton 2006; Hilton and Stoney 2009b).

The funding announcements and signage at construction sites were intended to provide the federal government with a visible presence in many rural and urban communities. Signs at construction sites large and small were, in effect, 'billboards' used as a means of trying to convince citizens that the federal government was relevant and played an active role in improving the quality of life in communities. The demand to promote "federal visibility" ramped up soon after the near-death referendum crisis in Quebec in 1995 and the negative fallout across the country following announcements of severe reductions in federal programming in order to reduce the deficit. The federal presence in communities started to wane through resulting efforts to curb spending, which included significant reductions in various social transfer programs to the provinces. Through its infrastructure programs, the federal government was endeavouring to "show the flag" in communities across the country. At the same time, the federal government began to assume a far greater share of infrastructure costs and demanded – except in Quebec – a greater role in the administration of program spending (Hilton 2006; Hilton and Stoney 2009b).

Despite these efforts and the significant overhead costs associated with "communications" activities in infrastructure programs, a poll conducted by the federal government in 2004 revealed disappointing results:

> This poll revealed that Canadians did not see the role of the federal government in communities. This finding heavily influenced the development of the communications annex of the GTF [Gas Tax Fund] agreement (Infrastructure Canada) was to sign with each Province and Territory. (Infrastructure Canada 2007, 1)

As a self-proclaimed "partner" in building local infrastructure, the federal government began to demand greater recognition for its involvement, requiring the recipients of federal funds to follow "communications protocols" outlining how media events and activities would ensure the participation of federal ministers and government MPs. Particularly for the Canada Strategic Investment Fund (and the Border Infrastructure Fund), recipients were required to be accountable to Ottawa not only for the how the funds were spent but also for progress reports at a *project level.* The federal government was now much more than a banker – it was becoming an active partner involved in project management. In order to garner political capital from its new role and increased funding, it continued to develop the branding and communications side of federal programs that would later culminate in the marketing and advertising of the Economic Action Plan (Hilton 2006; Hilton and Stoney 2009b; Stoney and Krawchenko 2012).

In 2000 the federal government endowed the FCM with $550 million to establish the Green Municipal Fund (GMF), designed to provide below-market loans and grants, education and training services to support municipal plans, studies and projects to improve air, water, and soil quality, and programs to protect the climate. Through the GMF, the FCM endeavoured to promote sustainable development and infrastructure innovation, enhance environmental performance, generate new efficiencies, increase municipal tax revenues, create jobs, and bolster economic development. In particular, GMF funding and knowledge are aimed at helping municipalities build better transportation, construct more efficient and resilient buildings, divert waste from landfill, make previously unusable land available for development, and improve soil and water quality. The FCM continues to administer this fund.

In 2001, the federal government, through its Infrastructure Canada Program and the National Research Council, partnered with the FCM to create the *National Guide to Sustainable Infrastructure*. "InfraGuide" was both a new, national framework of people and a growing collection of published best practice documents for use by decision-makers and technical personnel in the public and private sectors.

Based on Canadian empirical research and experience, the InfraGuide reports (2001–07) set out the best practices to support sustainable municipal infrastructure decisions and action in six key areas: municipal roads and sidewalks, potable water, storm and wastewater decision-making and investment planning, environmental protocols, and transit. The best practices were made available online and in hard copy. In spite of its innovative and forward-looking objectives, to build up and disseminate knowledge and enable better asset management, the program was ended in 2007 by the Harper Conservatives along with similar programs such as Infrastructure Canada's Knowledge and Outreach Awareness (KOA) program that funded research projects in various aspects of sustainable infrastructure.

On the revenue side, fuel taxes continued to provide a crucial plank in the federal government's funding of municipal infrastructure. In addition to providing an important fiscal tool, they are also seen to have "green" credentials because of their potential to penalize auto use and transfer the revenues to public transit or other types of sustainable infrastructure. The federal excise tax remained unchanged at a flat rate of ten cents per litre while the federal tax on diesel fuel (in effect since 1987) was also applied at a flat rate of four cents per litre. Although furnace oil, natural gas, and propane were exempt from this tax, the Goods and Services Tax (GST) (or Harmonized Sales Tax, HST) was applied to all petroleum products. With respect to gasoline, therefore, considerable government revenues are obtained both from the flat tax rate and as the percentage of the retail price (*ad valorem*) when the GST/HST is applied (Hilton and Stoney 2009b).

Totalling $11.2 billion in 2005–06, road fuel taxes (including gasoline and diesel) became the most important component of federal, provincial, and territorial government tax revenues from transportation. Total fuel taxes made up 75 per cent of total revenues by transport users. However, it was the introduction of the Gas Tax Fund (GTF), a crucial component in the Liberal government's "New Deal," that explicitly linked gas tax revenues with municipal infrastructure needs and "green" infrastructure in particular.

The Martin government's "New Deal for Cities and Communities" was ostensibly intended to address the need to enhance the fiscal capacities within cities and smaller communities and to address the infrastructure deficit in a meaningful and sustained fashion. In its first Budget, the Martin government committed "to share with municipalities a portion of the revenue from the federal excise tax on gasoline to help fund local environmentally sustainable infrastructure." Under the heading of "A Greener, More Sustainable Canada," the 2005 Budget outlined further dimensions to the New Deal for Cities and Communities, most notably the requirement that "at least half of the new revenues to be transferred through the gas tax will be dedicated to sustainable infrastructure" (Department of Finance 2005, 10). The main project categories identified included: Public Transit; Local Roads, Bridges and Tunnels; Active Transportation Infrastructure; Community Energy; Solid Waste; Water/Wastewater; and Capacity-Building/Integrated Community Sustainability Planning.

Unlike previous programs, municipalities received federal funding via the gas tax in advance – not for specific projects – but for *intended* capital spending, and were audited after projects were completed. Any spending on ineligible projects would result in the suspension of the subsequent allocation (Hilton and Stoney 2009b). Consequently, the gas tax is classified as one 'other transfer payment' because it does not conform to the federal Treasury Board's definition of previously existing transfer payment types. It was neither an unconditional transfer, where funds have no conditions attached and are not audited, nor a conditional transfer payment, where eligibility is tightly prescribed and individual projects must be approved and a considerable application outlining the 'business case' completed before funds are disbursed (Treasury Board 2008).

As a 'hybrid' instrument, the GTF is defined as a transfer payment "based on legislation or an arrangement which normally includes a formula or schedule as one element used to determine the expenditure amount; however, once payments are made, the recipient may redistribute the funds among the several approved categories of expenditure in the arrangement" (7). In addition, the annual funding can be spent or banked at the discretion of the municipality. This is significant because while it may encourage local assessment of priorities and longer-term or strategic needs, it may be less effective as a stimulus fund for rapid job creation should the funds be banked. However, the financial pressures on municipalities and the temptation for politicians to spend in the short term means funds in the GTF are usually spent in the same fiscal year they are received.

Another innovative aspect of the GTF was the proposed requirement that recipients of federal funding under the program develop a
long-term plan for sustainability within the first five years of receiving
gas tax funds. The Integrated Community Sustainability Plans (ICSPs)
were intended to be "long term plan[s], developed in consultation
with community members, for the community to realize sustainability
objectives it has for the environmental, cultural, social and economic
dimensions of its identity" (9).

Not surprisingly given the nature of Canadian federalism, jurisdictional tensions have continued to undermine the GTF's policy rationale
in a number of ways, particularly the goal of "building environmentally sustainable infrastructure." In addition to the patchy and sometimes perfunctory development of ICSPs using consultants, the federal
government has struggled to ensure that municipalities use the GTF
monies for the intended purposes. Imposing conditions on Quebec
municipalities proved particularly futile at times, but cities in other
provinces also objected to the limitations being placed on their spending of the gas tax funds.

In describing the consultation process used with stakeholders during
the development of the GTF, Infrastructure Canada (2007) also reveals
that "the Prime Minister told the big city mayors that he wanted them
to limit their GTF spending to one or two of the eligible project categories" (21). Bureaucrats followed the PM's lead in this regard:
Infrastructure Canada placed restrictions on investments in roads and
bridges. Municipalities with populations of over 500,000 were not
allowed to invest in roads and bridges as "such investments were
not deemed to lead to positive environmental impacts" (14). This edict
from bureaucrats did not go down well with some city governments:

> The Mayor of Winnipeg pushed strongly against the restrictions
> on the use of funds for roads and bridges and this dispute received
> heavy media attention from the outset ... The Government of
> Canada *denied Winnipeg's demands to use the money on roads
> and bridges.* The solution required multiple deputy minister level
> meetings and heavy involvement from Minister Godfrey and his
> staff. (24)

The arrival of the Harper Conservatives would eventually put an end
to the bickering, with their decision to allow Winnipeg to invest in
roads with gas tax funding. Nevertheless, these examples illustrate

that despite the federal government's attempts to direct municipalities to 'green,' 'innovative,' and 'transformational' projects, it has had to water down those conditions because of ongoing jurisdictional and enforcement challenges.

The GTF also illustrates the federal government's attempt to assume a more assertive role in decisions about what infrastructure is needed for local government. The federal government as *dirigeant* in decisions about municipal infrastructure marks a significant evolution in a role that began many decades ago when the federal government provided repayable loans and grants to local governments during times of crisis.

Lastly, the allocation formula for the GTF appears to contradict the program's rhetoric about the need to focus on building environmentally sustainable infrastructure, helping to drive economic growth and productivity, and putting in place "world-class infrastructure." By deciding to spread federal funding around the country – a policy described by Martin as "no hamlet too small" – valid concerns remain about the program logic. As Infrastructure Canada acknowledged, "It was widely recognized that the larger city-regions had the greatest ability to affect environmental change and therefore their investments should be very focused" – gains in productivity and growth are also maximized through investment in urban infrastructure (12). The failure of the federal government to concentrate program funds on those areas of the country generating the greatest revenues from gasoline taxes – cities and city-regions – may reflect another important focus of the GTF. As was evident in earlier infrastructure programs, the need to generate "visibility" and opportunities for federal politicians to engage in retail politics has become increasingly important in public policy design and implementation. This policy rationale appears to have been central to Canada's Economic Action Plan (EAP), launched in 2009 as part of the Harper government's policy response to the economic crisis.

5 Open Federalism: The Demise of the Cities' Agenda, but Infrastructure Dollars Continue to Flow, 2006–15

Soon after the Gas Tax Fund agreements were made, the Martin Liberals were defeated during a general election and replaced by the Harper Conservatives in 2006. During their first Budget, the Conservatives committed to retain the GTF over five years; in Budget 2007, they extended the GTF by another four years with an additional

$8 billion. The 2006 Speech from the Throne endorsed the GTF as part of a "historic investment of more than $16 billion over seven years in infrastructure – bringing federal support under a new long-term plan for infrastructure to a total of $33 billion, including the funding provided in Budget 2006" (Department of Finance 2007).

In Budget 2008, the government committed to launching a "permanent" transfer of gas tax revenues to municipal governments: $2 billion annually. The Conservative government's rationale for making permanent a Liberal policy initiative was explained as follows:

> [The Government recognizes the need for long-term funding for infrastructure to help drive economic growth and productivity, to achieve our environmental goals, and to build strong, competitive communities ... In response to ongoing requests for stable, long-term funding, the Government announces that the Gas Tax Fund will be extended at $2 billion per year beyond 2013–14 and become a permanent measure. This will allow all municipalities, both large and small, to better plan and finance their long-term infrastructure needs. (Department of Finance 2008)

Even if the Harper government had not wanted to extend the GTF, it had already proven so popular with municipalities that terminating it would have been very damaging politically.

The Liberals meanwhile were planning their way back to power on an environmental infrastructure funding platform marketed as the "green shift." However, Stéphane Dion's plan to introduce a carbon tax at the federal level following the 2008 election was not convincing and never materialized. Significantly, it was seen by many as a key factor in the defeat of the Liberal party. The "green shift" plan was designed to levy up to $15 billion in new taxes on carbon-intensive Canadian industries; the proceeds would then be used to cut income and other taxes for people facing higher energy costs and other rising prices. Although Dion's carbon plan would not have included new taxes on gasoline for cars, trucks, and buses (unlike the Green Party proposal, which hoped to raise up to $40 billion), the new tax on energy was still widely criticized by his opponents, including some within the Liberal ranks.

Aided by a looming economic crisis and Dion's own difficulties framing and explaining the carbon taxes to Canadians, critics were successful in demonizing the "green shift." Harper likened it to the

1980 Liberal National Energy Program and described it as a "tax grab" that would "recklessly harm the economy," penalize industry, and ultimately "screw everyone" (*CBC News* 2008). Following the 2008 Liberal defeat, leading members of the Liberal Party criticized the "green shift" as "too confusing, expensive and politically risky." Michael Ignatieff, the new Liberal leader, expanded on why he believed it to be a "vote loser":

> "You can't win elections if you're adding to the input costs of a farmer putting diesel into his tractor, or you're adding to the input costs of a fisherman putting diesel into his fishing boat, or a trucker transporting goods" ... Speaking of former leader Stéphane Dion's Green Shift plan, which would have sharply raised taxes on energy, Ignatieff told reporters: "You've got to work with the grain of Canadians and not against them. I think we learned a lesson in the last election." (Whittington 2009)

The 2008 defeat by the Conservatives was a chastening one for liberals; environmentalists feared that lasting damage may have been done to policy initiatives targeting sustainable development. Even if this were not the case, the worsening global banking and economic situation quickly reduced the environment as an issue in the minds of politicians and the electorate alike.

As the Canadian economy entered into recession in 2009, the federal government tabled an early budget to address the building economic crisis. The 2009 budget is significant, in part as the Canadian response to the historic global economic decline and the unprecedented Canadian deficit that the budget incurred as a result, but also for the level of fiscal transfers directed toward municipalities and the potential impact these transfers will have on multi-level governance in Canada.

Despite promoting "open" federalism and rejecting much of the Liberals' urban agenda, the Harper government described the 2009 budget as one of the largest infrastructure investments in Canada's history. The infrastructure-related components of federal stimulus measures in Canada were approximately $40 billion over two years. The largest portions of the infrastructure measures were tax credits for households – e.g., home renovation and energy efficiency tax credits administered through the Canada Revenue Agency.

Infrastructure stimulus funding was incorporated into the existing Building Canada Fund. The $8.8 billion Building Canada Fund (BCF) was established under the 2007 Building Canada Plan to fund projects until 2014. The Fund is intended to address national, regional, and local infrastructure priorities and supports projects designed to deliver results in three areas of national importance: a stronger economy; a cleaner environment, and strong and prosperous communities. The Fund invested in public infrastructure owned by provincial, territorial, and municipal governments, and in certain cases, private-sector and non-profit organizations. Funding allocated to each province and territory was to be based on population. All projects funded through the Building Canada Fund were to be cost-shared, with the maximum federal contribution to any single project being 50 per cent; municipal projects are normally cost-shared on a one-third basis, with the maximum federal share limited to one-third, and matching contributions from the province and municipality.

The BCF was made up of two components: the Major Infrastructure Component and the Communities Component. Funding for research, knowledge, planning, and feasibility studies was also available for projects financed under these components. The Major Infrastructure Component (MIC) of the BCF targets "larger, strategic projects of national and regional significance" (Government of Canada 2009). Under the MIC, at least two-thirds of funding supports projects that address national priorities and improve the lives of Canadians; these include projects related to drinking water, wastewater, public transit, the core national highway system, and green energy.

The Communities Component of the BCF targets projects in communities with populations of less than 100,000. The Fund "recognizes the unique infrastructure needs of Canada's smaller communities and focuses on projects that meet environmental, economic and quality of life objectives" (Government of Canada 2009, 5). Originally a $1 billion fund, Canada's Economic Action Plan expanded the Communities Component fund with a top-up of $500 million. By January 2014, the program had funded more than 1,400 smaller-scale projects to improve water, wastewater, public transit, local roads, and other types of community infrastructure (5).

Through Canada's Economic Action Plan, the Government of Canada also established the $1 billion Green Infrastructure Fund (2009–14). This program specifically targeted projects that would "improve the quality of the environment and lead to a more sustainable economy over the long term" (1). Specifically, the Green Infrastructure Fund

Table 2.2
Building Canada Plan programs and funds

Program	Amount
Municipal GST Rebate	$5.8 billion
Gas Tax Fund	$11.8 billion
Building Canada Fund	$8.8 billion
Public-Private Partnerships Fund	$1.25 billion
Gateways and Border Crossings Fund	$2.1 billion
Asia-Pacific Gateway and Corridor Initiative	$1 billion
Provincial-Territorial Base Funding	$2.275 billion
Total	$33 billion

Source: Government of Canada, Building Canada website, 2014, table 8.2.

(GIF) was intended to support projects that "promote cleaner air, reduced greenhouse gas emissions and cleaner water" (7). This includes new or rehabilitation infrastructure projects that fall into the following categories: wastewater infrastructure; green energy generation and transmission; and solid waste carbon transmission and storage (14).

The GIF was provided on a cost-shared basis to provinces, territories, local or regional governments, public-sector bodies, and other eligible non-profit organizations and private-sector companies, either alone or in partnership with a province, territory, or other government body (9). The fund, which ended in 2011, focused on a few large-scale, strategic infrastructure projects (3).

As noted earlier, the Building Canada Fund was part of the Building Canada Plan (Infrastructure Canada 2008), which remains even though the EAP stimulus funding has been wound down. The Building Canada Plan is directed towards "building a stronger, safer and better Canada through modern world-class public infrastructure." Launched in 2008, this seven-year plan was established to support projects that contribute to "cleaner air and water, safer roads, shorter commutes, and better communities" (7). The plan was intended to provide $33 billion in stable, flexible, and predictable funding to provinces, territories, and municipalities, allowing them to plan for the longer term and address their ongoing infrastructure needs, and combines a number of funds and institutions including Public-Private Partnership funds as well as the establishment of P3 Canada.

Following the launch of the Building Canada Plan, the federal government signed Infrastructure Framework Agreements with provincial and territorial governments. The aim of these agreements was to align the two levels of government to advance common goals – economic growth, environmental performance, and community interests – in the value of infrastructure projects. Canada's Economic Action Plan also focused on the Building Canada program with the intent of speeding up and streamlining approvals for projects in small communities and projects that were 'shovel ready.'

The updated Building Canada Plan (Infrastructure Canada 2014a) confirmed its standing as the largest and longest federal investment in provincial, territorial, and municipal infrastructure projects in Canadian history – over $53 billion in investments, including over $47 billion in new funding over ten years, starting in 2014–15 (7). This funding is to be delivered through three key funds:

- The Community Improvement Fund, consisting of the Gas Tax Fund and the incremental Goods and Services Tax Rebate for Municipalities, will provide over $32 billion to municipalities for projects such as roads, public transit, recreational facilities, and other community infrastructure. Gas Tax Fund payments will be indexed at 2 per cent per year starting in 2014–15, with increases to be applied in $100-million increments.
- The new Building Canada Fund will provide $14 billion to support major economic projects of national, regional, and local significance across the country.
- The renewed P3 Canada Fund will provide $1.25 billion to continue to support innovative ways to build infrastructure projects faster and provide better value for Canadian taxpayers through public-private partnerships.

An additional $6 billion was provided to provinces, territories, and municipalities under existing infrastructure programs in 2014–15 and beyond. In addition, the government committed to make significant investments in First Nations infrastructure and in federal infrastructure assets. Overall federal infrastructure funding was promised to total $70 billion over ten years.

In spite of the references to "green" infrastructure and the environment, the Harper government claimed that funding "will ensure that Canada's public infrastructure is world-class and a contributor to job creation, economic growth and productivity for years to come" (1–22). This rationale underlined the fact that the Conservatives' primary motivation for investing in infrastructure was jobs and economic growth, and these, along with delivering a balanced budget, would eventually provide the central thrust of the government's agenda heading into the 2015 election.

Of the billions of dollars the government had earlier earmarked for infrastructure in the EAP, it was the $4 billion Infrastructure Stimulus Fund (ISF) that emerged as the most high-profile and contested aspect of the 2009–10 stimulus measures. The ISF sparked a media furor concerning the decision-making process to select projects and accountability for the funds spent. The ISF was also the component of stimulus spending that had the greatest financial bearing on other levels of government, as it required joint contributions to infrastructure investments. Under the ISF program, the federal government contributed up to 50 per cent for provincial and territorial assets and not-for-profit private-sector assets, up to 33 per cent for municipal assets, and 25 per cent of eligible costs for non-profit-sector assets (Infrastructure Canada 2009).

The federal government intended the ISF to be "delivered in a flexible manner" with proposals having differing selection processes depending on each province and territory (1–2). Eligible projects were put forward through provincial and territorial governments to Infrastructure Canada, where the final decisions on which projects to fund were made. In this way, the ISF, along with a number of other stimulus-related programs, gave the federal government discretion over the final selection of projects. ISF project eligibility was guided by three major requirements: i) that project construction was ready to begin; ii) that the project would not otherwise have been constructed by 31 March 2011 without the federal funding requested; and iii) that the project plan be completed with all permits and necessary approvals in place.

The emphasis on 'timely' stimulus spending led to concerns that decisions were disproportionately advancing short-term, 'shovel-ready' opportunities at the expense of longer-term plans, as well as downgrading criteria such as sustainability and improved competitiveness. As the Public Policy Forum (2016) concluded from its review of recent federal funding, "there is no term more dangerous than 'shovel ready' when it comes to infrastructure ... Infrastructure can only be done well when it is done with due deliberation" (5). David Dodge, former governor of the Bank of Canada, was equally critical of the term and the process, stating that "shovel ready" is not "exactly the criterion you should use; the criterion the government should be using is 'What's going to produce the greatest opportunity for growth in the future'" (Dodge 2016).

There were also concerns that the due process normally associated with government programs was being compromised in the rush to begin construction. For example, some projects circumvented environmental screening practices and public consultation processes – an issue that was raised in the fall report of the Auditor General of Canada (2010). Specifically, the report found that, as part of the Economic Action Plan, the government introduced Exclusion List Regulations under the *Canadian Environmental Assessment Act* in order to eliminate the need for environmental assessments for a wider range of projects. These regulatory amendments were expedited and were not released in draft form for public comment prior to taking effect (5–16). Although the amendments were intended to be temporary and slated to expire on 31 March 2011, they were representative of the marked emphasis that the Canadian government placed on fast-tracking the flow of funding for infrastructure. In all, 93 per cent of the project proposals approved under the ISF were excluded from environmental assessment. While this may have been consistent with the primary goal of economic stimulus it clearly contradicted other federal policy goals including improving the environment.

In establishing the ISF, the federal government chose to use the application-based Building Canada Fund despite urging from a variety of municipal politicians to use the GTF mechanism to flow the money. In particular, the FCM lauded the Gas Tax mechanism as a "highly efficient" way to deliver funding "quickly, fairly and accountably" (Federation of Canadian Municipalities 2009a). Municipal governments urged the federal government to use the GTF as the transfer vehicle to deliver the stimulus money. In an open letter issued before the budget, Carl Zehr, chair of the FCM's Large Cities Mayors Caucus, argued that "to counter a recession this year we need a program that gets money to projects in time for the spring construction season. A program based on the gas tax funding model is the best tool for the job" (15). He further argued that the Building Canada mechanism would be "too slow to deliver the stimulus needed to fight the recession and create jobs" (15). Municipalities had been quick off the mark to show their willingness and ability to spend infrastructure money quickly, releasing a list of over 1,000 infrastructure projects. FCM members committed to undertake these projects starting in the spring of 2009 if the federal government made funding available in the budget. The FCM estimated that the funding would create over 150,000 new jobs (9).

Critics argued that the fund's aggressive spending and communications strategy was primarily political, and suspicions were fuelled when it emerged that despite job creation being a central policy rationale of the ISF, no effort was made to accurately track the number of jobs created through infrastructure stimulus programs. This of course made it impossible to accurately evaluate one of the key stated objectives of the stimulus program, as well as the much-trumpeted government claims of widespread job creation (Raj 2009a; 2009b; Scoffield 2010). When questioned, the then Infrastructure Minister John Baird stated that "it is not the federal government's job to track the results of stimulus funding" (quoted in Raj 2009b). This was a curious assertion given the government actively promoted the ISF as a highly successful program, based largely on its ability to generate jobs. Canada's then Parliamentary Budget Officer, Kevin Page, who provided a source of independent analysis on the usage and impact of the infrastructure stimulus funds, became a vocal critic of the federal government's own reporting on program results (Chase 2009). In a 2010 report on the infrastructure stimulus funds, the Parliamentary Budget Officer concluded:

> As we have indicated in previous reports on the ISF, parliamentarians have been poorly served with limited data architecture and information collection, especially when compared to the US practice. The lack of good data inhibits basic analysis let alone accountability. (Parliamentary Budget Officer 2010, 3)

The lack of reporting on job creation was also raised in the in the fall 2010 report of the Auditor General. The information on project level jobs was described by government officials as "anecdotal." There were no consistent measures or methodologies used to estimate the number of jobs created or maintained as a result of stimulus funding (Office of the Auditor General 2010, 63–4).

In a comparison of Australian, US, and Canadian stimulus spending, Stoney and Krawchenko (2012) concluded that the Canadian government stands out in terms of its failure to implement measures aimed at ensuring accountability and transparency in decision-making and in reporting mechanisms that aid in communicating program results. The lack of transparency in the Canadian case has led to allegations that the process has been politicized, with disproportionate funds going to Conservative (government) ridings. For example, an analysis by *The Globe and Mail* of infrastructure stimulus projects awarded through the Recreational Infrastructure Canada program found disproportionate rewards in Conservative ridings (Chase, Anderson, and Curry 2009). The lack of transparent reporting on funding commitments has made substantiation or denial of these claims difficult, and such analyses were beyond the mandate of the Office of the Auditor General in its review of the program. Nevertheless, the significant increase in program advertising, promotion, and branding of the EAP has continued to fuel concern that the ISF and other infrastructure funding programs were heavily influenced by short-term partisan interests.

6 2015–Present: Trudeau Liberals' Commitment to "Strategic" Infrastructure

In what resembled a high-stakes poker game with the Conservatives and NDP, the Trudeau Liberals gambled on increased infrastructure spending in the months leading up to the 2015 election campaign. With the economy steadily recovering from the 2008 financial crisis, the Conservatives were keen to reduce the deficit, while the NDP were eager not to scare away potential voters with high tax-and-spend policy promises. The Liberals, who had trailed in the polls for much of the campaign, took a calculated risk promising billions more in infrastructure spending than their political rivals even though this would lead to sustained deficits.

The Liberals promoted a plan that promised $60 billion in extra cash over ten years on infrastructure in addition to spending promised under the Conservatives, bringing the total federal budget for infrastructure spending to about $125 billion over ten years (Curry 2016). The policy appeared to strike a chord with many voters, with the Liberals duly elected to power with a surprising majority. Once in office, the Trudeau government wasted little time in preparing to ramp up infrastructure spending within an existing but also revised framework. In particular the prime minister was quick to reassure the public that short-term, politically driven infrastructure would now be directed at "strategic," lasting infrastructure that would help build the Canada of the twenty-first century.

As chapter 1 has revealed, within Trudeau's first month in office, mandate letters were sent from the prime minister to each of his ministers outlining the primary departmental goals; they were also made public in an effort to increase transparency and accountability as part of the "sunny ways" agenda. The minister of Infrastructure and Communities, Armajeet Sohi, was instructed by the prime minister's mandate letter (2015) to develop a ten-year plan focusing on:

- public transit;
- social infrastructure, including affordable housing, seniors' facilities, early learning and childcare, and cultural and recreational infrastructure;
- green infrastructure, including investments in local water and wastewater facilities, clean energy, and climate-resilient infrastructure; and
- making the Building Canada Fund more transparent and speeding up approval processes, including removing the P3 screen for projects. It should also be more focused on strategic and trade enabling infrastructure priorities, including roads, bridges, transportation corridors, ports, and border gateways.

In addition, the minister was also instructed to work with the minister of Families, Children and Social Development to create a housing strategy to re-establish the federal government's role in supporting affordable housing (see more in our analysis in chapter 7 on the Housing Regime). Sohi was also instructed to:

- support the minister of Public Safety and Emergency Preparedness in a review of existing measures to protect Canadians and our critical infrastructure from cyber-threats;
- support the minister of Indigenous and Northern Affairs to improve essential physical infrastructure for Indigenous communities including improving housing outcomes for Indigenous Peoples;
- work with the minister of Status of Women and the Minister of Indigenous and Northern Affairs to ensure that no-one fleeing domestic violence is left without a place to turn, by growing and maintaining Canada's network of shelters and transition houses; and
- move forward on a toll-free replacement for Montreal's Champlain Bridge.

The mandate letters also stressed that federal funding "should result in bilateral agreements with provinces and territories on infrastructure investments." As part of the overall infrastructure plan, $33 billion was subsequently earmarked to be delivered over eleven years through bilateral agreements with provinces and territories under four funding streams:

- $20.1 billion for public transit;
- $9.2 billion for green infrastructure;
- $1.3 billion for community, cultural, and recreational infrastructure; and
- $2 billion for wide-ranging infrastructure needs in rural and northern communities. In addition, the $400 million Arctic Energy Fund will be delivered under this stream to support energy security in the territories.

Federal government letters made it clear to provinces and territories that in order to receive funding they would need to demonstrate that projects would accelerate economic growth and benefit the environment by, for example, "reducing greenhouse gas emissions or improving resiliency against natural disasters" (7). To facilitate the former objective, provinces and territories were encouraged to engage in big thinking, focusing on new-build projects as opposed to renovations and projects that met national objectives and not just local interests (Curry 2016).

When the full Liberal infrastructure plan was announced in 2016, broad policy aims were again targeted and the amount announced had grown to "an historic $180-billion investments in infrastructure to support public infrastructure across the country over 12 years" (Infrastructure Canada 2017a). Given that in the 7–8 years since the global financial crisis Canada's economy has experienced steady (and more recently encouraging) growth, infrastructure investment on this scale took many observers by surprise and sparked concern about the implications for a growing fiscal deficit. Curry (2016), for example, noted that Canadians were already "staring down the barrel of a deficit which could hit $30 billion this year – and untold billions after that – designed to 'stimulate' the economy through public spending" (7). Sizeable infrastructure spending channelled through Ottawa also served to fuel speculation about the role of government: "Big government is back. Ottawa is positioning itself as the engine of economic growth and its chief tool is infrastructure, financed by debt" (7).

If debt-financed infrastructure spending is targeted at improving productivity, economic growth, and longer-term sustainability, the case for "strategic" investment is strengthened; but, in an interview with Bloomberg News, the prime minister acknowledged that during the most recent two years of his mandate, he sees government "getting creative by spending on new projects, including 'social infrastructure,' a term used in the Liberals' campaign platform which covers things like day care and social housing" (Kheiriddin 2016). While the economic impact of such investment is highly tenuous, it is evident that governments calculate the political pay-offs to be considerable, especially when programs are timed to roll out in periods leading up to an election and/or are made conditional on the re-election of the party in power.

The list of potentially contradictory priorities outlined in the mandate letters and subsequent programs also illustrates once again the wide range of policy aims and outcomes attributed to infrastructure spending. This was not lost on journalist and commentator Andrew Coyne:

> Once upon a time there were things called roads and bridges. Sometimes they were built by private capital, sometimes by government, but nobody pretended they were more than what they were: services, like any other, useful for getting from one place to another. But then someone got the idea of calling them infrastructure, and suddenly they were endowed with all sorts of miraculous powers: as short-term economic stimulus, as a longer-term spur to productivity, and beyond. Infrastructure was a jobs policy one day, an environmental policy the next, a national unity policy the day after that. (Coyne 2016)

Policies and programs announced to date suggest that infrastructure spending in the Trudeau era will serve a multitude of purposes and, despite rhetoric to the contrary, continue to be influenced by short-term political considerations at the expense of longer-term strategic planning. This was certainly a concern expressed by Aaron Wudrick, president of the Canadian Taxpayer's Federation (CTF), in response to the "much vaunted 'innovation' measures" (1) intended to overhaul and redesign the Stategic Innovation Fund as part of Budget 2017. According to Wudrick, the revamped fund amounts to little more than a repackaging of existing funds and a further extension of the boutique tax measures popular with the previous Conservative government.

The new Canada Infrastructure Bank, as we have referenced in chapter 1 and examine further in chapter 5, was also created during Trudeau's first term. Its structure and mandate indicate that potential for political interference would remain and could undermine the credibility of the bank's investment decisions as well as public- and private-sector confidence in the process. We explore the new bank in chapter 5, and also in chapter 4 where regular bank funding is central to the infrastructure story.

In spite of being returned to power with only a minority status and announcing a $26 billion deficit in its first fiscal update since the election, the Trudeau government's second term in office promises much the same as the first, with continued spending pledges on infrastructure and other key priorities. With fears for a downturn in economic activity looming and a budget deficit $7 billion worse than projected for the 2019–20 fiscal year, Finance Minister Morneau and the prime minister continued to downplay the disappointing update in favour of their preferred "debt to GDP ratio" and the importance of providing services and jobs for Canadians. Arguably, minority status in this second term could increase the tendency to grow deficit spending on infrastructure and social programs rather than limit it. Although the Conservatives form the opposition, the NDP and BQ effectively hold the balance of power in the new parliament and both are likely to favour more spending targeted towards their own constituencies and respective bases.

As for the direction of infrastructure spending, the second term mandate lettersreveal continuingand emerging priorities. A new Minister for Infrastructure and Communities, Catherine McKenna, is charged with implementing the "Investing in Canada Plan." Your focus must be on the successful, timely delivery of our growth-generating investments in public transit, green infrastructure and social infrastructure, as well as key strategic infrastructure that will increase trade. The key objectives of this plan are increasing economic growth and creating good middle class jobs with infrastructure that improves people's quality of life. (Prime Minister of Canada 2019, 2)

The minister is also required to create a "National Infrastructure Fund" to seek out and support major nation-building projects that will "benefit people across various regions, connect our country and improve quality of life," beginning with support for the Newfoundland-Labrador fixed transportation link (2). The minister is also responsible for the creation of an additional infrastructure fund by 2020–21 "to support priority projects and economic diversification for communities transitioning from fossil fuels," suggesting an emphasis on job creation in the increasingly "alienated" energy-rich provinces of Alberta and Saskatchewan. Furthermore, the minister is mandated to leverage infrastructure to contribute to "innovation, resilience and a low-carbon future, supporting the creation of Canadian jobs and attracting infrastructure investment into Canada" (2). In pursuit of these aims, the minister is mandated to continue progress on priority bridges, including the completion of the toll-free replacement for the Champlain Bridge and the rehabilitation of the Pont de Québec, and to provide support for the Windsor-Detroit Bridge Authority as it advances the construction of the Gordie Howe International Bridge.

In addition to investing in roads and bridges for private and commercial traffic, the mandate letter also makes specific reference to "green" infrastructure initiatives. In particular, the minister is instructed to target investment in public transit, including support for the minister of Transport to create high-frequency rail for the Toronto-Quebec City corridor and to continue working with the FCM to deliver the Green Municipal Funds as discussed earlier in this chapter. There is also specific reference made to the need to support the minister of Families, Children and Social Development to finalize the design and implementation of the "Housing Supply Challenge," which is intended municipalities as the main stakeholders targeted by the challenge (2). The minister is further mandated to work with the minister of Indigenous Services to co-develop and invest in "distinctions-based community infrastructure plans," and move forward with addressing "critical needs including housing, all-weather roads, high-speed internet, health facilities, treatment centres and schools in First Nations, Inuit and Metis communities by 2030." Interestingly these plans are also to include new investments to "support the operation and maintenance of this infrastructure" (2). The North is further targeted by the planned "Clean Power Fund," sourced through the Canada Infrastructure Bank, to help finance the "development and linking of clean energy to transmission systems" and to "support the transition of northern, remote and Indigenous communities from reliance on diesel-fueled power to clean, renewable and reliable energy." The infrastructure mandate letter also prioritizes rural communities, calling for 100 per cent high speed internet by 2030, and instructs the minister to use the Disaster Mitigation and Adaptation Fund to address the impacts of climate change on Canadians, "whether they are from small, rural and Indigenous communities or large urban centres" (2). Finally, it is interesting to note that the minister is asked to require that "all provinces and territories identify and approve all of their long-term infrastructure priorities" within the "next two years" and in accord with the signed bilateral agreements. Significantly, "[f]unds that are not designated for specific approved projects by the end of 2021 will be reinvested directly in communities through a top up of the federal Gas Tax Fund" (2). This is clearly intended to speed up the flow of infrastructure projects and address Liberal concerns that Infrastructure Canada is not distributing the funds quickly enough.

The health and economic crises resulting from the COVID-19 pandemic and lockdown have intensified pressure on the size, speed, and administration of stimulus funding and are already producing unprecedented spending and deficits across all levels of government. The fiscal snapshot provided by Finance Minister Morneau in July 2020 predicted the annual federal deficit will reach $343.2 billion dollars, an increase of approximately 1,000 per cent on pre-COVID-19 estimates (Snyder 2020a). Nevertheless, provincial premiers and local mayors have increased pressure on the federal government to do more financially and to reduce conditions on infrastructure funding to allow regional and local priorities to be met. The $187 billion Investing in Canada Infrastructure Plan (ICIP) has become a particular bone of contention, with provincial and municipal critics claiming that it is little more than a repackaged and ideologically driven public relations campaign that is too focused on "green" projects at the expense of jobs and economic growth, and predicting it will do little to address community needs for basic services such as roads or wastewater treatment centres (Snyder 2020b).

Further issues have already been raised by Prime Minister Trudeau's February 2021 announcement of an additional $14.9 billion in new federal infrastructure funding directed towards public transportation that includes $5.9 billion for shovel-ready projects and $3 billion per year towards establishing a permanent transit fund. Unlike other funding schemes, this would not be allocated through the provinces, but rather would provide a central fund that municipalities can access on a project-by-project basis. This would allow the federal government greater control in deciding which projects are suitable and align with the specific aims of the program. While reaction to the creation of a permanent fund has been mainly positive within municipal circles, the imposition of further conditions to federal funding project eligibility is likely to increase local frustration. It is also important to note that the funding is not intended to begin until 2026. This is significant because it would likely require the Liberal party to win two more elections for the funding to become a reality, providing a further illustration of the way that political parties use infrastructure funding announcements to further partisan interests.

The tensions, challenges, and complexity outlined in this chapter with respect to funding infrastructure across Canada will no doubt continue to surface as post-pandemic programs continue to roll out, particularly if local needs and priorities diverge further from federal goals, timelines, and political calculations.

CONCLUSIONS

In this chapter we have examined 1) the realities and evolution of multi-level federalism, and 2) six periods of federal-municipal infrastructure funding. We have seen the impacts of a growing fiscal imbalance on local infrastructure. Arguably, no other area of government spending has been subject to so many different and often conflicting policy goals and fiscal imbalances. In a democratic system such as Canada's, short-term economic imperatives are paramount because of their short-term political significance. Focusing on electoral success – usually a four-year cycle – limits long-term planning along with longer-term calculations of the public interest. It also defines the type of infrastructure that is built and funded, particularly when emphasis is placed on 'shovel-ready' projects. The growing tendency for federal, provincial, and municipal governments to jointly finance infrastructure projects further complicates and undermines strategic decision-making. Attempting to align interests and priorities on a multi-level scale also reveals diverse criteria (regional equity, urban versus rural communities, and social and environmental costs and benefits, for example) that further limits the willingness of governments to prioritize infrastructure projects on the basis of long-term returns or national or strategic importance, and to allocate funds accordingly.

These insights are neither new nor unique, but are intended to explain the findings of decades of research and analysis examining Canada's growing infrastructure gap. Despite the federal government continuing to pump billions into municipal infrastructure, the recurring and seemingly insurmountable problems of a complex governance framework – multiple and conflicting goals; partisan advantage; short-term horizons; mercurial funding programs; and a reluctance to accurately price infrastructure and usage – have each contributed to Canada's declining international standing. It is both ironic and crucial that this shift has occurred at a time when the pressures and demands on infrastructure have increased primarily because of global shifts beyond national control such as urbanization, immigration, climate change, security threats, technological innovation, and COVID-19. Individually and collectively, seismic shifts on this scale have daunting implications for future investment in infrastructure and present major challenges, but also generate transformative opportunities with respect to the governance and funding of programs and policies. We turn next to a closer look at these crucial and fast-changing international dynamics.

3

Canada-US and International Infrastructure Policy and Institutions

INTRODUCTION

This chapter examines Canada-US and international infrastructure policy and institutions as an important overall context for our later infrastructure regime chapters. Our focus is on the policy and institutional story, but necessarily linked to Canada-US and broader international relations and power, to overall pro- and anti-globalization and free trade forces, and to the more specific governance structures that have changed infrastructure policy for good or for ill. Indeed, as we have shown in chapter 1 and as we will see in each of the six regime chapters and in content regarding pandemic forces in 2020, the international aspects involve national and state and city-regional players on a continuous basis.

The analysis of international infrastructure policy deals with all kinds of conceptual and theoretical vantage points about international institutions and political-economic power (Baylis et al. 2014; Dryzek 2013; Wijen et al. 2013; Volger 2013; Elliott 2004; Held, McGrew, Goldblatt, and Perraton 1999). All these vantage points are different and overlap with each other. For example, with *international relations* (IR) theory, the focus is on power and on interpreting the international system through the lens of realism or "réal-politique." That applies to infrastructure policy as much as any other policy field. And *globalization* theory increasingly contends that all policy is influenced by strong and complex forces that need to be seen through the forces of economic liberalism and transformative technologies, global public interest, and the forces of civil society. This is epitomized through the ways they have been changed and challenged under the disruptive effects of the

UK's decision to leave the European Union (Brexit), and the coming to power of the Trump Administration in the US and its America First decisions and aspirations. Canada's international story in this chapter involves both its relationship with the US and an array of engagements with, and memberships in, international agencies with infrastructure policy and related research mandates. The United States functions in this and other policy fields as a neighbour, as Canada's main trading partner, as an investor, and as a global superpower. The global power structure has also been reshaped in multi-polar ways by the EU, China, Russia, India, Brazil, and other East Asian countries. The emergence of multiple new points of power and influence is symbolized by the decline of the G8 and the rise to prominence of the G20 bloc of relatively wealthy and large economies. These twenty countries determine most of the world's trade patterns and therefore impact infrastructure in direct though often mercurial ways. We have already examined in chapter 1 US trade policy and Canada-US trade relations historically as well as in the 2016 to 2019 Trump era of major trade conflict between Trump's America First agenda and the G6 allies, including (and perhaps especially) Canada. These too affect infrastructure.

Hoberg (2002) offers a framework for understanding Canadian-American relations that is useful in this chapter. His framework is anchored on six mechanisms of American influence on Canada-US relations: the physical environment; US policies and actions through emulation; diplomacy; trade agreements; economic integration and harmonization pressures; and cross-border lobbying (170–3).

All go through more complex processes for Canada because of the nature of the US political system and the sharp separation of powers in Washington, including the independent power of Congress, the frequent use of litigation through the courts, and the effect of very short electoral cycles – as little as two years for the House of Representatives. There is rarely one-stop shopping for any lobby in any democratic political system, but in the US federal system this is further compounded by sheer numbers: there are fifty state governments to contend with. Fourteen of them share the 3,000-mile border with Canada, and there is a dizzying array of border infrastructure, transport, environmental, trade, and regulatory concerns associated with the movement of people and goods that show up in diverse ways. Agenda-setting regarding how to recognize, address, regulate, fund, research, and hopefully solve problems and reach agreements are almost never easy to arrange in ways that suit both countries or interests in both countries regarding both content and timing.

We explore international infrastructure policy and institutions in three overall contextual sections: 1) US infrastructure policy and governance history, including the often-diagnosed US infrastructure deficit, leading to the possible $1 trillion Trump Administration plan and potential links to Canada's plans; 2) continuing and changing Canada-US infrastructure challenges and choices, including those related to a) bridges and border infrastructure, b) the Keystone XL pipeline, c) the St Lawrence Seaway, and d) the Arctic (virtually all our regime chapters in the second part of the book will add to this US-Canada picture); and 3) a selected sample of three international institutions with varied infrastructure policy, governance, and research roles; the European Union, the World Bank, and the Organization for Economic Cooperation and Development (OECD) feature prominently and other international bodies also enter the discussion in our regime chapters.

US INFRASTRUCTURE POLICY HISTORY, INFRASTRUCTURE DEFICITS, THE TRUMP ADMINISTRATION, AND OTHER PLANS

There are any number of examples of US infrastructure policy phases and eras, many captured in recent historical analyses such as those by engineer Henry Petroski (2016) and legal scholar Adam White (2012). Petroski's analysis in *The Road Taken* shows in different ways how in real terms infrastructure is both experimental and incremental in nature. White's analysis of infrastructure "lessons from America history" begins with post-Iraq War exhortations about the need to support "nation-building at home" rather than foreign policy nation-building abroad that "has left the United States in a condition of disrepair" (3) due to a failure to address varied infrastructure needs. But he immediately stresses that "the question of infrastructure (or 'internal improvements,' or 'public works') has bedeviled the nation since its founding" (3). It was a concern of the founding fathers and was explicitly linked to the establishment of the very core of the separation-of-powers US political system, with debates initially focused on how such a constitutional system would hopefully be constructed and mobilized to agree on nation-building roads and canals. In the 1930s depression era, President Roosevelt established a program of needed public works to create work and employment. In the 1950s in the post–World War II era, President Eisenhower fostered a national highway system infrastructure effort.

From the 1960s on, there have been proposals and studies that showed the need to deal with the growing infrastructure deficit, often because it was never clear how and when one could get infrastructure spending through the Congressional budgeting system, and its separation of powers fuelled political agenda calculus. The latest, more concerted effort came under President Barack Obama, who promised a program of "shovel-ready projects," but this was subject to approval in an eventually Republican-controlled Congress, and more specifically one controlled by the Tea Party subset within the Republican Party. A frustrated President Obama later sought executive branch action in 2011 to foster infrastructure action mainly via actions to "expedite permitting and 'environmental' review" (4). But earlier Obama as a senator had also advocated the establishment of a "national infrastructure bank" (7).

White's US infrastructure history ends on the theme of the national infrastructure bank, which was a frequently expressed reform idea in the early 2000s. His opposition to this idea draws on his sense from early and recent American political history as to why the infrastructure bank would not solve the key problems perpetually present. First, he concludes that such proposals "rarely offer any advance indication of exactly which projects, or which kinds of projects, would actually be supported" (30). In addition, the infrastructure bank would only "exacerbate the public's traditional suspicion that government-supported infrastructure is just pork-barrel, intended more to benefit the well-connected than the national interest" (30). Finally, it would "do nothing to transform today's regulatory landscape" (31).

A study published by the US Council on Foreign Relations (Thomasson 2012) began by stating that "federal infrastructure policy is paralyzed by partisan wrangling over massive infrastructure bills that fail to move through Congress" (1). Thomasson argued that first Congress "should give states flexibility to pursue alternative financing sources – public-private partnerships (PPPs), tolling and user fees, and low-cost borrowing through innovative credit and bond programs" (1). He also argued in favour of the need to streamline regulatory approvals so that they could be expedited into construction phases.

The most frequent analytical criticism of the weakness of the US infrastructure record comes from several report cards researched and published by the American Society of Civil Engineers (ASCE). Its report in 2017 gave the American system another basically failing grade of D+, unchanged since 2013 (American Society of Civil Engineers 2017).

Its work was conducted by a team of twenty-eight highly experienced civil engineers who assigned grades using the criteria of "capacity, condition, funding, future need, operation and maintenance, public safety, resilience, and innovation" (Walpole 2017). Seven of the sixteen infrastructure categories assessed did see improvement, but the D+ grade reflected "a continued dire need of overall" change (1).

While the above advocacy and research was by civil engineers, a recent and equally critical study of US federal infrastructure policy was more broadly interdisciplinary (Stanford Global Projects Center 2017). It begins with the view that in "recent years, chronic short-termism and inconsistent policies have led to underinvestment and a lack of maintenance in our national infrastructure networks" (2). Presented as a policy "white paper," the study argues that US federal infrastructure policies should and can "(1) support local infrastructure without prescribing it, (2) reform stakeholder engagement, (3) improve contracting and delivery models,(4) apply long-term approaches for long-term projects, and (5) increase federal capacity to implement megaprojects of regional and national significance" (2).

The coming to power in 2017 of the Trump Administration brought with it the possibility of a frequently mentioned $1 trillion infrastructure plan by the property-owning businessman president. His election and post-election agenda also included the building of a border wall across the Mexican-US border as a security and related trade protection matter (with the initial demands that the Mexicans would have to pay for the wall). It is not easy to predict the prospects for a big Trump infrastructure plan and agenda, given not only his unpredictability and volatility, but also given how it might proceed in a House of Representatives that his Republican Party does not control and that is also internally divided and more likely to seek budget cuts than to be avidly pro-spending. Moreover, this is occurring amidst the Republican Party's own reading of the Trump political tea leaves where there is no longer a dominant Tea Party faction but rather new factions favouring various policies, spending, and tax reform measures, though not all parts of the early Trump agenda. The results of the 2018 congressional elections were also critical. Nevertheless, the fact that the Trump executive is a government of millionaires, many in the property development industry, could also be significant in shaping infrastructure policy.

A Trump infrastructure agenda has included, dangled, and highlighted any number of possible measures and strategies for adoption in Congress and in relation to US federalism and local urban politics (Mufson 2017;

Thrush and Haberman 2017; Wise 2017; Yglesias 2017; Preston 2017; Penn 2018). These include: the use of tax credits to leverage private investment; selecting initial agreed "shovel-ready" investment projects to announce and get through Congress in 2018 before the then-being-strategized run-up to the 2018 Congressional elections; preferences for projects needing fast-track permitting and regulatory relief, not tax dollars; competing priority project lists suggested by federal agencies and/or by state and local government officials; key infrastructure funding arising from Obamacare health cuts; linking/selling infrastructure to tax cuts and tax reform; linking and financing via public-private partnership arrangements; and using infrastructure banks.

There has also been some analytical linkage and interest in the combined potential of a possible $1 trillion US program and Canada's $180 billion infrastructure plan. One international market reaction is that even these big sums are "unlikely to attract big global investors" (Deveau 2017). This assessment draws on the views of Sam Pollack, the head of Brookfield Asset Management Inc. in the US, who stressed that, regarding PPPs, "the amount of red tape involved, modest equity required and small returns investors will see ... will act as a deterrent for the world's largest investors" (2). On the other hand, Pollack argued that "there would be a 'feeding frenzy' of interest if the Canadian government decides to push ahead with plans to sell off the nation's airports" (2).

A further $3 billion planned project to turn the Hoover Dam erected in the 1930s into "a giant battery" is also in the works (Penn 2018). The Los Angeles Department of Water and Power wants to link the dam "with a pump station powered by solar and wind energy ... which "would help regulate the water flow through the dam's generators, sending water back to the top to help manage electricity at times of peak demand" (1) and also help "answer a looming question for the energy industry: how to come up with affordable and efficient power storage" (2). Approval and partial funding would have to come from the federal government but may not garner support from a Trump Administration, not sympathetic at all on matters and arguments regarding cleaner solar and wind energy (7–9).

FOUR CONTINUING CANADA-US INFRASTRUCTURE CHALLENGES AND CHOICES

To complement our initial overall US infrastructure policy picture, we now sample four continuing Canada-US infrastructure challenges and choices. These are located in diverse policy fields and also have complex physical and spatial features in the political-economic geography of the two countries and within each country. The infrastructure challenges and choices profiled are: bridges and border infrastructure; the Keystone XL pipeline; the Saint Lawrence Seaway; and Arctic infrastructure. Later regime chapters each deal with some Trump 2019–20 pandemic policies and the ensuing chaos.

Border and Bridges Infrastructure

Canada-US border and bridges infrastructure policy emerged more sharply and explicitly in the aftermath of the 9/11 terrorist events in the US in 2001. Canada-US relations, and, fully in step, Canadian internal policy priorities as well, shifted massively and immediately to national security concerns. This included national defence, transport, and border security measures. All of them were driven by trade and by keeping the Canada-US trade corridors secure and therefore open (Gattinger and Hale 2010; Whitaker 2003; Doern 2002; Hart and Tomlin 2002). The purpose was both to support the US as a neighbour, ally, and global power, and to protect Canadian access to its largest trade market. Gattinger and Hale's analysis, *Borders and Bridges*, describes an array of Canadian measures in trade policy, with "bridges" used both literally and metaphorically to refer to transport and border infrastructure that enables both countries to trade with each other.

All these developments hit the then freshly re-elected Chrétien Liberal government without warning. The most prominent measures taken by the government in this regard were anti-terrorism legislation, which featured new (and remarkably draconian) powers; changes to immigration law; new financial and personnel resources for the Department of National Defence, CSIS, and national police and border control; enhanced capacity at Health Canada to deal with anthrax infection and other forms of bio-terrorism; and measures to deal with airport safety and security. All of this had a powerful effect on domestic infrastructure and transportation – yet it was driven from abroad. Also established within the government was a Cabinet Committee on Public Security and Anti-Terrorism. Within days of the 9/11 attack, the US was demanding that Canada join in the construction of a North American security perimeter (Molot 2002).

New anti-terrorism legislation was introduced on 22 November 2001 by Transport Minister David Collinette. Called the *Public Safety Act*, it changed nineteen existing laws and greatly strengthened anti-terrorism measures. The federal government was empowered to collect air passenger data from airlines and reservation systems and share it with foreign governments. Such provisions in the law were criticized by opposition parties and privacy advocates for intruding into the personal details of people using the transportation system. In other words, international security issues found their way directly into the lives of individual Canadians.

Security measures were also a part of a comprehensive border agreement with the US. It included joint border policing, expanded international security teams, and coordinated immigration measures. All of these features came into sharp focus wherever people and goods were being transported across borders. Some of the pressure in the US came from the growing view there that Canada's borders were porous, even though it was conclusively shown that none of the 9/11 terrorists had entered the US via Canada.

The primary US legislative response to 9/11 was the *Patriot Act* and the establishment of the Department of Homeland Security. American insistence on a perimeter security arrangement raised questions about whether this was a US-Canada perimeter or a North American perimeter. One immediate response came in Canada when four major national business groups formed the Coalition for Secure and Trade-Efficient Borders that went on to lobby for what was, in effect, aimed at preserving the crucial gains in liberalized trade that had flowed from NAFTA and the WTO, while minimizing the costs to business of the new US measures (Whitaker 2003). The concept of "Smart Borders" also quickly emerged as a way of using technology-based infrastructure to raise confidence in security measures, mostly on the part of the US in respect of Canada, and thereby preventing delay in the transport of Canadian goods to American customers.

That mattered, because according to Globerman and Storer (2006), the new security measures were "producing significantly higher shipping costs and shipment delays" (1) and "both US exports to and imports from Canada were lower than they would otherwise have been in the post-9/11 period, given traditional determinants of bilateral trade" (1). The effects of the measures were anything but homogeneous, either geographically or by mode of transportation. Globerman and Storer report that "trade shortfalls are not uniform across land ports at the Canada-US border ... in part because of differences in the mix of transport modes serving the ports" (2) and that "ports that are more intensive users of rail as a transport mode are more likely to evidence a persistent import shortfall" (2). The study also emphasized that "bilateral trade is concentrated in a relatively small number of ports. Specifically, of the estimated 75 land ports along the Canada-US border, just three account for the bulk of bilateral trade" (3).

These were by no means the only bridges and border infrastructure issues to emerge. Another involved the key Windsor-Detroit crossing, whose Ambassador Bridge is the largest and most important transport piece of infrastructure in Canada-US trade and in the transport of goods. Over 25 per cent of Canada-US merchandise trade by dollar value crosses that 87-year-old span. Mainly because of Canadian concern and pressure, it was decided to establish a Windsor-Detroit Bridge Authority (WDBA) to "manage the procurement process for the design, construction, operation and maintenance of the new bridge between Windsor, Ontario and Detroit, Michigan through a public-private partnership (P3)" (Windsor-Detroit Bridge Authority 2016). Because of the complexity and delays on the US side (at the federal and state level), Prime Minister Harper in February 2015 gave up and made an extraordinary announcement, namely that Canada would build a new $4 billion bridge benefiting both sides of the river, without any financial participation from the state of Michigan or the US government. Canada undertook to pay for all the infrastructure, even on the American side of the bridge, including roads, plazas, and buildings and facilities for US Customs and Border Services.

The question of what "borders" are with respect to real or discursive infrastructure has taken on an interesting analytical shape in the Trump era, when early initiatives focused on banning illegal or unwanted immigrants from getting into the US or catching them if already in the country. Lalami (2017) points out that what "formally counts as a border, according to the United States government, is not just lines separating the United States from Canada and Mexico, but any American territory within 100 miles of the country's perimeter" (4). This includes all or most of fourteen US states, and as a result "the 100 mile border zone is home to two thirds of the nation's population" (4). Within these zones there are border enforcement officers or entities. Lalami concludes that "borders do not simply keep others out. They also wall us in" (5). Canada also has some similar extended realities about the internal reach of borders and what border infrastructure looks and feels like to foreigners versus Canadians in myriad individual socio-economic situations.

Keystone XL Pipeline

Pipelines are quintessentially infrastructure, and there are thirty-one oil and thirty-nine natural gas pipelines regulated by the Canadian federal National Energy Board (NEB) that cross the Canada-US border (Natural Resources Canada 2017). Indeed, Canada's first pipeline proposal and debate in the 1950s, and subsequent ones, were premised pivotally on selling the oil in US markets (Doern and Gattinger 2003). Later reforms to the NEB and its linked environmental assessment processes carried out jointly with Environment Canada's project assessment requirements also showed strong Canada-US links and learning (Doern, Prince, and Schultz 2014, 125–37).

The huge Keystone XL Pipeline was proposed in 2008 by TransCanada, a Calgary company, but this one was to carry hundreds of thousands of barrels of oil sands bitumen from Alberta to Texas. It encountered strong environmental opposition in Nebraska regarding its planned route in that state. This quickly became a partisan and pre-election issue in the United States in the run-up to the November 2012 elections, and afterwards, resulting in a decision by the Obama administration in 2015 to reject the proposal overall because of climate change impacts and concerns (McConaghy 2017; Laxer 2015). There were many phases of support and then disapproval at the state level in Nebraska, including court decisions and threatened legal measures (Avery 2013). In the US, the Keystone project also attracted opposition because of the policy paradigm that accompanied it, namely, regarding the oil sands, climate change impacts and the need to reduce, not expand, carbon emissions (Avery 2013).

The Harper government, presenting Canada as an "energy superpower," launched a strong criticism that labelled some opposing Canadian environmental groups as unpatriotic regarding both their opposition to Keystone XL and their alleged links to funding and support by US environmental groups (Toner and McKee 2014). Following the Obama decision to reject Keystone, TransCanada filed notice to launch a claim under Chapter 11 of the North American Free Trade Agreement, alleging the US government had breached its legal commitments under NAFTA. The company also filed a lawsuit in the US arguing that President Obama had exceeded his powers by denying construction of the project (CBC News 2017).

The Trump Administration announced on 16 January 2017 that it would grant a permit for the construction of the Keystone XL pipeline, saying that it was "the first of many infrastructure projects" that President Trump would approve (quoted in Dennis and Mufson 2017, 1). TransCanada thanked the Trump Administration and indicated it would continue to "invest in and strengthen North America's energy infrastructure" (1). Trump based his decision on the US State Department's supplemental environmental impact statement issued in January 2014 by the Obama Administration. It had concluded that "that the tar sands would be developed with or without the pipeline and that as a result the decision would not affect climate change" (2). Prime Minister Justin Trudeau has pursued a positive US decision on Keystone, partly based on his support for two other Canadian pipelines that he thought were sufficiently covered by his government's overall post-election climate change and energy-environment pipeline regulatory policy (Toner, Cherniak, and Force 2016), and of course by his own overall infrastructure agenda. We examine more recent Keystone XL features in chapter 9's examination of the energy-environment-resources pipelines policy and governance regime, including its links to a broader pan-Canadian pipelines infrastructure battle, and consider the broader ramifications of President Biden's swift action to rescind its construction permit and recommit the US to the Paris climate agreement.

The Saint Lawrence Seaway

The Saint Lawrence Seaway is an early major Canada-US infrastructure project and engineering achievement that took a decade to build, and that opened in 1959 and celebrated its sixtieth anniversary in 2019. It is a 189-mile system between Montreal and Lake Ontario that involved the building of seven locks, five in Canada and two in the US, in order to "lift vessels to 246 feet above sea level" (Great Lakes St Lawrence Seaway System 2016, 1). The project also involved a deepening of the Welland Canal in Ontario. The original building of the project was complex, innovative, and rooted in the longer history of the Saint Lawrence River in North America and trade with Europe.

An interesting dynamic between the two national Seaway entities that jointly operate the system occurred in the 1996–98 period. The Canadian lead agency is the St Lawrence Seaway Management Corporation (SLSMC), established in 1998 as a not-for-profit entity as a successor to the previous St Lawrence Seaway Authority (Jenish 2009). Its counterpart in the US is the Saint Lawrence Seaway

Development Corporation (SLSDC), which is a wholly owned US government corporation (SLSDC 2014). In the run-up to this decision, there had been pressure in Canada to privatize the Seaway authority, and there appeared to be one or two willing buyers/bidders (Jenish 2009, 88–90). The US Seaway authority, however, was a public corporation (the equivalent of a Crown Corporation) and it, and other parts of the US transportation government structure, were not ready to see Canada's entity become private if that meant it only had to behave like a private firm without public interest responsibilities. SLSMC also envisioned its then-sluggish 60 per cent capacity performance being greatly improved if it could move from its reliance on stable commodity shipments of grain, iron ore, and coal to have a greater capacity to ship container traffic.

Another relevant Canada-US process was the work and report of the Great Lakes St Lawrence Seaway Study (GLSLS) (2007). It involved seven departments and agencies as sponsors of and contributors to the study: Transport Canada, the US Army Corps of Engineers, the US Department of Transport, the SLSMC, the SLSDC, Environment Canada, and the US Fish and Wildlife Service. Its research and analytical work over three years was carried out by three working groups of subject matter experts: economic, environmental, and engineering (1). The central question the GLSLS was asked was "what is the current condition of the GLSLS system, and how best should we use and maintain the system, in its current physical configuration, in order to capitalize on the opportunities and face the challenges that will present themselves in coming years?" (1).

On its economic role, the study noted that "while grain still moves through the GLSLS, its volumes have been overshadowed by huge shipments of iron ore" (2). For these and other shippers, the system "offers significant savings" and it also "offers shippers considerable spare capacity," an issue of growing importance given road and rail congestion (2). The GLSLS can relieve some of these pressures "by offering complementary transportation routes through less busy ports and by moving goods directly across lakes rather than around them" (4) such as via so-called "shortsea shipping."

Regarding GLSLS infrastructure and its engineering systems consisting of "locks, shipping channels, ports, bridges, control and communication systems" (5), the key was the continued infrastructure maintenance of the system. In particular, the study stressed that "[r]eliability is critical because the GLSLS is essentially a series of structures that must be transited with no alternatives ... As a result, closure of one of the structures in the series closes the entire system." Increasingly a "proactive maintenance strategy" will be needed (6).

A study by Jetoo et al. (2014) maps and assesses "governance and geopolitics as drivers of change in the Great-Lakes-St. Lawrence basin." They begin with the not uncommon view that "the basic characteristic of governance is the migration of power from the central state up into supranational institutions, horizontally to non-state actors, and down to sub-national levels of government and non-state actors" (1). The analysis focuses on four central problems: institutional fragmentation; the changing relationship between federal and sub-national levels of government in Canada and the US; the governance capacity to implement decisions made within a governance regime "which includes expertise, resources such as funding and personnel, and an informed and engaged public" (2); and the "effect of geopolitics on Great Lakes region governance" (2).

While both the US and Canada and their co-governing Seaway institutions have ongoing challenges regarding market development and infrastructure change and refurbishment, they each separately and jointly have sought to develop new alliances and markets. For example, the us slsdc's annual report for 2015 headed the report with the statement that "[t]he Great Lakes St. Lawrence Seaway System is a binational waterway connecting world markets to North America's 'Opportunity Belt' – the Great Lakes Region" (Saint Lawrence Seaway Development Corporation 2015c, Table of Contents page). It stressed its own Great Lakes Regional Outreach Initiative, which centred on a delegation of Great Lakes stakeholders to a trade mission conference attended by 5,000 participants in Belgium (2). The Canadian slsmc annual report for 2014–15 struck some similar but more varied stakeholder initiatives, including three environmental ones (St Lawrence Seaway Management Corporation 2014–15, 26–7).

These are by no means the only voices and views concerning the state and adequacy of the Seaway. For example, Ontario grain farmers acted collectively as an interest group to draw attention to the routes and ports in the Great Lakes to the Seaway. These also have important consequences for centres such as Hamilton, Windsor, Sarnia, Goderich, and Oshawa. These feeder routes often are impacted by extended or delayed ice cover on the lakes. But they are also the location for quite large shipping vessels that function within the Seaway system as a whole (Telford 2015; Marowits 2017). Thus, overall, there is diverse awareness regarding how well the Seaway infrastructure stacks up against changing market and socio-economic needs on both sides of the border.

Arctic Infrastructure

Canada-US agendas, interests, and dynamics regarding Arctic infra-structure have also come into greater focus in the last twenty years, with both nations expressing concerns about Russia's strategies in a melting Arctic where year-round northern shipping and oil and gas development opportunities are driving politics and economics. Some of the relations regarding the Arctic are bilateral in nature between different pairings of northern neighbouring nations, but some are also multilateral in nature, especially through the work and auspices of the Arctic Council. We discuss the Arctic Council as an institution first and then look at more specific Canadian and US views of what Arctic infrastructure policies and needs involve.

The Arctic Council, whose member countries include Canada, the United States, Russia, Denmark (including Greenland and the Faroe Islands), Finland, Iceland, Norway, and Sweden, was established in 1996 as a Canadian-led initiative. It was both a Mulroney Conservative and **Chrétien** Liberal initiative and hence had full Canadian bipartisan international impetus (English 2013). The forerunner to the council was a 1989 meeting initiated by Finland to discuss with the eight countries cooperative measures to deal with the environment. Observer countries from other parts of the world were also involved, and as a result there are already broader dynamics regarding the further "inter-nationalization" of the Arctic Council because of the melting of the Arctic ice.

Environmental concerns were therefore pivotal, but the notion of climate change "adjustment" as a term for the melting Arctic did not do justice to the total task at hand, nor to the new worlds that other interests now see as exciting economic opportunities, including the opening of sea routes between the Atlantic and Pacific (Jones 2013). Concerns were also building about what Berkman (2013; 2010) refers to as the need to prevent an Arctic Cold War. Charles Emmerson's comprehensive assessment of the Arctic and its present and future concludes that "a battleground does not mean war, but it does mean conflict and competition: political, economic, cultural and diplomatic" (Emmerson 2011, 344).

This concern arises in part because, in the formation of the council, the crucial concerns by some about preserving peaceful relations were deleted in talks leading to the formation of the council (Berkman 2013). These concerns centred on US-Russian relations and history and their military capacities to back up sovereignty claims, but there is also NATO interest in the new sea routes and the possibility of conflict (Emmerson 2011). Indeed, the discourse used by some players is centred on *environmental security*. One of the latter concerns, published in *Nature*, reported on economic costs around the world due to the release of large amounts of methane, a powerful greenhouse gas, from the thawing permafrost (Whiteman, Hope, and Wadhams 2013; Connor 2013).

One of the first Arctic infrastructure initiatives in the Harper government era was the establishment of the Canadian High Arctic Research Station (Byers 2009; Coates, Lackenbauer, Morrison, and Poelzer 2008). Harper also gave considerable public emphasis to his plan that Canada would claim territorial jurisdiction of the North Pole under the UN Convention of the Law of the Sea. This stance was expressed despite expert opinion arguing that this claim was highly unlikely to be valid (Byers 2014).

One of the few Canadian reports that was infrastructure-specific and -focused was a Parliamentary Library analysis (Ruffili 2011). It focused on Arctic marine and intermodal infrastructure challenges and the federal government's responses. The responses related to: the Harper Conservative government's "northern strategy"; the Arctic Bridge and Arctic Gateway strategies centred on the Port of Churchill, Manitoba; and the Over-the-Top Route (Northwest Territories). As the Ruffili paper shows, there were now complex needs for new infrastructure related to ports, shipping, and intermodal transport related to dealing with the long distances between northern communities and southern ports, the high cost of air transport, and the lack of alternative transport infrastructure such as all-weather roads, paved airport runways, and rail lines (Ruffili 2012, 1). Other linked infrastructures such as telecommunications were also needed. The report showed that some new infrastructure investment commitments were being made by federal, provincial, and territorial governments but they were well below needed levels (4–5).

A similar but more recent and wide-reaching 2016 US study (US Committee on the Marine Transportation System 2016) focused on a ten-year prioritization of infrastructure needs in the US Arctic. Its suggested priorities were cast broadly as infrastructure related to navigable waterways, physical infrastructure (centred on the prevention of pollution from ships and port reception facilities), information infrastructure, and response services. The report stressed overall that "as sea ice retreats, the lack of US Arctic infrastructure to support increased maritime activity grows more apparent" (6). It also had many more related environmental rationales and concerns compared to the earlier 2011 Canadian report that made almost no such links or observations.

In Byers's (2009) definitive Canadian account, the central question is "who owns the Arctic?" in the sense of sovereignty, but also private property and the global commons where complex public goods have to be defended and managed. It involves infrastructure rescaling in major ways, including the fact that most southerners in each of the countries bordering the Arctic have never visited their northern and high Arctic realms. In many ways, they are out of sight and out of mind except for periodic media coverage of receding ice, snow, and endangered polar bears.

Meanwhile, the Arctic Council (chaired by Canada in the 2014 to 2016 period and later by the US), influenced by its member countries and their researchers and advocates, was also crafting infrastructure agendas, through various task force studies and reports and other related initiatives. Examples of the latter include *Arctic Transport Infrastructure: Response Capacity and Sustainable Development* (Arctic Maritime and Aviation Transportation Infrastructure Initiative 2012); the work of the Arctic Council's Task Force on Telecommunications Infrastructure in the Arctic (2016); Arctic Spatial Data Infrastructure (2016); and the Arctic Council Resilience Workshop (2016), which included work on risks to infrastructure from increased flooding and thawing permafrost.

As the Obama era ended in the US, there were also signs in some US quarters, well before the Trump election, that the Arctic Council itself needed reform because it was a discussion forum and not an actual international governing organization, and that it should not deal with matters regarding military security (Gourley 2016). A study by the Washington-based Center for Strategic and International Studies (Conley and Menno 2016) examines several scenarios for mandate and structural change for the Arctic Council. Its "complete redesign" model calls for "the creation of an Arctic Security and Cooperation Organization ... designed along the lines of the Consensus-Based

Organization for Security and Cooperation in Europe." The three Arctic dimensions "will cover economic issues, human/environmental issues ... and for the first time security issues" (4). Not for the first time, infrastructure issues and capacities are being built into the complexities of governance, power, and multiple policy fields simultaneously. We will see further discussion of the Arctic in chapter 6's regime analysis, which also includes transportation infrastructure in Canada's "many norths."

THREE SELECTED INTERNATIONAL INFRASTRUCTURE INSTITUTIONS

Our final contextual lens includes a sample of three important and relevant international infrastructure institutions with varied mandates, levels of funding experience, and research roles on infrastructure policy and governance. We look briefly in turn at the European Union (EU), the World Bank (also referred to as the World Bank Group), and the OECD. Canada is not a member of the EU but is part of the Canada-EU Free Trade Agreement. The EU is also important because its twenty-eight member states have been reduced to twenty-seven following Brexit, with the UK's decision to leave. EU member countries are broadly wealthy states but there are less wealthy countries among them and hence different infrastructure dynamics. Canada is a member of the World Bank, but the World Bank's infrastructure dynamics reflect a much larger set of countries globally, including some very poor countries that are supported by World Bank financing and banking initiatives. The wide disparity between rich and poor member countries places infrastructure in different economic growth contexts with a range of human capital needs and complexities. The OECD is a thirty-five-member organization of rich countries that Canada belongs to, and has also sought through studies and debate to shape infrastructure policy.

We explore these three international infrastructure institutions, but it must be stressed they are by no means the only international institutional players. Many other intergovernmental, public-private, and private-sector international entities are involved, including those in energy (oil, gas, nuclear, renewable), banking, telecommunications, the internet, transportation, and water, ports and marine. Each has core and changing infrastructure challenges and priorities as they frequently look to lobby and influence each other.

The European Union

The EU is relevant to Canada both with regard to its recent infrastructure policies and to the scenarios it developed in the process of a Brexit debate. We start with its 2017 *White Paper on the Future of Europe* (European Commission 2017), which set out reflections and scenarios for the EU by 2025. The five scenarios are cast as follows: scenario 1, Carrying On; scenario 2, Nothing But the Single Market; scenario 3, Those Who Want More Do More; scenario 4, Does Less More Efficiently; and scenario 5, Doing Much More Together (5).

The most explicit and immediate reference to infrastructure is in scenario 1, where the EU's linked focus on jobs, growth, and investment by strengthening the single market is to be bolstered "by stepping up investment in digital, transport and energy infrastructure" (16). Defence cooperation would be deepened in terms of "research, industry and joint procurement" (16). So would "high quality and high-speed broadband" (17). In scenario 2, infrastructure is border-related because the scenario implies greater mobility and immigration controls and therefore the need for "more systematic checks of people at national borders due to insufficient cooperation on security and migration matters" (18). Also mentioned is infrastructure related to dealing with large-scale "cyber-attacks" (19). Under scenario 4, the latter is referenced in enhanced terms by the expressed need for a "joint defence programme ... set up to protect critical infrastructure against cyber-attacks" (21). Scenario 4 also refers to the related need for a "European Telecoms Authority ... with the power to free-up frequencies for cross-border communication services such as the ones needed for the use of connected cars across Europe" (23). The "connected cars" infrastructure needs are also referred to in scenario 5 (25).

It must be stressed that these five EU scenarios, suggested to help discussion about the EU 27's future trajectory, are very briefly presented in the EU *White Paper*, but infrastructure issues nonetheless emerge illustratively within this visioning exercise. They emerge on top of more detailed infrastructure strategies and plans enunciated recently by the EU in the years before Brexit. As a complex functioning multi-member government entity, some of its infrastructure plans, in this case for the 2016–20 period, centre on the EU's Brussels Office for Infrastructure and Logistics (European Commission 2016a). These relate to its own buildings and space planning, and the quality of such infrastructure across many functioning European Commission directorates. But separate infrastructure-centred plans emerge in relation to the Directorate General Informatics (European Commission 2016b). The latter strategic plan for 2016 to 2020 had highlighted priorities related to creating the "Data centre of the future" and also "better IT Security." Earlier EU plans covering the 2014–20 period also were centred on mobility and transport (European Commission 2014). Indeed, it was cast as "the new EU infrastructure policy" because, for the first time, it articulated a vision for "a core transport network built on nine major corridors" across the EU. It will connect "94 main European ports with rail and road links; 38 key airports with rail connections into major cities, 15,000 km of railway line upgraded to high speed, and 35 cross-border projects to reduce bottlenecks" (2).

The World Bank

The World Bank shows an evolving view about infrastructure policy and development as it is seen by its wide-ranging membership of 189 countries, both rich and poor. An initial working paper by Estache and Fay (2007) reflected on then-current debates on infrastructure policy. It began by arguing that over the previous twenty-five years, the "received wisdom was that the private sector was going to take over" services such as electricity, telecoms, transport, and water and sanitation, "leaving only a residual role for governments (deregulation and restructuring)" (1). But this private-sector role did not materialize regarding infrastructure per se. The study then argued that "there is a strong and widespread sense among policy-makers that some of the differences in growth rates between East Asia and other parts of the world can be attributed to the failure to invest sufficiently in infrastructure" (1). The basic problem was "the insufficient stocks of infrastructure and hence the insufficient flows of associated services" (2). Unsurprisingly, the study also argued that there was "a long way to go still in meeting the infrastructure needs of the poorest countries" (5). When discussing what was then known about the "infrastructure-growth" nexus, the authors suggested that even if infrastructure is necessary, "it may not be the case that more infrastructures cause more growth at all stages of development" (6). It is also argued that "infrastructure services are mostly provided through networks, a fact that implies a non-linear relation with output" (6).

The progression of some of these ideas and arguments within the World Bank can be seen in an infrastructure strategy update for the period 2012–15 (World Bank Group 2011). Focused on "transformation through infrastructure," the update argued that the World Bank Group "will support client demand to address the more complex, second generation infrastructure issues" and "will leverage its capital by bringing more private sector financing into infrastructure" (2). Later, the update study took note of the pace of change in the world and argued that "uncertainty is increasing" and that these uncertainties for client countries need to be "integrated into infrastructure planning and design" (8), including uncertainties related to demographic changes, technological innovation, policy performance, and the environment. A further study (World Bank Group 2017) also captures the complexities of the main and increasingly diverse financing mechanisms for infrastructure projects. This built on an earlier study that had also examined its experience in client countries with public-private partnerships in the 2002 to 2012 period (Independent Evaluation Group and World Bank Group 2012).

While each of the above analyses linked their work to the mandate of the World Bank, none of them captured or contained the sense of priorities revealed and emphasized in its 2016 Annual Report (World Bank 2016). It opens with the stated goal that "ending extreme poverty by 2030 and boosting shared prosperity in a sustainable manner are the driving missions for the World Bank Group" (1). It stresses that "countries must grow their economies inclusively, so that everyone benefits: they must invest in their people: and they must ensure that those who have left poverty do not fall back into it" (1). It immediately links these undertakings to situations of global disruption, but states that "[m]illions of people have been forcibly displaced by conflict and live in ever-more fragile areas: the risks of pandemics can devastate the health of individuals, but also undermine countries' economies: and the threats of climate change are becoming ever more apparent" (2).

Diverse financial commitments, projects, and new alliances are mentioned but there is little explicit mention of infrastructure per se. Building on the above-stated core planned mandate are "investments in human capital" (18), cast in terms "education, health care, social protection, and jobs" (18), and measures targeted to "break the intergenerational transmission of poverty and to take advantage of the demographic trends in many countries where poverty is concentrated" (18).

Given its mandate and the wide of range of rich and poorer countries which it funds and supports, it is not surprising that the World Bank garners diverse kinds of praise and criticism regarding its infrastructure roles, concepts and financing. One commentary argued that the World Bank was "in the vanguard of an infrastructure boom" (Alexander 2015), with the bank also more interested in bigger projects that are "transformational." Another analysis (Gustin 2017) cites the bank's goal of reducing poverty, but in an examination of four countries in the 2007 to 2016 period the study argues that one of the bank's primary lending programs "has steered investment toward coal, gas and oil, while blunting efforts to advance renewable energy sources, including wind and solar" (2).

The OECD

The OECD has drawn on several strands of its research since 1998 that informed its overall 2015 report advocating its "framework for the governance of infrastructure" (OECD 2015b). It did so because "international good practices can help governments better seize opportunities and meet related challenges," given that "the interests and challenges in developing infrastructure are common across countries" (1). These were cast ultimately in the context of "five modes of infrastructure delivery," namely: direct provision; traditional public procurement; state-owned enterprises (in full or in part); public-private partnerships and concessions; and privatization with regulation (4).

The objective of the framework directed at its member governments is to "ensure that infrastructure programs: makes the right projects happen; in a cost-efficient, and affordable manner, that is trusted by users and citizens to take their views into account" (7). These are cast in relation to five "phases in the life cycle of an infrastructure asset project" (7). Its discussion of the coordination challenge stresses "that a multiplicity of actors across levels of government may ultimately derail a good project" (9). Attention is drawn to the multiple levels of government involved. Subnational governments "undertook 72% of total public investment in 2013 across OECD countries in terms of volume" and the OECD notes that "subnational public investment ranges from 13% in Chile to 88% in Canada" (9). A dozen or so governance challenges are then presented, including: the need for well-managed consultation with communities; the skills challenge with respect to the life cycle of infrastructure; uncertainty regarding revenue flows and sources; unstable or burdensome regulatory frameworks; the vulnerability of infrastructure procurement to corruption; and political and business cycles issues that impact the phases of infrastructure (8–15).

A related further study (OECD 2015c) also offered some lesson-drawing on the policies and processes for "fostering investment in infrastructure." Overall, the report concluded that "infrastructure investment needs to be substantially increased in most developing and emerging economies to meet social needs and support more rapid economic growth" (5). These were similar to the first OECD study cited above, but the later one also went into other lesson realms such as "an investment regime that provides clarity and predictability for investors"; "improving the public procurement regime"; and "unbundling vertically integrated supply chains in network infrastructure sectors" (5–6).

As we saw in chapter 1, the OECD has also offered research and advice on the protection of "critical infrastructure" and investment policies relating to national security (OECD 2008) and on pension fund investment in infrastructure, research that focused on Canada and Australia (Inderst and Croce 2013). Later chapters will also draw on OECD studies on "large research infrastructures" and their impacts (OECD 2014).

CONCLUSIONS

This chapter has provided a needed initial contextual look at the multidimensional nature of Canada-US and international infrastructure policy and institutions. Three institutional realms have been sampled: 1) US infrastructure policy and governance history, including the often-diagnosed infrastructure deficit leading to the possible $1 trillion Trump Administration plan and potential links to Canada's plans; 2) four selected examples of continuing and changing Canada-US infrastructure challenges and choices; and 3) a selected subset of three international institutions with varied infrastructure policy, governance, and research roles, namely the European Union, the World Bank, and the Organization for Economic Cooperation and Development (OECD). These examples illustrate growing international influences and imperatives, greater governance complexity, intermittent success and failure, and intense political pressures and changes that have to be interpreted, decided upon, implemented, or ignored or postponed.

Our account has been partly chronological, but it is also clear that there are overlaps and collision points among these developments in addition to diverse infrastructure types, dynamics, and interests. Together these influences change temporal senses of when new infrastructure is crucial to creating economic growth and when these links are downplayed. Infrastructure as pipelines, seaways, platforms, informational and institutional networks, and borders and border security have emerged. These bilateral and other multilateral international dynamics also inform in different ways and degrees the structure and analysis of our six regimes in part II of the book. In the regime analyses, the role and power of China also looms ever larger both for Canada and for US-China power relations in the post-2020 pandemic world. Canada-US conflict also reverts to the 2020 dynamics of President Trump's late-2020 election battle, driven by his gross pandemic failures whose consequences for Canada include closed Canada-US borders well into 2021 and possibly beyond.

PART TWO

Six Infrastructure Policy and Governance Regimes

4

The Business Infrastructure Regime

INTRODUCTION

This chapter provides a basic mapping and analysis of the business infrastructure regime, the first of our six regimes being empirically examined. This involves probing what business infrastructure means, or potentially could mean, and provides greater specificity on what types of business entities are involved, in addition to describing the sources and modes of funding business infrastructure. As our previous chapters have shown, we also need to be alert to examples of how diverse regulatory, tax, and policy systems impact on business infrastructure decisions, approvals, rejections, and timing and completion schedules for initial construction, maintenance, and renewal.

Actual or potential types of business infrastructure include: non-residential construction; buildings and physical plant (owned or rented); systems/facilities and equipment as assets for production, inventory management, and storage; information and telecommunication (IT) systems; energy/electrical systems; roads and vehicles; and banking/ financial systems. As already stressed in chapter 1, regime analysis means that businesses as owners and users of infrastructure are present in other regime chapters as well. An accurate sense of the business infrastructure regime also requires an appreciation of business entity types, including: non-incorporated owner-operated entities; large limited liability corporations; multi-national corporations (foreign- and Canadian-owned); small and medium-sized enterprises (SMEs); and start-up businesses. These in turn need to be related to the range of funding for business infrastructure: by business owners themselves; via tax and depreciation systems for assets; by normal bank loans; by share offers; via bonds; by shared funding with other partner businesses; by the regular big six Canadian chartered banks; and by specialized banks (such as the Business Development Bank of Canada).

The chapter is essentially a three-part journey. We start with three policy and governance histories regarding business infrastructure covering roughly a sixty-year period overall: 1) businesses and evolving core self-funding and banking system-funded infrastructure (1960s to present); 2) SMEs and start-up businesses and infrastructure (1970 to present); and 3) public-private partnerships (P3s) infrastructure (early 1990s to present). Chapter 5 on the infrastructure financing regime will examine the announced Canada Infrastructure Bank and also pension funds, already referred to in chapters 1 and 2, but will also cover key notions of banking and funding dating back to the 1930s. We then provide an analysis across the three policy and governance histories deploying the three elements in our analytical framework: ideas, discourse and agendas; power structures, democracy and governance; and temporal realities, cycles, conflicts and technology. Conclusions then follow.

In the three policy and governance histories, the meaning of "business" is in most respects relatively straightforward. The first history deals mainly with larger businesses. The second is focused on small and medium-sized enterprises (SMEs), which tend to be well-defined. It also includes start-up businesses as a more recent real and discursive category that typically refers to small (often very small) firms and involves some temporal ambiguity around what starting actually means and how long the start-up period lasts. The third policy and governance history focuses on public-private partnerships (P3s). This concept has been initiated by business and private interests through their advocacy of a greater needed business role in *public* infrastructure. We still have a business focus in this third history, since that is what some business interests are concentrating on in terms of benefits to themselves, but we also consider the claimed and actual benefits that business knowledge and expertise can bring to government-owned and initiated public infrastructure.

Alongside each policy and governance history, we also examine the impacts of selected regulatory and tax provisions that help to illustrate change or add additional notions of what business infrastructure assets include across an overall sixty-year period.

THREE BUSINESS INFRASTRUCTURE POLICY AND GOVERNANCE REGIME HISTORIES

1 Businesses and Evolving Core Self-Funding and Banking System-Funded

INFRASTRUCTURE, 1960S TO PRESENT

This policy and governance history relates to business policies and their own infrastructure decisions and thus is primarily a private-sector story – not entirely, however, since public policy and public money always influence investment decisions. This point notwithstanding, businesses remain the largest overall creators and funders of Canadian infrastructure despite "infrastructure" often not being the dominant discourse. Here we explore how the core business regime has emerged and has been examined.

Canadian analysts such as TD Economics (2015) and Statistics Canada (2016) characterize business infrastructure as *non-residential construction*. This includes "engineering construction" and "commercial and industrial building construction" that can be both business-centred and "institutional" since it deals also with health and education. TD Economics (2015) has noted cyclical changes for non-residential construction, including the recent and current ones caused by "weakness in oil-related investment" (1) in Alberta, but its report is mainly devoted to showing the cycles from 1990. The report shows that "the 1990s stand out as the toughest period for the sector in recent memory, with investment in non-residential structures plunging 15% during the 1990–93 period" and "remain[ing] subdued for another three years due to high interest rates" (2). Nevertheless, over the 2000 to 2014 period, "growth has been reasonably broad based across non-residential areas" (2). The fastest growth area in this period was a "135% jump in engineering construction led by the development of the oil sands and offshore petroleum, as well as mining infrastructure" (2). The Statistics Canada (2016) report showed smaller patterns of ups and downs for investment in non-residential building construction in the 2011 to 2016 period, with shifts from about $12 billion to about $13 billion annually (1). By mid-2019, the Alberta-centred oil sands economy was showing a major slump, and as already mentioned in chapter 1, federal Tory leader Andrew Scheer's 2019 election campaign was centred on a vision for Canada that included a "national corridor for energy and telecommunications" (Hunt 2019) and related concerns that were Alberta-centred.

A further common infrastructure-related policy regarding business, one that goes beyond actual construction, is that of tax policy and related discourse concerning *depreciation and capital cost allowances*. Operating costs associated with equipment lasting more than a year are a useful starting point to illustrate this. Businesses will set aside funds each year that will accumulate enough money to replace an asset when its economic life comes to an end because "Canadian tax law allows the company to deduct part of the machine's cost from its pre-tax cash flow every year" (Jones 2017, 1). Jones notes that the potential causes for depreciation of an asset include physical depreciation, functional depreciation, technological depreciation, depletion (related to consumption of a non-renewable resource), and monetary depreciation, but regarding overall Canadian tax law on depreciation, the key allowable depreciation expense is expressed as the "capital cost allowance" (CCA).

The legislation and related rules specify a small number of *classes of asset*, and a CCA *rate for each class* that must be accounted for separately. Only an accountant inside the firm, or advised by one outside the firm, would have the knowledge and tenacity to deal accurately with any of the potential 53 classes listed and/or illustrated in the Canada Revenue Agency (CRA) guide (Canada Revenue Agency 2017).

For example, classes 1, 3, and 6 (at a 4, 5, and 10 per cent rate respectively) could involve "a building, depending on what the building is made of" and the date acquired (1–2). They could include the parts that make up the building, ranging from electrical wiring and plumbing to elevators and escalators. Class 10 (30 per cent) includes "general purpose electronic data-processing equipment (computer hardware)" (4). Class 50 (55 per cent) involves property acquired after 18 March 2007 "that is general-purpose electronic data processing equipment and systems software for that equipment" (7).

The above basic features of depreciation must also be related to *how lending decisions are made by Canadian banks on a case-by-case basis*. The official banking industry view is that bankers "look at the total business package when making financial decisions and the ability to repay a loan is determined by factors such as the business plan, cash flow projections, asset base, sales and marketplace analysis and business viability" (Canadian Bankers Association 2016, 2). Thus, it is quite possible for other assets to be wholly or partly financed by banks in these case-by-case decisions. But these are not publically reported in a manner similar to the discussion above regarding non-residential building and its sub-categories.

A further way to gain insights into the nature of business infrastructure is via a sample of company annual reports. We have looked at about twenty large companies, but for our purposes here we take note briefly of just three large businesses, the Hudson's Bay Company (HBC), the Great-West Life Assurance Company (Great-West), and the Bank of Nova Scotia (Scotiabank). HBC states that it "is one of the largest department store retailers in the world, based on its successful formula of growing through acquisitions ... and unlocking the value of real estate holdings" (Hudson's Bay Company 2017, 4). It operates more than 480 stores and has a "global e-commerce presence" (4). In Canada, it operates 90 HBC stores "with an average of 166,000 square feet per store" (17), many owned directly but many others leased. Its facilities also consist of one owned warehouse and distribution facility and four leased warehouses under long-term lease control (36).

HBC also notes that its various means and modes of transport are entirely outsourced and typically the company does not enter into long-term contracts with their carriers. The report also draws attention to its digital and information technology as a crucial asset. It states that each of its "banners" (major product/sales offerings) "has suites of systems to support the performance of accounting, purchasing and inventory management, supply chain, and store systems" (37). The report also shows the regulatory matters it must deal with emanating from different levels of government in Canada, the US, the EU, and Japan. These laws and regulations include, among others, "securities laws, labour and employment laws, product safety laws, privacy laws and workplace safety regulations" (37).

HBC also highlights the extent to which, globally, retailers have been suffering and put out of business because of multiple closures of downtown stores and hence problems in keeping inner cities and towns surviving (Gonzales-Rodriguez 2019).

The above late-2019 analysis centred on the HBC decision that it is fully "exiting the Netherlands" by closing its fifteen stores, e-commerce site, and headquarters. The above analysis did stress that the closings were not expected to harm HBC operations in Canada. But other studies in business publications such as *Money Wise* did stress that many chains have announced "a ton of store closings in 2019" (Whiteman 2019).

Great-West Life Assurance Company (2016) is our second company to be explored in a brief basic way. Its report stressed that it "serves the financial security needs of more than 13 million people across Canada" by offering its customers an "array of choices for life, health, disability, and critical illness insurance for individuals and families, as well as investment, savings and retirement income plans and annuities" (1). Great-West also has "operations" in the UK, Germany, and Ireland. Great-West also draws immediate attention to the way in which it serves its customers through a "diverse network of financial security advisors and brokers" within its overall corporate structure "as well as independent advisors, brokers, and employee benefits consultants" (4). Its accounts show that in 2016 its "total assets under administration amounted to $420,421 millions" (4).

While Scotiabank is one of the big six Canadian banks (see more below), we are interested in it here as a business itself presenting itself and its assets to possible investors and customers (Scotiabank 2016). Posing the question of "why invest in Scotiabank," the bank's and its CEO's answers highlight "ongoing market volatility" and "historically low interest rates," but also how Scotiabank: has diversified by business and geography; has "earnings momentum"; has "attractive growth opportunities in our key Pacific Alliance markets"; is "focussed on digitization to strengthen customer experience and improve efficiency"; and has a "strong risk management culture" (1–2). "Digital transformation" was also one of the key features in discussion of its risk management culture (3) and the report refers to its launch of "digital factories" in its priority markets of Canada, Mexico, Peru, Chile, and Colombia, emphasizing that "at the Factories, employees from our business lines and corporate functions work together to reinvent the way our customers bank with us" (4).

The report also shows that Scotiabank has $896 billion in assets (132). Its corporate profile document (Scotiabank 2017) shows that in its Canadian banking operations it serves customers through "its network of 980 branches and more than 3500 automated banking machines (ABMs)." Thus "branches" and "automated banking machines" "are the infrastructure to be stressed." In some Canadian and global cities and communities, the closure of branches and the absence of automated banking machines are increasingly the object of sharp criticism. For Scotiabank, its international banking (an increasing part of its growth strategy) is described as a "well-established, diversified franchise" with 14 million "customers across our footprint" operating in "1800+ branches, and a network of contact and business support centres" (1).

Each of the above-sampled businesses is different and each has its own discourse for presenting its summary story, including what "infra-structure" may constitute its current or changing asset structure, and what different threats to it exist. To better comprehend and contextual-ize these narratives, we require some sense of how the banking system as a whole funds business assets/infrastructure. A study by Robert McKeown (2016) looks at the Canadian banking system from 1996 to 2015, noting that by 2014 it was made up of 25 domestic banks, 24 foreign subsidiaries, and 27 foreign bank branches operating in Canada. Overall, however, the Big 6 Canadian banks "controlled approximately 90% of banking assets" (2) during this period. The study also notes that recently "a number of Canadian banks have been expanding rapidly" in the US (3). In his highlights of the asset side of the bank's balance sheets, McKeown notes that the loan portfolio "had nearly doubled twice in the past twenty years" (7). Crucially, he also notes that the Canadian banking system "contains a smaller proportion of business loans and a greater proportion of mortgages and consumer loans than it did in 1996" (7). Mortgages "as a percentage of total assets increased by only 1.33% from 1997 to 2006 but increased 6.59% from 2006 to 2015" (12). This means that residential mortgages "accounted for 23.3 percent of total bank assets in 2015" (12).

Statistics Canada (2017b) also provides data on assets via the Canada Revenue Agency's Corporate Returns Act. Total assets went from $6,417,794 in 2010 to $8,848,493, with the figures for private enterprises increasing from $5,673,124 in 2010 to $7,972,377 in 2014. The other balances were assets owned by government business enterprises, which stood in 2010 at $744,670 and in 2014 at $876,116. As a further infrastructure indicator, Statistics Canada (2017a) also publishes data on building permits, with the total value of such permits for the 2012 to early 2017 period in the $7.0 to $7.8 billion range.

A further institutional presence in the banking and businesses infrastructure/asset nexus is the Business Development Bank of Canada (BDC), owned by the Government of Canada. The BDC traces its roots back to 1944 as a part of the Bank of Canada called the Industrial Development Bank, later succeeded by the Federal Business Development Bank (Layne 2016). Our immediate focus is on the BDC, but its institutional history reveals efforts in different eras to complement the main private banking system with a further lending and development focus, depending on how the key challenges were being posed and planned for. Our main interest is in the BDC mandate, and in teasing out what it may imply for business infrastructure.

A refurbished BDC asserts that it is the "only bank devoted exclusively to entrepreneurs" (BDC 2016, 1) to help them "in building strong and competitive businesses" (2). Its annual report states that it is "more pan-Canadian than ever before ... through 112 business centres across the country and online" (2), with 12 new ones recently opened. It supports 42,000 entrepreneurs and highlights how it deployed $5.1 billion to, among other linked features, "invest in information technology and other intangible assets, buy equipment to increase productivity, and transfer their companies to a new generation of owners" (2). The BDC support also led to loans "to majority women-owned businesses" (2). Later it also indicates that "to support innovative start-ups and help them commercialize their ideas, we continue to partner with top accelerators, tech clusters and private funds across the country" (5).

We indicated earlier in the discussion of the HBC that its report spoke briefly of the regulatory matters it must deal with emanating from different levels of government in Canada, the US, the EU, and Japan, including securities laws, labour and employment laws, product safety laws, privacy laws, and workplace safety regulations. Our intention now is to bring some of these issues into sharper focus, building on conceptual issues raised in chapter 1. We do this initially by referencing the *emergence of occupational health and safety policy*, and responses to hazards (including asbestos) with direct links today to older business buildings and infrastructure, especially those constructed before 1990. In infrastructure terms, this realm of regulation also involves discourse and infrastructure boundary issues regarding firms and any of their buildings seen and expressed as "workplaces."

The issues and policies regarding occupational health tended to emerge and sharpen in the mid-1970s, partly via inquiry commission reports (Doern 1977). Particular hazards were identified, but one of the easier ways to deal with such hazards was simply to ensure that the hazard was dumped or emitted outside the business plant or building. In effect, the occupational health hazard became an environmental problem, with "environmental" defined as anything near or outside the building. These and other related features were also seen as a part of the imperatives of "living with contradictions" (Doern, Prince, and MacNaughton 1982), including the use of asbestos as fire protection in the construction of buildings even though its hazards were increasingly well known and even though the federal and Quebec governments were major supporters and protectors of the Quebec-based asbestos industry.

Federally, in response to these and other hazards, the current Canadian Centre for Occupational Health and Safety (CCOHS) was formed in 1978. It functions as a federal departmental corporation but is governed by a "Council of Governors representing governments (federal, provincial and territorial), employers, and workers" (Canadian Centre for Occupational Health and Safety 2015, 1). Approximately "6% of the Canadian workplace falls under OH&S under the jurisdiction of the federal government" with the "remaining 94% ... under the province or territory where they work" (CCOHS 2017a, 2). A combined federal, provincial, and territorial Workplace Hazardous Materials Information System (WHMIS) also exists. It is important to stress that the CCOHS is not itself a regulator but rather is more of an exhortative researcher and consensus-building body. Federal regulation occurs via the administration of the Canada Labour Code.

At the federal level, the Canada Occupational Health and Safety Regulations (Justice Canada 2017) easily and in detail convey in its table of contents what they apply to and hence different senses and kinds of mainly business infrastructure. These include: permanent structures (division I), e.g. buildings; division II towers, antennas and antenna-supporting structures, etc.; temporary structures and excavations; elevating devices, boilers and pressure vessels, and lighting; levels of sound; and electrical safety. *Part X of the Regulations* contains key detailed features and provisions regarding hazardous substances (both those that are "products" and those that are not). Interestingly, the final two parts of the regulations deal with a hazard prevention program and with violence prevention in the workplace. Provincial and territorial government occupational health and safety laws and regulations have similar kinds of provisions plus others that relate to key provincial industries such as oil and gas, forestry, mining, and fishing (CCOHS 2017a, 2).

This first policy and governance history has sampled the field over several decades but it has tended to deal with larger businesses, including banks as funders, and with large workplaces and complex regulatory oversight, including occupational health and safety being enacted via respective federal and provincial governments. We now proceed to the business realm of small and medium-sized enterprises (SMEs) and start-up companies where overall digital policy and infrastructure are increasingly pivotal and disruptive (Johal and Crawford Urban 2017).

2 SMES *and Start-Up Businesses and Infrastructure, 1970 to present*

In policy and governance terms we need first to discuss the SME category and its main lobby, the Canadian Federation of Independent Business (CFIB), and contrast it both with emerging and active start-up business entities and networks and with earlier efforts to support firms that were not then labelled as start-ups though they were in the initial stages of development.

The CFIB states that it represents small businesses which are "powered by entrepreneurs" (Canadian Federation of Independent Business 2017a, 1). It states that it believes in "[t]he global value of the free enterprise system and the crucial role of small business within that system; the necessity of the entrepreneurial spirit to create hope and opportunity; eliminating obstacles at all levels of government which stand in the way of small business growth; and never giving up and never going away in advocating for small business" (1). It states that its "109,000 members mirror and reflect the regional and economic diversity of the country" (1). It lists 15 sectors and the percentage of its membership from these sectors, the largest being construction at 11.9 per cent and manufacturing at 11.1 per cent. Founded in 1971, the CFIB describes its membership as the "full range of enterprises in Canada from one-person, home-based businesses to firms employing hundreds of people" (1). It ranks its top national policy victories and achievements as:

- Introducing a special federal small business corporate tax threshold and then expanding it to every province;
- Increasing the Small Business Corporate Tax threshold to $500,000;
- Increasing the Lifetime Capital Gains Exemption to $813,600; and
- Influencing the federal government to commit to the reduction of the paper burden by 20 per cent. (1)

In short, the CFIB has been tax reduction–focused. Nothing leaps out of its own statements that focuses on infrastructure as such, but the vast majority of these businesses had buildings *and* capital assets to build and repair, and were also aided by the depreciation and capital cost allowance measures examined above in our first policy and governance history in this infrastructure regime.

A CFIB research paper by Parent and Poitevin (2016) examined small and medium-sized enterprises (SMEs) in relation to the evolving innovation agenda, anchored around a survey of CFIB members. The conclusions of the analysis are that "current narrow definitions of innovation exclude the vast majority of SMEs, and unintentionally reinforce the notion that Canadian businesses are not innovative enough. Contrary to these notions, over 80 per cent of SMEs report they have been innovative in their businesses in the past five years" (1). The authors argue that "governments must understand that high tech companies are not the only firms that *innovate*" (1). When asked about what kinds of things they had done during the past five years, a high percentage (in the 50 to 58 per cent range) of SME respondents in the retail and manufacturing sectors said they "improved existing internal business processes" and 37 to 49 per cent said they "created new internal business processes" such as marketing, logistics, and production (6). When asked "what type of investments will your business make in the next two years," the second highest percentage of responses (55 per cent) cited "acquiring machinery or equipment." Thus infrastructure-related issues emerge more explicitly in SME public discourse.

Another small business perspective focusing centrally on infrastructure policy emerges from an article by Catherine Swift (2016). A former CFIB president, currently president of the lobby group Working Canadians, Swift attacks both federal and provincial governments for their *procurement* approaches that require unionized labour. She argues that it is "the guaranteed reality that Canadians will be paying much more for infrastructure refurbishment than they should have to as a result of a simple policy," namely that "virtually all Canadian governments have over the past few decades enacted law to restrict bidding on government projects to companies that are either unionized, or that effectively pay inflated wages in some other fashion" (1). In short, "they will overpay for these projects by as much as 40 per cent" (1). They "bar the efficient competitive non-union companies from participating in the government work their taxes pay for" (1).

Historically, SMEs have also been the focus of the National Research Council of Canada (NRC) via its Industrial Research Assistance

Program (IRAP), a program established in 1962 with a view to "providing technology assistance to small and medium-size enterprises" (NRC 2017b, 1). It has evolved and been adapted across the decades in concert with other changes and challenges that the NRC was itself facing in the changing structure and funding of its labs, networks, and programs (Doern and Levesque 2002; Goss Gilroy Inc. 2012; Doern, Castle, and Phillips 2016). Its current stated mission is to "accelerate the growth of small and medium-sized enterprises by providing them with a comprehensive suite of innovation services and funding" (1). Its program goals include strengthening "technology-based communities," and its strategic objectives are to "provide support to small and medium-sized enterprises in Canada in the development and commercialization of technologies, and to collaborate in initiatives within regional and national organizations that support the development and commercialization of technologies" by SMES (1).

In terms of claimed impacts, the NRC states that IRAP currently "provides customized solutions to some 10,000 SMES annually" and also highlights how its "240 Industry Technology Advisors (ITAS) are a unique resource, the focal point of one-on-one relationships with companies that extend for years" (NRC 2017c, 1). NRC annual reports offer summary views of several IRAP "success stories" (NRC 2017e). Space does not allow systematic coverage of these in this policy and governance regime history, but each success story does capture the narrative and nature of what actual or potential "start-up" businesses might currently or increasingly mean. One success story centres on a math skill game developed by two graduates from the University of Waterloo, who in 2011 founded a company called SMARTTeacher. They turned to IRAP to "develop and scale-up their math game Prodigy, now used by millions of grade-school children in Canada and the United States" (NRC 2017e, 1–2). Another success story was centred on an established Alberta company created in 1991 but then, with IRAP assistance, was recast as a firm called Ideal Products seeking to "revolutionize the global mechanical insulation market" (infrastructure, without doubt) through various related products/technologies (NRC 2017a). This company was less a start-up in the sense that it was new, but some of its IRAP-supported product lines were.

An analysis by John Lester (2016) follows the policy trail of small business policy *partially* to the world of start-up business policy by arguing that in the innovation era Canada needs an "entrepreneurship policy, not a small-business policy" (85). He argues that most SME policy measures are available to all SMEs, but stresses that "a very small number of firms are responsible for the bulk of employment creation and innovation, so broad-based support for small firms runs the risk of harming rather than helping economic performance by encouraging small scale less efficient production" (85). The focus, he argues, should be on "high impact entrepreneurship" (86–8). Current overall federal measures include: financing programs, support for R&D, and tax measures for SMEs. Lester's proposed remedies are to: improve financing programs by eliminating the special low income tax rate for SMEs and restructuring the Business Development Bank of Canada; eliminate the gap between the federal R&D tax credit for large and smaller firms and restrict the 'stacking' of benefits from other federal and provincial programs; use the savings from the above measures to fine-tune some existing tax measures to benefit entrepreneurs; and implement general tax measures that would be of particular benefit to high-impact entrepreneurs (86).

Entrepreneurship is also the key analytical focus in an edited volume by Globerman and Clemens (2018). It examines the importance of entrepreneurship to economic prosperity with ever-greater links to technological change and "the introduction and widespread adoption of new ways of organizing business activity, as well as new or modified goods and services" ... that "are the primary means for making people healthier and wealthier" (i). However, the Globerman and Clemens volume overall is titled *Demographics and Entrepreneurship: Mitigating the Effects of an Aging Population*. In this larger analytical theme, they stress the work of Russell Sobel (in chapter 2), who provides "demographic data for a number developed economies (including Canada) which have been "aging and the aging process is set to accelerate beyond the year 2025" (iii). The essence of the looming or inherent concerns about impacts on entrepreneurship is three-fold: "relatively young people have supple brains that facilitate creative thinking" but "individuals need some business experience to successfully run a company," and "to the extent that senior and junior executives are relatively old, their continued participation in the work force can deprive young people of the business experience they need"; hence "an aging population can be a prominent barrier to entrepreneurship" (ii–iii).

Varied start-up discourse and strategies have emerged in several ways in recent years. One is the *Startup Eco-system Strategy for the*

City of Toronto (City of Toronto 2017). The report starts by referring
to the city's already established start-up support via its Enterprise
Toronto and Business Incubation programs in the broader context of
how SME success is crucial in Toronto "with approximately 98 per
cent of all businesses being small (under 100 employees)" (1). However,
the report then states that the proposed strategy's ambitious vision is
that of "making Toronto the start-up capital of the world ... which
can be "achieved by taking a planned approach to supporting the
infrastructure of the start-up eco-system." It would also address "sectoral gaps and building neighbourhood entrepreneurship capacity ...
so that ... a divide is not created between certain sectors or scales of
economic development" (1). Goal 1 of the strategy relates to strengthening the infrastructure of the system, characterized later in the report
as "Innovation Infrastructure: Business Incubators/Accelerators/
Co-Working Spacing" (15), with each of these then elaborated on in
more detail and with both "physical and virtual innovation infrastructure" described as crucial "in supporting a start-up through
various phases of growth" (16). Earlier in the report, the analysis had
divided SMEs into two segments, "traditional" and "fast growth,"
with the former including "main street businesses" and "professional
services" and the latter centred more on "technology, digital media,
life sciences and advanced manufacturing" (5).

Print and online media also increasingly cover Canadian start-up
business success stories. Buckner (2017), for example, examines
Reebee, a Kitchener, Ontario firm that is "taking retail flyers into the
digital age" (1). It was formed by two University of Waterloo grads
who had been childhood friends in London, Ontario and were delivery
boys dropping flyers on doorsteps. They established Reebee in 2012,
and it now employs twenty people and has "3.5 million users signed
up to their service" (1), which allows easy comparative shopping on
flyer items by big and small firms.

A different Waterloo University–related story centred on Embark
Technology has been examined by Wheeler (2017). Its twenty-one-
year-old CEO co-founded the start-up firm and "built one of three
companies approved to test autonomous 18 wheeler semis (trucking)
on roadways in the State of Nevada – along with Uber and Freightliner"
(1). He and a small group of Canadians went to Silicon Valley "to
partner with California's Y Combinator, one of the world's largest
start-up incubators" (2). The Embark staff also includes young
Americans from "Audi's self-driving division" (2). The two Canadian

Embark Technology co-founders had benefited early from Waterloo University's Velocity Residence, a program for selected students during their first year of study that helps them "develop their ideas into a business" (1).

Also noteworthy in this sample of varied start-up stories is the account by Allen (2017) of the announced decision by Uber to establish a research group "devoted to driverless car technology in Toronto" (1). The Advanced Technology Group will be headed by Dr Raquel Urtasun, who uses "artificial intelligence, particularly deep learning, to make vehicles and other machines perceive the world around them more accurately and intelligently" (1). Importantly, this kind of development grew out of a decade of internationally recognized work at the University of Toronto with both federal and Ontario provincial support. As reported in the *New York Times*, they have created a recognized global hub in the science and technology of artificial intelligence and automation and related robotics research (Lohr 2017). A further start-up-oriented development with a very different discourse is the "Creative Destruction Lab" (CDL), started in 2012 at the Rotman School of Management, University of Toronto with the "goal of helping its participating start-ups generate $50 million in equity value over the programs first five years" (Rotman School of Management 2017, 2). This led to the announcement of "cross-country expansion" including CDL-Rockies at the University of Calgary, CDL-Montreal, and CDL Atlantic at Dalhousie University, adding to CDL-West at UBC and the original CDL program in Toronto (1). The original Rotman CDL program's participants had already "exceeded $1 billion in equity value creation in 4.5 years" (2).

In the Canadian start-up policy and institutional story, an interesting dimension is provided by the formation of Startup Canada in 2012. A socio-economic non-profit entity and lobby, it describes itself as a group of "entrepreneurs working together to build a Canada for entrepreneurs and give a voice to the Canadian startup community" (Startup Canada 2017, 1). It has some modest start-up funding programs, but its overall mode of operation is to function as a "grassroots network of entrepreneurs" and to communicate via online platforms. It involves "120,000 entrepreneurs, 400 enterprise supporters, 300 volunteers and over 22 Startup communities coast to coast" (2) and is the result of early Canadian and international foundational institution-making by its two co-founding leaders, Victoria Lennox, a political science, governance, and public policy grad in 2006 and its CEO, and

Cypian Szalankiewicz, its vice president, a technology entrepreneur who has worked on robotics in the film and television industry. They had been the catalyst in an initial 2012 activist process six-month tour that brought together "more than 20,000 Canadians in town hall" meetings and consultations (2).

We have already cited the Uber example above, but a much bigger and more controversial Toronto-centred case is and has been the Google sister company Sidewalk Labs and its "smart-city community centred on a large sector of the Toronto waterfront … Sidewalk has a tripartite government development partner, Waterfront Toronto. Sidewalk in mid-2019 asked to have a hand "in planning a swath of lakefront land 16 times bigger than the 12-acre site it had won the right to plan" (O'Kane 2019), Other mid-to-late 2019 analyses also argued for a more "inclusive growth" approach (Golden and Broadbent, 2019) and expressed strong concerns that "Google will exploit the data" it acquires (Zochodne and Craig 2019). At the end of October 2019, Sidewalk "signed off on a radically reduced footprint, abandoned several preconditions and made concessions on data governance and technology sharing" (Oved, 2019).

3 Public-Private Partnership Infrastructure
(1991 to present)

Our third policy and governance history centres on Public-Private Partnerships (referred to also as PPPs or P3s). Their origin in Canada is traced to 1991 (Hobbes 2016). Two years later, in 1993, the Canadian Council for Public-Private Partnerships (CCPPP) was formed as a national advisory council and lobby (CCPPP 2017a). Hobbes's summary of P3s states that they "are partnerships between the government and the private sector to build public infrastructure like roads, hospitals or schools as well as deliver services" and that they "can be structured in different ways, allocating varying degrees of responsibility for design, construction, financing, maintenance or operation in the public sector, while always maintaining public ownership and control" (Hobbes 2016, 3). He also points out that the "facilities management component (of P3 contracts) covers a long-term concession period (25–35 years) with pre-defined hand back conditions" and stresses that "contracting arrangements are performance-based" (4).

As of 2016, over the CCPPP's twenty-five-year history, there have been 237 projects totalling $94.6 billion (13). Projects by jurisdiction add up to 175 provincial, 49 municipal, 12 federal, and 1 Aboriginal (16). By year, the number of projects is very small: fewer than 5 per year in the 1991 to 2001 period, modest growth in the 5 to 10 range from 2002 to 2006, and then stronger growth in the 2007 to 2015 period with projects in the range of 10 to 20 annually (17). The project history by sector ranges from 4 in information technology to 90 in health and 54 in transportation, and project numbers in the 15 to 20 range in education, water and wastewater, and recreation and culture and justice (14).

The CCPPP's vision of its role regarding P3s is "to influence the way in which public services are financed and delivered in Canada by: encouraging public-private partnerships; providing information … sponsoring conferences and seminars … stimulating dialogue between public and private sector decision makers … educating the public; and conducting objective research" (CCPPP 2017a, 1). The organization's website also gives early emphasis to its view about "P3 myths and facts" (CCPPP 2017b, 1–3). These include: whether "P3s are a form of privatization"; whether they "end up costing more than traditional procurements"; whether they "create big private-sector profits using public money"; and whether "P3s take longer than traditional procurement" (2).

Not surprisingly, some of the myths-and-facts responses are answered reasonably (such as why P3s take longer), and others are finessed with supportive advocacy discourse, such as its answers regarding traditional procurements. For example, none of its data summaries include similar data regarding how many infrastructure projects via traditional procurement have been processed over the same twenty-five-year project, nor why.

Of further interest is the CCPPP's 2016 federal budget submission. Not surprisingly, it is broadly supportive of the federal Trudeau Liberals' infrastructure-led economic productivity agenda, and gives examples of where P3s have been successful (Canadian Council for Public-Private Partnerships 2016, 1–3). It expresses considerable concern, however, about the planned federal Infrastructure Bank. It asks what the government's intentions are and stresses that there "is an abundance of private sector capital in the Canadian marketplace and a number of provinces and municipalities already have strong borrowing regimes in place. If not executed correctly, the creation of an infrastructure bank could have unintended consequences for existing institutions and on private lenders" (4). See further analysis in chapter 5.

Other related private research on P3s is also of interest. A study by the Canadian Centre for Economic Analysis (2016), commissioned by the CCPPP, focuses on "why building infrastructure 'on time' matters" and what "on time" means. It starts with commentary on the "curse" of the *megaproject* and frequent megaproject delays (5–7), assesses P3 strengths and weaknesses, and ends with interesting analysis and advice under the heading of "sensitivity analysis of timing certainty" which includes "optimism bias" about projects and their completion, and insights on the "economic value of delay" (26–30). An earlier paper by the Canadian Centre for Economic Analysis (2016) also provides a thorough examination of Ontario's public infrastructure showing "how standard economic models miss much of infrastructure's benefits, especially the multi-decade contributions to GDP, incomes, private investment and public sector revenues" (2) and how "systematic benefits are vitally dependent upon other things occurring" because "it is a measure of both benefits and what is at risk" (3).

Seventeen years into the P3 story, the Harper Conservative government established, in 2008, *Public Private Partnership Canada* (PPP Canada), partly via the lobbying of the CCPPP. Its 2015–16 Annual Report (PPP Canada 2015) stated its mandate "is to improve the delivery of public infrastructure by achieving better value, timeliness and accountability through P3s" (1). PPP Canada is described as a "knowledge-based organization of dynamic professionals who understand public infrastructure needs and the private sector's ability to leverage innovative and efficient approaches to generate results" (1). Its stated three business lines are: "P3 knowledge development and sharing; advancing provincial, territorial, municipal and First Nation P3s; and advancing federal P3s" (1).

The report highlighted its sixfold strategy, expressed as follows: "Increasing investment in public infrastructure that Canadians need; increasing value and reducing reliance on taxes through the effective use of P3s; demonstrating success in inexperienced jurisdictions, different sectors and new models; increasing knowledge development and sharing best practices and market intelligence; fostering economic growth through investments in projects that enhance competitiveness and productivity; and supporting a cleaner environment through improvements to aging assets" (2). From the report we learn that "in its first 7 years, the Corporation had been directly engaged in the development, procurement and operation of over 20 projects with capital costs in excess of $6.6 billion. More than $17 billion in incremental Value for Money (vfm) is expected to be generated through the use of P3s" (2).

Further statements by the corporation's CEO stress that PPP Canada "has matured into a leading source of expertise on" P3s. Its higher-volume involvement in projects is "driven by both an increase in the number of sectors in which P3s are being used" (3) and "the screening by PPP Canada of all federal capital projects in excess of $100 million is now well entrenched" (3).

Two evaluations and audits of PPP Canada (KPMG 2016; Auditor General of Canada 2016) were published subsequently. The KPMG study assessed the agency's performance in relation to the $1.2 billion P3 Canada Fund that PPP Canada administered and that was essential to its capacity to function, which was replenished for a further five years in 2014. The Auditor General's audit was of PPP Canada as a Crown Corporation. The reports were both mainly positive but also raised issues that were quite telling about how unusual this federal Crown Corporation is. Interestingly, PPP Canada only refers to itself as "the corporation" (see more below).

As an evaluation, the KPMG study used "multiple lines of evidence" in its methodology including "document and data review, interviews with stakeholder groups ... and the development of three case studies" (KPMG 2016, 1). It begins its conclusions about performance regarding the P3 Canada Fund with the view that it "has been successful in attracting 14 new and inexperienced jurisdictions to employ a P3 model for their projects ... and has invested in projects that brought $6.6 billion in capital to the Canadian infrastructure market" (3). It also concludes that the fund has "played a significant role in shifting the cultural views of the value of the P3 model ... however, there is still more to be done and it is recognized that the provinces have had an influence as well in this area" (3). The KPMG study recommended three areas for needed improvement. The first is "building the capacity" of stakeholders. The second is "project transition," which centred on needed "review processes and competencies to enable an efficient transition of PPP Canada staff either moving on or off recipient projects between project stages" (4). The third KPMG recommendation related to "recipient project processes," where there is a need to clarify "PPP Canada's involvement in directing recipient project processes upfront with the procuring authority ... It is unclear to some recipients the extent of PPP Canada's role in developing, in structuring and procuring P3 Canada Fund projects and funding approvals" (4).

The Auditor General of Canada audit is an audit per se and not a program evaluation, but despite several positives highlighted the core findings of its 2016 report into PPP Canada; the recommendations and responses on issues such as corporate governance and strategic planning and risk management stated that there were weaknesses. Regarding the final topic, "investment management," the AG concluded that "the Corporation had an investment policy in place, but it was missing elements such as *objectives, risk identification and investment guidelines*" (Auditor General of Canada 2016, 2). Interestingly, an earlier AG audit (Auditor General of Canada 2013) drew immediate attention to the fact that PPP Canada is a "non-agent of the Crown" when administering the Fund. Instead, *"use of the funds is governed by terms and conditions approved by the Treasury Board"* (3). As a non-agent of the Crown, when administering the P3 Canada Fund, PPP Canada "cannot bind the government by its actions and must therefore have cash in hand to commit funds" (3). But PPP Canada has "received yearly exemptions such that it is receiving P3 funds ahead of its disbursement needs" (3), a practice that the AG disagrees with fundamentally.

It is of considerable importance to take note of the analysis by Bordeleau (2012) which looked at PPP Canada and the P3 Fund and probed it in relation to how it was both a "new meso institutional arrangement" and that "there is a 'public administration malaise' with the way ... it has been drafted and how it operates" (145). He noted that its role is to "stimulate PPPs materially" (148), that it is a "hub" for a dialogue (149), and that this corporation is also "a school" but a flawed one (149). Bordeleau was looking at PPP Canada and the P3 Fund in its first three years, but it would not be difficult to see how his analysis is partly borne out after eight further years until the corporation's eventual demise in 2018.

Though a Crown Corporation, PPP Canada was not an agent of the Crown. It had a mix of roles that were PPP-related in addition to its status as a quasi-banker/lender. It also sought to be educative and voluntary but, backed by its money, it could in effect tell some provinces, some municipalities, and some federal departments what to do and when. It had features of *being* a mini-quasi-central agency but was also a kind of management consulting firm – a role that the CIB appears to have adopted, albeit with deeper pockets (as discussed in chapters 2 and 5).

Since 1991, P3s have emerged in Canada as a policy and as a governance and funding mix, with both considerable support and growing pains as policy- and decision-makers have had to learn on the job. P3s have also taken shape in different organizational forms in different provinces – for example, via Infrastructure Ontario (a differently structured actual Crown Corporation from PPP *Canada*), which in its first decade "completed more than $16 billion in projects with another $18 billion under construction and almost $10 billion more in the planning stages" (Infrastructure Ontario 2017, 1). Regardless of the level of government, P3s remain an important though controversial component of Canada's infrastructure story and are likely to play a crucial role in any future success of the CIB, as discussed in chapter 5.

ANALYSIS: THE THREE REGIME ELEMENTS

With the aid of table 4.1 we now look across the three policy and governance histories presented above by examining the three elements featured in the book's overall analytical framework. Regarding policy *ideas, discourse, and agendas* the analysis shows for businesses an evolving story and set of focal points. The initial focus was on conceptions of "non-residential construction" and related data. A second continuing idea and discourse centres on tax-related policies regarding "depreciation and capital cost allowances" relating to business buildings and equipment but with many "classes" of such assets. The issue of building permits is also present.

Ideas and agendas regarding occupational health and safety are also present as features and determinants of what the "business workplace" is or is changing to become. Also emerging are ideas, agendas, and discourse regarding IT and internet systems as assets and platforms.

Regarding the SMEs and start-up business policy story, there is the continued presence of technology assistance ideas and discourse centred on the NRC's IRAP program, including the use of some "start-up" discourse in some of its accounts of success stories. Also emerging is discourse advocating policies for "entrepreneurs" and even targeted policies at "high impact entrepreneurs." In both cases, these are increasingly differentiated from SMEs. As start-up discourse emerges, ideas

Table 4.1
The business infrastructure regime and the three analytical elements: highlights

Policy and governance histories	Policy ideas, discourse, and agendas	Power structures, democracy, and governance	Temporal realities, cycles, conflicts, and technology
Businesses and evolving core self-funding and banking system-funded infrastructure, 1960s to present	• Discourse and categories regarding "non-residential construction" comprising "engineering construction and institutional, commercial and industrial building construction." • Depreciation and capital cost allowances; with fifty-three different classes of assets and allowance rates for buildings, equipment, etc. • Bank lending to businesses on a "case-by-case basis" can include building and related equipment. • Different characterization of key assets by large firms. • Ideas and processes for granting building permits. • Expressed support for "entrepreneurs." • Recent discourse regarding "majority women-owned businesses." • Occupational health and safety laws and conceptions of "the workplace" and therefore sense of types of assets present and used.	• Canada Revenue Agency requirements/ support for depreciation and asset tax allowances. • Statistics Canada as source of public data on non-residential construction and on building permits. • Infrastructure is diverse in large businesses such as in the examples of Hudson's Bay Co., Great-West Life, and Scotiabank. • Tax and rules from other countries where Canadian firms operate (US a key example). • Banks as lenders and companies with own increasingly digitalized infrastructure. • Big Six Canadian banks have financing power and influence with Canadian businesses. • Business Development Canada (BDC) as federal government bank has supportive infrastructure funding but of limited scope.	• Types and time frames of CCA allowances increase and change each year as business assets and infrastructures change. • Emergence of occupational health and safety workplace law in 1970s but numerous changes and rates of introduction since. • Information technology and digital platforms have been fast-changing and complex from early 1990s on.

SMEs and startup businesses and infrastructure, 1970 to present

- IT and internet systems as assets and "platforms" for major businesses and banks as necessity and challenge.
- Hudson's Bay Co., late 2019, decides to "exit the Netherlands" by closing its fifteen stores there, but also in global context of store chains and a "ton of store closings."

- Role of Canada Centre for Occupational Health and Safety as advisory federal player on changing Canadian workplaces.
- Regulation of federal occupational health and safety via the Canada Labour Code.
- Provinces and territories are main regulators of occupational health and safety with diverse impacts on firms and their workplace assets.

- Ideas and characteristics of small and medium-sized business.
- SMEs also benefited from CCA/depreciation asset policies/rules.
- Technology assistance to SMEs by NRC's IRAP program.
- "Start-up" discourse emerges also in NRC IRAP processes in recent highlighted "success stories."
- Idea/argument recently that Canada needed an "entrepreneurial policy and not a small business policy."
- Also policies that target "high-impact entrepreneurs."
- Mitigating effects of aging population with adverse effects on young persons needing business experience but denied by longer presence of aging company management workforce.

- Role of SME tax reduction lobby and success of the CFIB.
- Limited infrastructure focus per se, regarding the CFIB's 109,000 members.
- But "construction industry" is one of its largest membership sectors.
- Different views of what infrastructure is.
- But some recent official surveys of members indicate SMEs need to "acquire machinery and equipment."
- Considerable opposition to union power in federal and provincial procurement bids, making it more expensive and unfair to CFIB member firms.
- "Working Canadians" formed as separate lobby against union power.
- City of Toronto Start-Up Ecosystem Strategy published/launched.

- SMEs in early temporal phase but often not referred to as "start-ups."
- NRC's IRAP program in place since 1962 and currently its 240 Industrial Technology Advisors (ITAs) are spread across Canada in one-on-one relations with companies "that extend for years."
- Physical and virtual innovation phases of growth are evident.
- Artificial intelligence and automation/robotics link to driverless cars and other technologies.

Table 4.1
The business infrastructure regime and the three analytical elements: highlights (*Continued*)

Policy and governance histories	Policy ideas, discourse, and agendas	Power structures, democracy, and governance	Temporal realities, cycles, conflicts, and technology
	• "Creative Destruction" Lab at University of Toronto. • Ideas about the infrastructure of the "start-up" system. • Discourse about need for "neighbourhood entrepreneurial capacity." • "On-line platforms" as infrastructure. • Toronto Sidewalk Labs and battle over Google smart-city monopoly in 2019.	• University of Waterloo influence is significant and growing via its students/grads in start-up firms/successes in Canada and Silicon Valley. • Rotman School of Management at University of Toronto in 2012 establishes Creative Destruction Lab (CDL) now expanded to five further cross-country CDLs. • Formation of Start-Up Canada in 2012 as voice for Canadian start-up firms and communities.	• "Disruptive technology" seen more often as fast-moving challenges as to how they are regulated or possibly cannot be regulated. • Start-Up Canada as a grassroots network of entrepreneurs, centred on fast-changing online platforms. • How fast is aging senior corporate management impacting on young business persons. • "Creative destruction" discourse and lab purpose/dynamic.
Public-private partnerships (P3) infrastructure, 2000 to present	• P3 or PPP as expressed early discourse in 1991 but can be seen as having links to 1980s notions of "partnerships" and "networks" and also "governance."	• Canadian Council for Public-Private Partnerships (CCPPP) established in 1993 as advocate and research body. • 287 P3 projects over twenty-five years. • CCPPP analysis of myths and facts regarding P3s.	• PPP Canada projects can involve long-term "concession period" (25–35 years) with pre-defined hand-back conditions.

- But defined as partnerships between government and business regarding "public" infrastructure.
- Structured in different ways to allocate various degrees of responsibility for "design, construction, maintaining, or operating in the public sector while maintaining public ownership and control." Contracting arrangements that are performance-based.
- Claims about being better than traditional procurement and in handling major projects.
- Ideas about what "on-time" completion means.
- P3s via Canada to "reduce reliance on taxes" to pay for public infrastructure.
- Increased support for P3s in "inexperienced jurisdictions."
- PPP Canada criticized as "neo-meso" institution with public administration malaise" built in.

- Critical of Liberal planned Canadian Infrastructure Bank.
- Canadian Centre for Economic Analysis studies of P3 features, e.g. "optimism bias" and potential "economic value of delay."
- PPP Canada formed in 2008 as Crown Corporation advocate of P3s and administrator of $1.2 billion P3 Canada Fund.
- Auditor General critical of some aspects because PPP Canada is a "non-Agent" of the Crown regarding the P3 Canada Fund.
- In 2018 PPP Canada is dissolved. Given the 2017 launch of an infrastructure bank the timing is surprising, but P3 expertise may have been incorporated into the CIB.

- Standard economic market analysis can miss many of the infrastructure benefits, especially the multi-decade contributions to GDP.

about the infrastructure of the start-up system are offered, in addition to conceptions of "neighbourhood entrepreneurial capacity" with both partly included in the discourse of "online platforms" as *infrastructure*. Start-up discourse also emerges in the form of the Creative Destruction Lab at the University of Toronto and its broadening network at five other universities across Canada. In the brief history of public-private partnerships, infrastructure as a discourse becomes more direct and explicit because P3s are to be a key feature of *public* infrastructure with, crucially, an increased role for *businesses in it.* Ideas and discourse also become more explicit as they relate to different P3 features and phases such as project design, construction, maintenance of public ownership and control, and completion "on time."

Regarding the analytical element of *power structures, democracy, and governance* the three histories capture important features and dynamics. The big business focus of the first policy history leads immediately to public data on non-residential construction published by Statistics Canada but analyzed mainly by private firms. Canada Revenue Agency requirements regarding support for depreciation and asset tax allowances are also a key feature of governance and power. The power and economic relations between the Big 6 Canadian banks and business funding, plus company funding of business infrastructure, has been sketched but is obviously complex with respect to which assets are funded by whom. The emergence since the 1970s of federal and provincial (mainly the latter) policy and regulation of occupational health and safety has also been highlighted, because it defines in key ways the nature of the changing "workplace." The roles of smaller entities such as Business Development Canada as a federal bank are also of interest in the mapping of this regime.

Regarding the SME and start-up business history, the nature of its power and interest group structure has provided important clues about business infrastructure. The CFIB has been the major player for SMEs but its focus has been decidedly on tax reduction issues with not much focus on infrastructure until quite recently. New lobbies such as Working Canadians have focused on what they deem to be the unfair role of unions (and unionized firms) as required features of who can bid on government procurement bids and contracts. The "start-up" lobby per se has been seen in the formation of bodies such as Start-up Canada in 2012, in the role of the University of Waterloo and its students in particular start-up successes and networks, in the formation of the Creative Destruction Lab system, and, more recently, the City of Toronto's Start-up Ecosystem Strategy.

In the P3 story the key institutional presence has been via the emergence and twenty-five-year role of the Canadian Council for Public-Private Partnerships as advocate for and analyst of P3s at the federal, provincial, and local government level (287 projects over 25 years). PPP Canada's role as a federal P3 Crown Corporation advocate and player in the decade 2008–18 has also been examined briefly, including its role vis-à-vis the P3 Canada fund. The institutional presence of the Auditor General of Canada has also been outlined regarding its concerns about how PPP Canada handled the P3 Canada Fund in questionable ways as a "non-agent" of the Crown. The critical and interesting published work on P3s by the Canadian Centre for Economic Analysis has also helped to shed light on these issues.

Regarding our final analytical element centred on *temporal realities, cycles, conflicts, and technology,* several features have been noted across the three policy histories. First, and crucially regarding the first policy history, we have seen the cycles of growth and contraction of non-residential construction. We also illustrated the types and time-frames of CCA allowances as they increase and change each year as business assets and infrastructure change. We also took note of the emergence of occupational health and safety laws in the 1970s and some of the realities of how these laws have defined and redefined the workplace. For major businesses it is also evident that IT and digital platforms have been fast-changing and complex, requiring investment and innovation.

Regarding the SME and start-up story, the NRC's IRAP program emerged and often dealt with what some now call start-ups, but which were not seen as a one-time-only IRAP involvement. As we have seen, the NRC's ITA staff often have one-on-one relations with companies "that last for years." Accounts have shown more generally that start-ups have other cycles centred on both physical and virtual phases. The more the start-up story emerges via technologies such as artificial intelligence and driverless cars, the more some analysts also speak of "disruptive technology" and how to deal with it, if possible, in regulatory or other governance ways. But players, as we have seen, also want to foster creative destruction of a fast-moving and opportunity-creating nature.

The P3 history has similar kinds of dynamics at play, but we have drawn attention also to studies that zero in on long-term tracking and analytical challenges in P3 *cycles* and projects. These include PPP Canada projects that could (and should) involve long-term "concession period" features of twenty-five to thirty-five years linked to "pre-defined hand-back" conditions. We also note observations by analysts that standard economic market analysis can miss many of the infrastructure benefits, especially the multi-decade contributions to GDP.

CONCLUSIONS

This chapter has mapped and examined the business infrastructure regime, the first of our six regimes. Through our three policy and governance histories covering six decades, and the three-element analysis across the three histories, we have traced what business infrastructure means or potentially could mean regarding large firms, SMEs and start-up businesses, and P3s that already exist or are being proposed with respect to business involvement in *public* infrastructure.

Actual or potential types of business infrastructure officially include non-residential construction and depreciation related capital asset classes of complex kinds as found in tax law and policy. In a broader sense, we also know that it consists of: buildings and physical plant (owned or rented); systems/facilities for production, inventory management, and storage; IT systems; energy/electrical systems; roads and vehicles; and banking/financial systems (related to banks, with the latter's own infrastructure systems as well).

We conclude that businesses in Canada are the largest continuous builders and funders of infrastructure assets. The qualifier has to be added because data on these assets and their nature and changing configurations are partly private, and also complex in terminology and rates of change. Public reporting on them by business groups, tax authorities, or Statistics Canada is rare and incomplete. We also know, as previous chapters have shown, that public infrastructure has had significant bursts of growth followed by decline, and the implication is that in different periods business infrastructure has been present and significant on a steadier large-scale basis.

5

The Infrastructure Financing Regime

INTRODUCTION

In this chapter we focus on municipal infrastructure, and specifically on the evolving ways it has been financed over the last several decades. In the second of the six regimes, we highlight how all three levels of government have sought to provide municipal infrastructure in urban centres and more broadly across the country. As chapter 2 explained, this has involved complex intergovernmental relationships characterized by varying degrees of cooperation and collaboration. At all times provincial and federal governments have looked to preserve their "power of the purse" and have been reluctant to devolve revenue-generating powers to municipalities. Both the higher levels of government have preferred to fund municipal infrastructure directly, usually in return for influence over projects and a share in political capital. Overtime policies and programs have changed, reflecting changes in public management and accountability and in ideological debates concerning the role of the private sector in project financing, construction, maintenance, and management.

In addition to capturing the broader debates, the ideological shifts, and the resulting policies and programs, we discuss the financial tools available to local governments to pay for the public infrastructure that underpins the delivery of a broad array of municipal services. While municipalities now rely on property taxes, user fees, and development charges as their primary sources of self-generated revenue, this has not always been the case. Decades ago, municipal governments benefited from revenues generated by income tax until their authority to collect it was removed during World War II through agreements between the federal and provincial governments. As will be explained in this chapter, what had been intended as a temporary loss of revenues became permanent, thus depriving municipal governments of a significant source of funds for infrastructure development and maintenance, including dedicated funds for life cycle repair and the replacement of public assets. These and other financing decisions have created the complex multi-level and inter-sectoral system we see today. This has produced serious and entrenched challenges with respect to coordination, the alignment of goals and priorities, transactional costs, political interference, and short-term funding and thinking. The COVID-19 pandemic and consequent economic crisis have exposed the challenges of these arrangements, with municipalities facing massive debt but possessing relatively limited tools to raise revenues themselves.

While local governments have received occasional funding through specific infrastructure programs[1] from senior levels of government, these transfers were more short-term injections of cash, particularly the programs launched by the federal government, which were often focused on economic stimulus and always subject to political changes in Ottawa. As discussed briefly in chapter 4, during the last two decades both the provincial and federal governments have also been championing the use of private-public partnerships (P3s) as a means of financing new municipal infrastructure and for providing alternate service delivery. However, there are limits inherent in such alternatives, and whatever their purported and actual benefits, these contractual arrangements have spawned further challenges and complexities. P3s are designed to include the private sector in financing, constructing, and/or operating new public assets with the clear intention of repaying the private-sector partner through the collection of user fees and other means that create a guaranteed dedicated revenue stream. Importantly, the repair and maintenance of many existing public assets do not lend themselves to a P3, as there is no capacity to generate an ROI (return on investment) for the private sector. As such, P3s do not address the significant municipal infrastructure deficit that has accumulated from years of deferred maintenance.

As mentioned in chapter 2, another funding model for major infrastructure has recently been introduced by the federal government, in the form of an "infrastructure bank" as a source of financing major projects. While details of how this "bank" will operate and the types of projects it will fund remain vague, there are serious concerns given the federal government's track record in providing loans – particularly repayable ones – to private-sector companies. Both the infrastructure bank and P3s will be examined further in this chapter as we outline three overlapping policy and governance histories in more detail, beginning with an overview of municipal infrastructure and the public financing of public assets over a seventy-year period. This is followed by a new era of Public Private Partnerships (1980s to present) and finally a new and potentially transformational era of an infrastructure bank (2018 to present). We then provide an analysis across the three policy and governance histories deploying the three elements in our analytical framework: ideas, discourse, and agendas; power structures, democracy, and governance; and temporal realities, cycles, conflicts, and technology. Conclusions then follow.

THREE INFRASTRUCTURE FINANCING POLICY AND GOVERNANCE REGIME HISTORIES

1 Managing and Paying for Municipal Public Assets, 1930s to 2003

According to data from Statistics Canada, municipal governments constitute the largest asset owners in the country, being responsible for more than half of public infrastructure. Of the remaining public assets, the provinces and the territories hold approximately 40 per cent and the federal government much less. Regardless of the size of a municipality, those who are elected to govern it are accountable to citizens for providing and managing the capital assets required to deliver public services and for meeting specific service standards. Levels of service incorporate the social and economic goals of the community in both capacity and maintenance or operation, and are usually measured according to several variables including safety, customer satisfaction, quality, quantity, capacity, reliability, responsiveness, environmental acceptability, cost, and availability. However, for many citizens of our municipalities there are misconceptions about costs. Infrastructure development and the adherence to adequate standards of service have long been treated as public goods that are provided by government, usually at no direct charge or charges that are far less than actual cost. While municipal governments are accountable for delivering levels of services according to what the majority of citizens are willing to pay, mandated service levels and their costs can also be driven by external factors such as regulatory requirements prescribed through provincial or territorial legislation. These normally include mandatory standards relating to the quality of potable water and the treatment of wastewater before it is released into a watershed. In such cases, senior levels of government may provide grants to municipal governments to offset the increased costs imposed by changes in legislation.

Although the types of services provided by municipal governments vary according to what is set out in provincial legislation, these typically include assets that involve the provision of transportation services (roads, bridges, and transit), environmental services (water treatment and distribution, wastewater – sewers and storm water – collection and treatment, solid waste collection and disposal), protective services (police and fire), social and health services (welfare administration, social housing, day care, homes for the aged, public health programs), and amenities such as parks, recreation, and cultural and community services. Because of this broad range of services and the infrastructure that is needed to support them, municipalities across the country argue that their share of the total taxes collected falls short of what is needed, producing the so-called infrastructure gap. With local governments averaging only 8 per cent of total taxes collected, while the provinces and the federal government share the rest (42 per cent and 50 per cent respectively), they appear to have a strong case. As mentioned in the introduction to this chapter, and earlier in chapter 2, the de facto limitation of municipal funding sources began several decades earlier with the removal of personal and corporate income tax powers.

Historically, income tax was a key revenue source for municipalities. The provinces and municipalities levied income taxes more than eighty years before the federal government started accessing these revenues in 1917.[2] In his research on the development of personal income tax in Canada, Robert Clark found that

> income tax levied at the municipal level was, in absolute
> amounts, more important than the provincial income tax in
> every year up to and including 1930 ... [and was] imposed
> in Canada (at least until 1930) both because of the need for
> revenue and because of the conviction that without such a tax
> persons who could afford to make contributions to municipal
> finances would not be paying their fair share of municipal taxes.
> (Clark cited in Silver 1968, 398–9)

As Kitchen (1982) observed, by the end of the 1930s "some form of municipal income tax had been accepted by every province in Canada" (781). As Silver (1968) points out, however, income tax was not administered uniformly as it "varied in form and rate and [was] often imposed at the same flat rate as the property tax" (399). While municipal governments relied on the revenues from personal and corporate income taxes, they suddenly and permanently lost access to them during World War II.

In 1941, the federal government proposed that each province 'rent out' its right to collect taxes as a means of supplementing revenues to pay for the war effort. Under the Wartime Tax Rental Agreement, the provinces – as well as municipal governments – temporarily renounced their rights under the Constitution to collect personal and corporate income taxes and succession duties.[3] However, the provinces did not embrace the proposal eagerly. As La Forest (1981) notes, "throughout this period, several provinces remained uncomfortable with the idea of ceding taxation powers to the federal government, even as part of a temporary rental agreement" (28).

The Tax Rental Agreements were expected to expire in 1947 but endured as part of the post war reconstruction. In 1962, the provinces ended the practice of renting out their taxing powers and in 1967 resumed collecting their own taxes (31–2). However, at the end of the tax rental agreements with the federal government, the authority to levy income tax was never reinstated for municipal governments. As Kitchen (1982) observed, "Since the signing of the first agreement, no municipality in Canada has levied a municipal income tax. Indeed, current provincial legislation states that local governments cannot implement a municipal income tax" (781).

In an article published in the *Canadian Tax Journal* in the late 1960s, Silver (1968) observed, "There is little doubt that municipal governments are rapidly approaching the limits of real property taxation and are under considerable pressure to find new sources of revenue" (404). More than forty years after Silver's warning of a potential municipal fiscal meltdown, municipal governments – apart from those in Manitoba that enjoy a revenue-sharing arrangement with the province – continue to be deprived of the revenues from income taxes.[4]

The origin of the shortfall in municipal revenues can be traced directly to the Wartime Tax Rental Agreements that removed income tax authority from municipal governments. In 1933, local governments accounted for 40 per cent of all government revenues, nearly as much as the federal government (42 per cent) and more than double that of the provinces (18 per cent). At the end of World War II, the Tax Rental Agreements had increased the federal government's share of all public revenues to 82 per cent (Bird and Vaillancourt 2006, 208). As La Forest (1981) pointed out, while the shift in federal fiscal clout was driven initially by a need to pay the costs of the war and post-war reconstruction, the demand for a greater federal share of government revenues evolved into a very different agenda:

> the [federal] government considered it essential to centralize tax-ation power to promote the Keynesian economic policies which it had proposed to embark on, and which it followed with con-siderable success for a long time during the post-war period with a singlemindedness that was probably unmatched in any other country ... During the last stages of the post-war period Parliament markedly expanded its activities in what had previ-ously been considered within the provincial sphere, notably in the welfare field, sometimes independently and sometimes in cooperation with the provinces ... Such activity, of course, effected a profound reorientation of power in the Canadian federation in favour of the central authority. (28–32)

This centralization has been consistent with what has taken place in other major industrialized countries during the twentieth century. As Lee (1994) observes, "The ideal of democracy may be the dispersion of power, but the tendency in democracies is the centralization of power; in politics centripetal forces dominate centrifugal forces" (1).

While the federal share of revenues eventually returned to pre–World War II levels (44 per cent), the provincial share increased to 45 per cent. Only 11 per cent of total government revenues are now allocated to local governments (Lee 1994, 208). According to the Federation of Canadian Municipalities (FCM 1985; 2006), the munici-pal share of revenues from taxes has continued to decline. In calculat-ing the municipal share of taxes – excluding other revenues – it argues that "currently 50 cents of every tax dollar collected in Canada go to the federal government, while 42 cents go to provincial and territorial governments [while m]unicipal governments are left with just eight cents" (FCM 2006, 2). TD Economics (2002) also examined the fiscal plight of municipalities, comparing their recent revenue growth with those of the senior levels of government. Between 1995 and 2001, the revenues for local governments increased by 14 per cent, far less than the 38 per cent and 30 per cent increases of the federal and provincial governments respectively.

During the past sixty years, while municipal governments have experienced a severe drop in their share of government revenues, they have faced an extensive and growing burden with respect to their responsibilities for providing public services and building the associated capital stock required to deliver them. The municipal share of public infrastructure increased from 30.9 per cent in 1961 to 52.4 per cent in 2002 (FCM 2006, 36). The expansion in the stock of municipal assets was particularly rapid from 1955 to 1977, when investment in infrastructure grew at an annual rate of 4.8 per cent (36). This period of intense capital investment closely matched Canada's population growth and rate of urbanization. As Tindal and Tindal (2000) note, "Canada's urban growth since the end of World War II had exceeded that of any Western industrial nation and three-quarters of the nation's population was concentrated on less than one per cent of its land area" (71, citing Gertler).

The costs of infrastructure have increased dramatically as Canada's population has shifted from rural communities to urban centres. Approximately 80 per cent of the population now lives in urban areas. Two-thirds of the country's population, employment, and real output are located in twenty-seven Census Metropolitan Areas (CMAS). The fiscal pressure on cities and city-regions has been particularly difficult for the larger centres that are experiencing the effects of urban sprawl.

To pay for the increased need for services, municipal governments have relied heavily on property taxes as their primary source of revenue since the 1940s. However, as TD Economics (2002) notes, property taxes "are inherently flawed as an instrument for funding cities' long-term needs" (2). Since they are based on the assessed value of property, these taxes are "only weakly related to ability to pay – which constrains governments' ability to raise tax rates to boost revenue" (2). Deprived of access to revenues such as income and sales taxes that grow with the economy, municipal governments have continued to increase their revenues through suburban green-field development.

As Lorimer (1978) points out, Canada's post-war land-development industry was created by the federal government's industrial development policy:

The federal government decided that it wanted more than just house-builders and houses; it wanted to see a new kind of

building industry, with large corporations each capable of producing a sizeable quantity of urban accommodation. The field
was no longer to be the exclusive preserve of small-scale independent businessmen as it had been up to the war. (16)

Federal policies provided special tax concessions that allowed developers to pay little or no tax on their profits (18). In addition, Ottawa
helped ensure the availability of the necessary investment capital to
finance residential construction through financial institutions and
investors: "potential homeowners could get mortgage money to enable
them to buy new suburban houses ... and developers could obtain
mortgage funds to build rental properties" (18). However, Lorimer
also observes that while federal policies were aimed at creating a
building industry, this is not what in fact was created:

> What they produced is a land development industry. A building
> industry, dominated by a few large, national, vertically and hori-
> zontally integrated corporations would make its money out of
> construction. The land development industry, however, makes
> most of its money not out of new buildings but rather out of
> urban land. (19, emphasis in original)

The federal government's strategy had a significant impact in shaping
the pattern of growth in municipalities, particularly urban centres. The
federal role in land assembly and the provision of financial assistance
for single-family homes reinforced the pattern of low-density sprawl.
As Goldrick observed, the federal government used urban growth as
a "prime instrument of public policy to stimulate and maintain high
levels of economic activity" (cited in Tindal and Tindal 2000, 75). As
the economy soared, both the federal and provincial governments
reaped the enormous benefits of increased revenues from personal
and corporate income taxes.

  Although municipal governments had the primary role in providing
the physical services needed to support economic development, they
were denied access to the tax revenues generated by this growth. When
property taxes became the principal source of their revenue after
World War II, municipal governments relied on the development of
'green space' in order to increase their revenues. Tindal and Tindal
(2000) point out that, as a consequence, municipal governments were
held hostage to land developers, becoming "servants of the development industry that they were supposed to regulate" (citing Lorimer,

77). The taxing and financing policies of municipal governments were shaped to encourage land development that inevitably led to more urban sprawl. As Slack observed, the higher property taxes accrued through this approach to land development provided incentives to create less dense housing projects. However, municipal governments eventually discovered that the costs to build and maintain the infrastructure needed to provide public services in lower-density configurations are much more expensive than those in high-density housing (Slack, cited in Tindal and Tindal 2000, 78).

Slack points out that the approach to land development in Canada has been costly. The unsustainable development of green fields and the consequences of increased urban sprawl have triggered a cascading effect on the costs of infrastructure needed to provide public services:

> Fragmented governments in metropolitan areas encourage scattered, leap-frog development that may be more costly to serve. Low densities of urban development are not only more expensive than more compact forms of development, but also undermine those aspects of quality of place ... that flow from higher densities and mixed land uses. (18)

In her report to the Panel on the Role of Government, Slack observed that, when combined with their increased responsibilities, municipal governments are fast approaching a fiscal precipice:

> Vibrant cities and city-regions do not have adequate resources to meet their growing expenditure requirements. Increased demands for services and infrastructure and the growing reliance on an inelastic property tax base, clearly threatens the future financial viability of the major city-regions. This situation is, at least to some extent, the result of a misalignment between expenditures and revenues. There is thus a need to *revisit the allocation of expenditure responsibilities and revenues* between the provincial government and its cities to ensure that there is an appropriate balance between them. Most significantly, funding social housing a portion [*sic*] of social services from property tax revenues needs to be reconsidered. (41, emphasis in original)

There is clearly a need for a permanent injection of revenues that grow with the economy, particularly for cities and city-regions of the country. One such solution would involve reinstating municipal income tax. In his research on this issue in the early 1980s, Kitchen (1982) argued that additional municipal revenues could be generated through increases to the residential portion of property taxes, although he admitted that such a policy would be highly unpopular. As for municipal income tax, he understood the basis for its popularity with local politicians:

> [f]rom a municipality's point of view, the revenue elasticity of the income tax is a major advantage ... Although it is recognized that there is no scientific basis for establishing an equitable tax that is unrelated to the value of the benefits received, it has generally been accepted that income, after allowance for exemptions and deductions, is the most acceptable base for measuring fairness or equity in the distribution of the tax burden. (781–2)

In reviewing the experience of municipal taxation in the US, Kitchen concluded that "any notion that (Canadian) municipalities might impose their own income tax ought to be quickly dispelled" (786). Rather, he suggested that municipal governments could 'piggyback' the administration of municipal income taxes onto the existing provincial income tax system.

Twenty years later, Kitchen (2002) remained cautious about a return to a municipal income tax regime, arguing that "the current practice in many developed countries, supported by most of the economic literature, is to lower reliance on income taxation and increase reliance on consumption-based taxes. This, it is argued, creates fewer distortions and reduces the deadweight costs associated with taxation" (173–4). Kitchen is more inclined to support a 'benefits-model' approach to paying for municipal services.[5]

Mintz and Roberts (2006) also argued against the idea of increasing the taxing authority of municipal governments. They note that expenditure and taxing powers vary from province to province and that "no single solution for improving municipal financing is necessarily appropriate for Canada as a whole" (2). In their search for a financial model that would improve municipal financing and encourage greater independence and responsibility, they conclude:

> Giving additional taxing powers to municipalities seems to be an inviting idea for those wishing to see cities with powers similar to other levels of government ... we find that an additional

tax field for municipalities in the provinces is generally not warranted, although it is important to provide municipalities with greater flexibility in financing their expenditure responsibilities. (1)

However, Mintz and Roberts miss the point. Rather than creating a new tax field and *increasing* taxes, a preferred option for reinstating municipal income tax could be accommodated through the transfer of tax points from the federal government, thus *restoring* a revenue source that was removed in 1941. A transfer of federal tax points is more easily accommodated than a transfer from the provinces. As Kitchen (2002b) observes, "provincial governments have shown no interest in sharing the income tax with their municipal counterparts" (224). Silver (1968) also agrees that the federal government is better placed to help municipal governments:

It is probably unrealistic to think that municipalities in Canada could persuade their respective provincial legislatures to pass legislation enabling the municipalities to levy an income tax without causing the provinces to consider the overall income tax burden. The trend has been for the provinces to levy income taxes only to the extent that the federal government has made 'tax room' available to them and, presumably, the provinces would authorize a municipal income tax only if tax room were made available by the federal government for this tax. (405)

Those who advocate the restoration of municipal income tax are not calling for a pan-Canadian, universal approach. Rather, there is a caveat to their endorsement of the concept. In researching this issue in 1948, Robert Clark found that a municipal income tax "was impractical for rural areas and was most successful in larger cities" (cited in Silver 1968, 399). More than fifty years later, Slack, Bourne, and Gertler (2003) concur with Clark's conclusion:

It is *not appropriate to give more taxing authority to all municipal jurisdictions* in the province. Large cities and city-regions are best suited to take advantage of new taxing authority; smaller cities are unlikely to be able to raise sufficient revenues from some of these sources to make the effort worthwhile. (42, emphasis in original)

Restoring municipal income tax would present administrative challenges. While a full exploration of these issues is outside the scope of
this chapter, the following example illustrates the complexity that
would be involved.[6] Kitchen (2002) commented on the need to connect 'work-based' income with the underlying municipal services that
support it: "[s]ince commuters clearly derive benefits from the provision of local services in the communities where they work, it could
be expected that they should contribute toward the cost of providing
the services that generate the benefits" (b 783). Calculating the costs
of the benefits in the tax to be paid would be challenging. As Silver
(1968) had observed, "Clark's study clearly indicates that the administrative aspect of a municipal income tax may well be the most
important factor in determining the success of the tax" (399). Silver
concluded that, since the administration of municipal income tax
would not be efficient at the local level, it was preferable to have the
tax administered on behalf of municipalities:

> The general consensus based both on the Canadian and United
> States experience appears to be that much is to be gained by hav-
> ing the municipal income tax parallel the federal income tax. In
> fact, there is much to be said for having the municipal income
> tax administered by the federal government. It is clear that if this
> were done, both the cost of administration and the burdens on
> taxpayers would be reduced. (402)

While there is a divergence of opinion about the need for municipal
income tax, there is general agreement that there is a need to improve
municipal financing and encourage greater independence and responsibility in municipal governments. Even dissenters who oppose municipal income tax – such as Mintz and Roberts (2006) – conclude that
"the key is to allocate appropriate expenditure and tax powers to
municipalities, which would also have greater autonomy in choosing
their tax policies" (1).

As McMillan (2003) points out, greater autonomy through decen-
tralization or subsidiarity is a central feature of fiscal federalism.
Responsibility for the delivery of services should be assigned to the
lowest level of government that is capable of providing effective levels
of service. Consequently, there needs to be "a close link between local
public benefits and local public levies ... the benefit principle should

prevail" (15–16). McMillan elaborates further on the cost of municipal services and the revenues necessary to pay for them, observing:

Maintaining the close connection between municipal services and municipal costs requires that *local residents* be responsible for meeting the expenses of local services. That is, municipal governments set the tax rates and charges to be imposed on their citizens (and electorate) to finance the costs of the municipal services. Benefit related finance and local determination of local levies are fundamental criteria. Addition [*sic*] criteria widely cited as desirable for municipal revenue sources (and often others) are that they should be adequate, predictable, fair, visible, not exportable and easily administered. (16)

The federal government has the opportunity to make the structural changes that are needed to modernize the fiscal framework for municipal governments, at least for those larger urban centres responsible for delivering municipal services for the majority of citizens. Rather than creating ad hoc programs that transfer revenues to municipalities, the federal government could provide municipal governments with the power to raise revenues on a more stable basis through a transfer of tax points. These revenues would be consistent with the principles of accountability and subsidiarity, allowing municipal governments to raise revenues "derived from the people who live and work in the municipality and who, presumably, have the primary responsibility for the financing of municipal services, [and] to bear the political burden of doing so" (Silver 1968, 405). The federal government has the opportunity to restore 'balance' to fiscal federalism. However, rather than taking steps in this regard, the federal government chose instead to support municipal infrastructure on a project-by-project basis by way of transfers carried out through program agreements with provincial and territorial governments. This policy choice has characterized federal funding for municipal infrastructure over several decades with important consequences for the type of infrastructure delivered and the politics that surround federal transfers and contributions. It has also defined municipal dependence on senior governments for funding, and in the process has transformed the FCM and municipal mayors into professional and increasingly effective lobbyists dependent on provincial and federal largesse.

During the 1970s, municipal governments undertook a robust lobbying campaign for increased funding that would allow them to address the growing "infrastructure deficit" across the country. A backlog of maintenance and replacement work had begun to mount due to the "bubble effect" of aging infrastructure: many of the postwar facilities were reaching the end of their lifespans. In addition, the economic morass that was ravaging the country during the decade was taking its toll on municipal budgets:

> the rapid inflation of the 70s was not matched by a concomitant rise in the rate of taxation. Municipalities were beginning to fund themselves with less money at precisely the same time that more facilities required repair or replacement. Meanwhile, allocations for capital works increasingly had to compete with demands to fund services designed to improve the quality of life. (Federation of Canadian Municipalities 1985, 7)

In the years preceding the repatriation of the Canadian Constitution in 1982, the municipal lobby argued strenuously "for increased autonomy and for larger shares of public funds" (Stevenson and Gilbert 2005, 532). The Canadian Federation of Mayors and Municipalities (CFMM), later renamed the Federation of Canadian Municipalities (FCM), published *Puppets on a Shoe String* in 1976, a polemic that predicted "the decline and fall of municipal government." Local governments blamed the provinces for their financial problems (1976, 1). As Hilton (2006) observed, "Not only was the organization seeking more money for municipal infrastructure from senior levels of government; it was at the same time seeking their support for a solution that would change the Constitution and the system of allocating revenues to all levels of government" (38). Fiscal pressures mounted as rates of inflation soared to double digits in the early 1980s. Municipal governments were reluctant to borrow at the high interest rates for fear of placing an even greater strain on their finances. Despite pleas for funding from senior levels of government, municipalities were unsuccessful for more than a decade in securing transfers to address needed infrastructure development and repair. The federal response to the calls for funding changed dramatically with the election of the Liberal government in 1993. Shortly after the election, the federal government began an intense period of funding for municipal infrastructure programs that provided transfers of federal funds through tripartite agreements with the provinces and territories. The first of these – the Canada Infrastructure Works Program – involved federal transfers totalling $2.4 billion; the combined share of the three levels of government was in excess of $8.3 billion. Although it was intended as a short-term program aimed at job creation, the success of the program quickly morphed into the creation of a series of transfer programs for infrastructure during both Liberal and Conservative administrations (see annex 1 at the end of this chapter).

In its interim report on infrastructure spending, the Standing Senate Committee on National Finance (2017) concluded that the federal government "needs to reduce the number and complexity of its programs, incorporate lessons learned from previous infrastructure programs, increase the flexibility of application-based programs, and ensure that provinces and territories respect municipal priorities (15)." A more fundamental problem, as alluded to in chapter 2, is that transfer payments from the federal government are politically driven, increasing or decreasing at the whim of the party holding the confidence of the House of Commons. As Hilton (2006) observed,

> in the absence of a clearly defined problem, the federal government created a policy framework founded on rhetoric rather than substance. In rationalizing the decisions to launch a series of ad hoc infrastructure programs that transferred billions of dollars in revenues to municipal governments, the federal government employed ambiguous language to define a vague public policy 'need.' While claiming that its investments in "strategic" municipal infrastructure had an impact on the economy, the environment and the 'quality of life' of citizens, the funding was allocated according to 'distributive politics.' In the absence of a clear plan or strategic policy, federal funding was sprinkled across the country for a myriad of infrastructure projects that served not as vehicles for the realization of policy objectives, but as opportunities to engage in retail politics and build political capital. (19–20)

From the perspective of municipal governments – particularly those of the largest urban centres – such a tenuous approach to funding infrastructure has long-term and potentially disastrous consequences, particularly in the planning and execution of large capital projects. The Senate Committee's report raised the administrative burden placed on local governments, stating that "the tangled web of programs is administratively burdensome and confusing" (20). While the focus on approving 'project by project' provides ample opportunities for federal politicians to engage in retail politics, there is a significant cost attached to providing communications resources to make these events happen.

Unfortunately, the Senate Committee's report was silent on the question of the utility of transfer payments as a solution to address needed funds for municipal infrastructure. As was discussed earlier in this chapter, rather than creating ad hoc programs that transfer revenues to municipalities, the federal government could have provided municipal governments – particularly the largest urban centres that serve as regional clusters – with the power to raise revenues on a more stable basis through a transfer of tax points.

2 Financing through Public-Private Partnerships, 1980–2020

During the 1980s the plight of municipal governments in dealing with the shortage of revenues for infrastructure development was seen as a golden opportunity for the investment community. Investing in municipal and provincial infrastructure projects would provide a means of growing capital within a relatively safe market. However, the potential marketplace – particularly municipal governments – needed to be "educated" about the benefits of partnering with the private sector in financing and building public assets.

Coincident with the fall of the federal Progressive Conservative government in 1993 and the election of a Liberal government that targeted investment in infrastructure as means of spurring job creation, the Canadian Council for Public Private Partnerships (CCPPP) (2017a; Hobbes 2016) was launched as a "national not-for-profit non-partisan, member-based organization with broad representation from across the public and private sectors." The organization functioned as a lobby for the investment community that would "educate stakeholders" (particularly local governments) on the benefits of public-private partnerships, "promot[ing] smart, innovative and modern approaches to infrastructure development and service delivery" (2).

As outlined in chapter 4, the Council ultimately hoped to influence the way in which public services are financed and delivered in Canada by connecting senior government and business leaders in the P3 community. Through an aggressive media campaign, the CCPPP began to sponsor conferences and seminars, organizing an annual conference "at which the most successful Canadian public-private partnerships are celebrated through CCPPP's National Awards for Innovation and Excellence." The Council also provides an online database on P3 projects – P3 SPECTRUM (2).

The Council quickly established close ties with politicians at the highest levels from both provincial and federal governments. P3 adherents such as former federal finance minister Michael Wilson (who chaired the Council), former premier of New Brunswick Frank McKenna, and Ernie Eves, minister of finance and later premier of Ontario, trumpeted the benefits of investments from the private sector in municipal and provincial infrastructure. Provincial governments across the country began launching specialized agencies charged with seeking and managing P3 projects as the procurement vehicles of choice.

In Ontario, SuperBuild Corporation began operating in 2000, with the mandate "to help the provincial government and its broader public sector partners be more strategic and be more creative in the financing and management of its physical assets" (Ontario Ministry of Finance 2000). The agency, which reported to Ernie Eves, then minister of Finance, set an ambitious goal of investing $10 billion in public funds in infrastructure projects that would be matched by an additional $10 billion "in partnership investments from the private and broader public sectors" (2). SuperBuild promised more than funding infrastructure: "SuperBuild's legacy will also be new ways of financing, developing and thinking about infrastructure." In 2001, when Jim Flaherty assumed responsibility for SuperBuild in his capacity as Ontario's Finance minister and deputy premier, the promotion of the P3 model of capital financing for infrastructure became paramount. As discussed below, Flaherty carried the mantra of promoting P3s when he later became the federal Minister of Finance in the Stephen Harper government. When SuperBuild's goal to match over five years with $10 billion from the public sector was achieved, the agency later morphed into a new entity – Infrastructure Ontario – under the Liberal McGuinty government in 2006. The new administration in Queen's Park also introduced a change in nomenclature: there were no longer references to "P3s." Ontario rebranded Public Private Partnerships as "Alternative Financing and Procurement (AFP)."

Other provinces followed Ontario's lead in creating agencies that promoted partnerships with the private sector, notably Partnerships BC (2002), Agence des partenariats public-privé du Québec (2004), Alberta Infrastructure (2006), and SaskBuilds (2012). In addition to creating new agencies, most provinces and the federal government created regulatory frameworks for P3s. Figure 5.1 maps the emerging regulatory environment for PPPs.

The vast majority of acts and regulations in Canada pertaining to PPPs are at the provincial level, which is unsurprising given the provincial authority over municipalities and the prevalence of PPPs provincially, particularly in transportation-related infrastructure projects. British Columbia stands out as having the most acts and regulations for PPP management and being both an early adopter and a province with a dedicated PPP office (Partnerships Canada). Significantly, for the discussion that follows, none of the acts or regulations set standards of practice for community consultation in the specific case of PPPs, which are instead generally seen as a procurement practice and treated as such, with much less emphasis on participation.

As figure 5.1 shows, the federal government's regulatory framework was set out under the *Strategic Infrastructure Fund Act* (2002), which was discussed in chapter 2. Six years later (as discussed in chapter 4), the federal government launched a special Crown Corporation agency to encourage P3s – PPP Canada (disbanded in 2017). The federal agency's purpose was defined as follows: "the Government of Canada has committed to supporting innovative public infrastructure projects, using the Public-Private Partnership (P3) model that deliver[s] maximum value for Canadians, stimulate[s] the economy, create[s] jobs and support[s] long-term prosperity" (P3 Canada). In explaining the reason for the dissolution of the agency, the federal government stated that "PPP Canada has fulfilled its mandate and Canada has developed a strong P3 market" (Infrastructure Canada 2017b).

This was a perplexing decision to take at a time when the planned Canadian Infrastructure Bank would presumably signal a raft of new P3 projects. While it could be that the role and expertise of P3 Canada will now be incorporated within the Infrastructure Bank, Armajeet Sohi, then minister of Infrastructure and Communities, suggested that PPP Canada was now effectively redundant given municipal access to provincial financing and expertise in addition to private capital. There is no doubt that P3s have been institutionalized at the core of infrastructure financing in Canada, but the strong support from provincial and federal politicians for private-sector financing of public infrastructure projects has also raised a key question: if a P3 arrangement presents an alternative to conventional procurement practices,

Federal
- Canada Strategic Infrastructure Fund

Provincial
- Alberta Infrastructure and Transportation P3 Policies
- British Columbia Transportation Investment Act (Part 2) [SBC 2002] Chapter 65
- British Columbia Transportation Investment (Port Mann Twinning) Amendment Act, 2008
- British Columbia Health Sector Partnerships Agreement Act [SBC 2003] Chapter 93
- British Columbia Capital Asset Management Framework
- Ontario Highway 407 Act, 1998
- Ontario Infrastructure Projects Corporation Act, 2006
- Quebec, An Act Respecting Infrastructure Quebec – came into force on 24 March 2010, replacing Bill 61 below
- Quebec, An Act Respecting Transport Infrastructure Partnerships (2000)
- Quebec, Bill 61: An Act Respecting the Agence des partenariats public-privé du Quebec
- New Brunswick Highway Corporation Act (1995)
- Nova Scotia Freedom of Information and Protection of Privacy Act

Municipal
- City of Edmonton P3 Policy – adopted 26 May 2010
- City of Calgary P3 Policy – adopted 15 December 2008
- City of Ottawa P3 Delivery Framework – adopted 7 June 2002

Figure 5.1 Regulatory Regime for Canadian P3s

what benefits do they offer the public sector? In *Understanding Public Private Partnerships* the Office of the Auditor General for the Province of British Columbia (2011) provides a useful synthesis of the main features:

Public-Private Partnership (P3) projects are publicly owned, publicly controlled, and publicly accountable. A private sector company may enter a lease/service agreement with the public sector to maintain or operate a public asset or service. Once the contract ends, the private sector must hand back the asset/service to the public sector in an agreed-upon condition. Underlying ownership always rests with the public sector even during the length of the agreement ... Typically in a P3, the [private-sector partner] would be responsible for securing its own financing. Under this arrangement, the consortium finances the upfront capital costs, then recovers its investment over the term of the P3 agreement. Although financing can be part of a P3, it is not a necessity: models such as Design Build ... are still financed by the public sector. When private financing is a part of the P3 agreement, it is normally in the form of project specific equity and debt. The proceeds from the public partner at the project's completion are used to repay the equity financing. With a conventional project, private financing is limited, so the project is often financed directly by government through capital contributions or debt. (2)

Since municipal governments have long complained about their share of revenues, it could be assumed that private-sector financing would offer an attractive solution to their problem. Private-sector investment would, in theory, provide needed cash to construct needed municipal infrastructure. However, the uptake on P3s from local governments has lagged that of provincial governments.

The Canadian Council for Public Private Partnerships' database on P3 projects (P3 SPECTRUM) reveals that, of a total of 272 "Active P3 Projects" with a market value of $125 billion, there were 52 municipal projects with a total market value of $11 billion. Under P3 Canada, federal funding in support of P3 projects totalled $1.3 billion, which supported 25 large infrastructure projects across the country. The focus of the funding was on provincial projects, which were mostly hospitals and schools (Office of the Auditor General of Canada 2015).

Rather than seeking capital from the private sector, municipal governments are able to use debt financing of large infrastructure projects through Provincial Municipal Financing Authorities/Corporations (known as MFAS or MFCS). The centralized provincial lending agencies with high credit ratings can borrow funds on behalf of municipalities at low interest rates. By providing loans that lower financing costs of capital projects, local debt charges and transaction costs are reduced. In addition, high-rated (low-risk) municipalities continue to fund many projects from reserves and through pay-as-you-go financing (Moody's Investors Service 2018).

In a *Globe and Mail* article, "The Hidden Price of Public-Private Partnerships," McKenna (2012) cites a study by Vining and Boardman that is critical of the "P3s are cheaper" mantra used by politicians:

These deals are politically seductive. Governments like them because they push spending down the road, pointed out business professor Aidan Vining of Simon Fraser University, who argued in a recent study with University of British Columbia business professor Anthony Boardman that taxpayers are too often getting a raw deal. "They get a service now and they get someone to pay for it later," Prof. Vining said. "From a political perspective, there's always an advantage to that." Governments are essentially "renting money" they could borrow more cheaply on their own because it's politically expedient to defer expenses and avoid debt, Prof. Boardman added. P3 has become a "slogan" with often dubious benefits, he said. (McKenna 2012, 3)

Another study on P3s (Siemiatycki and Farooqi) cited by McKenna found that public-private partnerships "cost an average of 16 per cent more than conventional tendered contracts." However, in calculating a "risk premium" compared with doing procurement the conventional way (referred to as a "public-private comparator"), governments assign a value to the premium that "reflects the risk shouldered by the private partner, including construction delays, cost overruns, design flaws and fluctuating future revenues. The result: The average premium is 49 per cent, making the P3 the better value on paper in every case, according to the Siemiatycki-Farooqi study." The researchers conclude that "no empirical evidence is provided to substantiate the risk allocations, making it difficult to assess their accuracy and validity" (3).

McKenna's bottom line on the hidden price of public-private partnerships: "Without putting a fair price on risk, taxpayers will never know whether P3s are any cheaper than building things the conventional way. Set the value too high, and P3s become vehicles for governments to subsidize inflated profits of powerful and well-connected contractors and financial institutions" (3).

A further reason why more P3s haven't been used in municipal infrastructure projects may result from the ingrained reliance on so-called "free money" provided by senior governments and discussed earlier in this chapter. The Canadian public remains relatively sceptical about P3s and is likely to place council under closer scrutiny for projects than if these are funded through traditional grants and contributions. Although advocates of P3s suggest that risks for delays and cost overruns are transferred to the private contractor, this is not usually the case. Politicians know, or at least fear, that they will ultimately be held accountable for delays and incurred costs by the public and media, who may perceive that the contract was badly drawn up or managed or both. Should a project run into trouble, it is the mayor and councillors who must face the media, not the contractor. The optics of this are often poor because the council are constrained in what they can say publicly by legal requirements in the contract and/or the need to ensure commercial confidentiality.

While financial penalties are usually built into the contract, council may be reluctant to enforce them, either because of the need to continue a healthy working relationship with the contractor or to avoid costly and protracted legal proceedings. Private firms will often dispute financial penalties by citing "unforeseen circumstances" or by claiming that the municipality itself contributed to or caused the delay, by, for example, changing the specifications of the contract or insisting on greater health and safety procedures that could slow down the pace of work. When faced with either managing a P3 project or lobbying for grants and funds from senior governments, the latter may be more appealing to local politicians.

A related concern, and a further potential barrier to increased uptake of P3s by municipalities, is the impact of commercial confidentiality on the level of citizen engagement. Local government is traditionally closer and more accessible to the public than either provincial or federal governments. Excluding or severely limiting public engagement is inconsistent with principles of local democratic participation. As Krawchenko and Stoney (2011) note:

> As the increasing institutionalization of PPPs in Canada leads them toward becoming a favoured method of financing, procurement, and operations, their role within the broader framework of governance and accountability will also need to be addressed, particularly for projects that demand elevated levels of public scrutiny and participation. Otherwise, the political and democratic costs of PPPs will not be fully captured or addressed, thereby adding to the so-called "democratic deficit" and fuelling calls for clarification of the policies regulations and laws that are supposed to protect communities and promote the public interest. (74)

The longevity of PPP contracts also means that they will usually outlast many election cycles. Unlike publicly delivered programs and services, PPPs (due to the nature of their contractual obligations) do not open themselves up to debate, particularly at election time, in the way that public services do.

Finally, municipalities may be reluctant to use P3s because the generation of a revenue stream is often required to entice private-sector partners to invest. Unlike many other countries, including the United States, Canadian politicians have been reluctant to establish user fees for the use of public infrastructure. Highways and bridges present the most obvious opportunities to charge given the inelasticity of demand, but Canada's system of municipal governance tends to favour the representation and interests of suburban and rural constituents over urban residents. As a result, the political costs of imposing tolls and fees on commuters have severely limited this option and undermined the business model for private-sector involvement in P3s.

We next examine the federal Canada Infrastructure Bank, but with needed links back to earlier periods regarding what banking and finance meant in relation to indemnification and loans.

3 Canada Infrastructure Bank: Indemnification, Loans, and Other Inducements, 1930s–80s, 2017–21

After more than two decades and billions of dollars in transfers supporting municipal infrastructure projects, the federal government recently launched another approach in providing funding for local governments and other potential recipients. The government will now provide loans, a financial instrument it has used in the past. As discussed earlier, during the decades after World War I until the 1980s, the federal government responded to various social and economic problems by creating short-lived municipal programs that provided loans and grants for local public works projects. Many of these problems were triggered by federal policies that had produced unanticipated negative effects on municipal governments. Federal assistance consisted largely of reactive countermeasures intended to provide short-term financial relief.

During the 1930s, the federal government responded to the dangers of severe unemployment created by the Depression. The threat of social unrest – particularly in cities – again warranted its involvement in providing financial support to local governments. Some municipalities had defaulted on their outstanding debt and were having difficulties in collecting taxes as a result of increased personal and business bankruptcies. Parliament passed the *Municipal Improvements Assistance Act* in 1938, using a provision of the *Bank Act* to authorize the federal government to provide municipalities with loans for construction projects, such as water and sewage improvements, that would create employment. In order to be eligible, projects were required to be "self-sustaining": municipalities were required to ensure that the interest and principal payments would not form part of the general tax levy. Under the *Municipal Improvements Assistance Act*, a maximum $30 million in loans was made available, of which approximately $7 million was actually paid out (Auditor General of Canada 1996). The *Act* was subsequently repealed by Parliament in 1948.

In addition to providing grants to municipalities, the federal government also launched a program to provide loans to stimulate employment. From 1963 to 1966, the *Municipal Development and Loan Act* established a $400 million fund to provide loans to local governments to encourage them to accelerate and expand their capital works programs. To be eligible for a loan, municipal projects had to constitute an addition to, or an acceleration of, an intended program of municipal capital works.[7] While the effect of the investment was intended to be incremental – increasing employment in the construction industry – the funds were allocated to provinces on the basis of population only. No consideration was given at the time to targeting federal funds to address the specific areas of the country where the need was greatest.

By 1969, the federal government had committed nearly $397 million in 2,429 loans to 1,262 municipalities, although not all of the loans were repaid. The Act authorized partial cancellation ("forgiveness") of the loan amount, with the degree of forgiveness related to the amount of construction work completed by a specified date (the repayment of up to 25 per cent of each loan could be forgiven based on the costs incurred by the municipalities). More than one-third of federal funding was directed to water and sewer infrastructure, with an equal amount applied to the construction of schools, roads and bridges, rapid transit systems, and civic administration buildings. A smaller portion of the loans was used for park developments, recreation facilities, hospitals, and power distribution projects. The federal government's loans to municipalities had effectively leveraged nearly twice their value – the provinces estimated that the total cost of the projects receiving funding surpassed $750 million (Infrastructure Canada 2003).

From 1975 to 1978, the federal government also introduced the Municipal Infrastructure Program, contributing over $1 billion in loans and $395 million in grants (Auditor General of Canada 1996). The rationale for federal funding for municipal infrastructure was linked principally to the increasing financial woes of local governments. As the Federation of Canadian Municipalities (FCM) pointed out, infrastructure that had been built immediately after World War II during rapid urbanization "seems to have been maintained at acceptable levels, partly because economic conditions were favourable, partly because so many facilities were new" (1985, 7). By the 1970s, however, the backlog of maintenance and replacement work had begun to mount due to the "bubble effect" of aging infrastructure: many of the post-war facilities were reaching the end of their lifespans. In addition, the economic morass that was ravaging the country during that decade was taking its toll on municipal budgets.

As outlined in chapter 2, subsequent decades saw the federal government develop a growing penchant for funding programs over municipal loans, resulting in a complex labyrinth of delivery mechanisms that could be packaged and branded with increasing sophistication. However, in the *Fall Economic Statement 2016*, the Trudeau Liberal government announced its intention to create an infrastructure bank that would use a wide breadth of financial instruments including loans, loan guarantees, and equity investments in infrastructure. Following Budget 2017, the *Canada Infrastructure Bank Act* came into force[8] as a Crown Corporation with the mandate to work with private institutional investors, such as public and private pension funds, to identify infrastructure projects and investment opportunities. The Bank is expected to use federal funding to leverage investment from the private sector by focusing on new "revenue-generating infrastructure projects that are in the public interest" (*Canada Infrastructure Bank Act* 2017). The goal of using federal dollars to leverage the "capital and expertise of the private sector" will allow the Bank to make "public dollars go further." This is expected to be achieved in part by screening projects and redirecting those "that are more appropriate for traditional grant funding mechanisms" (7).

The Bank is intended to operate at arm's length from government, governed by a Board of Directors that is "responsive and accountable" to the government and Parliament through the minister of Infrastructure and Communities. The governance for the new Crown Corporation is likely to be challenging, given the stated arm's-length relationship with the government and the political realities arising from major federal spending on infrastructure projects, especially those in lucrative "vote-rich" ridings across the country (8).

The initial federal funding available through the Infrastructure Bank is significant – $35 billion, of which $15 billion is sourced from the over $180 billion Investing in Canada infrastructure plan, including:

- $5 billion for public transit systems;
- $5 billion for trade and transportation corridors; and
- $5 billion for green infrastructure projects, including those that reduce greenhouse gas emissions, deliver clean air and safe water systems, and promote renewable power.

These are consistent with the four priority sectors, public transit, trade and transportation, green infrastructure and broadband infrastructure, identified by the C I B . and delivered in partnership with public-sector sponsors and private and institutional investors. All projects are bankable, revenue-generating, and satisfy commercial due diligence, including private-sector investment among other requirements.

Municipal governments are not the only intended beneficiaries of funds made available through the Canada Infrastructure Bank. Provinces, territories, municipalities, and Indigenous communities are expected to compete for funding infrastructure projects that "will contribute to … long-term economic growth" (Infrastructure Canada 2021). The resources available through the Bank may also be affected by the decision of the federal government to purchase the completion of the Trans Mountain (Kinder Morgan) expansion project, including related pipeline and terminal assets. The $4.5 billion transaction as well as required total project completion costs (which are estimated to be over $7.4 billion) will draw down nearly one-third of the funding committed to the Bank.

The rationale for investing in the pipeline project, which was deemed to be of "national interest," may have set a precedent for future projects funded through the Canada Infrastructure Bank. Will these projects, including those that involve municipal governments, also need to meet the threshold of "national interest?" The legislation creating the Bank makes no mention of or defines "national interest," but the C I B website states that it "promotes transformational projects that are in the public interest, linked to national economic priorities" (C I B 2020). As of February 2020, the C I B is participating in the eight projects summarized in table 5.1.

Table 5.1
Eight projects in which the CIB is participating

Project	Partner	Location	Sector	Commitment
Contrecoeur Port Terminal	Montreal Port Authority	Montreal, QC	Trade and transportation	Up to $300 million
GO Expansion – On Corridor	Infrastructure Ontario and Metrolinx	Greater Toronto and Hamilton Area, ON	Green infrastructure	Memorandum of understanding
Lulu Island District Energy	City of Richmond, Lulu Island Energy Company	City of Richmond, BC	Green infrastructure	Memorandum of understanding
Mapleton Water and Wastewater	Township of Mapleton	Mapleton, ON	Green infrastructure	Up to $20 million
Pirate Harbour Wind Farm	Port Hawkesbury Paper	Point Tupper, NS	Infrastructure [?]	Memorandum of understanding
Réseau express métropolitain (REM)	CDPQ Infra, Province de Quebec	Montreal, QC	Transit	$1.28 billion
Taltson Hydroelectricity Expansion	Government of Northwest Territories	Northwest Territories	Green infrastructure	Advisory services
VIA Rail	VIA Rail Canada, Transport Canada	Ontario, Quebec	Transit	$55 million

Source: https://cib-bic.ca/.

As important as these projects may well be to specific urban centres and communities across the country, it is difficult to determine why or how they were selected, or how they contribute to national economic priorities. The CIB does not provide documentation of cost-benefit analysis or factors used in the assessment of projects, providing instead only a perfunctory description of each one. Based on the CIB website and the choice of infrastructure projects to date, the criteria used remain as nebulous as ever regarding the distribution of federal funds. The CIB's promotion seems to acknowledge and confirm this:

These projects are located from coast to coast to coast, in the North, in small communities and large urban areas. They demonstrate our ambition to advise on, invest in and build knowledge about transformational infrastructure projects across Canada.

Given the geographical sprinkling of CIB funds, allied to the mix of urban, Northern, rural, major, and minor projects already established, it is difficult to conclude that the CIB funding of infrastructure indicates a radical departure from the politically influenced infrastructure that has characterized the history of Canada's infrastructure spending over many decades, as outlined in chapter 2. Though it is still early in the history of the CIB, there is little yet to suggest that the bank signifies a move towards the "strategic" approach to infrastructure investment promised by the Trudeau Liberals.

Concerns about the CIB's efficacy and future were reinforced by the recent changes in leadership and senior management. In April 2021, the Liberal government announced that the CIB's two most senior leaders – board chair Janice Fukakusa and CEO Pierre Lavallée – would be departing as part of a major shakeup at the organization. The changes followed criticism that "the bank had been slow to identify and fund projects" and occurred at a time when opposition parties were calling for investigations into the activities of the bank as well as the government's infrastructure spending in general (Curry 2020). Michael Sabia quickly took over as the new chair of the Bank's board, and in November 2020, Ehren Cory was appointed to the role of Chief Executive Officer. Despite new leadership and very public support from both the prime minister and the Infrastructure minister, scepticism remains about the role of the bank and its potential to deliver projects. In his ominously titled article "Farewell, Then, Canada Infrastructure Bank" Paul Wells questions the lack of detail regarding CIB projects as well as its independence from political meddling:

> So the project list the PM, his minister, and the inevitable Sabia announced on Thursday listed no projects, named no private-sector partners, and included no process for gathering private-sector capital before signing off. The Bank is, in no sense, a Bank any more. It's a pot of federal money, into which the federal government will dip to pursue the ends the federal government finds pleasing.

A further and longer-term question concerning C I B funding remains unanswered: will project partners in these projects also be afforded a guarantee of indemnification? In a backgrounder announcing the agreement to purchase the Trans Mountain project, the federal government committed to the following:

> Any purchaser of the [Trans Mountain] project would be covered by a federal indemnity protecting them against any financial loss posed by politically motivated unnecessary delays, in line with the indemnity offered to Kinder Morgan by the Government on May 16, 2018. (Finance Canada 2018)

Indemnification as such implies "no risk" or "derisking," which is antithetical to the argument for "shared risk" offered through Public-Private Partnerships. However, providing potential private-sector investors with a federal indemnity protecting them from any financial loss may be the only way to entice offshore investors in projects sponsored by the Canada Infrastructure Bank. The complications and delays witnessed in the Trans Mountain project have not gone unnoticed in the investment and political communities (see more in chapter 8).

ANALYSIS: THE THREE REGIME ELEMENTS

With the aid of Table 5.2, we now look across the above three infrastructure financing policy and governance histories by examining the three elements featured in our overall analytical framework.

Policy ideas, discourse, and agendas regarding infrastructure financing must capture the complexities of federal-provincial-municipal relationships as well as the politicized nature of infrastructure funding. In recent decades, infrastructure spending has been accompanied by a rationale that appears to have transgressed ideology, providing governments of all political stripes with irresistible opportunities to focus on spending announcements, "ribbon cutting," "photo ops," and egregious examples of partisan branding. Predictably, the discourse promoting increased infrastructure spending has developed into a compelling narrative drawing selectively on numerous virtues including economic stimulus (jobs), international competitiveness, regional development, "world class infrastructure," and similar hyperbole. The federal-municipal agenda has in recent decades morphed almost exclusively into funding for infrastructure. This provides federal governments

Table 5.2
The infrastructure financing regime and the three analytical elements: highlights

Policy and governance histories	Policy ideas, discourse, and agendas	Power structures, democracy, and governance	Temporal realities, cycles, conflicts, and technology
1. Managing and paying for municipal public assets, 1930s to 2003	• Infrastructure development and levels of service treated as public goods that are provided by government, usually at no direct charge or charges that are far less than actual cost. • Service levels regulated by regional and municipal governments often with funding from federal government to provide basic needs (e.g. potable water, safety, sewage treatment, roads, bridges, etc.). • Sustained by a rising share of public revenues, federal government policies play a key role in establishing the land development industry in Canadian cities. • The federal role in land assembly and the provision of financial assistance for single-family homes reinforce the pattern of low-density sprawl.	• Municipalities governed by provinces as set out clearly in the constitution. Provinces guard against federal "intrusions" but federal funding accepted – and difficult for Ottawa to attach "strings." • During the 1930s municipalities across all provinces establish income taxes as major source of local revenues. The federal government takes these away to raise funding for the war effort (Tax Rental Agreements). They are never returned and municipalities are left to rely on property taxes and user fees. • At the end of World War II, the Tax Rental Agreements had increased the federal government's share of all public revenues to 82 per cent. This share of overall taxation is gradually reduced as provinces increase their percentage of money for growing health and education costs. Municipalities historically limited to less than 10 per cent of the total state-levied taxes.	• During the 1970s municipal governments undertake a robust lobbying campaign for increased funding that would allow them to address the growing "infrastructure deficit" across the country. • Federation of Canadian Municipalities (FCM), publishes *Puppets on a Shoe String* in 1976, a polemic that predicts "the decline and fall of municipal government." Local governments blame the provinces for their financial problems. • Fiscal pressures mount as rates of inflation soar to double digits in the early 1980s. Municipal governments are reluctant to borrow at the high interest rates for fear of placing an even greater strain on municipal finances.

- Keynesian social welfare and countercyclical spending dominant ideology in 1960s to mid-1980s. Canada Infrastructure Works Program involves federal transfers totalling $2.4 billion; intended as a short-term program aimed at job creation, but quickly morphs into a series of transfer programs for infrastructure by Liberal and Conservative administrations.
- This approach continues to grow during 1990s and into the new millennium with confusing "tangled web" of funding programs placing administrative burden on local governments who become increasingly reliant on federal largesse. The "project-by-project" approval facilitates political interference and retail politics.
- In addition to stimulus, job creation, and nation-building, environmental agenda and discourse lead to growing emphasis on "green infrastructure."

- Despite losing income tax powers and a declining share of public revenues, the municipal share of public infrastructure increases from 30.9 per cent in 1961 to 52.4 per cent in 2002.
- The federal response to the calls for funding changes dramatically with the election of the Liberal government in 1993. Shortly after the election, the federal government begins an intense period of funding for municipal infrastructure programs that provides transfers of federal funds through tripartite agreements with the provinces and territories;
- Infrastructure Canada established as part of the Liberal government's New Deal for Cities and Communities. Provides the central hub for federal infrastructure funding.
- FCM provided with funding to administer the Green Municipal Fund on behalf of the federal government. Sustainable development and innovation emphasized as the key criteria for receiving the funds

- As the infrastructure gap continues to grow, federal government looks to invest more in municipal projects but Meech Lake and constitutional wrangling continue to limit the federal role in urban affairs.
- Growing body of science points to climate change and the need for sustainable development and improved asset management. "Infraguide" established to share technology and best practices between municipalities.
- Emphasis placed on sustainability and "green" infrastructure begins to fuel innovation and debate about how to do things differently. Funding programs begin to leverage transformational change but politics, stimulus, and short-termism continue to limit progress

Table 5.2
The infrastructure financing regime and the three analytical elements: highlights (*Continued*)

Policy and governance histories	Policy ideas, discourse, and agendas	Power structures, democracy, and governance	Temporal realities, cycles, conflicts, and technology
2. Financing through public private partnerships, 1980 to 2020	• Keynesian state planning and 'big government' are heavily criticized during the 1980s, prompted by a neo-liberal ideology and agenda promoting private-sector solutions including P3s. • International bodies such as the WHO and OECD, Canadian think tanks such as the Conference Board, and consultants including KPMG disseminate reports and evidence relating to the need for private investment in public infrastructure. • During the 1980s the plight of municipal governments in dealing with the shortage of revenues for infrastructure development is seen as a golden opportunity for the investment community. • The 2007 financial crisis provides the Harper government with rationale to embrace stimulus	• In Ontario, SuperBuild Corporation begins operating in 2000, with the mandate to help the provincial government and its broader public sector partners be more strategic and be more creative in the financing and management of its physical assets. Headed by Ontario Finance Minister Jim Flaherty, the P3 mantra and experience followed him into the Harper government. • Other provinces follow Ontario's lead in creating agencies that promoted partnerships with the private sector, notably Partnerships BC (2002), Agence des partenariats public-privé du Québec (2004), Alberta Infrastructure (2006), and SaskBuilds (2012). • In addition to creating new agencies, most provinces and the federal government create regulatory frameworks for P3s.	• P3s are increasingly institutionalized at the core of infrastructure financing in Canada, underpinned by strong support from provincial and federal politicians for private-sector financing of public infrastructure projects. • Conflict and questions remain about the benefits they offer the public sector. Notably, the uptake of P3s from local governments has lagged behind that of provincial governments. • The longevity of PPP contracts also means that they may outlast many election cycles. Unlike publicly delivered programs and services, PPPs (due to contractual obligations) do not open themselves up to debate, particularly at election time, in the way that public services do.

- funding for "shovel-ready" projects, launching the Building Canada Fund. However, environmental assessment requirements are reduced and all major projects required to explore P3 options.
- Trudeau Liberal government elected in 2015 promising to increase spending on infrastructure and commitment to "strategic" investment as opposed to the traditional approach.
- Mandate letter sent from PM to the Minister for Infrastructure and Communities (2015) outlines the new Liberal agenda, but specifies that Montreal's newly built Champlain Bridge is not to be funded by tolls – a decision that appears inconsistent with planned development of a new infrastructure bank designed to attract private capital.

- In 2009 the federal government launches a special Crown corporation agency to encourage P3s – PPP Canada (disbanded in 2017). The federal agency's purpose is to support innovative public infrastructure projects, using the Public-Private Partnership (P3) model.

- Municipalities may also be reluctant to use P3s because they often require the generation of a revenue stream to entice private-sector partners to invest. Unlike many other countries, including the United States, Canadian politicians have been reluctant to establish user fees for public infrastructure.
- In reality the political cost of imposing tolls and fees on commuters has severely limited this option and undermined the business model for private-sector involvement in P3s.
- Corruption unearthed during the Charbonneau Commission (2013–16) allied to several critical Auditors General reports increases calls for closer scrutiny of P3s, federal funding with respect to oversight and value for money.

Table 5.2
The infrastructure financing regime and the three analytical elements: highlights (*Continued*)

Policy and governance histories	*Policy ideas, discourse, and agendas*	*Power structures, democracy, and governance*	*Temporal realities, cycles, conflicts, and technology*
3. Canada Infrastructure Bank: indemnification, loans, and other inducements, 1930s to 1980s, 2017 to 2020	• Originally part of nation-building policies, infrastructure projects during the 1930s are seen primarily as a tool to get people back to work following the "great recession." Infrastructure funding has continued to provide "make-work" projects ever since, bolstered by Keynesian countercyclical ideology. • Having appropriated municipal income tax powers, the federal government has used a complex combination of loans, transfers and programs to invest in federal infrastructure rather than return those powers to local government. • From 1963 to 1966, the Municipal Development and Loan Act establishes a $400 million fund to provide loans to local governments to encourage them to accelerate and expand their capital works programs. Loans are agreed based on "partial forgiveness" and not the terms of a "true" bank.	• After the dollars in transfers supporting municipal infrastructure projects, the federal government launches the Infrastructure Bank in 2017. • Following Budget 2017, the Canada Infrastructure Bank Act comes into force as a Crown corporation with the mandate to work with private institutional investors, such as public and private pension funds, to identify infrastructure projects and investment opportunities. • The Bank is intended to use federal funding to leverage investment from the private sector by focussing on new "revenue-generating infrastructure projects that are in the public interest." • The Bank is intended to operate at "arm's length" from government, governed by a board of directors that is "responsive and accountable" to the government and Parliament through the Minister of Infrastructure and Communities.	• Following decades of federal funding in 'new' infrastructure projects since the 1970s, a growing backlog of maintenance and replacement work mounts, due to the 'bubble effect' of aging infrastructure: many of the post-war facilities are reaching the end of their lifespan. • In addition, the economic crisis suffered during a near decade of oil shocks of the 1970s is taking its toll on municipal budgets. • Following the launch of federal government purchases, completion of the Trans Mountain (Kinder Morgan) expansion project arises, including related pipeline and terminal assets. The $4.5 billion project completion costs, estimated to be over $7.4 billion, will draw down nearly one-third of the funding committed to the Bank.

- Funds are allocated to provinces based on population; no consideration is given to targeting federal funds to address the specific areas of the country where the need is greatest.
- From 1975 to 1978, the federal government also introduces the Municipal Infrastructure Program, contributing over $1 billion in loans and $395 million in grants.
- Infrastructure is seen increasingly as a state priority and a public good. Unlike the US, Canadians remain hostile to the notion of privately funded infrastructure and the accompanying tolls and fees.
- The 1980s witness an increased role for private sector through P3s but the vast majority of Canadians still expect infrastructure projects to be publicly provided and "free" to use.
- Using federal dollars to leverage the capital and expertise of the private sector is expected to allow the Bank to make "public dollars go further."

- The governance for the new Crown Corporation is likely to be challenging given the stated 'arm's-length' relationship with the government and the political realities arising from major federal spending on infrastructure projects, especially those that are in lucrative "vote-rich" ridings across the country.
- The question of governance is crucial to the effectiveness of the infrastructure bank. Given the politicization of infrastructure funding in Canada, political independence will be crucial to limit political interference and also to establish trust and credibility with private investors.
- The fact that the Infrastructure Bank reports to the Finance Minister suggests that the CIB will be a Crown corporation or agency as opposed to an independent bank. Allied to the early choices of projects by the bank, this raises questions about the strategic nature of funding, the criteria and definitions used in the process and the degree of financial risk of project partners.

- The rationale for investing in the pipeline project, which was deemed to be of "national interest," may set a precedent for future projects funded through the Canada Infrastructure Bank. Will these projects, including those that involve municipal governments, also need to meet the threshold of "national interest"?
- The legislation creating the Bank makes no mention or definition of "national interest."
- In 2018 the Bank provides federal indemnity to any company purchasing the Trans Mountain Pipeline. This protects investors against "any financial loss posed by politically motivated unnecessary delays."
- Indemnification promotes "no risk" or "derisking," which is antithetical to the argument for "shared risk" offered through public-private partnerships. However, the reality is that protecting investors from any financial loss may be required to entice offshore investors in

Table 5.2
The infrastructure financing regime and the three analytical elements: highlights (*Continued*)

Policy and governance histories	Policy ideas, discourse, and agendas	Power structures, democracy, and governance	Temporal realities, cycles, conflicts, and technology
	• The growing infrastructure gap leads the federal government to look for alternative funding sources. Internationally, pension funds investing in major infrastructure projects and appear to be an ideal fit given their resources and the need for long-term investment opportunities. • In 2015 election campaign the Liberal party commits to establishing an infrastructure bank for Canada. • The federal funding available through the Infrastructure Bank is significant – $35 billion, of which $15 billion is sourced from the over $180 billion Investing in Canada infrastructure plan targeting public transit, trade and transportation corridors, and green infrastructure.	• Following criticism of the CIB's capacity to spend money and deliver infrastructure projects, senior management of the CIB are removed by the government in 2020. It is expected that under new leadership the CIB will have a significant role to play in the post pandemic stimulus program promised by the Trudeau government. The immediate post-pandemic years will be crucial in determining whether the CIB has a longer-term future.	projects sponsored by the Canada Infrastructure Bank. The complications and delays witnessed in the Trans Mountain project have not gone unnoticed in the investment community.

with a way to intervene in urban affairs that is acceptable to provincial jurisdictional sensitivities. A relatively blunt policy tool, it has increasingly been used to advance the federal government's "Green agenda," though the enforcement of sustainable development criteria remains a challenge given provincial and municipal priorities and agendas and the scramble to fund "shovel-ready projects."

During the last two decades, the so-called "infrastructure gap" has become an increasingly common and powerful rhetorical device for justifying federal funding. While there are many widely varying opinions and estimates about the size of the deficit, the term and concept has become a largely taken-for-granted assumption along with climate change, globalization, and sustainability. The FCM has been highly effective in highlighting the dangers of Canada's "widening" infrastructure gap to leverage federal funding for municipalities. This has resulted in municipalities becoming increasingly dependent on federal funding, with mayors joining the FCM in actively lobbying for it. While the success of this strategy has produced significant and sustained federal funding, it is a narrative that has allowed municipal leaders to avoid the use of local user fees to help pay some of the costs of infrastructure. This unintended outcome may prove to be increasingly problematic, given that user fees are seen as an effective way of "pricing pollution" and will presumably be required to attract private-sector investment through the newly established Infrastructure Bank. The economic fallout from the pandemic will further increase pressure on municipalities to apply user fees and other revenue-generating tools to balance their books and reduce serious fiscal deficits.

Regarding *power structures, democracy, and governance* it was inevitable, given the massive growth in federal funding, that a multitude of new programs and institutions would emerge over time to streamline and accelerate infrastructure investment and provide appropriate oversight. Notably, these include Infrastructure Canada, Regional Development Agencies, P3 Canada, the Infrastructure Bank, the Gas Tax Fund, Canada's Strategic Infrastructure Fund, and the Building Canada Fund, to name but a few. This plethora of funding programs and agencies has made the funding of infrastructure highly complex, with significant transaction costs generated at each level of government. With larger municipalities receiving infrastructure funding from hundreds of programs and sources – all with different requirements and conditions – they have also had to hire extra administrators and in some cases create new departments to manage and account for the funding. This elaborate system of intergovernmental funding increasingly involves private-sector funding and partnerships, adding to the challenge of governance, accountability, and oversight. Whereas other areas of public spending have been pressured to focus on cost-benefit analysis, rigorous evaluation, and outcomes, infrastructure has been largely spared from recent accountability regimes with the emphasis on spending announcements as opposed to outcomes and value-for-money measures. This can mainly be attributed to the need to expedite spending in order to stimulate the economy and maximize political dividends within the current electoral cycle. However, it is also influenced by the federal government's inability to enforce and measure the outcomes of municipal projects and the difficulty in capturing and publicizing the political benefits. Each of these factors has contributed to the development of broad and often vague policy aims, which severely limits meaningful evaluation.

These multi-level infrastructure funding and governance arrangements also raise some fundamental questions of Canadian democracy. The involvement of several tiers of government makes it difficult for the electorate to know which level of government is accountable for spending on specific projects, and the potential for obfuscation is often fully exploited by politicians. The system of transfers and contributions also creates so-called "free money" whereby the municipal politicians responsible for spending public funds are not responsible for raising them through local taxation. A related concern is that this arrangement distorts local priorities and perceived needs. Federal and provincial conditionality can override local priorities, whereas the prospect of "free money" can encourage councils to create and demonstrate "need." Finally, in addition to blurring accountability, P3s have also reduced transparency and citizen engagement. The need for commercial confidentiality is widely used to limit information about projects and financing. While a lack of transparency is seen by some as an inevitable and justifiable cost of involving the private sector, it is something that politicians are only too happy to exploit when it is in their interests to do so, as it often provides a convenient shield. Information and transparency remain fundamental to a healthy democracy and recent reports focusing on municipal corruption have again exposed the dangers of "back room" deals and inscrutable contracts that have at times reduced public trust in infrastructure programs and projects.

As for *temporal realities, cycles, conflicts, and technology* relating to infrastructure financing, there emerge several related themes. Since the 1930s, infrastructure spending has been closely associated with economic cycles. Oddly, perhaps, government spending on infrastructure tends to be higher when the economy is in crisis as opposed to growing. Influenced by Keynesian thinking, infrastructure financing is regarded as a counter-cyclical tool by which governments can stimulate growth and put people back to work quickly. While there is merit in this approach, it has often led the funding of "shovel-ready" projects of dubious long-term benefit. The absence of strategic planning has been further undermined by the federal government's lack of constitutional powers with respect to municipal government, the vastness and diversity of the country, and the growing politicization of infrastructure funding. In the absence of a national strategy for infrastructure, Canadian infrastructure investment has been labelled "policy by project."

As discussed earlier in the chapter, infrastructure planning has also suffered from vague aims and unspecified outcomes. While job creation has often provided the underlying rationale for investing in municipal infrastructure projects, the federal government has failed to measure the number of jobs created. Similarly, when sustainable development has been used as to justify investment in "green" infrastructure, measures and evidence regarding outcomes are often lacking. This has made it difficult to learn from previous investment programs, with seemingly little feedback available to inform future policy and investment, resulting in a recurring cycle of potentially sub-optimal investments. In the wake of the pandemic, federal and provincial governments face another economic crisis and ready themselves to launch ambitious stimulus packages targeting infrastructure projects across the country. It remains to be seen if lessons have been learned from previous stimulus funding programs, in particular the development of a coherent national strategy that identifies projects based on merit rather than partisan advantage as demonstrated by transparent cost-benefit analysis.

Since the federal government removed municipal income tax powers prior to WWII, the reality for municipalities is that they have struggled to raise local taxes to invest in infrastructure and have grown increasingly dependent on federal and provincial funding, as highlighted by the pandemic crisis and its serious economic impacts on municipalities. Even when municipal leaders try to impose user fees for roads and bridges, they are often prohibited by provincial governments concerned about upcoming elections. Increasingly P3s and private-sector investment are seen as the most effective and affordable way to close the infrastructure gap, but this will require that Canadians accept user fees and tolls to make it financially viable. The notion of infrastructure as a public good has dominated Canadian thinking since federal investment in transportation and other "nation-building" infrastructure connected provinces and cities across the country. For many Canadians, the increasing use of private-sector investment, combined with user fees, effectively turns public goods into private goods and thereby conflicts with fundamental and ingrained expectations about the role of the state in providing infrastructure. The launch of the Infrastructure Bank will inevitably bring this debate into sharp focus.

Finally, advances in technology have created opportunities for rapid innovation. However, new technologies such as ride-share apps and autonomous vehicles will increase the challenge of governments to invest in the right kinds of infrastructure, with increasing risks that we will invest in out-dated or unnecessary infrastructure, leading to the so-called "white elephants" perhaps best epitomized by the federal government's ill-advised investment in Mirabel Airport during the 1970s. To limit these risks, policy-makers and politicians will need to develop a far more rigorous approach to project selection underpinned by a clearer vision and strategy for infrastructure needs in the face of rapidly changing technology.

As this history of infrastructure financing has outlined, more than forty years ago, municipal governments across the country complained vociferously about their less than fair share of revenues collected by all levels of government. Having lost their powers to collect revenues from personal and corporate income taxes, they sought a solution to a perceived fiscal imbalance that was negatively affecting their ability to provide needed services and related infrastructure. The federal government, always eager to announce new infrastructure projects, eventually responded by transferring billions of dollars, and later, during the second of the periods examined, encouraged municipalities to seek additional sources of funds by entering into partnerships with private-sector companies that would help pay for, build, and operate needed infrastructure. The recent creation of the Canada Infrastructure Bank presents such a significant shift in paying for public infrastructure that we have categorized it as a potential third era in infrastructure funding. Importantly, projects funded through the Bank will need to be "revenue-generating" in order to attract investment from the private sector. As discussed in this chapter, this is a challenging premise given Canadians' perception of the government's traditional role in providing public as opposed to private goods. Since projects will need to be large in scale and require revenue generation over decades (thirty to thirty-five years), the private sector partners/consortium would be expected to play an important role in the community in defining its future infrastructure needs and services. In other words, the partner/consortium would long outlive the councils that struck the initial partnership agreement and in effect provide a sense of permanence in the governance of the community. Municipal government may indeed still be "Puppets on a Shoe String" but the puppet master will change.

CONCLUSIONS

This chapter has illustrated the complex framework used to fund infrastructure in Canada. The involvement of multiple levels of government, numerous government departments and agencies, and, increasingly, the private sector has made strategic planning more difficult and blurred accountability for results. This complexity is exacerbated by the existence of myriad objectives related to infrastructure funding including economic stimulus, social, and environmental policy agendas, in addition to overriding political and partisan considerations and timelines. Cyclical programs, such as the Building Canada Plan and the Investing in Canada Plan, are confirmation that federal stimulus spending is now de facto a permanent source of government funding, regardless of the state of the economy. As we have indicated, federal governments of all political stripes have found infrastructure funding an invaluable political tool given the potential for branding, announcements, photo opportunities, and the discretionary nature of what type of infrastructure to fund, where and when. The economic and health impacts of COVID-19 will no doubt justify a significant ramping up of the government's already significant infrastructure stimulus spending as set out in the ICIP, and informal strategizing is already well underway under the direction of the minister of Infrastructure and Communities, Catherine McKenna. As discussed in this chapter and in chapter 2, the likely emphasis on green infrastructure will be controversial, particularly in the Western provinces and across many municipalities where local needs and priorities may not align with those in Ottawa. Also potentially controversial will be the role played by the private sector in influencing how the stimulus funding is spent and which projects are selected. While Boston Consulting Group have been invited to advise ministers on "charting the course for future-forward recovery" (Kirby 2020), it is the role played by SNC Lavalin that is likely to be most closely scrutinized, given its high-profile role in Prime Minister Trudeau's 2019 ethical violations and its own international reputation. In an article titled "SNC Eyes Infrastructure Spending in New Push to Governments," the *Globe and Mail* outlines how SNC–Lavalin Group Inc. plans to work with governments in Canada to "speed up their spending on infrastructure" (Van Praet 2020). Through its newly established service "Acceleration to Shovel-Ready Infrastructure," it has already begun to "approach government officials at all levels to help it quickly identify and accelerate high-impact projects" (Van Praet 2020).

A further and related concern regarding COVID-19 stimulus funding is the lack of oversight in the absence of a fully functioning parliament and political system due to physical distancing and other safety measures. Although opposition parties successfully pressured the federal government to pull back from its proposal to grant itself sweeping emergency powers to "spend money, borrow, and change taxes without parliamentary approval through to Dec. 31, 2021," normal levels of political scrutiny and oversight cannot currently be enforced (Aiello 2020). In this context, the WE charity sole-sourced procurement scandal, which sparked an investigation by the federal ethics commissioner, has raised serious concerns about the potential largesse built into the broader stimulus spending package. Although the Auditor General is currently conducting a review of the ICIP, results are not expected until 2022, and the continued erosion of funding for the AG's office by successive governments raises doubts about it capacity to fully investigate and evaluate a massive tranche of new stimulus funding. Ultimately, the infrastructure stimulus response to COVID-19 will test the Trudeau government's resolve to invest imaginatively and strategically in Canadian infrastructure projects based on need, evidence, and cost-benefit analysis rather than the short-term, partisan thinking that has been a hallmark of previous infrastructure stimulus programs.

ANNEX 1: FUNDING FROM FEDERAL INFRASTRUCTURE PROGRAMS

In response to the need for additional infrastructure investment in municipalities across the country, the federal Government of Canada committed substantial funds for infrastructure using a variety of initiatives as outlined below.

Canada Infrastructure Works Program
(CIWP, Phases 1 and 2)

Beginning in 1994 and ending in 1999, the CIWP contribution program involved federal transfers totalling $2.4 billion; the federal share provided up to one-third of the cost of each municipal infrastructure project. The total combined shares of the three levels of government was in excess of $8.3 billion. The program focused on job creation through the transfer of funds that supported thousands of construction projects.

Infrastructure Canada Program (ICP)

The ICP contribution program was introduced in 2000 for local municipal infrastructure projects. The federal government matched the provincial/territorial governments' contributions, providing up to one-third of the cost of each municipal infrastructure project. The $2.05 billion program was in effect until 2010–11.

Canada Strategic Infrastructure Fund (CSIF)

With a total of $4.3 billion starting in 2003–04 and an expected ending in 2018–19, the CSIF is a cost-shared contribution program for strategic infrastructure projects.

Municipal Rural Infrastructure Fund (MRIF)

The Municipal Rural Infrastructure Fund was allocated $1 billion as part of a "$3-billion federal investment over 10 years in strategic and municipal infrastructure." While 20 per cent of the $2 billion in funding for the CSIF from Budget 2003 was already targeted for projects that benefited communities of fewer than 250,000 people, the Chrétien government recognized the political benefits of providing more funding for smaller communities coast to coast. The Harper Conservatives were cognizant of these benefits as well, providing new funding in Budget 2006 that included an additional $2.2 billion over five years for the Municipal Rural Infrastructure Fund.

Public Transit Fund

Budget 2005 established the Public Transit Fund (PTF) as a new $800 million infrastructure program (although the funding was subsequently reduced to $400 million by the Harper Conservatives in Budget 2006.)

Public Transit Capital Trust

While cutting in half the $800 million in funding for the Public Transit Fund provided under the previous Liberal/NDP Budget, in Budget 2006 the Harper Conservatives introduced a new instrument for transferring federal funding for transit as well as four other "short-term pressures." Rather than creating a new program or adding funds to an existing program, the Budget provided $900 million in "one-time additional funding" for transit as part of an envelope of funding for the provinces and territories that was described as a measure that focused on "Restoring Fiscal Balance in Canada." The combined $1.3 billion in funding for transit aimed to "strengthen and expand Canada's public transit systems from coast to coast to coast" (Finance Canada 2006a).

Building Canada Plan

The Building Canada Plan was launched in 2007 as a $33 billion, seven-year plan to support projects that contribute to cleaner air and water, safer roads, shorter commutes, and better communities. It was comprised of the following initiatives:

- Gas Tax Fund: provided $11.8 billion over seven years to municipalities.
- Municipal Goods and Services Tax (GST) Rebate: a 100 per cent rebate of the GST paid by municipalities, which amounted to $5.8 billion over seven years.
- Building Canada Fund: consists of two components:
  - Major Infrastructure Component: $6.8 billion for larger, strategic projects of national and regional significance; and
  - Communities Component: $1 billion for projects in communities with populations of fewer than 100,000 (a $500 million top-up was provided in 2009).
- Public-Private Partnerships Fund: $1.25 billion to support the development of public-private partnerships (P3s) by PPP Canada.

- Gateways and Border Crossings Fund: $2.1 billion to enhance infrastructure at major border crossings between Canada and the United States.
- Asia-Pacific Gateway and Corridor Initiative: $1 billion for strategic transportation infrastructure projects across Western Canada.
- Provincial-Territorial Base Fund: provides each province and territory with $25 million per year over seven years (2007 to 2014) for a total of $175 million per jurisdiction, or $2.275 billion in total.

Additional Infrastructure Funds

Subsequent to the Building Canada Plan, several other infrastructure funds were announced:

- Infrastructure Stimulus Fund: $4 billion announced in January 2009 as part of Canada's Economic Action Plan. It supported over 4,000 projects as a short-term boost to the Canadian economy during a period of recession.
- G8 Legacy Fund: $50 million for infrastructure that supported the G8 Summit in June 2010 in Huntsville, Ontario.
- Green Infrastructure Fund: $1 billion, launched in 2009, for infrastructure projects that improve the quality of the environment and lead to a more sustainable economy over the long term.

New Building Canada Plan

Announced in Budget 2013, the New Building Canada Plan allocates $53 billion over ten years for provincial, territorial, and municipal infrastructure. It combines the following initiatives:

- New Building Canada Fund: consists of two components:
  - *National Infrastructure Component*: $4 billion for projects of national significance.
  - *Provincial-Territorial Infrastructure Component*: $10 billion for two sub-components:
    - *National and Regional Projects*: $9 billion for projects prioritized by provinces and territories; and
    - *Small Communities Fund*: $1 billion for projects in municipalities with fewer than 100,000 residents.

- Community Investment Fund: consists of the renewed and indexed Gas Tax Fund and the incremental Goods and Services Tax Rebate for Municipalities, which together would provide over $32 billion over 10 years to municipalities.
- PPP Canada Fund: an additional $1.25 billion to the fund managed by PPP Canada for P3 projects.
- Other: $6 billion in funding for existing and ongoing legacy infrastructure programs, including the National Recreational Trails Program, the Canada Strategic Infrastructure Fund, the Border Infrastructure Fund and the Green Infrastructure Fund.

Budget 2016

In Budget 2016, the federal government committed to investing $120 billion over ten years in infrastructure. The government's infrastructure plan will be implemented in two phases. Phase I of the infrastructure plan proposes to spend a total of $11.9 billion over five years, beginning in 2016–17, to address immediate infrastructure needs, including:

- $3.4 billion over three years to upgrade and improve public transit systems;
- $5 billion over five years for investments in water, wastewater projects, and green infrastructure projects; and
- $3.4 billion over five years for social infrastructure initiatives, which includes:
  - $1.219 billion for investments in First Nations, Inuit, and Northern communities;
  - $342 million for cultural and recreational infrastructure;
  - $400 million for early learning and child care; and
  - $1.481 billion for affordable housing.

The government also plans to spend $3.4 billion over five years to maintain and upgrade federal infrastructure assets, such as national parks, small craft harbours, federal airports, and border infrastructure, as well as to clean up contaminated sites

Fall Economic Statement 2016

The government provided more detail for phase II of its infrastructure plan in its *Fall Economic Statement 2016*. It committed to spending $81 billion over eleven years, as follows:

- $25.3 billion for public transit;
- $21.9 billion for green infrastructure;
- $21.9 billion for social infrastructure;
- $10.1 billion in trade and transportation projects; and
- $2 billion in infrastructure in rural and Northern communities.

Additionally, the government will create an infrastructure bank to provide loans, loan guarantees, and equity investments in infrastructure.[9]

Second Trudeau Administration (2020)

Under the second Trudeau administration, the Liberals intend to focus on investments in infrastructure that support the implementation of the $187 billion *Investing in Canada Infrastructure Plan (ICIP)*: public transit, green infrastructure, and social infrastructure, as well as key strategic infrastructure that will increase trade. The Mandate Letter of the Minister of Infrastructure and Communities states that "the key objectives of this plan are increasing economic growth and creating good middle class jobs with infrastructure that improves people's quality of life." The funding will be delivered over twelve years by fourteen federal departments and agencies including the Canada Infrastructure Bank, CMHC, Canada Heritage, Crown Indigenous Affairs and Northern Affairs, and Employment and Social Development Canada. This funding is intended for key infrastructure such as public transit systems, clean water and wastewater systems, and social infrastructure such as affordable housing. Over the next decade the plan will support five priority areas: public transit, green, social, trade and transportation, and rural and Northern communities' infrastructure, and focuses on large-scale transformational projects.

To be eligible for the funding, provinces and territories are required to identify and approve all of their long-term infrastructure priorities by 2021 according to the signed bilateral agreements. Funds that are not designated for specific approved projects by the end of 2021 will be reinvested directly in communities through a top-up of the federal Gas Tax Fund.

NOTES

1 Includes contributions, a conditional transfer whereby specific terms and conditions must be met or carried out by a recipient before costs are reimbursed and grants, an unconditional transfer payment where eligibility

criteria and applications received in advance of payment sufficiently assure that the payment objectives will be met.

2 The Canadian government was a latecomer to the practice of levying income taxes. Like in the US, the need to levy these taxes was driven by the need to pay for the costs of war. Federal income tax in Canada started in 1917 to pay for World War I. Congress imposed the first US federal income tax in 1862 to finance the Union's waging of the Civil War.

3 There were a series of Wartime Tax Rental Agreements: 1941–1947, 1947–1952, 1952–1957, and 1957–1962. For an overview of the terms of the agreements, see R.M. Burns, *The Acceptable Mean: The Tax Rental Agreements. 1941–62* (Toronto: Canadian Tax Foundation, 1980).

4 Through a revenue-sharing agreement, Manitoba transfers a portion of the revenues from provincial-levied personal and corporate income taxes to its municipalities as unconditional per capita grants (2 per cent and 1 per cent respectively). While Manitoba is the only jurisdiction in the country to share its revenues from income tax, the arrangement neverthe-less is a "transfer" of revenues rather than a permanent sharing of tax points that would permit municipalities to levy their own income taxes. For details on the Manitoba arrangement, see http://www.gov.mb.ca/chc/press/top/2005/07/2005–07–27–02.html.

5 See Kitchen (2004), "Financing Local Government Capital Investment."

6 Some examples of the complexities involved in the administration of municipal income tax include its structure, the rate, exemptions and deductions and who should pay (residents and non–residents).

7 For details on the history of the *Act* see the Research Note "Canada's Municipal Development And Loan Fund (1963–1966)," prepared by Infrastructure Canada in November 2003. Available at http://www.infrastructure.gc.ca/research–recherche/result/alt_formats/pdf/rn03_e.pdf.

8 Canada Infrastructure Bank Act, SC 2017, c. 20, s.403. Assented to 22 June 2017.

9 *Report of the Standing Senate Committee on National Finance*, February 2017 (amended with supplemental data).

6

The Transport Infrastructure Policy
and Governance Regime

INTRODUCTION

Our third regime analysis deals with transport infrastructure policy and governance. Not surprisingly, transport infrastructure has already featured illustratively in chapters 1, 2, and 3. The specific transport infrastructure policy and governance regime explored in more depth in this chapter builds more explicitly on the observed reality of global transport infrastructures to deal with change and inertia (Van Wee, Annema, and Banister 2013; Stopher and Stanley 2014). The chapter begins with, and is centred on, three infrastructure policy and governance histories, namely those dealing with: 1) transportation infrastructure in freight-rail and trade-related supply chains (1990s to present); 2) transport infrastructure in Canada's many Norths (1970 to present); and 3) transit infrastructure in cities (early 1990s to present).

Each brief history necessarily also deals with different spatial/geographic realities about Canada as a massive coast-to-coast-to-coast country; each thus features different initial modes of transport infrastructure, and though this quickly becomes multi-modal and inter-modal in nature, it does so in different ways and with changing and widely diverse population imperatives. The first history centres initially on the mainly east-west freight-rail mode in southern Canada, but with increasingly lengthened supply chains that are international and propelled by liberalized markets and free trade. The second history is centred on the vast and thinly populated spatial realms of Canada's many Norths as governed by a complex web including the three territorial governments, the federal government, the norths of each province, and small and often isolated communities in the more southern provincial "north" and the high north. The third history covers transit in cities, where the spatial imperatives are much smaller and more compact compared to the first two, but still vary widely with respect to size, population mobility, and congestion. While the biggest cities are getting bigger, smaller cities are getting smaller; but together they are the centres where almost three-quarters of Canadians now commute, live, and work. Issues also emerge regarding what constitutes "rural" development and inadequacy in the context of major trends and challenges such as aging populations, changing mobility needs, aging infrastructure, and a shrinking tax base (see more below).

We then provide an analysis across the three transport infrastructure policy and governance histories deploying the three elements in our analytical framework: ideas, discourse, and agendas; power structures, democracy, and governance; and temporal realities, cycles, conflicts, and technology. Conclusions then follow.

THREE TRANSPORT INFRASTRUCTURE POLICY AND GOVERNANCE REGIME HISTORIES

1 Transportation Infrastructure in Rail Freight Trade-Related Supply Chains, 1990s to present

As an infrastructure policy and governance analysis, transportation infrastructure in our first history relates initially to infrastructure *in motion*, in this case products being shipped mainly by CP and CN as Canada's current freight rail market duopoly. But earlier in Canadian history it was CP as rail transport that led to the settlement of the Canadian West and CN that later anchored transport and settlement in Eastern Canada (Murray 2011; Langford 1976; Gwyn 2011). In the period from the 1990s to the present, we look at *fixed* infrastructure owned and operated by CP and CN and by some shippers (Doern, Coleman, and Prentice 2019; Doern 2015; Coleman and Doern 2014). There is also rail freight infrastructure cast as forms of *surge capacity* or *smaller capacity* or just *capacity* related to the extra rail freight rolling stock provided by CP and CN.

Canada's fifty private *short-track railways* also deal with supply and capacity challenges (Cairns 2015, 7). For example, the Canadian Association of Railway Suppliers (2017) notes that "the current freight car loading standard for the North American railway industry is

286,000 lbs. The short-line infrastructure cannot handle these loads and are unable to privately fund the upgrade on their own as their profit margins are limited" (1). One such short-line railway company featured in the 2013 Lac-Mégantic disaster in Quebec (see more below). In this policy history, we focus first on infrastructure per se, but as expressed with diverse discourse by analysts and the freight rail-shipper industry. The analytical journey, roughly from the 1990s to the present, is also necessarily bound up in complex rail-shipper relations as well as with shippers and their customers seeking delivery of their products and goods.

The service problems identified by shippers are usually not network-based (Canada 2011). In fact, as Coleman (2015) shows, the two are interconnected. Whenever freight cars are picked up or delivered at customers' sites, they enter or leave the main-line network. The full effects of this intermixing of traffic are not very well understood outside the railways themselves. Most shippers have little or no interest in or concern about the specifics of "network operation," or the train on which their traffic is carried (Coleman and Doern 2014; 2015).

Infrastructure in motion refers in this policy and governance history first to freight rail trains moving on fixed tracks, shipping and delivering goods. Historically, this relates to the railways, and the building of Canada and the east-west trade within its borders. This history is also linked to Canada-US development and rail in cross-border trade, and the development of common carrier protections and obligations to ensure fairness and to deal with abusive railway monopoly power. In this infrastructure policy and governance history, the focus, especially in the last twenty years, is on how this historical system has been transformed into a Model 21 system by the two main railways' pursuit of a transformative system optimization strategy (Coleman 2015; see more below).

Surge capacity infrastructure refers to transportation assets that are needed to handle unexpected sharp up swings in various kinds of traffic, or possibly to deal with individual shippers whose needs are different, or who are unable or unwilling to provide their own infrastructure for such surges, partly because of the costs (Coleman and Doern 2015). Under Model 21, railways try to keep just enough extra capacity to handle random events, and to cope with upswings in traffic, but some of these may be seen or defined as surges, with smaller infrastructure capacity implications/needs. If a railway tries to handle the full amount of a surge on its existing network, harmful and avoidable congestion occurs (Coleman 2015). Among shipper interests, there are some who believe that the railways should pay for all or some of this infrastructure.

The first of the above infrastructure types, infrastructure in motion, is the most pivotal and has direct impacts on the second and third. The two main railways' concept of optimization is "now based on what used to be counter-intuitive principles of lean production, as manifested in certain things like removing locomotives and especially freight cars from the network to drive out (and prevent) congestion, especially in classification yards. The concept also includes driving relentlessly to keep the freight cars moving to destination and back for reloading faster and faster" (Coleman 2015, 2). Optimization logics and logistics now involve striving for *uniformity* and *consistency* in everything railways do, especially regarding traffic movements. Coleman also makes clear that "the way Model 21 was introduced was an exercise of raw monopoly power" (8) but he also argues that "it is wiser to provide strong incentives to good-faith negotiating and respond to abuses of market power when it occurs, than to intervene directly in the decisions made by railway traffic managers" (8).

The reality of *just-in-time production*, and the growth in the length and complexity of supply chains, which depend on clockwork deliveries and un-congested handling of cargo at ports and elsewhere, is also a part of this optimization business and infrastructure dynamic. The supply chain as a conceptual and practical idea emerged in the early 1980s. As previewed in chapter 1, it captures the idea of a system of companies, organizations, logistics, information, and expertise involved in moving and transforming resources, products, and services and delivering them to end-customers and users domestically and internationally, increasingly in the context of liberalized trade and trade agreements (Baldwin 2012; Council of Supply Chain Management Professionals 2015; Wieland and Handfield 2013). Since the advent of containerization infrastructure and the opening of Asian markets, supply chains have grown in length and complexity worldwide. Increasingly, many supply chains do not end in the same country in which they start.

This is our initial core focus on infrastructure in motion. To deal with it accurately, however, we need to look briefly at the presence of several connected transport policy and related infrastructure dynamics (Doern 2015). These include: freight rail being subject to *common carrier law and "required service levels"* as a replacement for historic common carrier ideas; *rail-shipper disputes* in Canada and the role of the Canadian Transportation Agency (CTA) as a private dispute arbitrator; and the infrastructure dynamics when transportation movement is necessarily slowed or stopped because of rail safety laws, including provisions dealing with the shipment of dangerous goods. Each of the three overall types of freight infrastructure play out differently in these contexts.

COMMON CARRIER POLICY VERSUS REQUIRED SERVICE
LEVELS AND FIXED INFRASTRUCTURE IMPLICATIONS
In the US, "common carriage" as a concept and provision had its roots in two different sources of law: the law of bailment "under which carriers were responsible for goods that they carried, and the law of franchise and monopoly, under which companies allowed by the state to provide general transport (and later communications networks) were required not to discriminate and to serve each customer equally" (Crawford 2010, 878). Cramer's historical account of North American freight rail is also of particular interest here (Cramer 2007). He shows how railways "were crucial to the integration of national territories from the mid-1850s through the 1920s" and how common carrier policy was forged to deal with early abuses by railways. He also traces how a dramatic shift began in the 1970s "as three prongs of economic liberalization were implemented: deregulation of the industry, privatization of state owned firms, and liberalization of controls in foreign investment" (1), albeit in different ways in the US, Canada, and Mexico (the three NAFTA countries). And these are ultimately drivers of the development of supply chains.

Currently, in its provisions on rail transport, the *Canadian Transportation Act* refers not to the common carrier principle *per se* but, in section 113, to provisions regarding "level of services" as follows:

113. (1) A railway company shall, according to its powers, in respect of a railway owned or operated by it,
(*a*) furnish, at the point of origin, at the point of junction of the railway with another railway, and at all points of stopping established for that purpose, adequate and suitable accommodation for the receiving and loading of all traffic offered for carriage on the railway;
(*b*) furnish adequate and suitable accommodation for the carriage, unloading and delivering of the traffic;

(c) without delay, and with due care and diligence, receive, carry and deliver the traffic;

(d) furnish and use all proper appliances, accommodation and means necessary for receiving, loading, carrying, unloading and delivering the traffic; and

(e) furnish any other service incidental to transportation that is customary or usual in connection with the business of a railway company.

(2) Traffic must be taken, carried to and from, and delivered at the points referred to in paragraph (1) (a) on the payment of the lawfully payable rate.

(3) Where a shipper provides rolling stock for the carriage by the railway company of the shipper's traffic, the company shall, at the request of the shipper, establish specific reasonable compensation to the shipper in a tariff for the provision of the rolling stock.

(4) A shipper and a railway company may, by means of a confidential contract or other written agreement, agree on the manner in which the obligations under this section are to be fulfilled by the company.

The items in section 113.1 above could easily be forms of fixed infrastructure provision, and section 113.3 could be a form of surge infrastructure capacity (small surges probably but possibly large as well). Qualifier words, however, such as "adequate and suitable," "customary or usual," and "reasonable compensation," are important because they are features of service provision that easily invite differences of view and interpretation, challenges, and disputes in negotiations between shippers and railways. The stated *levels-of-service provisions* are very public in the statute but very private in commercial cases involving railways and shippers most of the time (Doern 2015). Items 1(a) and (b) are actually or potentially infrastructure issues that seemingly are the railway's responsibility but with shippers apparently having no such obligations as an efficient business functioning in a modern rail network. That means, for example, that shippers seem to bear no responsibility in the eyes of the law for furnishing adequate infrastructure to load and unload rail cars at specific juncture points.

Coleman's definitive detailed analysis of the core Model 21 system identifies several infrastructure-like features, but none of them are directly called infrastructure. Instead, Coleman refers to the concept of "buffers," notions of "capacity," and also, because of modern technologies, "synchronized handoffs" (3, 7, 110) to capture key possible juncture points in a system that is driven ever more by optimized motion to minimize and avoid congestion in complicated just-in-time supply chains. Heaver (2009) had earlier highlighted the widened application of "interswitching" and also the greater role of information and computer systems linked to logistics.

The Coleman and Doern (2015) analysis of the common carrier principle concludes:

> The principle appears to have negative effects, now that railways sometimes operate at capacity on at least some parts of their networks. To avoid congestion, railways must ration their services at least some of the time. That contravenes the common carrier principle.
>
> Another way railways avoid congestion is by planning their capacity and their operations based on forecasts of traffic. But some shippers interpret common-carrier provisions in the law as giving them a dispensation for not providing railways any forecasts at all. This complicates the planning and management of the rail system, with negative consequences for everyone who uses the rail system or depends on its performance. (19)

Many of these kinds of arts of judgment and discretion in relation to the content of actual service agreements and how they are negotiated were also highlighted in the Dinning Report (Dinning 2012, see pages iv, v, 11, 14, and 26). However, the Dinning Report was not very specific about rail freight–supply chain infrastructures in the triple sense being probed and highlighted here.

The difficulty of this task, and the fact it was not resolved particularly well in the Dinning process, therefore signifies that the common carrier idea is now simply a residual unmentioned concept, and that service levels are used to define something that is no longer mentioned as a principle. It makes little practical sense unless all parties recognize publically, to a much greater extent, that the new North American model of system interrelationships among capacity, congestion, system optimization, and levels of service is the overriding feature of Canadian freight rail transportation. And crucially, it makes little sense that dispute mediation and resolution is a private confidential process (see more below) when it should be an open and accountable system of administrative justice (Doern 2015).

Two rail-shipper disputes and decisions are significant in that they each led to legislative change: Bill C-52, *The Fair Rail Freight Service Act*, and Bill C-30, the *Fair Rail for Grain Farmers Act* (Coleman and Doern 2015, 12–14). The first dispute event and process centred on Bill C-52, the *Fair Rail Freight Service Act*. It arose from shipper complaints and contained two main features: mandatory service agreements if a shipper asks for them, and third-party arbitration if a shipper insists on it. Neither shippers nor railways claimed to be particularly satisfied with the legislation. It has left room for abuse because the *Act* has loopholes such as that arbitrators are obliged to take into account the effect of a decision on other users of the rail network.

The Canadian Transportation Agency does not allow external arbitrators to talk to each other, or to talk to staff in the Agency (apart from administrative matters on the case). So, when it comes to understanding the effect of their individual decisions, they have no one to fall back on but themselves regarding knowledge of the dynamics of how railways operate (Coleman 2015). Government regulation contributes to the failure because it empowers a party, the CTA, to instruct railways to add traffic to their networks – at times, and over corridors, where the railway may well be rationing its services to avoid congestion. But the CTA does not know about the susceptibility of the network to congestion and it is likely to misjudge situations (Doern, Coleman, and Prentice 2019; Coleman 2015). But for our purposes in the context of this chapter it is also true that particular rail-shipper agreements which are not made public may involve agreed fixed infrastructure measures available for some shippers but not for others in similar situations.

The second dispute, centred on Bill C-30, the *Fair Rail for Grain Farmers Act,* was the result of actions by the Western grain industry seeking to ship one of the largest grain harvests in history. The legislation agreed to by the Harper Conservative government in 2015 obliged the railways to double their weekly grain movements, or in essence to provide *surge capacity infrastructure.* The tonnage was subject to revision by Cabinet on advice from the Canadian Transportation Agency. The *Act* has ancillary provisions giving every railway access to business in certain regions from shippers on any competing railway's tracks up to 160 km away; and making railways liable to pay penalties for breaching the terms of a service agreement without the complainant having to make their case in a commercial court.

Aspects of these Harper-era challenges in infrastructure terms remain in the Justin Trudeau Liberal plans and policies under the *Transportation Modernization Act* (Bill C-49) being debated in Parliament where the Senate and its Standing Committee on Transport and Communications report re-raised many of the same Harper-era issues under the guise of Liberal government policy and restated shipper and air industry protests (Standing Senate Committee on Transport and Communications 2018; Tomesco 2018).

SHORT-LINE FREIGHT RAIL, SURGE CAPACITY, RAIL SAFETY, AND THE LAC-MÉGANTIC DISASTER

While the focus thus far has been on the two big rail freight companies as an oligopoly and their shipper relations, other forms of rail capacity are also found in the role of smaller short-line rail firms, in this case with a different dynamic for surge infrastructure capacity. This dynamic was graphically demonstrated in a July 2013 runaway train disaster in Lac-Mégantic, Quebec, in which forty-seven persons were killed by an out-of-control train carrying a shipment of oil in seventy-two tanker cars. The resulting derailment, explosions, and fire also destroyed the town centre and therefore its critical infrastructure (Bishop 2013; Mackrael 2013).

The short line rail company involved was the Montreal, Marine & Atlantic Railway (MM&A). Investigations showed that the MM&A train was carrying 7.7 million litres of petroleum crude oil in seventy-two Class 111 tank cars (Transportation Safety Board of Canada 2016). The federal safety board's review examined: fire in the locomotive; the braking force, which included hand brakes plus two types of air brakes (automatic and independent brakes); the Class 111 tank cars, manufactured between 1980 and 2012; the safety culture at MM&A; Transport Canada's own monitoring and auditing practices regarding MM&A; the issue of single-person crews; and the inadequate testing, monitoring, and transport of dangerous goods.

Safety actions following the accident included the need for "critical safety information on the securement of unattended trains, [and] the classification of petroleum crude oil, and rail conditions at Lac-Mégantic" (7). Transport Canada introduced an "emergency directive prohibiting trains transporting dangerous goods from operating with single person crews," among other initiatives (7). In 2015, the federal government laid criminal charges against six members of MM&A, under provisions of the *Railway Safety Act* and *Fisheries Act* (Atkins and Stevenson 2015, 1). Five years later, on 19 January 2018, "after nine days of deliberations, jurors … acquitted the three former MM&A railway employees" who had been charged with criminal negligence causing death" in the accident (Laframboise and Brunette 2018). The acquittal was supported by many town residents. But those residents, including local businesses, bore the brunt of the massive costs of the accident, and there are still no decisions to rebuild the railway track in a way that bypasses the town.

Also crucial is the way in which the Lac-Mégantic disaster entered the ever-widening Canada-US institutional mix of court processes and decisions, Quebec government actions, and also US bankruptcy law as a weapon of choice to protect MM&A, an American rail company, from accident liabilities (Laframboise and Brunette 2018; Rousseau and Rivest 2018; *CBC News* 2018; *CBC News* 2013). MM&A initiated "proceedings for Chapter 11 bankruptcy protection in a U.S. court while its sister firm in Canada presented a petition in Quebec Superior Court" (*CBC News* 2013, 1). The parent company said that "it has between $50 million and $100 million in estimated assets and between $1 million and $10 million in estimated liabilities" (1). Quebec Justice Martin Castonguay granted an application for bankruptcy protection in Canada for its sister firm in Canada, saying that "this decision is to prevent anarchy," and added that he was not impressed with the railway's application for bankruptcy and believed that the people of the town "have a right to know what is going on" (1). Quebec and town authorities meanwhile "had also sent legal notices to MM&A for almost $8 million in environmental mop-up costs" (1).

The need for better classification of petroleum crude oil was directly linked to the development and use of fracking technology to produce shale oil in the US (Prud'Homme 2014) and the movement of significant volumes of shale crude oil by rail since 2008, including into Canada in the above accident. Cairns (2013) points out that the recent growth in crude oil by rail (rather than pipelines as the normal infrastructure) is due to three factors:

- The rapid development of shale oil – particularly the Bakken formation in North Dakota, which has insufficient feeder pipelines;
- Associated transmission pipeline capacity constraints; and

- The ability of rail to serve many markets across the continent, and to reach underserved markets. (11)

INFRASTRUCTURE DYNAMICS UNDER TRANSPORTATION
SAFETY REGARDING DANGEROUS GOODS

The Lac-Mégantic accident was also about safety regarding dangerous goods, but freight rail as a *moving* and *fixed infrastructure* system is also impacted by dangerous goods policies and regulation and by where enforcement most has to take place, which is on fixed rail infrastructure. Governance is centred in Transport Canada's Transportation of Dangerous Goods Directorate (TDG) (Transport Canada 2016). The report of the Standing Committee on Transport, Infrastructure and Communities (2015) shows how overall Canadian policy on dangerous goods impacts on fixed transport infrastructure in particular. Early in the report the committee noted that, in 2011, the minister of Transport had assured the committee that "99.997% of dangerous goods shipments in Canada arrive safely without any incidents" (2). But the committee itself drew attention to the fact that "over 72% of all reportable dangerous goods accidents across all modes of transport since 2008 happened in *facilities where the goods were prepared for transit*, unloaded or stored (e.g. transload facilities)" (2). It was, in short, at points of fixed infrastructure, which indicated that the goods' final destination was not the key performance indicator. In addition, "at 56%, human error was determined to be the main underlying factor contributing to these accidents followed by equipment problems (34%)" (2). The committee had already reported Transport Canada's data showing that there are 40,000 dangerous goods sites in Canada (1).

Interestingly, the committee report argued that the system "encompasses the entire supply chain for products identified as dangerous goods" including "the producers and consumers of the regulated products, the transportation services and transfer points between them, as well as the organizations that are involved in the production of the standardized means of containment used" (1). *Containment* is also fixed infrastructure. Transport Canada informed the committee "that the department has 35 dangerous goods field inspectors who conduct approximately 3000 inspections of the 40,000 dangerous goods sites across all modes per year" (3).

In freight rail and related supply chain infrastructure terms, there is little doubt that rail freight infrastructure *in motion* has been the dominant type in the overall story conveyed under the logic and logistics of the rail companies' optimization policies/strategies. But in other terms, freight rail fixed infrastructure issues arise both in stated service-level discourse and in unknown ways in rail-shipper agreements and disputes as adjudicated in private by the Canadian Transportation Agency. Infrastructure in motion is also a feature in basic rail safety dynamics and dangerous goods regulation. Surge capacity infrastructure was most evident in the grain dispute and legislation, but it could arise in smaller, more compact contexts as well. In either case there is no doubt that it was pivotal in the short line rail context of the Lac-Mégantic story.

While it is important to tell the transport infrastructure story via rail as *one mode* of transport, it is not possible to ignore the fact that transport is also *multi-modal* as an industry and as competing and linked infrastructures. For example, Canada's airport infrastructures are a complex system of joint public-private major airports and de facto competing US airports that, located near the Canadian border, are key infrastructure that draws Canadian passengers with low fares (Doern, Coleman, and Prentice 2019, chap. 7). In 2018, the growth of a few new Canadian low-cost airlines such as WestJet's offshoot, Swoop, in addition to international European low-fare airlines moving into the Canadian market on key routes, are "giving a boost to secondary airports in Canada" (Marowits 2018) such as Hamilton, Ontario. This is occurring in part because "airlines are attracted to Hamilton due to fees that are 30 to 50 percent lower than [Toronto's] Pearson" (2–3). However, Pearson has chosen to lower its fees considerably to be a location point for this market.

2 Transport Infrastructure in Canada's Many Norths, 1970 to present

The title of this second policy and governance history reveals the task at hand. We need to map, through various studies, what transport infrastructure in the north involves regarding new infrastructure and the repair and upkeep of deteriorating infrastructure. The notion of "many norths" is pivotal in the spatial context of the Canadian north's vast territorial expanse (39.3 per cent of Canada's total land mass) and its small northern populations (in all, 0.3 per cent of Canada's total population). The notion of many norths is also pivotal in terms of governing authorities, including the territorial governments, the north of each of the ten provinces as governed by the provinces, varied rural local governments, and multiple federal government departments. INAC (Indigenous and Northern Affairs Canada), for example, described itself as "one of 34 federal government departments for meeting the Government of Canada's obligations and commitments to First Nations, Inuit and Metis, and for fulfilling the federal government's constitutional responsibilities in the North," which "are largely determined by numerous statutes, negotiated agreements and relevant legal decisions" (Indigenous and Northern Affairs Canada 2017, 1).

It is multi-level government and governance incarnate, even more so than the previous system headed by the former Department of Indian Affairs and Northern Development (DIAND). In addition, as we have seen in chapter 3's discussion of the high Arctic, it also includes international governance dimensions vis-à-vis the United States and other northern democratic countries within and outside of the Arctic Council. We begin this policy and governance history by looking first at efforts to describe and assess northern transport infrastructure per se, before returning to the above-mentioned 'many Norths' governance imperative.

A study report by the governments of the Yukon, Northwest Territories, and Nunavut (2008) is probably still the most complete single mapping of transport infrastructure in the territorial North covering each mode (roads, airports, marine, and rail), in addition to other details of what infrastructure actually is or ought to be. The report followed and was designed to complement an earlier study by the Council of the Federation (2005), but such strategies that are pan-provincial and national were immediately stated by the three territorial governments to be insufficient because they "must account for northern needs and priorities, which would be largely overlooked using nation-wide criteria only" (Yukon, Northwest Territories, and Nunavut 2008, 3). The report by the three territorial governments stresses from the outset the fundamental reality that the territorial North "comprises 40 percent of Canada's land mass, contains two-thirds of Canada's marine coastline, shares 14 percent of the US/Canada border and interfaces with European interests in the Eastern Arctic. Despite this geographic reach, historically there has been limited Canadian political interest in the North" (4).

While there is some greater southern Canadian political-economic and social interest in northern resources and northern communities, the report's lead-off argument is that, "[f]irst and foremost, the north has transportation systems and corridors that are under-developed and, in the case of Nunavut highways non-existent. Where this infrastructure does exist, much of it was built decades ago, well below the standards required for large-scale development. Where infrastructure was originally built to standard, significant rehabilitation is now required" (6). The study early on also stresses that while "the three territories face similar challenges, the mistake should not be made of categorizing Canada's northern territories as one single entity" (8). Pivotally, the descriptive profile of each territory stresses its very small population living and functioning in vast terrains, and these features help in presenting and understanding key specific infrastructure features as well as gaps/weaknesses. For example, within the Yukon's 4,800 kilometres of roads, "250 kilometers are paved and 1900 kilometers surfaced with … a thin asphalt membrane. The remainder is gravel" (8). Nunavut has no road system, and its twenty-six communities each have a small airport, "of which only two have paved runways, with the remainder gravel" (13).

Not surprisingly, the territorial governments as of 2008 advocated greater infrastructure funding, envisaging then a needed $25 billion over ten years. They supported "a special northern component of the then existing Strategic Transportation Infrastructure Fund reflecting unique northern needs – and the strategic importance of northern infrastructure – that will likely be missed using investment criteria of larger southern jurisdictions" (16).

Related further studies emerged, including one by the Northern Development Ministers Forum (2010). It made similar arguments, but in this case the analytical and advocacy scope extended to other related infrastructure needs such as telecommunications. Another 2009 report focused on adapting infrastructure, much of it transport-related, to climate change in northern Canada (National Round Table on the Environment and Economy (2009). A Natural Resources Canada study (Hunter 2013) reported briefly on work lead by NRCan's Climate Change Geoscience Program (CCGP) to help "reduce risk and develop adaption solutions for land-based and coastal transportation infrastructure" (1). It cited, as an example, "a 'winter road' that leads to diamond mines north of Yellowknife. The road is built each winter over permafrost, frozen lakes and land portages and was subject to unseasonably warm temperatures in 2006" leading to "deteriorating road conditions, prompting a premature road closure for trucks hauling fuel and goods to remote camps" (2).

A Canadian Polar Commission (CPC) research review report (2013) focused on research advances and knowledge gaps in northern communications, infrastructure, and transportation systems, again many climate change-related. Some research and advocacy (Prentice 2016; 2010) has also focused on the potential for developing and using transport airships and related logistics for filling some key gaps in the northern transport system and related networks. The potential for airships has been touted, for example, as a possible way to deal with the longstanding "washed out sections of the Hudson Bay Railway to Churchill, Manitoba" (Cash 2017, 1). Churchill's status as a "fly-in" community "puts them in the company of hundreds of other communities in Canada, including several in Manitoba with larger populations" (2). An all-weather road would be possible but expensive. Indeed, the many norths and transport infrastructure dynamics of Churchill as a town and northern Arctic Port, with transport links south into mid-northern parts of Manitoba and with the prairie grain trade, have been the subject of study and controversy for decades (Montsion 2015; Canada and Manitoba 2013; Financial Post 2017).

The Jozic (2006) analysis had summed up northern transportation in 2006 as "snowmobiles, airplanes and the occasional road," with snowmobiles remaining "the most economical to transport people and light loads over the northern snow. Bombardier had been formed and invented technology centred initially on the ski-do [sic] snowmobile vehicle which revolutionized some aspects of northern transport technology and which also in Canada's various norths was adapted, as markets changed, to popular recreational vehicles" (McQuarrie 2016, 1–3).

Also of interest in specific northern air transport infrastructure terms is a Standing Senate Committee on Transport and Communications (2013) report on Canadian air travel growth and competitiveness. Its specific diagnosis and comments focus on "northern and regional air transport infrastructure," defining it as including "airports, terminal buildings and runways, as well as air navigation systems" (5) but also including related infrastructure such as "the roads and rail lines linking airports to the communities they serve" (5). The first priority identified is the "state and availability of runways," most of which are unpaved. Also highlighted is the fact that many are "1200 meters or shorter" due to "geographical constraints," which has become an issue now that "a minimum distance of 1520 meters is required to land the newer generation of small aircraft" (6).

Also brought out in the Committee's research and hearings are infrastructure components such as: the lack of meteorological information; climate change impacts on the softening of the permafrost on which airport runways are built; and the fact that some airports are not equipped with a "modern instrument approach system, making it impossible for aircraft to land there under foggy conditions" (6). Regarding infrastructure funding, the committee drew attention to the inadequacies of funding and to instances where funding criteria were quickly changed such that airports that were too small or too large "are not eligible" (7).

A different but interesting take on northern transport (and related) infrastructure is offered in a University of Calgary study by Sulzenko and Fellows (2016) centred on what they advocate as a "Northern Corridor right-of-way." It would establish "a new multi-modal (road, rail, pipeline, electrical transmission and communication) transportation right-of-way through Canada's north and near north" (1–2). It would "prepare the way for privately funded and economically driven projects to, for example, transport a full range of export commodities efficiently to port facilities on all three coasts, while improving economic development" (1–2). The 7,000-mile corridor would "have room for roads, rail lines, pipelines, and transmission lines, and would interconnect with the existing (southern-focused) transportation network" (1–2). In infrastructure development terms, Sulzenko and Fellows argue that such a corridor concept would create "the environment in which private investment, properly regulated, can be applied to projects without intransigent 'one-off' regulatory processes for a new right of way for each project" (2). In the 2019 federal election campaign, federal Conservative leader Andrew Scheer, as noted in chapter 1, outlined his vision for Canada that included a "National Corridor for Energy, Telecommunications" (Hunt 2019). Consequently, the corridor analysis has key aspects of the infrastructure as *platform* concept, as discussed in chapter 1, but with a different process for each project that may emerge over a longer time period.

Sulzenko and Fellows (2016) believe that the shared transportation right-of-way will enable a system in which "multiple modes of transport can co-locate in order to realize economies of agglomeration," but they also note that such decisions are "in some ways separable from actual infrastructure investment" (2). The bulk of the paper then shows how Canada's north-south export economy has changed in key ways and that the relations between Canada's south and north are more complex to define and envisage in precise ways. But the analysis ends with the useful reminder that various versions of a corridor concept in the past "have been proposed and to some extent implemented" (14). These include the 1950s Roads to Resources program and the late-1960s rail-centred Mid-Canada Corridor (Rohmer 1970).

Further recent evidence and views about infrastructure in the north can be found in the Auditor General of Canada's independent audit on *Civil Aviation Infrastructure in the North – Transport Canada* (Office of the Auditor General 2017). It draws on a series of past reports and studies (some of which we have cited as well), but crucially it involved discussions with a wide variety of stakeholders involved in civil aviation infrastructure in the north, in addition to interviews with Transport Canada officials and stakeholders (18–19).

For audit purposes, remote northern communities were defined as "those communities for which the only reliable year-round mode of transport was by air," with this definition including "many communities in the territories and northern parts of the provinces" (3), comprising 117 airports in total. Covering the audit period from 2013 to 2016, the audit objective "was to determine whether Transport Canada assessed and addressed civil aviation infrastructure needs in Canada's north to ensure a safe and efficient civil aviation system" (18). The OAG concluded that

Transport Canada had the information needed to assess the infrastructure challenges remote northern airports face. However, the Department did not take the lead with others to address these infrastructure challenges. The Department's role in addressing infrastructure needs centred on the Airports Capital Assistance Program which provided funding for safety-related projects at remote northern airports. However, the funding available through the program will not be sufficient to meet remote northern airport needs. (18)

The OAG made two overall recommendations. The first is that "Transport Canada, in collaboration with stakeholders should lead the development of a long-term strategy for northern airport infrastructure" and the second that "Transport Canada should work with stakeholders to determine what sources of funding would meet the infrastructure needs of remote airports" (19–20). The broader issues raised here highlight small rural communities and the important challenges they face such as aging populations, changing mobility needs, aging infrastructure, and the impacts of a shrinking tax base.

As the Trudeau Liberal government began its overall infrastructure policy in 2015, it announced a transportation infrastructure program focused on communities across the Northwest Territories (Canada 2016). The $80.9 million program is jointly funded by the federal government and the Northwest Territories government ($60,675,000 federal money and the rest from the NWT). Its purpose is to "improve accessibility to and from remote communities in the North and to ensure the movement of goods across major trade routes" (1).

While our focus is as much as possible on northern transport infrastructure per se, there is little doubt, as stressed from the outset, that the broader politics and governance of the north is also crucial. Key overall historical analyses (Phillips 1967; Wonders 2003) are replete with the complex and varied stories of how the North, variously defined, was settled and discovered. The north of each province had both separate and linked histories and socio-economic features. The territorial North, as we have seen earlier, has sought to be thought of in ways that are unlikely to be captured by criteria of the more southern parts of the north governed by the provinces and by Ottawa. Hamelin (2003) has written about efforts to "regionalize" the Canadian north in various ways. In the 1950s Ottawa launched the previously mentioned "Roads to Resources" program and related discourse.

Recent prime ministers have all had variously expressed northern visions and selected priorities and funding in relation to them. They each knew Canada's North is vast, and that the various norths separately and in total do not have large populations and therefore do not pay most of Canada's taxes that support spending in national politics. Consequently, there is often rhetorical support for the North but not real or sustained support, and these often-repeated dynamics have led Gilmour (2016) to characterize Canada and support for the North as the "great Canadian lie."

On the other hand, the *Centre for the North* based with the Conference Board of Canada in Ottawa has carried out research and analysis on the North over the five-year period extending until 2015 (Jeffrey et al. 2015). Its report discusses how the North matters to all Canadians and to northerners and in that context goes on to discuss "three starting points" for northern policy-making, namely: northern complexity; dimensions of northern security; and northern community resilience (see chapter 3). This leads to discussion of three priority areas: Aboriginal youth; upgrading northern infrastructure; and good governance to steer growth (see chapter 4).

A related Conference Board of Canada (2017) study focused on the need to rethink infrastructure funding regarding Canada's northern and Aboriginal communities. The highlighted key challenges include "the sheer size and complexity of Northern and Aboriginal infrastructure gaps [that] makes it hard for decision-makers to plan and prioritize," and the fact that "Aboriginal communities and Aboriginal businesses continue to face capacity challenges that diminish their ability to participate in infrastructure development and management" (7). In addition, and in relation to the life cycles of infrastructure development, the study concluded that program "funding levels are inadequate for closing the infrastructure gaps" (7).

The various notions of corridors and Indigenous populations will also be impacted by how resource company projects and developments are reviewed under Liberal government policies revealed/previewed in a discussion paper on *Environmental and Regulatory Reviews* in June 2017 (Canada 2017). The report's themes were partly a strong reaction against Harper-era efforts to favour and speed up resource project approvals, as already discussed in chapter 1. The Liberal proposal says that through its new proposals "it is committed to deliver environmental assessment and regulatory processes that regain public trust, protect the environment, introduce modern safeguards, advance reconciliation with Indigenous peoples, ensure good projects go ahead, and resources get to market" (Canada 2017, 3).

As we have seen in chapter 3, in 2019 then Minister of Foreign Affairs Chrystia Freeland set out new policies and strategies to defining Arctic leadership to secure legal "international recognition of the outer limits of Canada's continental shelf in the Arctic Ocean" (Global Affairs Canada 2019, 1). These measures were deemed crucial given both the US's and China's power and ambitions vis-à-vis each other to transport and move through the melting Arctic year-round, and also to recast the nature and role of the Arctic Council. Other analysis by Levinson-King (2019) also showed how there was a "superpower fight for internet near the Arctic" with involvement by the Chinese firm Huawei. This analysis cited Canadian data about satellite-dependent communities, which included 5.4 million people, or 15 per cent of the Canadian population, in the high and low North of Canada who, in short, did not have "high-speed internet" (2).

This policy and governance history reveals multiple and very real examples of what northern transport infrastructure is in very specific and vast spatial contexts and situations, and also reveals needs for new infrastructure and for infrastructure repair. We have stressed the number of governance levels and players in the various norths. The studies we have drawn on come from a variety of particular federal and other bodies, but each enters the debate from specific and definitional starting points rather than from overall views. We have seen the presence of particular northern transportation infrastructure funds, but we also know that the funds are not even close to adequate, and those that are available are subject to the classic distributional politics already seen in previous chapters.

3 Transit Infrastructure in Cities, early 1990s to Present

As in the first two transport infrastructure policy and governance histories in this regime chapter, we will first characterize what "transit infrastructure" is variously defined to include. We then look at its overall evolution over the last three decades in relation to municipal and city development in Canada. This is followed by a brief look at two sample cities: first, Canada's largest and fastest-growing city, Toronto, and second, Winnipeg as a mid-sized city. We then gradually build in the impact on these two sample cities of more recent transit infrastructure policy and funding initiatives of the federal government under the Trudeau Liberals aimed at city transit but with projects selected and developed through processes involving both the provinces and their cities/municipalities and the federal government.

The 2016 and 2017 federal Liberal government infrastructure plan was cast as a *Transformational Infrastructure Plan* (Canada 2017). Promised overall was a public transit investment of $25.3 billion over eleven years. Its stated intent was to have a "greater focus on new, transformative construction and expansion projects that build the new urban transit networks and service extensions that will transform the way that Canadians live, move and work" (1). Other infrastructure plans and projects may also impact on transit (Canadian Urban Transit Association 2017), and as we see further below. It must also be noted that the federal budget of 2016 had a smaller initial $3.4 billion funded through a Public Transit Infrastructure Fund (Infrastructure Canada 2017a).

Table 6.1
Pan-Canadian city network features, 2013

Transit authorities	37
Serviced population of transit authorities	17.2 million
Per cent of Canada's population served by transit	67 per cent
Total ridership of transit authorities	1.84 billion
Per cent of Canada's transit ridership	88 per cent
Total vehicles	15,666
Estimated per cent of Canada's total transit vehicles	82 per cent
Total technology assets	9,898
Total assets (non-linear)	142,380
Total fixed assets (linear)	4,206

The *definitional scope* for transit infrastructure is broad because the transit assets involved, mainly municipally owned, include: "buses, streetcars, ferries, heavy railcars; light railcars, mobile technology, security systems, rail signal systems, terminals, transit shelters, tunnels, exclusive rights-of-way, tracks, parking facilities and service facilities" (Canadian Infrastructure Report Card 2016, 127). We have already provided, in chapter 1, the core dynamics of the Report Card 2016 study. The Canadian Urban Transit Association (CUTA) had been a key player and was given its own "sector analysis" position in the report (126–40). The above study's summary (130) of the pan-Canadian city network features is shown in table 6.1.

The report's transit summary is also useful regarding some of its overall ratings and conclusions. For example, it concludes that the "physical condition of transit assets is Good; adequate for now: in acceptable condition" (127). The survey asked respondents "to provide data on the replacement value of assets and the annual renewal budget, which is how the report derives reinvestment rates. However, very few were able to provide both" (127). Regarding the assessment overall, the study concludes that the physical condition "of transit assets in large and medium-sized transit authorities was good: adequate for now. In small transit authorities, the condition rating was fair: requires attention" (128). Such an assessment could be taken as further evidence that important, transit-related, rural challenges continue to be overlooked, including aging populations, changing mobility needs, and a shrinking tax base. A further complicating trend is that "villages" find themselves increasingly located within expanding networks of urban and suburban growth as many become "bedroom communities" with changing transportation needs. The above CUTA study also triggers such concerns, given the different and growing types of detailed and integrated operational infrastructure that this necessitates.

The report also sought information from transit authorities regarding the extent and nature of the "*asset management*" approaches/practices they had regarding the various *asset sectors* such as vehicles, technology inventory, and fixed asset inventory both non-linear and linear (131). Not surprisingly, there were divergent practices/performance, such as 6 per cent indicating that "climate change adaptation strategies" were evident. Overall, however, 71 per cent "used asset management systems for transit assets" (131), albeit with diverse percentages for particular asset types.

Slack and Bird (2018) focus on a particular transit subset, namely regional public transit in Ontario and its financing. They contrast how it is financed with how it ought to be financed. Among their concerns is the need for a system that delivers both new and replacement investment. Linkages between expenditures and revenues and decision-making are stressed. The issue of who can and should pay is crucial, and they use rapid transit in the Toronto region as a pivotal example. They argue for the greater deployment of user charges but see little prospect of them at present, linked overall to weaknesses in the formation and deployment of regional government.

Transit in cities is impacted by findings in the Canadian 2016 census, released early in 2017. The headline summary is "big cities getting bigger and smaller cities getting smaller" (Press 2017, 1). Toronto, Montreal, and Vancouver "are now home to more than one third of Canadians with a combined population of 12.5 million," half in the greater Toronto area. Calgary and Edmonton "were the fastest growing cities between 2011 and 2016" (1).

A Pembina Institute (2014) study focuses on rapid transit defined as "rapid and express and transit infrastructure – transit systems that are capable of moving riders quickly, frequently and reliably" – but the study immediately cautions that "this distinction between rapid, express and other forms of transit is not always clear, and it has become increasingly blurred in recent years as new technologies and hybrid systems have proliferated" (3). Focusing on Toronto, Calgary,

Vancouver, Ottawa, and Montreal, the factors examined include "the length of rapid transit networks – that is, subways, SkyTrains, light rail, right-of-way streetcars and right-of-way rapid buses – along with express bus networks" (1). The study also examined "ridership levels and the proximity of each city's population to transit stations or stops" (1). Its highlighted five key finds are that: 1) Toronto has the highest rapid transit ridership per capita; 2) Calgary leads Canada's cities in rapid transit infrastructure per capita; 3) Vancouver has built the most rapid transit over the last twenty years; 4) over the past decade, Calgary and Vancouver have built the most transit; and 5) Montreal leads the way in access to rapid transit (1). We now look briefly at the Toronto and Winnipeg situations, starting in each sample city with initial transit infrastructure fund allocations and then necessarily viewing them in the larger context of transit and overall city transport infrastructure governance.

TORONTO

The distribution of federal transit infrastructure funds to Toronto following a federal government-Ontario 2016 agreement on a $1.49 billion transit funding program saw 61 different projects with the Toronto Transit Commission (*CBC News* 2016). These involve infrastructure projects such as bridges/structures maintenance, a subway escalator overhaul program, and Union Station. The costs of these projects ranged widely, with several in the $5 to $6 million range, but with others, such as a skylight replacement program, costing $85,000 (1–2).

The Toronto Transit Commission (TTC) anchors the city's transit operations and evolution (Transit Toronto 2015). Its history in the 1970s and 1980s has been described as a period of growth and success, but during the 1990s "it fell on hard times," in part due to "political foot-dragging" that "slowed subway development to a crawl, and budget cuts, the recession, and the inability to service the rapidly growing areas outside Metro Toronto cut ridership by almost 20 percent" (3). Some of these problems were partly dealt with as the twenty-first century began, but new ones arose and government restructuring occurred as Toronto-area amalgamations transformed the city into the Greater Toronto Area (GTA). Again, this impacted on the adequacy of its transit and related governance, with financing never matching urban ambitions on infrastructure and other matters (Galvin 2012).

There are any number of conflicts and funding and shared funding constraints as new transit initiatives are announced but run into intra-GTA disputes. One example is the case of Bombardier's long "delayed streetcar deliveries" (Spurr et al. 2017). The TTC's $1 billion contract with Bombardier is for 204 low-floor Flexity streetcars to be delivered in 2019. By May 2015, only 35 had been received, and thus "almost eight years into the deal, Bombardier has repeatedly failed to meet its delivery deadlines, demonstrated quality-control problems that have dragged on for years and promised that improvements that would double or triple the speed of delivery were around the corner" (1). The delays have also forced the TTC to pay extra to keep its existing fleet in operation (8–9).

Another example among many is the 2016 decision of the Toronto City Council to proceed "with the Bloor-Danforth (subway) line extension to the Scarborough Town Centre" (James 2017). James's analysis centres on mayors in the politics of transit planning, and he argues that instead "of going where the evidence takes him or her, our mayors declare a position on the campaign trail, get elected, claim the mandate of the electorate, marshal the city's compliant bureaucrats, commission studies that support the prevailing position, ignore evidence to the contrary" (2). He argues that this kind of transit planning "has been trending this way for decades" but "is particularly galling now … because the region is on the cusp of a grand transit expansion and massive expenditure. And we are deliberately making critical and costly 'mistakes' that will bedevil commuters for generations" (2). The availability of new funds has indeed upped the ante for the politics of the federal-provincial-city nexus as well. Mayor John Tory has directly lobbied the federal government to put pressure on the Ontario government to ensure that appropriate funds are provided (Ballingall 2017; Ivison 2017; Selley 2017).

In addition to the above types of complex GTA multi-level governance transit sagas, there is also overall regional governance overlap regarding Metrolinx, the Ontario government agency created in 2006 "to improve the coordination and integration of modes of transport in the Greater Toronto and Hamilton Area," whose stated mission is to "champion and deliver mobility solutions which connect people, places and communities throughout our region" (Metrolinx 2017, 1). Its operating programs include the previously existing Go Transit that serves the region, as well as the recent Union Pearson Express (service from Union Station in downtown Toronto to Pearson Airport).

The above-mentioned Bombardier dispute has also featured in the recent Ontario Transport department decision to have Metrolinx sign a $528 million contract with French firm Alstom as an extra *backup* fleet to complement what happens or might happen in the Bombardier case (Spurr 2017).

Following the election in June 2018 of a new Conservative Ontario government under Premier Doug Ford, Rushowy and Spurr (2018) draw attention to Ford's early statements of his view that commuters "from the 905 should have an easy ride into downtown Toronto" and that "we are going to build a rapid transit system that's going to extend not only in Toronto but we are the first government that's going to run a regional transportation system" (1). But, in the "long term," Ford as premier wants to build "*subway lines* to Pickering and Markham," a much costlier goal, as pointed out by the Toronto Transit Commission when it noted that the cost of extending "into York Region, its most recent expansion[,] was roughly $380 million per kilometre" (2). And it was not a belowground subway, but rather, as we have seen, a rapid transit way.

The Ford Conservative government's 2019 Budget, *Protecting What Matters Most*, promised eventual balanced budgets by 2023–24, but among its new spending commitments is $11.2 billion for various new rail lines across the GTA, along with a possible $17.3 billion from the federal and provincial governments. There are also cost estimates and timelines for four lines in the GTA, another two lines in Toronto, and one in Mississauga (Compete Prosper 2019, 3–4). There are also plans to increase GO Transit rail service across southern Ontario. All the GO Transit and the transit agenda overall was intended to "unlock value from its assets, reduce the burden on taxpayers and promote residential development close to transit" (Denton 2019, 3). As these kinds of transit and transport infrastructure policy and governance dynamics are observed and thought through, it is also useful to keep in mind an analysis from the Institute on Municipal Finance and Governance at the University of Toronto (Schabas et al. 2019). They ask from the outset "why is transit so difficult" and then list the wise answers, namely: that "each city has unique characteristics; legacy investments constrain technology and service choices; geography and development patterns affect cost and viability of different services; limited knowledge of own city; vague awareness of how cities differ from each other; and challenges of working in any complex technical area" (5).

WINNIPEG

The story of Winnipeg as a mid-sized city centres initially on Winnipeg Transit as a long-established entity within the city government. As a transit authority, its conception of "how it works" stresses the importance of "transitways," "also known as Bus Rapid Transit (BRT) Corridors," defined as "high-speed roadways for buses, physically separated from the regular street system. Buses operate at high speed, free of other traffic, providing fast, reliable service that is unaffected by traffic congestion and other incidents that might occur on the regular street system" (Winnipeg Transit 2017, 1). The development of a rapid transit system can be traced to the Winnipeg Transportation Master Plan (2011) and the proposals in it to develop "four rapid transit corridors in Winnipeg by 2031" (8). Winnipeg Transit 2017 also links such plans as a way to "provide citizens with a viable alternative to the automobile" (1). Rapid transit is presented as a service that "operates into the heart of the downtown in very close proximity to major employment, shopping, medical, dental, cultural, and entertainment centres. It creates more pedestrian activity on downtown sidewalks, reduces parking needs, and frees up land currently used for surface parking for higher value uses" (1).

While the city of Winnipeg gets its expected significant proportion of the federal Liberal government public transit infrastructure investment, key announcements tend to draw attention more to the politically distributive spending via "43 new public transit projects across Manitoba" in smaller cities and rural municipalities (Canada 2017d, 1). They involved $6.6 million in combined federal and provincial funding. The backgrounder list (Canada 2017a), for example, showed the City of Brandon receiving six project approvals, most of them in the "replacement" category such as "transit bus replacement," but also including "bus wash equipment replacement" (2).

Federal funding for longer-term Winnipeg transit has not been finalized. As we have seen, Ottawa had promised $25.3 billion for transit projects across the country over the coming eleven years. Winnipeg's deputy mayor, Jenny Gerbasi, has said that "now we know for x number of years, we'll have this funding to rely on it and can actually do long term planning for things like rapid transit" (quoted in Jones 2017, 1). Gerbasi also said that the funding formula "that determines funding amounts will depend on ridership and population numbers – which means Winnipeg should get a proportionate share" (2).

Of some importance here is the fact that in Winnipeg, transit authorities do not have full control because the much larger city public works department has key roles regarding *major projects*, current and past/recent, as well as construction studies and *specific capital projects* (City of Winnipeg 2016). These impact on multi-modal transport and related infrastructure spending that can easily impact adversely, or also positively, on decisions and budgets, and completion and delay dynamics for transit infrastructure.

Analysis in 2019 shows aspects of changed dynamics and advocacy for Winnipeg as a faster-growing city. Kavanagh (2019), for example, focuses on new "rapid bus lines" that "could mean massive changes as dozens of routes are cancelled, added, or changed" (1), with Winnipeg Transit hoping "its new spine and feeder system in southwest Winnipeg will move passengers faster and more completely." Under the planned/proposed system there are eighteen "proposed cancelled routes," ten "proposed changed routes," and fifteen "proposed new routes (5–8). Related research and advocacy reported by Bernhardt (2019) focused on why "Winnipeg's car culture is unsustainable. The analysis stresses that Winnipeg as a city was "originally designed around public transit" (8) but then the car became dominant as the suburbs grew in the 1950s and 1960s. Kavanaugh draws in arguments centred on the need for pressure to be taken off ... road infrastructure ... by establishing a multi-modal network – whether that uses buses, subways, trains, or monorails – that respects bicycles, cars, and pedestrians" (10).

Also relevant in this context is the lobbying role in Ottawa of the ideas and priorities of the Canadian Federation of Municipalities (CFM) (2016), and within it the Big City Mayors' Caucus, composed of mayors of 22 of Canada's biggest cities. CFM membership includes 1,976 municipalities and associations representing 80 to 100 per cent of municipal populations in most provinces and territories. The CFM membership captures both small- and medium-sized municipal governments, but its internal dynamics are largely driven by the more powerful Big City Mayors' Caucus (2). The latter's advocacy theme is "nation-building through city-building" (2). Its priorities in lobbying the federal government are climate change, transit, partnerships, and housing. Regarding city transit, the Big City Mayors' Caucus calls for funding and action for "reducing gridlock and cutting commutes" (3).

In fact, one also needs at this point some sense of the broader dynamics at play as revealed in the growing policy, political, and governance literature on Canadian cities and urban places and spheres. Transportation overall or city transit in particular is not a major focus in this literature because the urban space is where multiple policy fields and ideas are shaped by city agencies and fall under different academic disciplines (Horak and Young 2012; Bradford and Bramwell 2014; Graham and Andrew 2014; Filion et al. 2015). The above kinds of literature are also often centred on multi-level governance as an idea per se, in part because cities and municipal governments are the constitutional creations of the provinces, and the provinces' ideas about them include limited revenue-raising powers and capacities focusing mainly on property taxes. This very top-down, paternalistic governance structure highlights the point made earlier in the chapter regarding the challenges facing villages (in or near cities), which often have to function with little minimal autonomy, few resources, and little discretion to find place-based solutions.

Our third policy and governance history reveals again the complex array of transit and rapid-transit infrastructure, including buses, streetcars, heavy railcars, light railcars, mobile technology, security systems, rail signal systems, terminals, transit shelters, tunnels, exclusive rights-of-way, tracks, parking facilities, and service facilities. It also involves intricate realms of asset management practices and needs. There is considerable optimism about transit funding reaching a high point historically in infrastructure agendas. But it is also evident that higher figures spread across many years will yield highly competitive battles for various priorities and fair shares within cities, among cities, and vis-à-vis multi-level government.

ANALYSIS: THE THREE REGIME ELEMENTS

With the aid of table 6.2 we now look across the above three policy and governance histories by examining the three elements featured in the book's overall analytical framework.

Regarding policy *ideas, discourse, and agendas* we have seen that each reveals transport infrastructure in detailed and complex discursive ways and in relation to both assets per se and their repair and maintenance. In the freight-rail case, *infrastructure in motion* was central as the two national railways sought to put into place system optimization policies and strategies in the context of related just-in-time production systems and supply-chain development in the liberalized economy. *Fixed infrastructure* of various sizes and types was

Table 6.2
The transport infrastructure regime and the three analytical elements: highlights

Policy and governance histories	Policy ideas, discourse, and agendas	Power structures, democracy, and governance	Temporal realities, cycles, conflicts, and technology
Transport infrastructure in freight-rail-trade-related supply chains, 1990s to present	• Freight trains as pan-Canadian *infrastructure in motion.* • But set in history of CP Rail as pivotal in nation-building settlement of the Canadian west and CN as key in settlement of the Canadian east. • *Fixed transport infrastructure* of diverse sizes and extent, and described in such terms as "buffers," "capacity," "inter-switching," and "synchronized handoffs." • *Surge capacity infrastructure* of various sizes and degrees, by CP and CN and by small short-line freight rail companies. • Model 21 as CP and CN system optimization network approach for efficiency, uniformity, and consistency around traffic movement and congestion avoidance and minimization. • Required Service Level obligations include rail company to: a) furnish, at the point of origin, at the point of junction of the railway with another railway, and at all points of stopping established for that purpose, adequate and suitable accommodation for the receiving and loading of all traffic offered for carriage on the railway;	• CN and CP power as oligopoly with Model 21 system optimization approach/strategy. • Transport Canada as multi-modal policy maker but also rail safety and risk authority. • Freight-rail versus shipper disputes under auspices of market agreements and private/secret dispute arbitration by the Canadian Transportation Agency. • 2012 Dinning Report on aspects of rail-shipper disputes. • Decline of common carrier law and rise of "required service level" provisions. • Shipper responsibilities to build own fixed infrastructure links not clear-cut. • *Fair Rail Freight Service Act* passed. • *Fair Rail for Grain Farmers Transportation Act* passed. • Related new 2017–18 legislation, the *Transportation Modernization Act* (Bill C-49), being debated in response to air and rail interest pressures and concerns.	• System optimization strategy designed to ensure faster, efficient freight transport and avoidance and elimination of congestion. • Just-in-time production imperatives, daily and longer time frames. • Notions of surge capacity. • Continuous and lengthening supply chains and needed logistics. • Containerization innovation and technological rapid change. • Delayed but then sudden emergence of low-cost air carriers in multi-modal dynamics.

Table 6.2
The transport infrastructure regime and the three analytical elements: highlights (*Continued*)

Policy and governance histories	Policy ideas, discourse, and agendas	Power structures, democracy, and governance	Temporal realities, cycles, conflicts, and technology
	b) furnish adequate and suitable accommodation for the carriage, unloading, and delivering of the traffic; c) without delay, and with due care and diligence, receive, carry, and deliver the traffic; d) furnish and use all proper appliances, accommodation, and means necessary for receiving, loading, carrying, unloading, and delivering the traffic; and e) furnish any other service incidental to transportation that is customary or usual in connection with the business of a railway company. • "Just-in-time" production systems fostering or requiring supply-chain systems within Canada and vis-à-vis liberalized trade systems and corridors; also made more possible by containerization innovation and technology. • Hand brakes and air brakes for defined type of tanker cars; securement of unattended trains; facilities where goods are prepared for transit; and standardized means of containment.	• Rail safety governance and key accident disasters such as the Lac-Mégantic, Quebec crash and fire involving short-line rail company and defective rail car equipment/infrastructure with numerous deaths due to fire and explosions that destroyed town centre and its infrastructure. • Impacts of Dangerous Goods law and enforcement especially at fixed rail infrastructure sites. • Growing low-cost airlines giving boost to secondary airports such as Hamilton. • Infrastructure is multi-modal in key and changing ways.	

Transport infrastructure in Canada's many Norths, 1970s to present

- Transportation systems infrastructure and corridors that are undeveloped.
- In Nunavut, highways are non-existent but its twenty-six small communities each has small airport.
- For all transport modes (road, air, rail, marine) all infrastructure needs significant rehabilitation.
- Linked infrastructure also needed such as related telecommunications and also climate change adaptation for impacts of melting permafrost in winter.
- Air infrastructure cast as including airports, terminal buildings, runways, and air navigation instrument approach systems.
- Idea/concept of establishing 7,000-mile Northern Corridor *right of way* for Canada's north and near north.
- Spatial vastness of the many norths (in three territories; northern spheres of the provinces; and under jurisdiction of the federal government).
- Minister of Foreign Affairs Chrysta Friedland sets out 2019 plan to secure legal recognition of the outer limits of Canada's continental shelf in the Arctic Ocean.
- Conservative leader Andrew Scheer outlines 2019 election campaign Vision on "National Corridor for Energy, Telecommunications."

- Indigenous and Northern Affairs Canada describes itself as *one of thirty-four* federal departments with roles and responsibilities regarding both its Indigenous and its Northern Affairs mandate.
- Pressures to ensure that one should not categorize Canada's northern territories as one single entity.
- Frequent call not to use infrastructure investment criteria of larger southern jurisdictions in the north.
- Territorial governments advocate greater infrastructure funding but such spending has to be spread across particular communities and modes.
- Bombardier impact early on in 1960s–70s snowmobile/Ski-doo development and use.
- Pressure/need to deal with condition and availability of runways, most unpaved.
- Frequent infrastructure funding and eligibility rule changes.
- Auditor General's 2017 critical audit report of Transport Canada's failure regarding civil aviation infrastructure.
- There are 117 northern airports in total.
- Town and Arctic port of Churchill, Manitoba as historical and current set of transport infrastructure choices and dilemmas.

- Potential for future use of technologically advanced airships in various norths.
- Infrastructure funding criteria often quickly changed to make some infrastructure needs "not eligible."
- Earlier federal northern initiatives such as 1950s Roads to Resources program and 1960s rail-centred Mid-Canada Corridor.
- Frequent cycles of infrastructure development and repair and never enough funding.

Table 6.2
The transport infrastructure regime and the three analytical elements: highlights (*Continued*)

Policy and governance histories	Policy ideas, discourse, and agendas	Power structures, democracy, and governance	Temporal realities, cycles, conflicts, and technology
		• Various infrastructure funding programs hard to get established and always subject to distributive politics in the north, and nationally centred on question of which southern taxpayers pay most of the taxes. • Need to have better processes to directly consult array of market and social stakeholders. • Centre for the North formation and research. • Need to differentiate and fund Aboriginal communities and non-Aboriginal northerners. • Liberal *Environmental and Regulatory Reviews* reforms of June 2017.	
Transit infrastructure in cities, 1990 to present	• Transit "assets" include buses, streetcars, heavy and light rail cars; exclusive "rights-of-way"; tracks, mobile technology; terminals, etc.; and linear and non-linear assets. • "Asset management" approaches vis-à-vis asset sectors. • Distinction between rapid, express, and other forms of transport not always clear.	• Canadian Urban Transit Association as lobby. • Canadian Federation of Municipalities and Big City Mayors' Caucus within it. • Federal Liberal $25.3 Public Transit Infrastructure Fund over eleven years. • Federal Minister of Finance as power centre.	• Large 2017 Transit Infrastructure Fund over eleven years but annual amounts are small as a national total, and strong short-term distributive pressures/needs.

- Subways in larger cities such as Toronto.
- Subways and bus-lane extensions.
- Transit corridors.
- Asset replacement (minor and major).
- 2016 census shows big cities in Canada getting bigger and small cities getting smaller.
- Multi-level government as desirable idea itself.
- "Nation-building" through "city-building."
- March 2021, federal infrastructure minister announces funding for public transit beginning in 2026–27. Initially set at $3 billion annually, the programming is intended to provide a permanent source of revenue.
- Infrastructure Canada will work with provinces, territories, municipalities, local governments, Indigenous communities, transit agencies, policy experts, and other stakeholders to develop programming for the $3 billion in permanent public transit funding in a manner that offers the greatest benefits to Canadians from coast to coast to coast.

- Infrastructure Canada role amidst larger full federal 2017–19 "Transformative Infrastructure" programs.
- Thirty-seven big versus small transit authorities.
- Transit riders as direct interest.
- Canadian Infrastructure 2016 report on transit.
- Pembina Institute research report on Fast Cities.
- Toronto amalgamation into Greater Toronto Area (GTA).
- Toronto Transit Commission (TTC) – Bombardier streetcar contract multi-year order delay dispute.
- Mayor roles/politics in determining fast transit routes or new stations, etc.
- Ontario provincial agency Metrolinx role on transit among GTA and other nearby cities, and corridors.
- Conservative Provincial Government led by Premier Doug Ford wants subways built "in the long term."
- Winnipeg Transit focus on "Bus Rapid Transit (CBRT) Corridors.
- Early evidence of transit project allocations and distributive politics in Manitoba vis-à-vis smaller cities and rural communities.

- No guarantee that federal (and related provincial and city) budgets will not be changed (reduced especially) as annual fiscal policy contexts change, economically and politically.
- Asset delivery contract delays, including issues regarding technical reliability.
- New mobility and other technologies emerge that affect service and also what "rapid" transit actually means.
- Ready, timely, reliable access in cities and different parts of cities to rapid transit service.
- Ridership populations as drivers of who gets what share of transit asset funding among and within cities over time.
- Debates continue concerning public transit service levels during the pandemic. With normal ridership and revenues down to 80 per cent, many urban centres continue to run at full capacity with losses being subsidised through provincial and federal funding.

Table 6.2
The transport infrastructure regime and the three analytical elements: highlights (*Continued*)

Policy and governance histories	Policy ideas, discourse, and agendas	Power structures, democracy, and governance	Temporal realities, cycles, conflicts, and technology
			• Policy debates also emerge concerning public transit needs beyond the pandemic and the extent to which ridership levels and transit requirements will return to "normal" or will be transformed. With path-dependent funding, planning, and construction continuing apace, the numerous "unknowns" and uncertainties present a severe challenge to strategic investment.

known, but was also increasingly buried and obscured in obligations between diverse shippers and the railways. Many of these were discoverable only in relation to concepts of *required service levels* under common carrier and rail transport law. *Surge capacity infrastructure* also emerged in different kinds of rail-shipper market disputes, including a major one regarding the politically powerful Western Canadian grain industry.

In the story of *transport infrastructure in Canada's many norths*, infrastructure is partly cast in terms of corridors that are highly undeveloped in the spatial vastness of the different norths. Road, air, rail, and marine are the transport modal infrastructures on the analytical and practical checklist, but then the sharp peculiarities leap out, such as the total non-existence of highways in Nunavut resulting in each of its twenty-six small communities having small airports that can only service small aircraft. Air infrastructure overall in northern locations is seen to include airports, terminal buildings, runways, and air navigation instrument approach systems, but also shows practical gaps and local logistics of how airports are paved or not. The many norths story has also seen recent proposals to establish a 7,000-mile Northern Corridor right-of-way for Canada's north and near north within which regulatory systems could later be devised.

In the *transit infrastructure in cities* analysis, infrastructure centres on *transit assets* of specific kinds such as buses, streetcars, and heavy and light rail, in addition to the key role of "rights-of-way." Linear and non-linear assets are also part of the analytical discourse. The definitions of what rapid, express transit might be can also be problematical, given the emergence of related linking technologies, including fast-changing ones. The transit realm also draws attention to *asset-management* approaches: assets need to be replaced and updated as technology changes, at the same time as upkeep is still required for existing older assets playing important connector roles.

The *power structures, democracy, and governance* at play in this regime are diverse and, not surprisingly, different regarding transport infrastructure. Regarding freight rail, the power structures centre on CN and CP as an oligopoly seeking to foster and implement its system optimization strategy. Transport Canada has multiple involvements in rail, and links with multi-modal transport involving road, truck, and air transport as well. The power, democracy, and governance nexus for freight rail plays out in rail-shipper relations and disputes and also in regards to private/secret dispute arbitration via the

Canadian Transport Agency. But Transport and other federal ministers had been involved in major rail-shipper disputes that led to the Dinning Report of 2012 and later legislation passed by Parliament. Actual or possible disputes regarding the obligations of shippers versus rail companies to build smaller fixed infrastructure and links are not generally settled in particularly open or clear ways. Dangerous goods and rail safety laws and processes also impact on particular kinds of infrastructure locations, and relate to major accidents; the example given is the 2013 Lac-Mégantic (Quebec) disaster, which involved a short-line train whose safety infrastructure on rail engines and cars failed to work, and which killed 47 Lac-Mégantic residents and destroyed town buildings and homes via fire and explosions.

The power structure regarding infrastructure in Canada's many Norths involves the three territorial governments, the provinces regarding Canada's more "southern norths," and the government of Canada as instantiated in both the current Indigenous and Northern Affairs Canada (INAC) and its predecessor Department of Indian Affairs and Northern Development (DIAND). But all of these Norths have to manage transport infrastructure in contexts of truly vast spaces and terrains and very small populations and communities, many very isolated. Indeed, in the federal government it is asserted that thirty-four federal departments have roles and responsibilities in the North. Transport Canada is one of these, but the core transport infrastructure dynamics centre on pressure in the three northern territories, not to characterize them as one single entity, but also not to use the infrastructure investment criteria of larger southern jurisdictions. The governance structure shows the need for federal infrastructure funding, but also shows that such programs are difficult to get started and when started they are rarely adequate and are subject to frequent changes. The Auditor General's analysis stresses the need for better processes to directly consult an array of market and social stakeholders rather than just working through governmental departments solely or even primarily.

Regarding transit infrastructure in Canadian cities, the structure of power and democracy is propelled increasingly by the dynamics of big cities getting bigger and small cities getting smaller, but also by the fact that overall there are thirty-seven big and small transit authorities with diverse transit asset needs. The Government of Canada's current transit infrastructure funding program has generated optimism, but the early processes of project selection and timing involves a triple dynamic of distributive politics involving the federal, provincial, and city governments. The lobby structure has centred on organizations such as the Canadian Urban Transit Association with more specific transit expertise and, more broadly, on the Confederation of Municipalities and the Big City Mayors' Caucus within it. The Toronto and Winnipeg examples show also the role of mayors in determining some fast transit routes or new stations in addition to very different configurations of transit authorities.

The third analytical element, *temporal realities, cycles, conflicts, and technology,* emerge in some similar and different ways across the three transport infrastructure histories. In the freight-rail case, the system optimization strategy drives the double temporal dynamic of both faster continuous freight transport but also the avoidance on a continuous basis of congestion. Just-in-time production imperatives in the larger liberalized economy also yield the underpinnings of, and requirements for, ever-lengthening supply chains. Technological impacts have certainly impacted on transport infrastructure in the north, initially with Bombardier snowmobile and ski-doo technologies in the 1960s and 1970s, and currently there is research on and advocacy of the use of technologically advanced airships. Temporal dynamics and cycles are present in federal northern infrastructure project funding initiatives such as the 1950s Roads to Resources program and the 1960s rail-centred Mid-Canada Corridor development. There have been other short and smallish cycles of transport infrastructure funding, some for initial development and some for needed repairs, but never adequate funding. We have also seen that northern transport infrastructure funding criteria are often quickly changed, rendering some infrastructure needs suddenly no longer eligible for funding. Regarding the transit infrastructure story, new mobility and other related technologies are increasingly and frequently a part of how linked transit infrastructures are defined, and they are also changing the determinants of what kind of "rapid" transit actually exists. In temporal/cyclical terms, one can see currently that the large federal Transit Infrastructure Fund has plans for funding over eleven years, but the government itself may not last that long, given four-year election cycles and its current minority status. Even if a government remains in office for longer, its fiscal policies and those of the provinces may not be in sync overall or even annually or in two- or three-year cycles. The risks of this are obviously increased by the pandemic and its massive impact on Canada's economic outlook and transportation needs. Temporal constraints have also been evident in the multi-year delays that occur in major asset-delivery contracts, including concerns about technical reliability. The transit infrastructure story also involves the growth of transit ridership populations as the impetus for which transit authorities get what share of transit funding among and within cities. Once again, short and longer-term changes arising from the pandemic will necessarily influence and intensify decisions about who gets what, why, and when with respect to future transit funding.

CONCLUSIONS

Our account of the transport infrastructure policy and governance regime reveals at least fifty examples/types and discourse of what transport infrastructure is said to include across the three policy and governance histories. The types of assets relate to building and modernizing core assets (those that are in motion and those that are more fixed and stationary, as well as those that have extensive needs for repair and renewal). We have seen that each of the three histories deals with different spatial realities and imperatives about Canada as a massive coast-to-coast-to-coast country and with different initial modes of transport infrastructure featured, which quickly becomes intermodal in nature but in different ways with diverse and changing population imperatives.

The first history centred initially on the mainly east-west freight-rail mode in southern Canada, but with increasingly lengthened supply chains that were international and propelled by liberalized markets. The second history centred on the vast but thinly populated spatial realms of Canada's many norths as governed by the three territorial governments and the federal government, but also including the norths of each province, and small, often very remote communities in the more southern "north" and the high north. The third history covered transit in cities where the spatial imperatives are much smaller and more compact compared to the first two. Our examples focused on cities and communities of different sizes, illustrating how both coped with urban mobility challenges, including under population imperatives where the biggest cities were getting bigger while smaller cities have been getting smaller.

One can see in this regime's analytical story that policy about transport infrastructure per se, in all its intricate detail, resides partly with government bodies that are significantly different – in the freight rail case, ranging across several federal departments and agencies. It also involves "private" infrastructure public policy-making by CP and CN in relation to their "market"-centred system optimization strategy, in contrast to short-line rail companies, as partly revealed in the Lac-Mégantic accident examined earlier. There are, however, different and overlapping dynamics regarding which parts of the government and the freight-rail firms pay for infrastructure. The clashes and mismatches between public-private infrastructure policy and the policies for the funding of infrastructure also emerge in intricate ways both regarding transport in the many norths and in relation to rapid transit in the differently sized and funded cities, as well as in relation to diverse kinds of transit authorities. For transit authorities, the dynamics also include their relations (direct and indirect) with mayors, the province involved, and the federal government. This is especially true when major multi-year infrastructure funding is promised and subject to distributive retail politics involving new extended infrastructure assets in addition to infrastructure repair and renewal. This is particularly challenging for smaller infrastructure needs, which may perhaps be known and understood only by operational personnel and professionals in many different public and private bodies. These challenges have been discussed not only in the context of Canadian cities, but also with respect to smaller rural towns and villages, where local needs and priorities are often overlooked in the design and implementation of largely top-down, centralized funding programs. Smaller communities are also subject to demographic, technological, and environmental trends that impact infrastructure and transportation needs and require federal, provincial, and municipal policy-makers to incorporate place-based planning while simultaneously maintaining a strategic lens that focuses on the coordination and integration of urban, rural, and regional transportation systems.

The short- and longer-term impacts of the pandemic on the economy and on transportation needs and settlement patterns will intensify the need for a strategic lens, but will also increase the number of variables, many still unknown, that will have to be examined and understood if infrastructure investment is to prove optimal. Rapid technological changes have the capacity to transform work and mobility needs post-pandemic, but, as we have seen in chapters 2 and 5, a strategic approach to infrastructure planning is often undermined by short-term economic pressures to stimulate the economy and reinforced by short-term political calculations and thinking. Path dependency provides a further barrier to strategic investment, with many Canadian cities and all levels of government already committed to and heavily invested in particular public transit systems, including LRT. These capital-intensive and city-wide projects were predicated on pre-pandemic needs, assumptions, and growth models, but it remains to be seen how closely aligned these transportation services are with future transit needs and demand.

7

The Housing Infrastructure Policy and Governance Regime

INTRODUCTION

Our fourth regime analysis deals with housing infrastructure policy and governance. It builds on some contextual analysis in both chapters 1 and 3 regarding observations that housing is rarely referred to as infrastructure, seemingly because it ought to be obvious. We refer to housing infrastructure in part because of the different kinds of housing being built, renovated, or abandoned/changed across time as populations and sub-populations have shifted within cities, and more recently to key fast-growing cities such as Toronto, Vancouver, and Calgary.

The chapter begins with three policy and governance histories: federal mortgage and housing policy and the Canada Mortgage and Housing Corporation (CMHC) (1940s to present); provincial and city housing and social housing infrastructure (1970 to present); and the globalization of housing: foreign ownership/investment impacts and Airbnb technology and market impacts (1980s to present).

We then provide an analysis across these policy and governance histories deploying our analytical framework of ideas, discourse, and agendas; power structures, democracy, and governance; and temporal realities, cycles, conflicts, and technology. Conclusions follow.

THREE HOUSING INFRASTRUCTURE POLICY AND GOVERNANCE REGIME HISTORIES

The three policy and governance histories involve different time periods, and in each the primary focus is on different levels of government, although all three levels of government are present in each of the three histories. The first history has a federal focus centred on the CMHC and spans the longest time period, covering mortgages and housing from the 1940s to the present. The second history shifts to a focus on provincial and city governments, looking at more recent developments across a forty-to-fifty-year period, and the third centres on global and foreign dynamics, in the last thirty years or so. Because of these focal points and time frames, we draw on diverse kinds and samples of literature, some academic and some drawing on analysis by key interests and advocates. Many analyses are recent but have considerable historical scope as they marshal evidence about what housing means as infrastructure or about how it is linked to other values and ideas across time. There is also a tendency in the second and third histories to focus illustratively and necessarily on the fast-growing and largest cities in Canada, such as Toronto, Vancouver, and Calgary.

1 Federal Mortgage and Housing Policy and the Canada Mortgage and Housing Corporation, 1940s to Present

In the CMHC's name, "mortgage" comes first and "housing" comes second. The way analysts have assessed it depends partly on what they consider the key eras/periods and macro Canadian policy and political agendas as they change, and on exactly how its role has been examined historically. We start this policy and governance history with the CMHC's own "History of CMHC" (CMHC 2011). Its online history ends with the rhetorical assertion that the "CMHC is truly home to Canadians." Though this is undoubtedly a questionable claim, made on the organization's own website as it celebrated sixty-five years in 2011, it has valid reason to take pride in its achievements. The summary headings of its history proceed as follows, with its own chosen emphasis and discourse:

- The 1940s: a new beginning for housing in Canada;
- The 1950s: from home building to community building;
- The 1960s: the renaissance of Canada's cities;
- The 1970s: the focus on social housing;
- The 1980s: laying a new foundation for quality and affordability;
- The 1990s: a new era for building science; and
- 2000 and beyond: leading the way home.

First called the Central Mortgage and Housing Corporation, and then in 1979 changed to the Canada Mortgage and Housing Corporation, the CMHC history points to several initiatives of its own in each period and, increasingly, those at provincial, city and community levels. Although its early wartime and post-war origins saw it focus on housing for returning war veterans and later as well on funding public housing for low-income families, the essence of the CMHC was its role in mortgage lending and loan insurance guarantees via federal borrowing and fiscal powers. It also involved, as the above summaries capture, federal spending to provide grants to cities and other entities. Even more crucially, "in 1954, the federal government expanded the National Housing Act to allow chartered banks to enter the NHA lending field, via Mortgage Loan Insurance, taking on mortgage risks with a 25% down payment, making home ownership more accessible to Canadians" (2). The CMHC history later shows how housing affordability "received a boost in 2001 through CMHC's introduction of Canada Mortgage Bonds aimed at ensuring the supply of low-cost mortgage funding and keeping interest low" (3).

The limits of the CMHC and some criticisms of it (and of the federal government) inevitably emerged, as in discourse relating to "community-building," "municipal planning," "social housing," and "quality and affordability" (see further core discussion below). CMHC records also show its own sponsorship, funding, and publication of studies that were critical of its own activities and record overall. Some of this reporting, discussed further below, also enters into our second policy and governance history, which is focused on more recent provincial and city housing and social housing.

Analyses by Bacher (1986; 1993) are relevant regarding this mortgage versus housing trajectory of challenges and causes. He argued that "one of the ironies of Canadian housing policy is that homeownership assistance programs for middle income groups and subsidies for private investors have continually emerged in the midst of political demands for publically subsidized rental housing for low income groups ... Starting in the 1930s a unity between government and business emerged while a wide gulf remained between federal housing officials and advocates of social housing," and "this tilts Canadian housing policy in favour of those Canadians who are least in need of government assistance in securing decent accommodation" (Bacher 1986, 32). Bacher (1993) later developed this argument in more detail. Titled "Keeping to the Marketplace," his history showed that the ownership sector of Canada's housing system had strong lobbying power with key ministers and officials and also support from a majority of the electorate, centred on federal mortgage insurance and risk guarantees.

Writing a decade later, Hulchanski (2004) argues that Canada's housing system is based on "policies that privilege ownership" (223). He analyzes the housing system via a three-part conceptual framework: first, "the need to recognize that each country develops a housing system – a method of ensuring (or not) that enough good-quality housing is built, that there is a fair housing allocation system, and that the stock of housing is properly maintained"; second, "the dynamics of the jurisdictional issue in the housing system"; and, third, understanding "why and how some groups and some housing terms/tenures benefit from public policy decisions more than others. To do this we need to situate housing within the context of the full range of social benefits that we call the 'welfare state' and the housing-relevant sociopolitical dynamics that shape it" (222). The central feature regarding policies that "privilege ownership" is that by 2004, in concert with the above-mentioned Bacher 1993 analysis, "95 percent of Canadian households obtain their housing from the private market. Two thirds of all households own their house in which they live. They are merely passing through the rental market. Only 5 percent of Canada's households live in non-market social housing ... the smallest social housing sector of any Western nation except for the United States" (223). This relates, therefore, to ideas of social infrastructure and market/economic infrastructure.

The social housing weaknesses and vulnerabilities stressed in the Hulchanski analysis are tied to federal-provincial-municipal government relations and political and fiscal capacities (229–33). But facets of these realities had been pointed out and argued for some time (Banting 1990). A relevant analysis is also offered by Prince (1995), especially because of his focus on how social housing does and does not relate or is not examined in the context of larger social policy developments in Canada in the period he covers. Prince examines the "three purposes of social housing in: macro-economic stimulus; community development and family self-sufficiency" (721). He begins with the powerful valid argument that a "house, as everyone knows, is far more than a roof over one's head" (721). He stresses that housing's various purposes/functions "are a complex bundle of descriptions of activities; expressions of beliefs, and claims for public intervention," but also emphasizes from the outset how "these programs have generally operated quite separately from other social policies and services" (722). After a summary look at federal social spending, Prince concludes that "housing is still a small kid on Canada's social policy block" (724).

The analysis by Prince examines the impact of Keynesian thinking on housing policy, including how "after the 1973 and 1980–81 slumps, there were major surges in market housing assistance" by the CMHC (726). He then examines the values of "social housing policy and community" with the concept of community, seen as "an important concept in the value systems of nations," that "people should live in a place from which they draw satisfying social relationships and adequate developmental opportunities" (729). This discussion of social housing policy and "family self-sufficiency" relates to how social "housing can provide security of tenure, safety, and stability for people with mental disabilities, the frail elderly, the homeless, youth at risk, single mothers, and women (and their children) who are victims of abuse" (741–2). Prince then examines how crucial social housing programs "have operated in a manner detached from the overall social policy system" (747). The analysis shows that the "problem is not only the lack of coordination but also a lack of wanting to be coordinated. Canadian housing policy in general, and the CMHC in particular has a history of remaining distant from other federal government policy processes" (748). These themes also emerged in the Rice and Prince (2013) book on *Canadian Social Policy* (249–87).

A further comprehensive analysis of housing policy and governance regarding the time periods and analytical complexity deployed came in research by Carroll and Jones (2000). They dealt with "devolution in housing policy in Canada" by analyzing "policy shifts during five stages of housing policy development which have occurred in post-war Canada" (278) and how "each of the stages developed in response to different demographic and economic conditions, was driven by differing ideological values, [and] has fitted within the more general changes in the pattern of intergovernmental relations in Canada" (278).

Their analysis shows that while "the first two stages emphasized building, the latter three stages have been more concerned with constraint and targeted assistance" (279). The five housing policy stages encompassed: "1945–1968 (Economic Development); 1968–1978

(Social Development); 1978–1986 (Financial Restraint); 1986–1994 (Disentanglement) and 1994–2000 (Disengagement and Privatization)" (279). But, of interest, little of this analysis said anything about the CMHC's mortgage insurance roles per se. Carroll and Jones argue that the "clearest pattern across the five phases was in the delivery of programs. Initially, the federal government funded and delivered programs. But, as programs gained acceptance the government would gradually withdraw, passing the financing costs to the private sector, and the delivery and regulation costs to the provinces" (280). A further key underlying feature was that "the provinces criticized the federal government for "being insensitive to particular provincial ... housing conditions" (281). In terms of theories of policy development and change, Carroll and Jones wisely related these changes and outcomes across time to policy and institutional dynamics that could produce any or all of innovation/change, convergence, or inertia (283–6).

A further example of commentary is on the CMHC itself and its mortgage role in the global banking crisis of the 2008 to 2014 period. One analysis in the middle of this period referred to the CMHC as "Canada's mortgage monster" (Sorensen and Kirby 2011). Four critical themes were stressed, namely: that CMHC "policies have inflated the housing bubble" because its "main function is to provide mortgage insurance for prospective homeowners who put less than 20 per cent down on their housing, protecting banks in the event of defaults"; that key players are reluctant to "criticize the CMHC because of the agency's reputation for snuffing out dissent"; and, worst of all, that "the public knows next to nothing about what lurks inside the CMHC's books, aside from the smattering of details in its annual report. And unlike every other major insurance provider in the country, the CMHC doesn't answer to Canada's top financial services regulator" (1). That regulator is the Office of the Superintendent of Financial Institutions (OSFI), about which more later. The analysis also warned that CMHC practices could result in a similar housing market collapse as hit the US. The argument overall was that the CMHC needed much more supervision.

It is instructive to move forward a mere four years and look briefly at the Crown Corporation's 2015 annual report (CMHC 2015) and how it presented itself there. Its initial highlight items/boxes began with "market analysis and research" regarding progress in assessing data gaps; assisted housing; mortgage loan insurance; and securitization (securing access to funds for mortgage funding). These items were in reverse order, from smallest to largest, in relation to the financial size and scale of its mandate realms. The message of former CMHC chairperson Robert Kelly, on the other hand, begins in the reverse risk order. He states:

> Housing markets across Canada indicate increasing evidence of overvaluation with prices and household debt levels again rising faster than wages most notably in Vancouver and Toronto. As a result, the Board was very supportive of the federal government's announcement in December of an increase in the minimum down payment for mortgage loan insurance and OSFI's intention to increase capital levels for mortgage assets held by lenders. Slowing global growth, deflation, debt levels, and declining oil prices present material risks to our national economy and to oil provinces in particular.
>
> We are pleased to note that residential mortgage arrears rates remain low and credit scores were good. CMHC's profits and capital levels remain strong. The Board supports CMHC's ongoing efforts to enhance its financial disclosures, market analysis and commentary for Canadians. Strengthening risk management practices continues to be a priority, particularly in this environment. (4)

Only then did Kelly revert to a brief mention of supporting "Canadians in housing need," including a visit by some board members to Nunavut and a reference to the need for targeted measures for "Northerners and other Canadians whose housing needs are not being met in the market" (4). The following section of the report by the CMHC president, Evin Siddall, covered some similar points but began with the ways in which the CMHC was continuing with its "CMHC in motion" framework, "launched in 2014," to build "an organization that Canadians can count on in good times and bad" (5).

Regarding the OSFI-CMHC relationship, by the end of 2016, under the Trudeau Liberal government, the OSFI (2017, 6) "released the final version of new capital requirements for mortgage insurers that aimed to ensure these firms can withstand a major downturn in the housing market. The new requirements were more risk sensitive." The OSFI was also given the authority to examine the CMHC's commercial programs. A key qualifier to that oversight authority was added, however, justified by the reasoning that because the CMHC is a Crown Corporation "it is the government that establishes rules governing the CMHC's activities, such as its size and shape, and sets the rules on insured mortgages. The OSFI's role is to report its findings and recommendations to the CMHC board of directors and to the relevant federal ministers for their follow-up" (6). Thus, there is a clear assertion of authority for and by the CMHC.

Over the years the Federation of Canadian Municipalities (2016) has set out for the federal government calls for and solutions offered for a national housing strategy. The FCM urged Liberal ministers for federal funding of an overall agenda. In order of importance from the Federation's own sense of past and recent history, this housing agenda sought to: protect existing social housing; invest in new social and affordable housing; grow the rental housing sector; enable innovation for sustainable solutions; support distinct Indigenous housing needs; support distinct Northern housing needs; engage municipalities to address challenging markets; and finally review the CMHC's mandate (11–18).

In the 2019 election, many of these issues, plus numerous other emerging housing issues, were presented by the FCM to all federal political parties, calling on them to "commit to eight targeted measures that address Canada's housing affordability crisis" (Federation of Canadian Municipalities 2019, 1). Among the eight measures were the launching of a new intergovernmental forum on housing affordability and the provision of housing for low- and moderate-income Canadians (2), including establishing "a supportive housing construction fund" such as a "dedicated fund to construct supportive housing for people experiencing homelessness and struggling to live with mental illness, substance abuse or other challenges" (3–4). Also stressed was the need for a new "Indigenous social and affordable housing initiative" (4–5). The FCM also called for the initiation of a "market rental housing preservation program ... to preserve and improve aging low-cost market rental housing (privately owned) using a combination of federal tax incentives and grants" (7–8). Also proposed was a "new housing adaptations program for seniors" such as one that "offsets the cost of home adaptations (grab bars, ramps and lifts) that help seniors safely and affordably age in place" (9–10).

While the FCM array of linkages were broad and valid, they all predate the COVID-19 pandemic and post-pandemic period which began in early-to-mid 2020. But a federal Senate Committee report (Jordon Press 2020) showed in several ways how Canada was ill-prepared for a second wave of COVID-19. The focus, it was argued, simply now had to be on long-term care homes and on the social needs of seniors and key related issues.

2 Provincial and City Housing and Social Housing Infrastructure, 1970 to present

Our second housing infrastructure policy and governance history takes us to provincial and city levels of Canadian government in more direct ways, with cities being where 70 per cent of Canadians live and work. We obviously can only sample a small subset of cities and provinces. The basic time frame of coverage is from 1970 to the present. The recently published analyses we draw on highlight provincial-city examples, and situations and analytical entry points covering this longer period.

For example, a research study by Glenn Miller called *No Place to Grow Old* (Miller 2017) advances three arguments in a multi-decade context:

- "With Canada's population aging rapidly, municipalities must refocus community planning efforts to deal with the impact of decades-old car-dependent suburban sprawl that leaves less mobile seniors isolated";
- "Although most of Ontario's largest cities have declared their intention to become 'age-friendly', none have yet taken the basic step of amending their land-use plans to reflect that commitment"; and
- "Amending provincial planning policies to make age-friendly planning a municipal priority would complement other provincial policies favouring compact, walkable development and promoting aging at home." (1)

The study also cites other surveys that showed that "none of the 25 cities that committed to becoming age-friendly have to date acknowledged this commitment in their official plans" (5). In his detailed analysis, Miller points to examples of seniors' mobility obstacles "when residential sub-divisions are approved with sidewalks on only one side of the road or with no sidewalks at all. This can happen because development charges (fees charged to the developer by a municipality) cover only the capital costs of constructing elements in the public realm (such as sidewalks) but not maintenance costs" (11). This limited coverage from development charges threatens or limits the ability of municipalities to maintain and repair their local infrastructure.

Another analysis focuses on the need for new governance in "big cities" (Keesmaat 2017). She argues for a "new relationship between large cities and provinces." Crucially, she stresses that "whereas the City of Toronto is the sixth largest government in Canada, responsible for the well-being of some 2.8 million inhabitants, it lacks the constitutional powers and rights of self-government afforded to many smaller governments a fraction of its scale – and by that I mean most provinces – across the country. In Canada, large-scale cities remain to this day 'creatures' of their province ... This lack of autonomy hamstrings governance in a global age defined by cities. And while this is about governance, it is also about something else that is far weightier – money" (2). Keesmaat relates the money factor to the example of road tolling and its continuing difficulties in acceptance and implementation (3). She concludes that a new model of governance and intergovernmental financing is needed because the "old model is a 19th century one" that "sees cities as service delivery agents, providing access to roads, sewers, parks and schools" (4).

The "renovation" of housing has also been examined in several ways. Of initial interest is a report by the Canada Mortgage and Housing Corporation (2012) based on its renovation and home purchase survey of 2011. Renovations in the study "are categorized into two groups: alterations and improvements, and maintenance and repairs" (2) with the former defined as "any work made to add value or extend the useful life of the property," and the latter as "any work made to keep a property in working condition or maintain its appearance" (2). The study reported that in 2011, "75 percent [of Canadians/survey respondents?] undertook some form of alteration and improvement in their homes, while 46 percent performed maintenance and repairs. Twenty-one percent ... undertook both types of renovation" (2). Approximately 1.7 million households performed renovations. The study, moreover, highlighted the finding that "most renovations (68 percent) were paid for using household savings ... and [respondents] did not see their debt level increase as a result of the renovations" (1). On a comparative city basis, renovation percentages were highest (40 to 43 per cent range) in St John's, Halifax, Quebec, Ottawa, and Winnipeg, and lowest in Toronto (37 per cent), Calgary (35 per cent), and Vancouver (33 per cent) (1).

Analysis by Atchison (2016) reported on various data on "home improvement" investment in 2015, with Canadians spending "more than $71-billion ... an increase from $45-billion in 2006" (2). Developments were also linked to the "about 800,000 jobs in Canada related to the home renovation industry" (3). The analysis drew on other earlier developments including how, prior to the 2008 recession, a "surge in renovation spending ... was propelled partly by an increase in the construction of single-family homes to accommodate the influx of new Canadians and those looking to upgrade their accommodation" (3). Also stressed was the fact that single-family "housing construction dwindled during and after the recession as rising land costs and development restrictions pushed developers to focus on multistory apartment and condominium development" (3).

Housing for an aging population is another pivotal infrastructure and related policy and governance theme analyzed by Welsh (2018). Her focus is on dementia care, which is undergoing major needed change inside the Redstone Unit at Peel Region's Malton Village long-term care home. But Welsh adds that the changes underway "could transform the way Ontario cares for its aging population, proving that a warm, lively nursing home is not that difficult to create" (1). What needs to change is the fact that "Ontario's 630 homes are controlled by 300 provincial regulations that keep staff focussed on the tasks of feeding, scheduling and cleaning, all documented for government collection ... It is a detached antiseptic end to life" (1). In a word, it is "efficient." For our purposes, the infrastructure issues deal partly with what the care home looks like and feels like to the aging seniors living in it, but it also ultimately and pivotally deals with what values ought to exist, and what staff should be there to implement them. Welsh deals with a transformation in the last two years, when a nursing home specialist from England "was invited by Peel Region, David Sheard, to assess its dementia unit. His view "declared it empty of laughter, or any semblance of kindness" (2). Sheard stressed that the new model is a place where "we get love back into care ... we give staff permission to stop being detached. It's a place where people with dementia are busy, in their own ways that we don't understand, but you know it's linked to something in their past. And to be busy you need a place full of the stuff of life – not an empty building called long-term care" (3). Key parts of the analysis, with accompanying videos, show how "the building" has now been transformed into a place of vibrant diverse colour and brightness. Thus "it shouts familiarity. It's not scary, it's like a hallway at home" (17).

The Welsh analysis and the story it conveys opens with "long term care," which is "the not-so-distant destination for the great mass of Boomers who are all hurtling toward their fragile years" (1). Then the focus shifts to dementia. But there are, of course, long-term care needs and infrastructure for other housing needed by, for example, elderly cancer patients – and indeed middle-aged and also young cancer patients. A further example of dementia-related housing reform has been achieved in the city of Hamilton (Fragomeni 2019), based on a Netherlands care model by a former McMaster University engineering professor, Nafia Al-Mutawaly. He added the innovation of the living units being all in one building, and introduced "smart sensors and AI (artificial intelligence)." The "first floor is reserved for the McMaster Institute for Research on Aging and McMaster University's engineering researchers" (2–3).

Another housing market examined is *student housing*, with a key proposal in Calgary (Crowther 2017) of considerable interest. Toronto-based developer Campus Suites had applied to build in an existing site a "28-story residence, aimed primarily at undergraduates" (1). The plan is to better utilize land by "densifying," which "coincides with an intention from the city to increase transit-oriented development in this community" (1). The nearby University of Calgary and the Southern Alberta Institute of Technology "collectively educates around 80,000 students a year" (1). Campus Suites operates student housing developments in Ontario, Ottawa, and Quebec. The proposed tower in Calgary "would add 328 units to Calgary's apartment rental pool, with approximately 500 beds, with each unit averaging 340 square-feet." Apartments would come with private bathrooms and kitchenettes, while amenities in the tower would include "a fitness centre, social spaces and gaming tables, private studies, laundry, bike parking and 135 underground parking stalls" (2). The Campus Suites strategy is linked to fast-growing university enrolment, including international student enrolment. Existing student housing includes "'student ghetto' housing in old houses that are not code compliant, they're badly wired, they don't have windows that open, and often that's worrying for parents" (2). The Campus Suites president offers the view that everyone "wants to see these rundown student ghettos convert back to single family housing. And developments like this help do that … by putting college kids in concentrated areas, you also tend to improve community relations because we're a management company and we have more ways of dealing with the kinds of issues that can come up" (2).

Student housing is only a starting point for the Calgary story. Analysis by White (2018) shows that 6,500 condo units are being built throughout Calgary, but "the planning, designing and financing of current condo projects started several years ago, before the oil price crash" (2). The analysis shows the condos shifting role vis-à-vis "millennials and retirees," and with respect to the ways in which people and families are "buying lifestyles" (4–6). In the "northeast of the city, is something that could be called Calgary Airport City, with new condo projects feeding off the growth of airport expansion and nearby mega-warehouses" (9).

As the above account on Calgary student housing shows, tower housing raises key issues about building safety. But the issue of apartment tower blocks and condos took on an immediate impact after the huge Grenfell fire in the UK that resulted in about thirty deaths in a twenty-four-story public social housing structure located near an area of housing for the wealthy in London. The local council was condemned for its incompetence and failure to respond in anything close to appropriate ways. Through global media coverage it quickly became a Canadian issue (Bozikovic 2017), where immediate questions were posed regarding how "Canada's thousands of aging towers [can] be kept safe" (1) given that their state will "affect the lives and safety of more than a million Canadians" because of the retrofitting of apartment towers "usually through the sort of 'overcladding' that took place at Grenfell" (1). The mainly privately owned Canadian towers were built between 1950 and 1980. The overcladding of such structures had already begun "and would be a common practice in the next 20 years" (1). Toronto Mayor John Tory immediately asked the city's fire chief to review the city's emergency and future practices. One initial response is that the Canadian Standards Association would be asked to review what it classes as "non-combustible" materials. The Ontario Ministry of Municipal Affairs would also be involved because "the Ontario Building Code does not permit this type of cladding on buildings over six stories in height" (2). The analysis suggests that any new operational "Tower Renewal" plan must take "a broad approach to the construction, zoning, and planning of tower sites and tower neighbourhoods, which supply a large portion of Canada's purpose-built rental housing" (2).

Challenges in cities also involve issues such as "unlicensed group home operators" and their dangerous and repeated health and safety violations (Pagliaro and Powell 2017). The operator of one such group home in Scarborough had eight people living in the home, including "a number of people living in the basement where there is only one exit." A second inspection visit a few days later found thirteen residents. The owner was charged with breaking fire code rules. Convictions "under the Ontario Fire Code can result in fines of up to $100,000 or up to a year in prison. Planning Act charges can lead to a maximum of $50,000 in fines" (3). The analysis points to "a systemic problem throughout the province of people turning regular residences into homes for vulnerable occupants. The situation has arisen as a result of the housing shortage in the GTA" (3).

Pagliaro and Mathieu (2018) examine the purchase by the City of Toronto of "prefabricated structures" for emergency shelter housing. Even the title of the company manufacturing the shelters is infrastructure discourse–laden. The firm is "Sprung Instant Structures Limited." The four temporary structures are places where "anyone in sudden need of a place to stay can rest, access food, showers and support services," but there is also a need by the city "to secure appropriate, vacant city properties that will be used for these structures" (1–2). These sites need to be "solid and level like parking lots and not parks" (2). To illustrate further the need and nature of this kind of infrastructure, the authors also note the role of a drop-in site called Sistering, which operates year-round, "where women line up to sleep on about a dozen reclining chairs and the rest are left to find mats or free space on the floor" (2–3). The issue of the city having to deal with larger numbers of refugees also emerges in the analysis.

A further example of modern housing dilemmas centres on how climate change "is making some homes uninsurable" (Armstrong 2019). This is an increasing risk for both home owners and insurance companies, and indeed the insurance industry. In cities where flooding has obviously increased, owners of homes may find that earlier modes of building construction are vulnerable to permanent flood damage in and around windows and other locations. The CEO of Intact Insurance, Charles Brindamour, has seen the insurance issues escalate to such an extent that his company "now funds one of the biggest academic facilities on this issue in Canada, the Intact Centre on Climate Adaptation, a research centre at the University of Waterloo" (3–4).

Consider also an affordable housing strategy published by the Alberta government (2017). In the strategy's introduction, the former NDP provincial government's minister of Seniors and Housing stressed that as "a social worker for more than 25 years, I saw first-hand the fundamental importance of housing – and the hardships families face when this basic human right is neglected … our new Provincial Affordable Housing Strategy goes beyond the bricks and mortar of a house – it puts people first, ends backward measures and helps Albertans achieve their dreams" (1). Affordable housing is defined in the strategy as "government supported housing available for Albertans, who because of financial, social or other circumstances, cannot afford private market rental rates … Housing is considered 'affordable' when a household spends no more than 30 percent of its gross income on shelter" (1–2). This is the classic CMHC standard of affordability for housing.

The strategy focuses on several elements. Investing $1.2 billion over five years to build more affordable housing for those who need it is a foundational measure. Other elements comprise integrated housing and supports where tenants are given the tools they need to have every chance to be successful in life, including effective transitions and aging in community; and where "applicants and tenants will no longer be penalized for improving their financial circumstances. Housing providers have the flexibility required to respond to community needs" (2).

Ontario also has sought to craft strategies for affordable housing. The first was in 2010, followed by an update in 2016, and by a separate initiative on Affordable Housing and Ending Homelessness (Ministry of Municipal Affairs and Housing 2016) and then by a plan announced by the Ontario Ministry of Finance (2017) dealing with *Ontario's Fair Housing Plan*. The 2010 initial *Long-Term Affordable Housing Strategy, Building Foundations: Building Futures* was described by Minister of Municipal Affairs and Housing as a strategy "rooted in the conviction that a home is more than a mailing address, more than just a roof over your head" and that "good housing lies at the heart of any vision of a fair and prosperous society. It consolidated five formerly separate homelessness-related programs into a single flexible, outcome-focussed program" (quoted in Ministry of Municipal Affairs and Housing 2016, 1). An *Update* on Ontario's *Long-Term Affordable Housing Strategy* (1) was announced following the 2016 Ontario Budget, when $178 million was available over a three-year period. The update initiatives involve: more than $17 million to pilot a portable housing benefit targeted towards survivors of domestic violence; up to $100 million in operating funding for housing allowances and support services to assist up to 4,000 families and individuals in new supportive housing for the next three years; and supporting the construction of up to 1,500 new supportive housing units over the long term (1).

The Ontario Ministry of Finance's measures in *Ontario's Fair Housing Plan* focused on the housing price surges (see discussion below in our third policy and governance history). Then again, the plan also included: "expanding rent control to all private rental units in Ontario including those built after 1991; actions to increase housing supply; and actions to protect homebuyers and increase information sharing" (Ontario Ministry of Finance 2017, 1–2).

Each province in Canada has examples of particular housing governance entities. A useful further illustrative example is the Saskatchewan Housing Corporation (SHC) (2016). The SHC is a Treasury Board Crown Corporation and is "accountable to Cabinet through the Minister of Social Services and operates under the authority of the Saskatchewan Housing Corporation Act which establishes a Board of Directors (the Board) to govern its affairs and business of the Corporation" (7). The SHC "promotes independence and self-sufficiency by providing housing and housing services to people who could not otherwise afford or access adequate, safe and secure shelter," and it "manages financial contributions from the provincial, federal and municipal levels of government, and plays a lead role in the development of housing policies on behalf of the Government of Saskatchewan" (6). Its range of housing programs and services includes: social and affordable rental housing; development of new housing; home repair, renovation, and adaptation programs; home ownership options; and support for housing planning (6). Crucially, it has to manage "operating agreements with approximately 485 organizations" (6–7). This is an example of networked governance arrangements in this regime/field. The SHC-owned rental housing portfolio consists of "18,232 units located in communities throughout the province," but SHC-owned units "are managed by local housing authorities and are targeted to low- and moderate-income families, seniors and persons with disabilities ... and, in addition, 10,031 units, including 6,274 rental units and 3,757 special purpose housing units (i.e. special care and group home beds) are owned and operated by nearly 250 different non-profit groups and cooperatives" (2). The distribution of the SHC portfolio is summed up to be: "45 percent seniors, 33 percent families; 13 percent special care/group home beds; and 9 percent singles" (2). The SHC's expenditures in 2016 totalled $178.1 million and its revenues of $183.9 million are shown to come from "federal spending 27%, provincial 7%, municipal and other 6%; and client 60%" (21). These client revenues come from rents, user fees, and other charges.

The recent academic published work of urban scholar Richard Florida is also of interest. He addresses what he calls *The New Urban Crisis* in the US (Florida 2017a), but, as an American scholar based for some time at the University of Toronto Rotman School of Management, Florida also published an article on what the Canadian equivalent looks like (Florida 2017b). He argues that in "recent years, the young educated, and affluent have surged back into cities, reversing decades of suburban flight and urban decline. And yet, all is not well. The very same forces that power the growth of our great cities have generated a crisis of gentrification, rising inequality, and increasingly unaffordable urban housing" (1). In Florida's view, "the new urban crisis is different from the older urban crisis of the 1960s and 70s" which was "defined by the economic abandonment of cities and their loss of economic function. But the new crisis is, in many ways, an outgrowth of urban success. The predicament can be seen in the dramatic growth in housing prices and even more the dramatic decline in housing affordability, especially in cities like Toronto and Vancouver" (1–2). As a result, he argues, "Canada's major metropolitan areas are fragmenting into a new kind of 'patchwork metropolis', with small areas of concentrated advantage surrounded by much larger spans of concentrated disadvantage that span city and suburbs alike" (2). A key feature of the new crisis is "the decline of the middle class and of once sturdy middle-class neighbourhoods" (2).

A further analysis in a Toronto context comes via the Toronto Region Board of Trade (DeSilva 2017). Its CEO, Jan de Silva, advocated a plan/strategy for building badly needed rental stock by "removing barriers to private sector rental construction" (2), especially condos. He argues that at present 80,000 people move into the GTA each year and "to house them, we should have 30,000 homes a year coming on stream, instead of the fewer than 2,000 built in a typical year" (2). He points to the problem of development charges and taxes that are distortions for rental builders. Recent rent controls, or other forms of controls, are also argued to be barriers to private-sector investment.

So are delays due to getting planning approval. The Board of Trade's central argument is to put "condos and rentals on an equal footing." Its top priority is "to amend the Condominium Act so rental developers can use the same tools to their advantage" and the second is to "allow condo towers to be developed explicitly and entirely as 'rent-only condos' packaged with slightly different rules, services and governance structures to attract rental-oriented investors" (2). DeSilva concludes with his view that our "rental market is a mess because policy-makers forgot the business side of rental development over decades of policy changes" (3). It would not be difficult to find similar situations in other Canadian cities, large and smaller, with their analogous local business lobby groups.

3 Globalization of Housing: Ownership/Investment Impacts and Airbnb Technology and Market Impacts, 1980s to present

Our third policy and governance history is centred on the globalization of housing, examined in a two-part manner: global ownership/investment ownership impacts, and Airbnb technology and market impacts.

The *global ownership/investment impacts* emerged visibly in Canada in 2016 and 2017, with home price surges in Vancouver and Toronto that resulted in immediate analytical efforts to determine whether and to what extent the surges were due to supply-side versus demand-side factors, and, in the latter case, how much of this was foreign/global demand (TD Economics 2017a; 2017b). The first of these analyses was on housing in the GTA, where home prices "have risen by an average of 19% over the past 12 months, marking the fastest pace since the late 1980s" (TD Economics 2017b, 1). Both supply constraints and demand factors are involved, but the TD analysis asserts that having "a debate on whether there's a housing bubble is a distraction, since this tends to be confirmed only retrospectively" (1). And to determine whether a market is sustainable, a "logic check is required against domestic fundamentals. Two of the most common cited underpinnings to the Toronto housing market are insufficient supply, often attributed to obstructive government policies and land usage and permit processes; strong demand, often attributed to population growth" (2–3). Regarding Toronto's "lure to foreign investors," the analysis pointed out that surveys "of realtors and condo corporations suggest that foreigners account for roughly 5% of GTA market activity" (4).

The second TD Economics analysis (published five months later) explored the Canadian regional housing outlook (TD Economics 2017a), with better data on what happened in the Vancouver and Toronto surges, both initially and in response to provincial policies to deal with them, and, overall, providing a better account of what was happening regarding foreign investment. Regarding Vancouver, the study showed that "the B.C. government started tracking foreign buyers in 2016 ... and found that between June 10–July 14 of that year, 9.7% of all sales transacted in the Greater Vancouver Area were tied to foreign nationals"; but it also found "the number plummeted to 1% following the (provincial) non-resident tax implementation in August, but recovered to near 4% by the end of 2016" (3). As for, the analysis showed the provincial government "started tracking the share of foreign buyers in total transactions in May of this year and found the figure to be 4.7% in the Greater Golden Horseshoe region" (3). The study additionally noted that following "the implementation of the non-resident's tax in Ontario, there has been little evidence of a jump in foreign activity in other regions. Ottawa and Montreal ... have heated up in recent months but they are not yet exhibiting the typical signs of increased foreign investment activity" (4).

The *Economist* (2017) has drawn lessons from Canada's global house price boom, especially the Vancouver and Toronto situations, with reference to cities in Australia and the US. Unlike the other accounts above, the *Economist* cites China in particular for the ways in which it has helped "drive a wedge between the price of homes and the local fundamentals of incomes and rental payments" (16) in China. It argues that in "only a few decades China mastered the manufacture of high quality goods. But it takes far longer to be able to manufacture safe stores of value" (16). Key in the *Economist*'s investigation is the conclusion that Chinese "affluent citizens seek out rich-country assets including houses. This fundamental mismatch limits the ability to stop bubbles from inflating" (16–17).

An analysis by Gordon (2017) assesses the demand factors behind Toronto's housing affordability problem, including the "new global real estate reality" (17). He argues that "what distinguishes Toronto and Vancouver is the phenomenon of wealth-based migration, which was actively encouraged by Canadian governments since the late 1980s." He focuses on one of "the primary conduits of foreign capital into the Canadian housing market ... the Immigrant Investor Program (IIP) established in 1986" (19–20). This program "allowed wealthy aspiring migrants to front the Canadian government a five-year interest-free loan in return for permanent resident status ... path to citizenship (prior to 2010, $400,000; afterwards, $800,000)" (20). Gordon shows that the IIP was cancelled in 2014 "because the Canadian government realized that the program was not working as intended" and stresses that after its cancellation, one could see that "Canadian governments, [and] the Canada Mortgage and Housing Corporation (CMHC) failed to gather good data on foreign ownership in the housing market" (20).

Each of the above studies in its own way looks at both supply and demand and stresses the realities of policy and governance complexity. This is underscored by a 2017 study by the Canadian Centre for Economic Analysis (CANCEA). Focusing on "shelter affordability" in Ontario and the GTA, it emphasizes that the affordability challenge "is complex, rife with data limitations, and poses risks associated with both action and inaction by policy makers. Unfortunately, most of the existing commentary is singularly focussed, ignoring this complexity and the interrelatedness of factors and behaviours that are actually driving the issue" (1). The CANCEA paper uses a "systems approach" to socio-economic analysis that draws on current and changing "major computing and analytical innovations" (1), including hundreds of data sources linked to the objects that generate the data (see also v, vi).

With respect to data, the 2016 Canadian census offers further insight on housing use in Canada with relevance for this policy history. As noted by Galloway (2017), a key change is that "for the first time in the country's history, the number of one-person households has surpassed all households last year, more than the percentage of couples with children, couples without children, single parent families, multiple family households and all other combinations of people living together" (1). The census data also showed significant changes in "living arrangements of young adults aged 20 to 34," indicating that "in 2016, more than a third of Canadians between the ages of 20 and 34 lived with at least one parent" (6). Regarding housing infrastructure, these kinds of changes create different needs regarding the need for certain forms and sizes of housing as well as also complex affordability issues. For example, Warren (2019) starts with similar data to the above "one third" figure but then links it to Toronto's housing crisis and to experts who are "seeing a new divide taking hold among the younger generation: those who can live with their parents – and save for a down payment – and those who can't" (2).

The Airbnb story is a global "disruptive" technology as defined in chapter 1. It began in 2008 when the company, based in San Francisco, was created by three tech founders, Joe Gebbia, Brian Chesky, and Nathan Blecharczyk. The company in 2017 described itself as a "trusted community marketplace for people to list, discover, and book unique accommodation around the world – online and from a mobile phone or tablet. Whether a flat for a night, a castle for a week, or a villa for a month, Airbnb connects people to unique travel experiences, at any price point, in more than 65,000 cities and 191 countries. And with world-class customer service and a growing community of users, Airbnb is the easiest way for people to *monetize their extra space* and showcase it to an audience of millions" (Airbnb 2017a, 1, our emphasis), including over 3 million listings worldwide.

The "Airbnb Story" year-by-year highlight section on its website shows its quite modest early stages, including an "airbed and breakfast" phase and then its initial expansion "beyond just rooms to apartments, houses and vacation rentals" (Airbnb 2017b, 1). "Its international expansion began in 2011 with the opening of an office in Germany and in 2017; it launches the Airbnb Chinese brand Aibiying" (1). On 5 August 2017 the website celebrated the fact that that night was "Airbnb's biggest night to date, with over 2.5 million people staying *on the platform*" (1, our emphasis). Indeed, there is also a thirty-page section listing new initiatives and opportunities in cities and locations across the globe, including some with specific social goals regarding women in the Airbnb community marketplace. By 2021, Airbnb had established twenty-three offices globally, and it is estimated that there are seven million accommodations listed globally, accounting for about twenty per cent of the total lodging market in the US. These figures do not take into account smaller competitor sharing platforms such as HomeAway, which accounted for a smaller but still sizeable eleven per cent of the US lodging market in 2019–20 (Kovachevska 2020).

The Airbnb developments were occurring at the same time as the unfolding of the transport-centred Uber ride-hailing technology and economy, as well as those of other firms dealing with the on-demand or gig economy (*Economist* 2015; 2016a). Some analysts support the burgeoning need for a light-touch pro-innovation approach rather than a hard regulatory one on such development. Still others are deeply critical of the implications for workers in the claimed part of the commercially branded "sharing" economy on the grounds that little is "shared" in a normal social context, but rather it is the exact opposite, namely one of exploitation via technology (Hutton 2016; Slee 2016; Hill 2015). Even more in-depth analyses such as those by Botsman and Rogers (2011) regarding "collaborative consumption" and that of Arun (2016) on the "sharing economy" are crucial. Interestingly, they each start illustratively with the example of Airbnb, but quickly and necessarily have to proceed to an array of developments and their digital determinants that emerged earlier. In Arun's book, the focus is on the shifting landscape of regulation and consumer protection in a digital economy and society.

A McGill University School of Urban Planning report (Wachsmuth, Kerrigan, Chaney, and Shillolo 2017) provides an initial and significant assessment of the implications of Airbnb for housing infrastructure. Titled *Short Term Cities*, it assesses Airbnb's impacts on Canadian housing markets and the early tentative efforts to regulate it, with a focus on Montreal, Toronto, and Vancouver, and with cautionary advice on the need for "new methodological techniques for spatial analysis of big data" (2) regarding Airbnb activity. The report leads off with its summary view that

> [s]hort-term rentals are expanding rapidly across Canadian cities. In May 2016, there were approximately 50,000 Airbnb listings in Montreal, Toronto and Vancouver regions which had been active at some point in the previous 12 months. A year later, there were over 81,000. In the same period the number of entire homes rented more than 60 days a year had increased from 8,900 to 13,700 across the three cities. Meanwhile, Airbnb revenue has become *ever more concentrated among a small set of large-scale operators*. Hosts with multiple full-time, entire home listings now earn more than a third of all platform revenue, despite only controlling eight per cent of active listings. (5, our emphasis)

In the three cities, Airbnb hosts earned "a collective $430 million in revenue last year, an average of $5,310 per listing and a 55% increase over the year before" (16). The study then shows the housing that *is removed from the market* by Airbnb growth and dynamics. Airbnb as a business is cast as a "triple threat" centred on evidence that a "third of all active Airbnb properties are 'multi-listings,' whose hosts administer two or more entire homes or three or more private rooms. The most successful of these hosts earn millions of dollars per year running commercial short term rental services across dozens or even hundreds of homes, most of which are no longer able to support a long-term resident" (27). As a result, Airbnb has a growing negative impact on rental housing in each of the three cities studied.

The report ends with a tentative look at the "state of short-term rental regulation in Canada," stressing that short-term "rentals often operate in legal grey zones, able to avoid existing accommodation regulations and taxes" (40). Drawing on some international experience such as that of Amsterdam, the authors offer "three simple principles" for short-term rental regulation. These are "1) one host, one rental; 2) no full-time, entire home rentals; 3) platform responsibility for enforcement" (44). Platform responsibility means that Airbnb and other such platforms are "required to proactively enforce" these rules (45).

Further related research by Combs, Kerrigan, and Wachsmuth (2019) show that revenue "is highly concentrated amongst a small number of hosts at all scales of analysis" (1) and similar levels of concentration in each settlement type. But the analysis also shows that "entire home listings make up a higher proportion of active listings (83%) and revenue (95%) in rural areas "than in other sized/ types of cities and communities" (1).

Not surprisingly, other studies and lobbying are in play. A study by Jamasi and Hennessy (2016) on Airbnb in Toronto reported its fast growth in the 2013–16 period, and showed how Airbnb listings in Toronto "are highly concentrated in three areas" (6), including the Toronto waterfront. An article by Israel (2017) surveyed efforts by various cities in Canada to map and regulate the socio-economic market. One group that formed in Toronto, the Fairbnb Coalition, "comprises a hospitality workers union, a variety of urban issues advocacy groups, hotel industry groups and others" (1). One of its reports (Fairbnb 2017), titled *Squeezed Out*, diagnoses how other businesses are being adversely impacted, functioning in rental and hotel industries where they are regulated but Airbnb is not. The report proposed model legislation and argued that "voluntary compliance leads to sub-optimal results" (36). The Fairbnb story in Toronto has been extended by Valverde (2019), who refers to proposed but disputed stronger licensing rules by Toronto as a city that would, if they came into force, mean that "more than 8200 listings would have to be removed, and up to 6500 whole houses would be available to boost [the] supply of long-term family rental housing" (3).

In other Canadian cities, lobbying campaigns are directed against Airbnb and other vacation rental services. Calgary was experiencing changes that prompted the Alberta Hotel and Lodging Association, representing about 800 hoteliers and campground operators, to lobby the provincial government to regulate (Stephenson 2017, 2). Its president is quoted as saying, "our concern is the degree to which their operating like hotels but not on the same level playing field ... we have licensing and insurance and health and safety regulations that right now don't exist for those types of regulations, and those are all extra costs that are on the backs of our industry" (2). Similar proposals and protests are emerging in Manitoba, in this case from the Manitoba Lodges and Outfitters Association (Pursaga 2017).

In British Columbia, a further configuration of dual Airbnb property right conflicts and enforcement issues have become public. An owner, Emily Yu, is "using her three-bedroom, five-level North Vancouver home as an Airbnb hostel" (Proctor 2018, 1). Battles arose "with other residents in her townhouse complex," and they, "the city and the courts have all told Yu to stop using her ... home as an Airbnb hostel" (1–2). Her strong reply and belief is that "this is my home. I have a right to enjoy my property. My [neighbours] can say whatever they want, but they don't have the right to take away my civil right of enjoying my property" (2). Airbnb is also investigating the situation.

Meanwhile, globally, other evidence and strategies are being deployed and examined as well. Sherwood 2019 notes that Airbnb is "moving into the hotel business" in cities such as New York. She also draws attention to Fairbnb, which will launch in five European cities to establish a "new category of urban lodging" and a way for cities to develop "community-based tourism" (4). COVID-19 will of course cause further changes to housing strategies and infrastructure priorities. As discussed in other chapters, evidence is emerging of demographic changes that will have major short- and longer-term implications for the supply of housing. The demands for "affordable housing" will need to be balanced with competing demands for "age in place" options, as well as entrepreneurial and real estate investment opportunities provided by a pandemic-fuelled housing boom and the state-sanctioned Airbnb rental market.

ANALYSIS: THE THREE REGIME ELEMENTS

With the aid of table 7.1 we now look across the above three policy and governance histories by examining the three elements featured in our overall analytical framework.

Regarding policy *ideas, discourse, and agendas,* the federal mortgage and housing policy ideas, discourse, and agendas are bound up in the very name of the CMHC, where "mortgage" comes first and "housing" comes second. The former privileges mortgage risk-protected lending that centres on private home ownership. But the CMHC's long history shows that it has articulated smaller housing ideas, variously expressed, in order to show concern and foster support when needed in the discourse of community-building, social housing, and related ideas. Our second policy and governance history samples more recent provincial and city housing, in which the array of ideas, discourse, and agendas include "age-friendly" housing and urban structure; "renovation" as two groups of activities; "affordable housing" and tower housing and building safety; removing barriers to private-sector rental construction on condos; and academic overviews such as the modern Canadian big city as a "patchwork metropolis." In our third policy and governance history on the more recent globalization of housing ownership investment, including the Airbnb emergence, the discourse centres on home price surges in Vancouver and Toronto and ideas about how to discuss and understand supply-side versus demand-side ideas and dynamics in short-term "housing bubbles." Airbnb casting itself as a technology-centred "trusted community marketplace" and as a global "platform" also emerges.

When it comes to related relevant *power structures, democracy, and governance,* the CMHC–centred story is very much federally centred in part by the inherent political support from the pan-Canadian private ownership majority sector. More recently, there is also some pressure, albeit limited, from critics of the CMHC for it to be regulated by the OSFI. The array of provincial and city initiatives and actual responses/delays is shown regarding delays in basic land use plans; links of the home improvement lobby to the 800,000 jobs in the renovation industry; Calgary student housing reform and changing markets; and the unique lobbying and structure of the Saskatchewan Housing Corporation. The power structures, democracy, and governance dynamics in the global housing ownership/investment context were Vancouver- and Toronto-focused, but then actions by the British Columbia and Ontario provincial governments to impose non-resident taxes on foreign property buyers reduced the levels of housing price surges immediately and effectively. Cities such as Montreal, Toronto, and Vancouver, as well as provincial governments, grapple with Airbnb's impacts, positive and negative, as they try to work out how,

Table 7.1
The housing infrastructure regime and the three analytical elements: highlights

Policy and governance histories	Policy ideas, discourse, and agendas	Power structures, democracy, and governance	Temporal realities, cycles, conflicts, and technology
Federal mortgage and housing policy and funding and the Canada Mortgage and Housing Corporation (CMHC), 1940s to present	• Mortgages versus housing. • CMHC as "home to Canadians." • From "home-building to community building." • Social housing focus. • Returning war veterans. • "Public housing for low income families." • But primacy of mortgage lending and loan insurance guarantees • "Housing affordability in 2001 through Canada Mortgage Bonds. • But primacy of marketplace centred on federal mortgage insurance and risk guarantee function. • Policies that "privilege ownership." • Housing in the welfare state. • Federation of Canadian Municipalities (FCM)'s 2019 election plan for 8 targeted housing measures regarding affordability, such as for "moderate-income Canadians" etc.	• Ownership sector in marketplace had strong lobbying power. • Two-thirds of all households own the house in which they live. • Social housing problem is not only the lack of coordination but also a lack of desire to be coordinated. • Devolution in housing policy linked to stages tied to demographic and economic conditions and patterns of intergovernmental relations in Canada. • CMHC as "Canada's mortgage monster" in global housing crisis. • Reluctance of key players to criticize CMHC. • CMHC was not regulated by Superintendent of Financial Institutions (OSFI) but now is partly as of 2016.	• Changes and outcomes across time could produce innovation/change, convergence, or inertia.

| Provincial and city housing and social housing infrastructure, 1970s to present | • Ontario cities declaration to be "age friendly" but little follow-up.
• Support compact "walkable development" and promote "aging at home."
• New governance in big cities compared to provinces (e.g. Toronto bigger than several of the small provinces and needs greater powers).
• "Renovation" of housing as two groups of activities: "alteration and improvements" and "maintenance and repairs."
• Discourse of "home improvement."
• Student housing "densifying."
• Calgary 6,500 condo units vis-à-vis millennials versus retirees, buyers buying lifestyles, etc.
• Tower housing and building safety in aging towers regarding "non-combustible" materials in cladding.
• "Dangerous unlicensed group home operators" as a result of housing shortage in GTA.
• Alberta provincial "affordable housing" strategy; beyond "bricks and mortar."
• Ontario "affordable housing and ending homelessness."
• "Expanding rent control to all private rental units in Ontario." | • Delays in amending basic land-use plans.
• Charges to developers cover capital costs of construction elements such as sidewalks but not maintenance costs.
• Toronto as sixth-largest government in Canada and bigger than most provinces; but constraints in acting on this policy and governance thesis.
• CMHC renovation study in 2012 shows 68 per cent of renovations paid for with household savings.
• Lobbying and link of home improvement to about 800,000 jobs in renovation industry.
• Housing construction dwindled during and after recession that started in 2008.
• Calgary student housing and role of Toronto company Campus Suites.
• Growing university enrolment, Canadian and international students.
• UK 2018 Grenfell fire disaster and immediate Canadian safety debate on building safety in aging towers.
• Saskatchewan Housing Corp (SHC) as complex entity with its revenues of $183.9 million coming from feds (27 per cent), province (7 per cent), municipal and other (6 per cent), | • Cycles of housing construction such as decline after the 2008–14 recession.
• Provincial and city varied social housing programs and announcements but with small funding bases due to budget cycles.
• Sluggish regulatory response to handle diverse condo and rental needs.
• Grenfell tower fire in UK and immediate Canadian city condo response needed.
• Growing aging population needing diverse seniors' needs, staff, and new buildings. This is brutally exposed by the pandemic and impact in long-term care homes (LTCs). Ideological debates and blame intensify concerning private versus not-for-profit and state-run LTC homes.
• The pandemic also has severe impact on housing affordability due largely to the falling supply, the demand for larger houses |

Table 7.1
The housing infrastructure regime and the three analytical elements: highlights (*Continued*)

Policy and governance histories	*Policy ideas, discourse, and agendas*	*Power structures, democracy, and governance*	*Temporal realities, cycles, conflicts, and technology*
	• "Independence and self-sufficiency regarding moderate-income families, seniors, and persons with disabilities" in Saskatchewan. • "Removing barriers" to private-sector rental construction, condos. • Metropolitan areas (Toronto, Vancouver) cast as "patchwork metropolis." • "Small areas of concentrated advantage surrounded by large spans of concentrated disadvantage." • Armstrong 2019 analysis of how climate change is making some homes uninsurable because of flood damage.	an "client" (hundreds of entities at micro local level, 60 per cent). • Toronto Board of Trade as lobby. • Academic analysis and advocacy by Richard Florida. • Reform evidence and pressure regarding types and scales of seniors' housing infrastructure needs, including dementia, and bringing both care staff and "buildings" to life, and celebrating life at its end stages.	beyond urban centres, and rising domestic and growing international investment. Governments at all levels face mounting pressure to take action and address the looming housing crisis.
Globalization of housing ownership/ investment impacts and Airbnb technology and market impacts, 1980s to present	• Home price surges in Vancouver and Toronto. • Causes debated in relation to supply-side and demand-side, the latter including global demand. • "Housing bubble" notion as distraction. • "Domestic fundamentals." • "Wealth-based migration" encouraged by federal government since late 1980s.	• BC government in 2016 tracked foreign buyers in Vancouver area: 9.7 per cent of all sales tied to foreign nationals. • Number plummeted to 1 per cent following provincial non-resident tax. • Ontario tracked foreign buyers at 4.7 per cent in Greater Golden Horseshoe region.	• Interrelatedness of factors and behaviours actually driving the issues. • Needs "systems approach to socio-economic analysis." • Need for "new methodological techniques" for spatial analysis of big data.

- Supply and demand sides of "shelter affordability."
- Analytical census 2016 ideas/findings regarding one-person households, couples with and without children, persons between twenty and thirty-four years old living with at least one parent.
- Airbnb as "trusted community marketplace" providing people with unique travel experiences.
- "Monetizing their extra space."
- The Airbnb "platform."
- Part of the "sharing economy," "on-demand economy," and "gig economy," like Uber.
- Light touch pro-innovation appeal versus hard regulation.
- Part of "collaborative consumption."
- Sherwood 2019 shows how Airbnb is moving into the hotel business in New York and so is Fairbnb moving into cities to foster tourism based on community values.

- Little evidence of foreign buyer growth in cities such as Ottawa and Montreal.
- Federal Immigration Investor Program (IIP) established in 1986 and cancelled in 2014.
- CMHC did not gather good data on foreign ownership in housing market.
- Airbnb formed in 2008; now in 65,000 cities and 191 countries.
- Has nineteen offices globally.
- Academic studies of Airbnb impact in Montreal, Toronto, and Vancouver.
- Focus on housing that is removed from the market by Airbnb growth and dynamics.
- Negative impact on rental housing.
- Need for short-term rental regulation.
- "Platform responsibility should mean that Airbnb are "required to practice enforcement themselves.
- Fairbnb Coalition of hospitality workers and union and hotel industry.
- Alberta Hotel and Lodging Association lobbying Alberta government to regulate Airbnb.

- "Short-term rental regulation" needed for Airbnb.

to what extent, and by whom Airbnb and its "platform" should be regulated. Within this fluid and contentious housing context, a Fairbnb Coalition lobby has emerged.

Regarding *temporal realities, cycles, conflicts, and technology*, each policy and governance history reveals relevant observations/theories. In the CMHC–focused history, observed changes and outcomes across time produce in complex ways "innovation/change, convergence, or inertia." The "crisis" timelines of the Canadian and global housing situation in the 2008 to 2014 period are also relevant in the second policy history on provincial and city housing, where provincial and varied social housing programs and concerns are announced but with small funding bases, due themselves to underlying budget cycles. In the globalization of housing and Airbnb's recent history, the obvious temporal/technological speed of the Airbnb impacts, globally, nationally, and within major cities in Canada, are obvious; sooner or later pressures for the "short-term rental regulation" of Airbnb also began. The larger globalization of housing ownership led to calls for technological and temporal systems of analysis: on the interrelatedness of factors and behaviours actually driving the issues; the needs for a "systems approach" to socio-economic analysis; and the need for new methodological techniques to improve the spatial analysis of big data.

CONCLUSIONS

This chapter has examined the housing infrastructure policy and governance regime, passing through three multifaceted policy and governance histories across a period starting in the 1940s and extending to the present. A long time frame was needed for these analyses in order to understand housing in changing circumstances. The first policy and governance history provides a federal focus centred on the CMHC and spans the longest time period, covering mortgages and housing from the 1940s to the present. The second history shifts to a focus on provincial and city government, looking at more recent developments across a forty-to-fifty-year period, and the third centres on global and foreign dynamics in the last thirty years or so. We also stressed, however, that all three levels of government are present in *each* of the three histories.

Because of these focal points and time frames, we have drawn on diverse kinds and samples of literature and analysis, some academic and some drawing on analysis by key interests and advocates. Many of the analyses are recent, but they in turn have considerable historical scope as they provide evidence about what housing means as infrastructure or about how it is linked to other values and ideas across time. There is also a tendency in the second and third histories to focus illustratively and necessarily on the fast-growing and largest cities in Canada such as Vancouver and Toronto.

Housing as overt infrastructure, we conclude, is often not central but rather emerges as a diverse array of expressed and often vague approximations. Thus, we have seen that housing is more than a roof over one's head and "more than an address," going well beyond simply bricks and mortar. In social housing and community settings, it involves a place where people and families can and should live in places from which they can develop meaningful social relationships. Governments at all levels have been both sensitive and insensitive to particular housing conditions. These include places to grow old, and housing infrastructure dependent directly and indirectly on land-use planning. Housing and home location can be tied to the capital costs of constructing elements in the public realm such as sidewalks, but not the maintenance costs of sidewalks. Renovations of houses as buildings can be cast as "alterations and improvements" but also "maintenance and repairs." Significant sections of housing and types of buildings/towers are for fast-growing student populations. Tower housing, including condos, generates visible concerns about safety regarding fire and other dangers/threats. Houses need to be "affordable" and safe, with policies needed to "end homelessness" and support "persons with disabilities." The Airbnb business approach was to allow people who own housing and property to "monetize their extra space." Airbnb is also a "platform" and allows citizens and tourists to pay to stay in other people's homes and property for varied time periods. It also has, as a disruptive technology, adverse effects on "rental" and affordable housing. In all of these housing and potential and actual infrastructure features, the question of who pays (governments at all three levels) and the interests of homeowners or beneficiaries, or businesses, emerge. They are almost always accompanied by the dynamics of payment for duration and how to regulate between competing demands. There are also issues centred on whether needs are real or driven by existing cycles of budgetary politics and fiscal gestures that fall well short of the mark for many players most of the time. As with most other chapters in this book, given the impact of COVID-19 and the subsequent economic crisis, housing demands, needs, and trends could be fundamentally changed in both the short term and the longer term as Canadians adapt to new ways of working, travelling, and living and as real estate prices respond, household debt increases, and immigration falls. Funding programs for housing will also be an important part of government stimulus packages, and it will be important to align that funding with the changing reality and needs of Canadians, including both housing affordability and affordable housing. In an era of unprecedented low interest rates it is tempting, but ultimately short-term policy thinking, to promote real estate investment opportunities and Airbnb entrepreneurship above the needs of new or younger Canadians, or homeless people, looking to access the housing market. Such policies will disproportionately impact women and disadvantaged and racialized groups. It will also undermine other policies currently being developed to improve LTC for seniors and those aimed at increasing opportunities to age in place. It is impossible to "age in place" if you have no "place" to age in, making sharply increased institutionalization rates inevitable as Canada's "boomer" generation retires over the next fifteen years.

8

The Energy-Environment-Resources Pipelines Infrastructure Regime

INTRODUCTION

We now examine the energy-environment-resources pipelines infrastructure regime. Its initial three-word hyphenated policy and governance title is an entry point into a nexus of ideas, values, institutions, and complex change and inertia, but with a particular focus on pipelines. It is a nexus because each needs discussion and understanding of different types of energy, concepts of environment, and interwoven natural resources and resource industries and contours across Canada. This nexus features multiple institutions within key multi-level governmental ministerial, departmental, and agency realms and vis-à-vis economic and social interest groups and networks, some key features of which have already been previewed in chapters 1 and 3. We examine these dynamics and then relate them to pipeline battles and survival for competing/colliding and threatened major pipeline projects.

With these two core linked accounts in place, we then provide a summary analysis by deploying again our analytical framework centred on the interplay of the *three interacting elements*: ideas, discourse, and agendas; power structures, democracy, and governance; and temporal realities, conflicts, cycles, and technology. Conclusions about the regime then follow.

1 Energy, Environment, Resource Policy, and Institutional Nexus Dynamics and Complexity, 1970s to present

The content of "energy-environment-resource" policy involves types and subsets within each element and across its hyphenated discourse

and terrain. Thus "energy" includes oil, oil sands, natural gas, liquefied natural gas, hydroelectricity, and fracking. "Environment" evokes
meanings and discourse such as pollution control, safety, sustainable
development, climate change, carbon capture, and carbon pricing.
"Resource" policy and discourse embraces safe drinking water, rivers,
lakes, canals, oceans, and key aspects of nuclear power and safety.
Climate change challenges and environmental regulation are vast
realms with regard to both global and Canadian debate, successes,
failures, and half-measures (Klein 2014; Helm 2012; Doern, Auld,
and Stoney 2015) (see more below).

The institutional nexus at the federal level initially involves the
prime minister, the minister of Finance, Natural Resources Canada,
Fisheries and Oceans Canada, and Environment and Climate Change
Canada (with "climate change" added to the departmental name in
2015 by the Trudeau Liberals). Indigenous and Northern Affairs
Canada was a changed name, as we saw in chapter 1, because the
Liberals added "Indigenous" as a virtual constitutional imperative,
and was a replacement of the earlier long-term name of Indian Affairs
and Northern Development. The other key agencies involved include
the Canadian Environmental Assessment Agency, the National Energy
Board, and the Northern Pipeline Agency. As we also saw in chapter
1, more recent agency change has involved the Trudeau Liberals'
creation of the Impact Assessment Agency of Canada and the
Canadian Energy Regulator. This overall institutional nexus encompasses literally hundreds of laws, regulations, and guidelines that we
cannot cover in detail here. We stress simply that the institutional
nexus did not recently become complex. It has been so for the entire
period being looked at here in infrastructure policy and governance
regime terms.

The key Alberta story is also similar, functioning at the heart of its
energy and oil sands economy and society, but with seven similar
ministries involved in this regime (Alberta Government 2017a). It is
also anchored in a political system characterized by long-term multi-
decade Progressive Conservative Party rule and dominance until 2015,
when the NDP surprisingly and shockingly won power (Urquhart
2018), but with the United Conservative Party (UCP) returning the
Conservatives to office in May 2019 (see further discussion of Alberta
below). Space does not allow coverage of other provinces in detail,
but again the situation is similar regarding ministerial range and
administrative institutions, the provincial regulatory state, and civil

society and policy networks (Atkinson et al. 2013) and regarding the interplay of Canadian federalism and infrastructure (Allan et al. 2018).

Analysis of overall business-government relations in Canada, such as the research by Hale (2017; 2018), also stress such relations in and across many policy sectors interacting with federalism, regionalism, and provincial diversity in addition to the "political marketplace" of interest groups, policy communities, and lobbying. Canadian electoral federalism also produces political situations where there is greater turnover among political parties in power, a factor of some importance both here and in our second infrastructure policy and governance regime history regarding key pipeline battles.

In this infrastructure policy and governance regime history, we look first at the federal National Energy Board (NEB) and interpretations of its changing energy and environmental-resource dynamics at the federal and intergovernmental level. This is followed by a needed look at the energy-environment-climate change realm in Alberta as the leading provincial/national energy producer and player. We then explore recent conceptual and advocacy efforts by selected academics, think tanks, and interest groups to understand the complexity of both policy discourse and multiple core and changing institutions in this regime. We end with an account of studies that are focusing on Canada's weaknesses regarding energy and resources and other sources as critical infrastructure and international and national infrastructure security realms.

Regarding the NEB, the Doern, Prince, and Schultz (2014) analysis, centred on arguments about "rules and unruliness," included a historical look at the NEB in five periods (125–37): its origins and initial core mandate from 1959 to the late 1970s; its relative demise as a player in the 1980 to 1984 National Energy Policy era; its role in the dominant Mulroney era of liberalized energy markets; its consolidation in the 1990s to 2006 period of shared environmental and expanded safety mandates, although often disconnected from the climate change and Kyoto Protocol debate and larger regulatory failure in the Liberal Chrétien era; and its place in the oil sands and Alberta-dominated period in the Harper Conservative era, couched as "responsible resource development." In each of these periods, the NEB's core public utility regulatory function is at the centre of what it does and how it sees itself, but its mandate reaches much further, as do its changing regulatory grasp and its approaches to ever-more-complex market-centred and social and environmental conceptions of the public interest.

In the decade from 2002 to 2012, the NEB's changing view of itself is captured in sample annual reports, as it both chronicles and responds to new pressures and energy-environment dynamics during the later Chrétien years and then in the context of the Harper minority and majority governments. Thus, the 2007 NEB annual report highlights, early on, the board's risk-based life-cycle approach, which "relates to a company's performance as well as the scope of regulatory oversight required through the life cycle of a project" (National Energy Board 2008, 1). But, given the NEB's then location in Calgary, the board also refers to its establishment of a Land Matters Consultation Initiative, a response to the growing problem of angry and aggressive land owners, mainly in Alberta, defending their property rights against development encroachments by energy companies. Such property rights issues, and related land and resource management and boundary issues, had often been important in Alberta politics (see more on Alberta below).

By the time of the 2011 annual report, the NEB was stressing its needed and broadening approaches to public engagement (National Energy Board 2012, 1–2). This pre-eminently included consultations regarding Canadian Arctic offshore drilling. A report late in 2011 set out the information that the board would need to assess in any future applications for Arctic offshore drilling (National Energy Board 2011). The previously mentioned Land Matters Initiative had by 2011 resulted in the board forming a Land Matters Group that was drafting approaches to "company involvement programs." More broadly, the board drew attention to how it had taken steps in getting companies to develop "a strong safety culture through a management systems approach" (National Energy Board 2012, 2, 14). The dynamics of the oil sands era was also revealed through the fact that applications to the board for various approvals and licenses had doubled over the previous year.

In its 2016–17 Annual Report, the NEB was presenting its own more diverse ways of expressing the current and future regulatory challenges and priorities it and the country faced (National Energy Board 2017). Its opening description was that "we regulate pipelines, energy development and trade in the public interest with safety our primary concern" (3). The NEB "is a lifecycle regulator. We oversee the safety and environmental protection of a pipeline project from the application assessment phase, through to construction and operation," and due to the passage of the *Pipeline Safety Act* in 2016, "even after they are no longer in operation to make sure they remain safe" (3). On its safety and environment core mandate tasks, the report highlighted steps based on public input, such as strengthening *emergency management*. For this reason, the NEB issued an order in 2016 "requiring all NEB-regulated companies to make their emergency procedure manuals publicly available" (5).

In a 2017 presentation to a Safety Culture Summit in Halifax, the NEB's CEO, Peter Watson, made a keynote presentation that was quite frank about how the NEB was responding to the new Trudeau Liberal government's agenda, and also to changing energy and environment imperatives (Watson 2017a). Watson had come to be the NEB's head after a long and diverse career in the energy, environmental, and utility aspects of the Alberta regulatory governance and policy system. He opened his remarks with the following key items stressed: "the NEB is a lifecycle regulator"; the NEB "is in the middle of it all," namely "the most important public policy debates in Canada ... from pipeline safety, to controversial pipeline projects, to the relationship Canada has with Indigenous Peoples"; the NEB "strives towards excellence in all that we do" (1).

Watson, however, then spoke about "our journey" on that path when he stated that "our experience over the past months has resulted in us getting 'unstuck' from a way of thinking that had hindered us from asking 'what can we do better' ... and asking 'what does regulatory excellence mean to us?'" (2). This led directly into Watson's and the NEB's focus on "preventing harm," an approach "to move beyond traditional transactional business towards awareness and understanding of the big picture," including having an impact "on safety, security, innovation and prosperity for Canadians" and also pushing for "opportunities – beyond monitoring and compliance at the company level – to influence the broader system at an industry level" (2–3). This in turn led Watson to a discussion of how the NEB is fostering a "safety culture" that is broader than minimum standards and that operates at the organizational level.

It is also crucial to mention the evolution of Alberta's energy and related environmental regulatory policy and governance system and its infrastructure implications. The Alberta Energy and Utilities Board (AEUB) emerged in the mid-1990s out of a merger of two previous separate bodies (see Doern and Gattinger 2003, 135–41). Its mandate responsibilities were aimed at ensuring the "safe, responsible and efficient development of Alberta's energy resources" (135), including pipelines and transmission lines. The AEUB's "facilities" include regulated wells, pipelines, batteries, and plants (136). Overall, the AEUB's processes were governed by more than forty pieces of legislation. As stressed above, it was also governed by a Progressive Conservative government long in power and used to power and how to manage it.

A decade later, in 2010–11, a further restructured Alberta energy-environment-resource regulatory system emerged (Doern 2012). It came after a 2010 Regulatory Enhancement Task Force report and process, and then a follow-up Enhancing Assurance discussion document. But the discussion of regulatory "enhancement" and enhancing "assurance" showed how general and managerial the Alberta government and the Alberta ministry discourse were, even as they sought to move further into an ever-more-complex energy and resource nexus that now explicitly included the oil sands economy, the environment, related resources such as water, and overall climate change. In a review of proposals as they headed into a pre-legislative phase in 2012–13, Doern argued that "greater clarity in law and policy is needed to ensure that substantive mandate values rather than management principles are the main basis for defining the public interest and for governing and regulating in the new integrated system" (5). This analysis also argued that "the Alberta reform's intermittent reference to the need for life-cycle approaches needs further clarity when thought of, or presented in policy or regulatory terms" (6). The eventual new governance structure was the Alberta Energy Regulator (AER).

Under the New Democratic Party led by Premier Rachel Notley, the AER had been recrafted as a regulatory body with a "mandate to provide for the efficient, safe, orderly, and environmentally responsible development of Alberta's enery resources" (Alberta Energy Regulator 2017). As for what it does, the AER said then that it is "responsible for regulating oil, oil sands, natural gas, and coal projects in Alberta from application and constructionto production, abandonment and reclamation" (2). Also highlighted are "advancements in technology, such as horizontal wells and multi-stage hydraulic fracturing, that have enabled the economic development of previously unattainable 'light' oil and gas resources" (2). Unmentioned, not surprisingly, was the massive extent to which fracking had already transformed the US energy industry and infrastructure and fundamentally harmed Canada's energy exports to the US (Prud'homme 2014).

The Notley NDP government, however, announced early on a Climate Leadership Plan that included a carbon levy and rebates, ending coal production, developing renewable energy, capping oil sands emissions, and reducing methane emissions (Alberta Government 2017b). Some authors such as Berman (2017) felt this gave them a positive early view of the government, but he also stressed that "even under this government, the cumulative effects of fossil fuel develop-ment are growing and industry continues to obtain sweeping approvals that are shocking for their lack of environmental rigour" (2). He showed in particular how the Notley government "approved a tailings management plan for Suncor Energy Incorporated, the oldest company in the Canadian tar sands. By approving this plan, Suncor will get an additional 70 years after their operations shut down to clean up the environmental mess that they have created over 60 years of oil extrac-tion." The toxic mass of sludge in these ponds "contain[s] a unique cocktail of toxic chemicals and hydrocarbons that will remain in molasses-like suspension for centuries if left alone" (2).

Oil sands tailings environmental regulatory inadequacies have remained a focal point for critical analysis by the Pembina Institute (McNeill 2017). The analysis by Urquhart (2018) also provides a broad comprehensive look at Alberta's oil sands, casting its birth as "market fundamentalism," but also looking at its myriad environ-mental weaknesses and damage (chap. 7–8). It also cast the NDP government as "new government, same approach" (chap. 9).

Pipeline politics and conflict also hit the Notley agenda, especially in 2017 when, after a tough political battle lasting over a decade, the Alberta Progressive Conservative Party transformed itself into the United Conservative Party (UCP), devoted to ousting the NDP from power in the 2019 Alberta election. In this pre-election context, the pipeline politics compelled Notley to make greater explicit efforts to develop a pro-pipeline campaign. This was centred on the Kinder Morgan pipeline expansion in British Columbia, but was also a defence of the now-threatened/cancelled Energy East pipeline (see a more detailed look in our second policy history on the main pipeline battles in the Harper era and the current Trudeau Liberal context). Interestingly, the latter included the dangled plans of a special review team that advised the Trudeau Liberals to move the NEB headquarters from Calgary back to Ottawa (Alberta Minister of Energy 2017). But before proceeding with more on the Alberta UCP government and the post 2019 federal election, which saw theTrudeau Liberals weak-ened by voters converting them to a minority government, it is worth looking at the nature of other accounts and challenges.

Priorities in energy-environment-resources infrastructure can take widely diverse directions. For example, the *Alberta Oil Magazine*'s 2010 focus on Canada's top twenty-five energy infrastructure projects started off with its top three (Jaremco 2010). Each was centred on carbon capture and storage (CCS) aimed overall at disposing of up to 1.3 million tonnes per year of greenhouse gas emissions. This garnered considerable interest in Alberta, where it played into views that it would show environmental and climate change awareness. It was also of some interest to the federal Harper Conservatives and thus led to a 2008 CCS task force study. CCS seeks to capture emissions of CO_2 from industrial facilities before they are released into the atmosphere. The CO_2 is then compressed and transported by pipeline or tanker truck to a storage site and injected into deep geological formations between one and five kilometres underground, where it will, it is argued, be safely stored for the long term.

Thus some CCS work was underway, but progress was not yet demonstrable, only potential. Meadowcroft and Hellin (2010) refer to the dynamics of a technological transition versus an enhanced "carbon lock in." The lock-in can easily occur as societies become bound to a carbon-intensive energy trajectory under which "early competition over the purposes and orientation of new technologies typically settles down after the emergence of a 'dominant design'" (239–40).

Three very different climate change analyses are also useful in indicating scope and content in terms of this regime analysis regarding federal, Albertan, and more complex international parameters. The first is a brief but insightful analysis by Craft, Howlett, Crawford, and McNutt (2013). It examines the "infrastructure policy sector's capacity to respond to climate change "adaption" through an analysis of the Canadian case" via "a three-level" examination of capacity at the macro, meso, and micro levels. The macro level involves a "virtual policy network analysis." The meso level focuses on the "lead department's evolving mandate and resources" and the micro level involves an "analysis of survey data related to departmental workers policy tasks and attitudes" (42). The authors conclude overall "that the policy capacity in the Canadian infrastructure sector will be unable to meet the demands placed upon the sector to respond to the increasing challenges of climate change adaption" (61).

At a very different scale of coverage and scope is a study by the Canadian Academy of Engineering (2016) centred on understanding current and future transformations "for major reductions in GHG emissions." The full technical and modelling results cover the greenhouse gas challenge overall and sector-by-sector opportunities. These sectors and sector opportunities include "oil, natural gas, coal, LNG supply and trade" but also the transport sector, residential, commercial, and agricultural sectors, and others, extending to biomass feedstocks, biofuels, and carbon capture (67–126). Scenarios are offered on each, including economic impacts.

Regarding the fossil fuels sector, the study concludes that "this is the sector that will be subject to the greatest change in Canada and around the world ... there will be a need to greatly reduce dependence on burning fossil fuels for providing energy-related services" (295). The study also comments on the nature of "institutional development" because of the need to derive corresponding unit costs and limits for respective transformation options. These options need to be analyzed in a comprehensive integrated multi-sector and multi-jurisdictional context and over a long time horizon" (297). The *Economist* report on the geopolitics of energy (*Economist* 2018d) has a similar focus on what it calls the "new power superpowers" as they variously develop and compete with and for diverse energy sources (3–11), including the US and shale, renewables in numerous countries, and the decline of oil in petrostates.

Significant too is the global analysis of climate change by Naomi Klein (2014). Her book, *This Changes Everything: Capitalism vs the Climate*, ties climate change to a fundamental failure of capitalism and democracy. It can only be, in her view, met by a new model of human progress that will confront the economic policies of deregulated capitalism and endless resource extraction. Her analysis includes chapters on Indigenous rights and also the "atmospheric commons." Klein is not alone in seeing democratic failure. Analysis within and about Alberta by Shivastava and Stefanic (2016) also sees close ties between Alberta oil and the decline of democracy. The notion of a needed atmospheric commons also emerges in the November 2017 global climate change discussions in Bonn, Germany, and is summed up and interpreted in the *Economist* (2017) analysis as the need for "sucking up carbon" as a crucial element in actually reducing the total amount of carbon dioxide.

Also important in understanding this regime are a series of academic and think tank studies that seek to understand and embrace complexity and identify weaknesses and opportunities for policy and institutional nexus realities. For example, the analysis by Noble (2016) of

eight policy case studies across Canada involving Aboriginal participation in environmental assessment argues in part for the need for
regional assessments by governments that are more comprehensive,
rather than being triggered by a given project. Related analysis by
Maclean (2016) argues for more comprehensive scope and governance
change, the former based on root-and-branch change in Canada's
weakened environmental governance system, due to the problem of
identifying and escaping regulatory capture. Hughes (2016) argues
for tougher looks at contaminated sites and the dynamics of the
rough-and-ready nature of the allocation of liability.

A further study by Cleland, Nourallah, and Fast (2016) focuses on
how to understand local communities' trust and confidence in energy
authorities. Among its findings are that "there is a lack of adequate
forums for community involvement and a lack of adequate and accessible information, all well upstream of individual project applications and regulatory decisions, often involving regional level,
multi-project and long-term considerations" (2).

Also of interest analytically is a study by Iacobacci (2017) on "business cases" for major infrastructure projects in Canada. It focuses
empirically on urban public transit Projects, but the analysis is underpinned by a useful and necessarily complex typology of "business
cases in public infrastructure space" (5). The framework centres on
lists of asset classes, project types, evaluation questions, and stakeholders. Asset classes include privately owned infrastructure for energy
and pipelines. On the "stakeholders" list, Iacobacci includes: sponsors/
owners; regulators; communities affected; other funders/investors;
taxpayers; and other interest groups (5). Under "project types" one
finds: new builds; refurbishments; regulations; pricing decisions; and
other policies and programs. His "evaluation questions" are those
that are "strategic" such as "what is the problem?" or "economic"
such as "are we better off? (And by how much?)" But "deliverability"
overall is also tagged, in addition to socio-economic "distributional/
equity considerations" (5).

An analysis by the Canada West Foundation (2017) focuses on
modernizing the National Energy Board (NEB). But it opens by saying
that de facto "it is as much about entire energy decision making as
it is about the NEB" (5). It then stresses that the "unresolved political
questions such as climate and Indigenous policy … have found their
way into the NEB process *where they do not belong*. In a representative liberal democracy, political and policy questions are best addressed

by elected representatives, not regulators" (6, our emphasis). The analysis then seeks to argue about the importance of differentiating and keeping separate the values/criteria of *legitimacy* versus *trust* (7–17). Thus, the report reiterates that "climate change decisions should not be made by the NEB" (8) because they are "political."

But procedural fairness, which is based on trust, can be advanced, in part because "Canadians believe that the NEB process is fair" (10). But "trust" needs thought regarding reforms because "trust involves something more; it is highly subjective and constitutes a leap of faith for each individual" (3). A number of specific changes are then advocated or illustrated in the study. For example, on the trust front, the study recommends that the "NEB's energy information function should be housed ... in a respected trusted federal body such as Statistics Canada ... [thus the NEB] will avoid the perception of conflict of interest and build trust in both energy information and the NEB" (3).

A follow-up study by the Canada West Foundation (2018) was centred on a reponse to new legislation by the Trudeau Liberals that contained proposals for a new Canada Energy Regulator (CER) to replace the NEB, and also a new Impact Assessment Agency for project assessment, previewed earlier in this chapter and in chapter 1. Titled *Unstuck*, the Canada West Foundation report reiterated, regarding the CER, its central argument that the "regulatory process is not the place to debate government policy ... It is not set up to deal with policy debates, nor should it ... and the legislative framework should define clear mandates, roles and responsibilities of the regulator, minister(s) and cabinet" (3).

A valuable study published by the University of Ottawa (Cleland and Gattinger 2017) also examined energy decision-making in Canada, characterizing it as a "system under stress" and needing "informed reform" because it is "reaching the point of dysfunction" (4). The initial key policy gaps highlighted by the authors relate to "climate, reconciliation with Indigenous peoples, and cumulative/regional effects of energy development" (4). The three main "stress points" that are high priorities for reform and for reformers are identified as: "the policy-regulatory nexus: the two energy solitudes; who decides? the balance between local and higher level decision authorities; and, how to decide: engagement, information and capacity" (6).

The study shows how "the number of players in the energy decision-making system and the complexity of their interdependencies and interconnections has grown considerably," and that "in particular actions by Indigenous and municipal governments have shown that more attention needs to be paid to these entities" (25). The authors ultimately argue that the system needs a "systems-based approach." But key limits are also stressed by a final declaration that "first of all, big unresolved policy – decarbonization and reconciliation with Canada's indigenous peoples – will be chaotic, politically messy and expensive. It would require human resource capabilities far greater than Canada devotes today to managing energy policy and regulation" (41). The Cleland and Gattinger analysis does not highlight or use the discourse of "infrastructure" per se, but it does make a brief reference in its discussion of "planning scales" to "physical and market energy systems," "innovation … and aging/renewal/replacement of capital stock," and "specific energy project decisions" (25). Much of this kind of reform and massive complexity is inherent in the Trudeau Liberal 2018 announcements and proposals regarding both the new Canadian Energy Regulator and the Impact Assessment Agency of Canada (Duke 2018; Canada 2018a; 2018b).

The Canadian Energy Pipeline Association (CEPA) is a business lobby whose recent views and discourse about energy pipeline regulation and governance are also worth citing. Its 2015 "Pipeline Industry Performance Report" (Canadian Energy Pipeline Association 2015) is its first "public performance" report. CEPA "represents Canada's transmission companies who operate approximately 117,000 kilometres of pipeline in Canada," cast as "energy highways" for 97 per cent of Canada's natural gas and onshore crude oil production from producing regions to markets throughout North America. The report states that CEPA's "Vision" is "a safe, socially and environmentally sustainable energy pipeline industry for Canadians" (1).

Its "Mission" is to "continually enhance the operating excellence, business environment and recognized responsibility of the Canadian energy transmission pipeline industry through leadership and credible engagement between member companies, goverments, the public and stakeholders." CEPA's "Values" are stated to be "accountability, transparency, respect, and leadership," and are instantiated via a process whereby CEPA members "have set competition aside and are working together to improve performance in three broad areas: safety, environment, and socio-economic" (2). The CEPA president also stresses that energy transmission pipelines "are part of Canada's critical infrastructure." The CEPA board of directors leads off with its view that "we must earn the public's trust and the continued right to operate." This view is linked immediately to the CEPA goal of "zero incidents" and to its stated view that when "it comes to safety, CEPA members don't compete, we cooperate and collaborate" (2–3). This in turn is tied to the CEPA Integrity First program, begun in 2012 and tied to the previously mentioned ideas of safety, environment, and socio-economic improvement.

It is also important to locate in this macro "pipeline" mapping some basic contours of the *natural gas industry* and its related infrastructure. In its 2018 pre-Budget Submission, its main lobby group, the Canadian Gas Association (2018), said that "[t]hrough over 450,000 kilometers of transmission and distribution gasline, supported by a robust energy storage network, natural gas is delivered to just under seven million unique residential, commercial and industrial locations ... Ultimately, over half of all Canadians benefit from affordable, clean burning, safe, and reliable natural gas solutions to heat buildings, generate electricity, fuel vehicles, and power appliances. Today, natural gas meets 36% of Canada's energy needs" (1). The discourse here is not pipelines, but it is a crucial infrastructure network that is almost four times bigger than pipelines and far more pan-Canadian, but with enormous local impacts. Not surprisingly, therefore, in any macro energy infrastructure agenda, its lobby, the Canadian Gas Association, has a permanent capacity to be heard federally, provincially, and locally across Canada. The natural gas industry was indeed "heard" late in 2018, as per our discussion in chapter 1 of the announcement of a $40 billion LNG project for a pipeline carrying natural gas from Dawson Creek in northeastern BC to a new processing plant in Kitimat, where the gas would be liquefied for overseas export (Schmunk 2018; Morgan 2018; Bundale 2018).

Finally, and complex in a different sense, are the issues of *critical infrastructure* (already previewed briefly in chapter 1) and *critical energy protection and security*. An analysis by Jacques Shore (2008) builds on the post-9/11 concept of critical infrastructure (CI) via a focus on *critical energy infrastructure (CEI) protection*, in this case with a look at what the legal imperatives are to protect such infrastructure. It begins with his mapping of Canadian CI, which is made up "of a number of sectors that include energy and utilities, communications and information technology, finance, health care, food, water, transportation, government, and manufacturing" (2). These sectors face "a range of physical and cyber threats that include terrorism, natural phenomen[a] such as earthquakes, floods, ice storms, accidents and cyber attacks" (2). Shore also stresses how "Canada is vulnerable to attacks on energy infrastructure aimed at disrupting service to the United States" (2–3). For these and other reasons, "protecting national security, which encompasses CEI security, is a task for which government has primary responsibility" (3), even though "most oil production and transmission systems are owned and operated by the private sector" (3). Shore is leery about the extent to which these challenges are being dealt with in Canada, but points to how the "peace, order, and good government" provision in the *Constitution Act* will be pivotal. This may be most manifest in the basic need to reduce government liability relating to the "legal imperative to protect CEI" (6). He relates this to issues of negligence under tort law as decided by the Supreme Court of Canada. But case law decisions may implicate private players in the CEI domain as well.

Critical energy infrastructure protection is the focal point for analysis by Angela Gendron (2010). She begins by noting that various "governments have claimed that emergency management and critical infrastructure protection are major priorities" but that "the reality appears rather different from the rhetoric" (iii). She argues that neither "is there any consistency in the identification, regulation, or application of security standards from one sector to another," and that while "complex and emerging threats respect no boundaries, different jurisdictions in Canada adopt a variety of countermeasures against threats to national critical infrastructure" (iii). The Gendron analysis stresses that energy sector products are highly diverse but also function in a "regionally concentrated" supply infrastructure context that is "closely integrated continentally with the United States" (iii). The notion of an "integrated 'all-hazards' risk management" system is not even close to a reality, nor to an agreed-on definition (iii).

The analysis of how Canada does and does not manage threats to critical infrastrastructure by Quigley, Bisset, and Mills (2017) examines the social context that shapes the Canadian government's ability to prepare for and respond to emergencies. It includes capacities to deal with industrial failures, natural disasters, pandemics, cyber attacks, and terrorist threats. An analysis edited by Balleisen, Bennear, Krawiec, and Wiener (2017), titled *Policy Shock*, examines the recalibration of risk and regulation after oil spills, nuclear accidents, and financial crises in several countries. It does so in the context of dynamics tied to the insurance industry, exploring how narratives shape risk, and the dyanamics of "policy regret." It argues that after "the immediate challenges of disaster management, crises often reveal new evidence or frame new normative perspectives that drive future events of a similar magnitude. Such responses vary widely – from cosmetically masking inaction, to creating stronger incentive systems, requiring greater transparency, reorganizing government institutions and tightening regulatory standards" (1).

It makes sense, as we end our first policy and governance history, for us to capture an initial sense in late October 2019 of the Jason Kenney era and how the United Conservative Party (UCP) leader was dealing with the previously mentioned Alberta Energy Regulator (AER). First, it was announced in the UCP's first budget that the AER would face "cuts of up to $147 million," cuts seemingly in the 50 per cent range over the budget period of four years (Jones 2019a). Even more tellingly, it was announced that senior staff of the Alberta Energy Regulator faced a scandal on their departure, and relating to more recent behaviour in Alberta's troubled oil sands economy (Jones 2019b). A more detailed account in early November 2019 (Seskus 2019) said that "weeks after the provincial government launched a review of the agency, three investigations detailed gross mismanagement and a culture of fear inside the industry watchdog" (1–2). This was connected to earlier regulatory struggles where "industry complained of slow approval times, while environmentalists brought attention to the growing and costly legacy of aging energy infrastructure like orphaned pipelines and oil wells" (3).

In the same time period, November 2019, after the federal election and with the federal Liberals newly under the constraints of governing as a minority, the Alberta government and other key interests stressed the need for Alberta to gain more provincial autonomy (Rieger 2019). Their proposals included the creation of "a new Fair Deal Panel" that went well beyond the oil and gas industry and climate change to include areas such as pension plans, ending the province's relationship with the RCMP, and establishing a formal provincial constitution. The panel submitted its final report to government in May 2020. It recommended numerous ways to ensure Alberta has a strong voice in Confederation, including fairer funding allocations from Ottawa, better representation for Alberta in the House of Commons, and exploration of an Alberta Pension Plan and Alberta Police Force. We disscus the UCP and Jason Kenney political dynamic in more detail below.

Our first infrastructure policy and governance history shows compellingly that the energy-environment-resources policy and institutional nexus starts with complexity but also leads to efforts to broaden it even further by an array of reform arguments and possible focal points for change and experimentation. It also shows that climate change responses and discourse are seen as inadequate, even as they challenge the primacy of fossil fuel economies in Canada and in the Alberta heartland for the now threatened oil sands. These issues and dynamics are crucial as we proceed to a multi-pipeline-focused second infrastructure policy and governance history.

2 Pipeline Battles and Survival
for Competing/Colliding and Threatened
Major Pipelines, 1980s to present

While our ultimate focus in this second regime-centred infrastructure policy and governance history is on major pipelines, it is useful initially to have a sense of what oil and gas pipelines imply as infrastructure. Revie (2015) and his contributing author/practioners look at pipelines in terms of both *design* issues and issues of *manufacture, fabrication, and construction.* Space does not allow a review of both sets of issues, but an illustrative look at the design realm includes analysis of: the pipeline integrity management system; supervisory control and data acquisition, material selection for fracture control; and both strain-based and stress-based design of pipelines (chap. 1–5). For oil and gas pipelines to function and adapt, there are specific features that are part of the overall story.

Crucially, we also need a macro look at Canada's pipeline system. Natural Resources Canada (2017d) provides a useful mapping. It begins with needed distinctions between oil versus natural gas pipelines, stressing that "both are coated steel pipe buried underground," but "natural gas transmission pipelines transport gas at higher pressures of 1000 psi or greater" (2). Also important is the fact that natural gas pipelines service most major cities in Canada with *connections to individual homes.* Historically, Canada's pipeline system *as* a system began in the 1950s following "major crude oil and gas finds in Western Canada" (2), especially in Alberta.

At present, there are "an estimated 840,000 kilometers of transmission, gathering and distribution lines in Canada with most provinces having significant pipeline infrastructure" (2). About 73,000 kilometres are federally regulated pipelines. Canada-US cross-border oil and gas pipelines are a key feature of the NEB's work in this regard, given that there are "31 oil and 39 natural gas" cross-border pipelines (3). The NEB regulates about 100 pipeline companies in Canada (inter-provincial and those involving international boundaries, mainly Canada-US). Pipelines that are intraprovincial (entirely within one province) are regulated by each individual province. These crucially include "the smaller natural gas distribution lines which go to every house with a natural gas furnace or water heater" (7). Those furnaces and heaters are also infrastructure.

The NRCan mapping also examines why "parts of Eastern Canada import oil when there is supply in Western Canada" (3). The answer is that eastern refineries (which are also infrastructure) are not con-nected by pipeline to western Canada. Instead, many eastern refineries "import oil from a variety of oil-producing countries" (4), with the US recently becoming the largest source of imported oil. The Organization of Petroleum Exporting Countries (OPEC) also supplies oil, and so do some North Sea countries such as Norway. Nonetheless, it is true that "Canada has the third largest crude oil reserves in the world" (4). In a further key mapping comment, Natural Resources Canada 2016 stresses that "Canada has an enormous endowment of oil and gas resources but only one significant export customer. 100 percent of our natural gas exports and 97 percent of our oil exports currently go to the United States … However, Canada will need to find new markets … to reach these markets, we will need additional pipeline capacity" (2).

Given these demands and choices, it is also important for any pipeline infrastructure story to have a brief core sense of how Alberta characterizes and maps its own pipeline and related infrastructure. Regarding natural gas, Alberta (Government of Alberta 2015) high-lights that it "has one of the most extensive natural gas systems in the world as part of its energy infrastructure, with more than 400,000 kilometers of energy related pipelines" (1) and that "about 71 per cent of Canada's natural gas production is from Alberta." Regarding oil, it has created "an extensive infrastructure that facilitates the continued drive to locate, drill for and transport the oil to market" (Alberta Energy 2017, 1). Again, "most of the crude oil produced in Alberta is exported to other markets" (1).

Regarding the massive oil sands resource, Alberta (2017) defines the oil sands as a "mixture of sand, water, clay and a heavy oil called bitumen. Once extracted, bitumen must be diluted or heated to enable it to flow or be pumped," and notes that the oil sands underlie

"142,200 square kilometers of land in northern Alberta" (1). Extraction from them involves, depending on the depth, one of two bitumen recovery methods: "surface mining" (about 20 per cent) or "in-situ" production (80 per cent). Also of interest in terms of our regime analysis overall is the data on oil sands investment, which was $23.4 billion in 2015, but "estimated at $16.6 billion in 2016, and is forecast at $12.1 billion in 2017" (2). Interestingly, writing in the US, Struzik (2016) stressed that "in the summer of 2014, when oil was selling for $114 per barrel, Alberta's tar sands industry was still confident in earlier predictions that it would nearly triple production by 2035. Companies such as Suncrude, Royal Dutch Shell, and Imperial Oil Limited were investing hundreds of billions of dollars in new projects to mine the thick, highly polluting bitumen" (1).

With the above national and Alberta pipeline infrastructure mappings as a crucial starting point, we can now begin to focus on the current/recent pipeline battles and dynamics. The federal Trudeau Liberal government initially listed the following six energy pipeline projects (NRCan 2017c) and the decision stages they were at.

- 2017 NGTL System Expansion Project
- Northern Gateway Project
- Line 3 Replacement Project
- Trans Mountain Expansion Project
- Towerbirch Expansion Project
- Energy East Pipeline Project

Not mentioned here is the Keystone XL pipeline, which, as we discuss below, is bound up in Canadian political-economic pipeline concerns but whose fate ultimately rested in US regulatory processes, as we have already previewed in chapter 3 and chapter 1.

Accompanying the summary discussion of each project are the Trudeau Liberals' January 2016 *five decision principles* "for project reviews which were designed to restore trust in the environmental assessment process" (NRCan 2017f) but are in fact more than that. These principles are: 1) no project proponent will be asked to return to the starting line; 2) decisions will be based on science, traditional knowledge of Indigenous peoples and other relevant evidence; 3) the views of the public and affected communities will be sought and considered; 4) Indigenous peoples will be meaningfully consulted, and where appropriate, impacts on their rights and interests will be accommodated; and 5) direct and upstream GHG emissions linked to the projects under review will be assessed (2). There is no doubt that these decision principles were an immediate declaration of what the Liberals and many others viewed as being the serious weaknesses of the previous Harper era (Toner, Cherniak, and Force 2016). They are inherent in the previsously mentioned Liberals' announced establishment of the Canadian Energy Regulator and the Impact Assessment Agency of Canada. We now look briefly at each pipeline project and the implicit and explicit agenda battles among them, nationally, regionally, and internationally, some of which cross over both the Harper and Trudeau eras and indeed earlier.

The lead pipeline battle examined centres on the Kinder Morgan *Trans Mountain Expansion Project* (NRCan 2017b). The Trudeau Liberal summary starts with its initial decision statement that it has "approved ... the project ... subject to 157 binding conditions that will be enforced by the National Energy Board before construction can begin, during construction and during operation" (2). The project involves building a new pipeline along the existing Trans Mountain pipeline route between Edmonton, Alberta and Burnaby, British Columbia, "which will increase the pipeline's capacity from 300,000 barrels to 890,000 barrels per day. The project will also expand the Westridge Marine Terminal in Burnaby to permit it to increase the number of tankers per month it can receive from five to 34" (2). Liberal highlights (on the pipeline, not on the Burnaby tanker capacity) also include: 89 per cent of new construction along existing rights-of-way; $6.8 billion capital investment; strategic access to new global markets will unlock the true value of Canada's natural resources; the project fits with Canada's climate plan to 2030; projected GHG emissions are within Alberta's 100 megatonne cap; more than $300 million is committed to Indigenous groups under mutual benefit and capacity agreements; $64.7 million is earmarked to fund an Indigenous pipeline environment committee to ensure ongoing monitoring of the project; the Oceans Protection Plan is the most significant investment ever to protect our oceans and coastlines; and there is a targeted action plan to promote the recovery of the Southern Resident Killer Whale population (1). Regarding the above-mentioned access to new global markets, it is later stated that the project "will diversify Canada's export market access for oil to markets in Washington State and northeast Asia ... and to secondary markets in the United States such as California, Hawaii and Alaska. It will also help address an emerging bottleneck in Canada's pipeline network which might otherwise drive producers to greater reliance on transportation by rail" (2).

The already complicated set of issues and processes inherent in the above summary features were further politicized when BC Premier Christy Clark's Liberal minority government, which had supported the project, was defeated by an NDP and Green Party coalition in late June 2017. NDP Premier John Horgan immediately announced that they would oppose the pipeline project (Harrison 2017). The new BC government knew that the pipeline, as an interprovincial pipeline, was under federal jurisdiction, but its core objections were that the project massively benefits Alberta economically while all the environmental costs and dangers reside in British Columbia (Bains 2017). The legal cases begun were centred on the argument that the NEB review and consideration "failed to consider the environmental impacts of increased tanker traffic" and that in real terms the expanded pipeline would be the "proverbial pipeline to nowhere" (Bennett 2017, 1). Other cases were centred on weaknesses and inadequacies regarding consultations "with First Nations" and in relation to environmental assessment processes (Penner 2017). Thus it was possible for the BC government and others to delay the project in several ways, but the BC Attorney General is quoted as saying that government "won't unduly delay permitting" the project (2).

The second key pipeline to examine is the *Energy East Pipeline Project (EEP)* proposed by TransCanada (Major Projects Management Office, 2017). It is a massive "4,500 kilometer pipeline proposed to carry 1.1 million barrels of crude oil per day from Alberta and Saskatchewan to refineries in Eastern Canada" (1). It involved "converting 3000 km of existing natural gas pipelines to oil and constructing 1600 km of new pipeline" as well as "over 70 new pump stations, 4 tank terminals and a marine terminal in Saint John, NB" (1), with the marine facilities enabling access to other international markets by ship. The Eastern Mainline project involved a separate application. On 5 October 2017 TransCanada notified the NEB that it was *withdrawing* its two applications (National Energy Board 2017). Thus both the proposal and its withdrawal are a part of the overall regime story.

Again, the EEP was met with the Trudeau era's new additional pipeline decision principles mentioned above. The first was the need to "undertake deeper consultations with Indigenous peoples," which, given the expense of the pipeline, would require that there would be "five Regional Consultation Coordinators" (Major Projects Management Office 2017, 1). Also indicated was the proviso that once the NEB issued its report, the "MPMO will lead whole-of-government consultations with Aboriginal groups on outstanding issues related to potential or established Aboriginal or Treaty rights" (2). Also now required would be work and actions by Environment and Climate Canada to "assess the upstream greenhouse gas emissions associated with this project and make this information public"(2).

The unexpected cancellation of the project by TransCanada on economic grounds produced a range of reactions and attributions of blame and credit. A basic reponse asserted that "big business and big oil lose climate battle in pipeline review" (McSheffrey 2017). A key to this criticism is that the NEB would be "agreeing for the first time in its history to consider both upstream and downstream greenhouse gas emissions while reviewing a major project" and thus both direct and indirect emissions would be assessed (1). McSheffrey reports that earlier both TransCanada and the Canadian Chamber of Commerce sought to discourage the NEB because, for starters, the huge pipeline "would cross some 3000 streams, rivers and waterways on its way from the oil patch to eastern Canada" (3). In short, many of these issues are out of the control of TransCanada. Not surprisingly, the cancellation decision was toxic in Alberta, with some claiming that it was "an attack on Alberta" (Graney 2017, 1). Alberta Premier Notley was criticized about it, but also began mounting her own campaign to save it and other pipeline projects.

Other responses to the cancellation, such as by Beer (2017), argued that TransCanada was fortunate to have it cancelled because the "basic reality faced by projects like Energy East is that, like it or not, the fossil fuel era is rapidly drawing to a close" (1). Beer poses questions such as "is there any realistic scenario in which a 30 to 60 year piece of fossil fuel infrastructure is *not* going to be a recipe for controversy, litigation, and eventual bankruptcy?" He goes on to say that "no one is suggesting that oil and gas consumption will fall to zero tomorrow, next week, or even next year. But a new, multi-billion-dollar pipeline isn't about today's markets. Such pipelines only have a purpose or a business case if its proponents can confidently anticipate steady demand through the middle of the century and beyond" (2).

Columnist Chantal Hebert (2017) was not looking that far ahead in 2017, but she did suggest that the end of the Energy East project "could mark the start of federal-provincial turmoil" (1) when one considers *changing interacting electoral cycles*. She focused initially on Quebec politics and the contending parties in a 2018 election, and argues that "from a partisan perspective, its demise is a net loss to a sovereignty movement in search of a defining irritant between Quebec and the rest of Canada" (3). She stressed that "for all the harsh words exchanged between Quebec, Saskatchewan and Alberta over Energy East, the main political result of its demise is to shift ground zero of the pipeline debate to Western Canada" (3).

Third in the top three pipeline controversies and battles we look at is the *Keystone XL pipeline* and its conditional approval in the state of Nebraska on 20 November 2017 (Smith 2017). On a 3–2 vote the Nebraska Public Service Commission gave its approval of the TransCanada Coproject, but on a nearby alternate route that would itself require further hearings and review. That route "veers east to follow the path of the existing Keystone Pipeline" (1). We have discussed the Keystone XL infrastructure saga in chapter 3 as a feature of Canada-US energy development, including under the Trump Administration, which had given the pipeline federal approval regarding environmental safety matters under US federal jurisdiction. The Obama government had previously denied approval of Keystone XL on climate change and related grounds, much to the disapproval of both the Harper government and the Trudeau Liberals. The XL designation meant that the pipeline was to provide an extention to existing TransCanada lines that bring Canadian/Alberta oil sands petroleum 1,100 miles to the US Gulf coast to connect there with existing pipelines. Supporters of Keystone XL in the US include "many labour unions and business groups" (2) but its opponents in Nebraska include "a bipartisan coalition of landowners, Native Americans and environmentalists" (3).

In Canada, both Alberta Premier Notley and Prime Minister Trudeau applauded the decision but also knew that more delays would follow. As Haavardsrud (2017) observed, however, "in the current supercharged world of pipeline politics, no decision was ever going to be that straightforward" (1), and indeed the "shrugging off of even seemingly good news on the pipeline file is, by now, a standard reaction from Canada's energy industry, which has seen its hopes for a major export pipeline stymied by several cancelled projects, years of delays, and what many see as unnecessary regulatory and government foot dragging" (1). It came as no surprise when President Biden effectively cancelled the Keystone XL pipeline project with an executive order signed on day one of his presidency.

In fairness, the three "other" current pipline projects on the NRCan master list, while nominally less controversial, deserve mention because of their infrastructure importance in other ways. Thus the *Towerbirch Expansion Project* involves a NOVA Gas Transmission Ltd (NGTL) application to expand its current "natural gas pipeline system in northwestern Alberta and northeast British Columbia to connect new gas fields to the system to meet growing demand" (NRCan 2017f, 1). Two pipeline sections, one fifty-five kilometres long and the other thirty-two, are involved. The NEB will require the company to meet twenty-four conditions, including the regeneration of the Old Growth Forest Bird Habitat, a project-specific environmental protection plan, Indigenous monitoring, and waterways authorizations under the Fisheries Act (2–3).

The *Line 3 Replacement Project* by Enbridge involves a $4.8 billion capital investment to replace an existing five-decades-old pipeline from Hardisty, Alberta, to Gretna, Manitoba (NRCan 2017e). It will have more modern technology and safer standards and thicker pipeline in many sections; Line 3 "serves as a vital link from North American production regions to Minnesota, Wisconsin and other North American refinery markets" (2). Other required provisions are: GHG emissions "must operate with[in] Alberta's 100 megatonne cap"; "$21.6 million to fund an Indigenous environment committee"; and "over 27 million in engagement agreements for Indigenous groups committed by proponent" (1).

The *2017 NGTL System Expansion Project* is a Nova Gas Transmission Ltd's request to expand its existing "current natural gas pipeline system to northern Alberta in order to connect new gas fields and to continue to supply local customers and North American markets – 91 percent of construction will be on land already in use for pipelines and roads" (NRCan 2017a). The concerns and conditions being reviewed/required include: emergency response; waterways (under the Fisheries Act); caribou habitat restoration plan; wetlands and wildlife; and engaging Indigenous communities (2).

While it is important in infrastructure terms to look at and appreciate each pipeline separately, it is also crucial to draw on Hoberg (2013; 2016) for analysis of the political and institutional dynamics of *multipipeline* processes, outcomes, delays, and resistance. Hoberg's 2013 article looked at the political risk features of pipeline alternatives. He argued that risk is a function of the number of "institutional veto points," such as: whether opposition groups have access to veto points;

whether the project can take advantage of existing infrastructure; the salience of concentrated environmental risks; and the jurisdictional separation of risks and benefits (371). Hoberg (2016) has also looked at the Trans Mountain Pipeline as a single key case, but this time relates it to the "politics of structure" or the "struggle over defining the institutional rules of the game" (1). It is also tied to "the political dynamics of energy in Canada in the 2010s," thus covering at the federal level both the Harper era and the current Trudeau era.

As already highlighted, Alberta Premier Rachel Notley's position, both in Alberta and nationally, caused her to offer a much more aggressive campaign in the pipeline political economy, especially now that the Alberta economy was again growing at a 7 per cent rate. When speaking to a Calgary business lobby and audience, she garnered strong applause for the following points she made and the discourse used:

- "We need a Canadian pipeline built to a Canadian coast."
- "I reminded those folks out east that there is not a school, not a hospital, not a road, not a bus station and not a port ... that doesn't owe something to a strong Alberta energy industry."
- "To my political colleagues in the federal NDP, I said: 'You can't write working people and their jobs out of climate action. You need to start writing them in, so please, smarten up.'"
- "To the federal Liberals, I said, and I say again today: 'You have to step up.'"
- "The NEB's decision to include downstream emissions in evaluating pipeline proposals – like with Energy East – was an historic overreach, something that no other industry is subject. It should not, it cannot be a precedent in the future" (Quoted in Fletcher 2017, 1).

Pipeline battles as infrastructure sagas are by no means over. Notley also spoke in Vancouver a few days later to do battle in support of the coastal pipeline she most wants to see supported in the national interest, rather than rejected in the environmental interest of BC alone. Her battle strategies included initially a plan to ban BC wine in Alberta, but she decided on a partial pullback from this plan, choosing to instead use a direct action on limiting oil and natural gas exports to BC (Bennett 2018). Saskatchewan Premier Scott Moe added to this pressure by saying that he would stand by Alberta "if the province decides to restrict oil exports to pressure British Columbia to abandon its opposition to the Trans Mountain pipeline expansion project" (von Scheel 2018, 1).

Premier Notley escalated the Kinder Morgan and overall Alberta-BC pipeline battle when Alberta passed legislation "giving the province's energy minister the power to choke off gasoline shipments to British Columbia if that province continues to throw-up barriers to the Trans Mountain pipeline expansion" (Bellefontaine 2018, 1). This "turn off the taps" strategy was premised on the fact that "Vancouver drivers are currently payng about $1.57 per litre for gasoline and blocking shipments could push prices even higher, putting political pressure on B.C. Premier John Horgan" (2). The BC response to date has been to mount a legal challenge.

The pipeline battles increased further in interesting ways as later 2018 political-economic developments paved the way for the 2019 federal election. Public pressure came from CEOs in the oilpatch who blamed high costs and red tape for the erosion of Canada's competitive edge, especially vis-à-vis much lower costs in the US in the Trump-era context (Bakx and Seskus 2018). Following the 2014 oil price crash, profits have returned but "the inability to construct new oil and gas export pipelines is front and centre" (2).

As a result, the federal minister of Environment and Climate Change announced that a new federal Impact Assessment Agency (IAA) will be created to lead all federal reviews of major projects. Under these provisions, the existing *Canadian Environmental Assessment Act* (2012) is in the process of being repealed. The Canadian Environmental Law Association (2018) review of the legislation supported the idea of a new independent agency to conduct and coordinate impact assessments for "designated projects," including a new "early planning phase that seeks Indigenous and public input on the proponent's project description" (2). But it also argues that the legislation "is marred by a number of serious flaws," including the continued use of "ad hoc review panels rather than establishing the new Agency as a quasi-judicial commission" (3).

Among other energy interests, the Canadian Energy Pipeline Association (CEPA), citing the "poison" of the array of existing pipeline battles and foibles, offers an overall summary view that "CEPA does not see anything within the Impact Assessment Act that will attract energy investment to Canada" (2018, 2).

Also present on the complex Trudeau Liberal agenda was Bill C-48, an Act respecting the regulation of vessels that transport crude oil or persistent oil to or from ports or marine installations located along British Columbia's north coast (Library of Parliament, Chong, and Sweeney 2018). The BC north coast extends from Vancouver Island to Alaska. Introduced by the federal minister of Transport, Marc Garneau, the bill "formalizes a crude oil tanker moratorium ... and sets penalties for contravention of this moratorium." It related to earlier policy and agreements in the 1970s and 1980s but re-emerged in the context of the battle over the Northern Gateway Pipeline project.

Crude oil and persistent oils are defined, with the latter's fourteen types "including partially upgraded bitumen, one of the products from the Alberta oil sands" (3). The Bill is "binding on the provinces and the federal government" and there are also "prohibitions and exemptions" and "reporting requirements" and offences and punishment, such as "conviction on indictment: a maximum fine of $5 million." Support for the Bill has come from the Coastal First Nations – an "alliance of First Nations on British Columbia's north and central coasts, as well as on the archipelago of Haida Gwai." Opposition came from the Chamber of Shipping of British Columbia, and the Canadian Association of Petroleum Producers (7). But Natural Resources Canada's 2019–20 Departmental Plan was also locating these kinds of developments in an even broader plan centred on "creating a sustainable resource advantage" (Natural Resources Canada 2019, 2).

Of interest also was the opposition expressed by the Chief's Council for the Eagle Spirit Energy Projects – a First Nations-led energy corridor proposal. The Eagle Spirit Energy Pipeline, developed and financed over the previous five years, needed to be added to the national working list of pipelines. Its proposed route "would run about 1562 kilometers from Fort McMurray to a terminal at either Grassy Point, BC or Huder, Alaska" (Laanela 2018, 1) and "carry up to two million barrels of medium to heavy crude oil a day from Fort McMurray to tide water on the West Coast," and it has the backing of the Vancouver Aquilini Investment Group, at $16 billion (2). The intent was to bypass the legislative ban or to arrange to have the pipeline hosted by a landowner in the US border town of Hyder, Alaska.

The Kinder Morgan pipeline is also not the only issue fuelling the previously discussed Alberta-BC battles. Also present are the roles and strategies of Indigenous peoples in BC whose traditions and locations are water-based and island- and land-based in complex ways. They involve a territory that is "home to 17 First Nations bands and the world's only inland temperate rainforest" (Kassam 2018, 2). It stretches "across a wide swath of south-central British Columbia" (2), but the "territory is unceded, meaning no treaties were ever signed between Canada and the Secwepemc" (2). Central to their strategy vis-à-vis Kinder Morgan was the work of the Tiny House Warriors to build ten tiny homes, strategically placed to show how "our land is our home" and to thwart the pipeline; moreover, the tiny houses were based on wheels to avoid being caught up in injunctions. It was hoped that the "small homes will offer a big platform" (3).

The intensity and ferocity of the Alberta-BC but also national debate was made more evident when Jason Kenney, the leader of the United Conservative Party, announced to his party members an attack on the "green left" (Bennett 2018b) in the province and nationally. This included those who "secretly fund and support the demonization of Alberta's oil" (2). Kenney, a former senior minister in the federal Harper government, promised that "we will fight back for economic survival." Deploying the classic Harper strategy, he plans to create a special legislative committee "to probe the sources of foreign money funding any groups working against Alberta's interests" (3) and to use the courts to ensure that Ottawa deny charitable status to "bogus charities" such as "the David Suzuki foundation" (3).

Think tanks such as the Fraser Institute were also marshalling research evidence showing the growing costs of "pipeline constraints in Canada" (Aliakbari and Stedman 2018). The analysis showed these constraints included "an overdependence on the US market and reliance on more costly modes of energy transportation" (1). It showed that between "2009 and 2012, the average price differential between Western Canada Select (WCS) and West Texas Intermediate (WTI) was about 13 percent of of the WTI price" but by 2018 it was 42 per cent (1). Overall the "depressed price for Canadian heavy crude oil has "resulted in CA$20.7 billion of forgone revenues for the Canadian energy industry" (1). The report stressed that these changes, when linked to the pipeline constraints, mean that "nearly 99 percent of Canadian heavy crude gets exported to the US, meaning that the US is essentially still Canada's only export market" (6).

In late May 2018, the politics and economics of the Trans Mountain expansion project shifted markedly in ways that would not have been easily predicted just a few months previously. Federally, the power centre shifted to Minister of Finance Bill Morneau with a further key role played by Jim Carr, the Natural Resources minister. Negotiations focused on how to ensure the project proceeded. Central was the fact that the "Government of Canada has reached an agreement with Kinder Morgan to purchase the company's Trans Mountain Expansion Project and related pipeline and terminal assets for $4.5 billion (Department of Finance Canada 2018, 1). The project will "proceed under the ownership of a Crown corporation"; however, "at the appropriate time, Canada will work with investors to transfer the project and related assets to a new owner or owners, in a way that ensures the project's construction and operation will proceed in a manner that protects the public interest" (1).

The government did not want the building BC-Alberta conflict to fester, hence the sudden change in strategy. But also part of the political trajectory was the fact that elections both in Alberta and federally in 2018 and 2019 were looming. In addition, the Trans Mountain project was increasingly unpopular in British Columbia; thus columnist Thomas Walkom (2018) argued that the "federal government's decision to nationalize the Trans Mountain pipeline is deeply flawed ... because it doesn't solve the real problem – which is that a good many British Columbians oppose any project that would increase the likelihood of heavy oil spills along the Pacific Coast" (1). Walkom (2019) also later wove into his analysis the growing inability of the BC pipeline "to navigate the maze of Indigenous politics," one that now included a Supreme Court decision that "Indigenous communities do not have a formal veto over resource developments affecting their lands" (3). As McQuaig (2018) had already argued argued, even "if the economics of the project worked, there would still be the devastating environmental impacts, including the potential sullying of BC coastal waters with oil that is exceptionally difficult, if not impossible, to clean up" (2).

In chapter 1, we referred to the varieties of nimbyism and its politics, and cautioned against quick deployment of the term, but did suggest that environmental and coastal oil spills would be highly relevant impacts of the Trans Mountain project. These are easy to *visualize* in Vancouver when one sees large container ships already queueing in area waterways, a crowd that would be tripled in number by much larger container ships.

Also increasingly relevant was the prediction that the federal Liberals would likely lose several of their BC seats in a coming 2019 federal election, given that protests were rampant by diverse groups objecting specifically to the federal government's $4.5 billion purchase of the pipeline. Author Michael Harris (2018) immediately typecast

Prime Minister Justin Trudeau as one who is "confirming a miserable axiom of Canadian politics," namely that "when companies with iffy projects begin to lose their nerve, they can always turn to government – the investor of last resort." He also added that "history shouts from the leaky rooftops of multiple mega-flops" (1) which he then goes on to sample across a fifty-year period (1–3). The Liberals did indeed lose most of their MPs from BC and indeed across Western Canada in the 21 October 2019 federal election.

The Alberta UCP's coming to power early in 2019 has already been referred to earlier in this analysis. Premier Jason Kenney's Throne Speech was cast by promises to "undo much of the Notley government's work" (Frenson 2019). Its first legislative item, Bill 1, promised to end the province's carbon tax. In more specific ways in late October, Alberta announced rule changes on oil production limits to spur more conventional drilling (Kucerak 2019). The UCP Energy Minister announced that "starting immediately any oil produced from a new well will not be subject to limits" and that "the change will spur producers to drill hundreds of new wells and … each well will create about 145 jobs" (2).

Meanwhile, even by mid-2019, analyses showed that the core politics regarding the Trans Mountain pipeline was changing in a more supportive direction in British Columbia, including and even especially Vancouver Island (Green 2019). In late 2019 and early 2020, the overall political economy of the pipeline battles is very much caught up in the current and future fate of several governments and political parties in a world where climate change continues to accelerate, where the ensuing politics are increasingly and fundamentally more intergenerational, and where Canada's record is not nearly good enough. Prime Minister Trudeau said as the Alberta UCP won power that he would work out the details "of a federal carbon tax in Alberta" (Kaiser 2019, 1) and that what "we're going to ensure is that nowhere across the country will it be free to pollute" (1–2). Intergenerational climate politics will ensure that different voters gain ascendency but in ways that are not in the least formulaic amidst pipelines and in public and private decision-making.

The intergenerational dynamics were borne out in the visit by Swedish climate science activist Greta Thunberg to Alberta just before the November federal election. Two useful accounts of her visit to Edmonton reached similar but differently crafted views about its impact, both immediate and potentially in even the short-term future (Markusoff 2019; Staples 2019). Markusoff argued that the sixteen-year-old Thunberg "laid out a science-driven case to rapidly draw down emissions" and asserted that climate change's main enemy is physics, not politics or any given political party. Thunberg had been making this her main argument in her series of speeches at global centres just prior to her Edmonton visit. She drew a good crowd in Edmonton and Markusoff concluded that "by stoking a movement – yes, even in Alberta – stands to leave something legitimate behind" (5). The analysis by Staples noted that "Thunberg's speech came off without interruption free from catcalls from the civil Canadian crowd, even as it was peppered with folks holding pro-oil and gas signs" (2). Staples also stressed her uniting "behind science" message but then went on in a more critical fashion to say that "her speech was short on answers" and that "more homework is in order" (2). He then went on to cite other scientists globally who were marshalling and advocating different science-based answers or partial answers (3–5). He also concluded Thunberg "can play a huge role by championing their best ideas" (5).

By late June 2020, UCP Alberta Premier Jason Kenney, in the context of the COVID-19 pandemic and also the global oil price wars that had damaged the Alberta economy, announced that he would spend $10 billion on projects that would immediately create jobs, including health-care facilities, pipelines, schools, drug treatment centres, and more, making this in effect the largest infrastructure build in Alberta history (Anderson 2020).

Also on the Alberta agenda was a COVID-19 outbreak at the Cargill meat processing plant south of Calgary that had forced the facility to be temporarily closed (Rieger 2020) and was later linked to dozens of COVID-19 cases among its employees, raising serious questions about working conditions and the treatment of employees before and during the crisis. These vulnerabilities, along with numerous other structural and systemic inequalities, have been ruthlessly exposed by the pandemic and will require urgent remedial action by federal and provincial governments with respect to infrastructure and employment as part of the much-vaunted promises to "build back better."

ANALYSIS: THE THREE REGIME ELEMENTS

With the aid of table 8.1 we now look across the two policy and governance histories presented by examining the three elements featured in our overall analytical framework.

Regarding policy *ideas, discourse, and agendas,* there is in one sense a natural division of content in the two histories but also some crossover. Regarding energy-environment-resources as a linked trio of normative content and debate, we see across time an array of ideas and discourse regarding energy as oil, the oil sands, and natural gas; environmental agendas and discourse include sustainable development, safety, and GHG reduction; and the resources category includes ideas and content regarding safe drinking water, rivers, lakes, and oceans.

The complexity of agendas is presented as a given because it has been present throughout the period covered and includes notions of life-cycle scope and regulatory coverage, in addition to landowner rights and more recent expressions of critical energy infrastructure as policy ideas and needs.

While there is crossover content with the second policy history, the latter because of its pipeline battle focus, the agenda and discourse content is about what oil and gas infrastructure are in more specific terms, including kilometres of scope and coverage and high vs lower pressure content in pipelines. It also concerns infrastructure types nationally and within Alberta as the dominant energy province, and in relation to Canada-US cross-border pipelines. And of course, agendas are driven by the specific nature and content of a given set of pipelines seeking approval or being repaired and upgraded.

With regard to *power structures, democracy, and governance,* each policy and governance history reveals relevant content. The first history is necessarily broader, hence the mapping of the six or so leading federal cabinet departments and also multiple regulatory bodies. This complexity and scope is evident both at the federal and provincial levels, although our provincial discussion is necessarily focused mainly on Alberta. The power and democracy story in Alberta cannot help but stress the long Progressive Conservative Party dominance, including in the latest oil sands era. The new presence of the NDP as a force in Alberta also features in both of the policy histories.

In the first policy history, the advocacy and influence of a selection of key think tanks and interest groups are important. As our attention shifts to the pipeline battles and to pipeline infrastructure in specific, the interests tend to be infrastructure interests and players, including Eastern refineries and proponents/owners of current and changed pipeline proposals. The dynamics of pipeline battles also engage real old and new federal-provincial and interprovincial partisan battles and strategies in an Alberta-BC context regarding the

Table 8.1
The energy-environment-resources pipelines infrastructure regime and the three analytical elements: highlights

Policy and governance histories	Policy ideas, discourse, and agendas	Power structures, democracy, and governance	Temporal realities and conflicts and technology
Energy-environment-resource policy and changing institutional dynamics and complexity, 1970s to present	• Energy as oil, oil sands, natural gas, etc. • "Responsible resource development" as overarching discourse in Harper era. • Environment as sustainable development, safety, GHG reduction. • Resources as safe water, rivers, lakes, oceans. • Community support. • NEB life-cycle approach; landowner rights in Alberta; safety culture and "preventing harm"; moving beyond traditional transaction business. • Alberta AEUB "safe, responsible and efficient development" and also regulatory enhancement. • Current Alberta AER, "life-cycle" references; more than "management principles." • Alberta Notley NDP government "climate leadership" including capping oil sands emissions and reducing methane emissions. • Some advocacy of need to keep agency separate; issues of "legitimacy" versus "trust."	• Range of key ministers/departments involved federally: prime minister, minister of finance, Natural Resources Canada, Environment and Climate Change Canada, Indigenous and Northern Affairs Canada, Fisheries and Oceans Canada. • Similar ranges of key minister involvement in each province. • Natural gas infrastructure and lobby is also relevant in that its infrastructure is four times longer (450,000 kilometres of transmission and distribution gasline and key lobbies such as the National Gas Association). • Also multiple regulatory bodies at each level. • NEB shifts and evolution in last five federal political-PM eras. • Alberta power longevity by dominant Progressive Conservative policy rule before and across oil sands era. • But then the NDP is in power.	• Fracking technology and rapid impacts. • Carbon-capture technology with early carbon "lock-in." • Big, unresolved policy such as "decarbonisation" and reconciliation with Canada's Indigenous peoples will be "chaotic, politically messy and expensive." • "Planning scales." • Aging and renewal/replacement of capital stock. • Interacting/changing federal and provincial electoral cycles and changes or longevity in power. • Diverse policy and infrastructure budgetary cycles.

Pipeline battles and survival for competing/colliding and threatened major pipelines, 1980s to present	<ul><li>Avoiding the perception of conflict of interest.</li><li>"Canada's critical energy infrastructure protection."</li><li>"Regionally concentrated supply infrastructure."</li><li>"Integrated all-hazard risk management."</li><li>Physical and cyber threats and terrorism.</li><li>Jason Kenney UCP government's major cuts to Alberta Energy Regulator in October 2019 and scandal of the AER senior staff announced.</li><li>Climate change as explicit issue sharpened by visit by young Swedish activist Greta Thunberg to Edmonton just before 2019 federal election.</li></ul>	<ul><li>Key agenda and discourse to understand what oil and gas infrastructure is in real asset terms.</li><li>Design features include: material selection for fracture control; strain-based versus stress-based design.</li></ul>	<ul><li>Alberta-federal carbon capture initiatives.</li><li>Analysis and advocacy by think tanks and interest groups (e.g. Canadian Engineering Academy; Canada West Foundation: Pembina Institute; Canadian Energy Pipeline Association; Canadian critical infrastructure centres; and individual scholars/advocates).</li></ul>	<ul><li>Eastern refineries as infrastructure are, via Eastern Canadian decisions, not connected by pipeline to Western Canada.</li><li>US as dominant/too-dominant foreign market for Canadian oil and gas.</li></ul>	<ul><li>Canada's pipeline system began in 1950s with major oil and gas finds in Western Canada, especially Alberta.</li></ul>

Table 8.1
The energy-environment-resources pipelines infrastructure regime and the three analytical elements: highlights (*Continued*)

Policy and governance histories	Policy ideas, discourse, and agendas	Power structures, democracy, and governance	Temporal realities and conflicts and technology
	• Goal to increase Canadian oil and gas as Alberta-centred infrastructure to reach international markets to both seacoasts and beyond. • 800,000 kilometres national transmission, gathering, and distribution lines, of which 73,000 kilometres are federally regulated. • NRCan mapping of oil versus natural gas pipelines, with the latter at higher pressures. • Natural gas pipeline service in most cities with connections to individual homes. • Thirty-one oil and thirty-nine gas Canada-US cross-border pipelines. • One hundred pipeline companies in Canada. • Key parts of Eastern Canada import oil. • Alberta dominant with 400,000 kilometres of energy related pipelines and 71 per cent of Canada's natural gas production. • Oil sands/bitumen underlie 142,000 sqare kilometres of land in northern Alberta.	• Dominance of Alberta Conservatives in continuous power in both the pre-oil sands and oil sands eras in Alberta. • NDP in power in Alberta since 2015 added climate change emphasis but also, via Premier Rachel Notley, fought for key pipelines, especially Trans Mountain and Energy East; the two projects with coastal/export features. • Trudeau's five decision applications were exercises in federal government Liberal power; which in turn saw them as antidote to Harper era which critics had cast as being: anti-science; weak on environment, including weak on Fisheries Act; practitioners of wedge politics; and little concerned about Aboriginal issues on energy. • TransCanada corporate power/ influence shown in Energy East proposal and then weakened in its cancellation decision; also important in Keystone and Keystone XL dynamics in US.	• Energy East proposal was for pipeline changes and reversals whose effective life economically would be over fifty years; its decision to cancel was taken in weeks in response to Trudeau decisions. • Pipeline technology changes occur regarding pipe construction features and improvements in different time frames. • Some institutional dynamics of multi-pipeline processes, as per Hoberg analysis, can effect outcomes, delays, and resistance related to the number of "institutional veto points." • US Nebraska decision on Keystone XL had approved it, but also due to short-term politics required a nearby route change in the pipeline due to a bipartisan coalition

- Recovery methods are 20 per cent surface mining and 80 per cent "in-situ."
- Trudeau Liberals' five *decision principles* for current pipeline project reviews; two major and three other pipeline infrastructure decisions.
- Major pipeline project decisions/battles are:
  a) Trans Mountain; and
  b) Energy East.
- Three other projects:
  a) Towerbirch expansion;
  b) Line 3 replacement; and
  c) 2017 NGTL system
  d) expansion.
- Separate Keystone XL in the US key for oil sands international exports to and through the US via the larger Keystone Pipeline.
- Harper-era "responsible resource development" ethos strongly favoured pipelines but was not inclined to engage in federal-provincial battles.
- Trudeau's five decision principles: no project proponent will be asked to return to the starting line; decisions based on "science, traditional

- Alberta-BC politics intensifies over Trans Mountain project, especially when BC government was defeated in the legislature and replaced by an NDP government in power with the direct support of the Green Party (very much a first for BC and Canada regarding direct leverage of the Greens).
- Alberta legislation passed in May 2018 to "turn off the taps" regarding gasoline shipments to BC if it continued to throw up barriers to the Trans Mountain expansion project.
- Energy East as proposal and vis-à-vis its cancellation caught up in potential Quebec-West politics regarding the run-up to 2019 Quebec election, including separatism issues and timing.
- New federal Impact Assessment Agency (IAA) planned under Trudeau legislation, as well as new legislation to control tanker traffic on north BC coast.

- of landowners, Native Americans, and environmentalists
- Temporal arguments that the fossil fuel era is rapidly drawing to a close.
- Fast-moving Alberta legislative measures against BC.
- Unexpected quick measures introduced by Trudeau Liberals on Impact Assessment Agency and vis-à-vis tanker traffic on BC north coast.
- Sudden unexpected decision by federal Finance minister to buy Trans Mountain Expansion project for $4.5 billion.
- Inauguration of President Biden results in immediate cancellation of Keystone XL pipeline extension. Scant objections from the Trudeau government fuel sense of Western alienation.

Table 8.1
The energy-environment-resources pipelines infrastructure regime and the three analytical elements: highlights (*Continued*)

Policy and governance histories	Policy ideas, discourse, and agendas	Power structures, democracy, and governance	Temporal realities and conflicts and technology
	knowledge of Indigenous Peoples"; views of public and affected communities will be sought and considered; Indigenous peoples will be meaningfully consulted; and direct and upstream GHG emissions will be linked to the projects under review. • Alberta UCP sets up • Fair Deal Panel to help get "fair deal" for Alberta from new minority Trudeau Liberal government. • Alberta UCP premier calls for "5 Point Plan" from Ottawa that includes a "firm, fixed and fast deadline" for the completion of the Trans Mountain expansion pipeline project and also includes Indigenous equity in the project.	• Federal Finance minister's decision to buy TransMountain Expansion project for \$4.5 billion.	• In early 2021, US-Canada pipeline tensions continue with Michigan Governor Gretchen Whitmer's attempt to shut down the Enbridge Line 5 pipeline due to the environmental threat to Lake Michigan and other Great Lakes. This pipeline is crucial to Eastern oil supplies and the Prime Minister states that keeping it open is non-negotiable.

Trans Mountain pipeline and a Western-Quebec context over the Energy East pipeline.

Regarding *temporal realities, cycles, conflicts, and technology*, each policy and governance history reveals relevant observations, features, and theories. In the first policy history, these are highlighted with regard to fracking as a technology that rapidly created new infrastructure, but also with examples such as carbon-capture technology including observations about its early "lock-in" features and potential. Predictions of current big policy complexities are also noted, including that they are highly likely to be "chaotic and politically messy." The temporal dynamics of interacting/changing federal and provincial electoral cycles and changes or longevity in power join up with numerous policy and budgetary cycles. When one shifts to the history of pipeline battles, there is a need to understand the way that Canada's pipeline system began in the 1950s with a Western Canadian and especially Albertan focus and dominance that has continued into the present. The world of pipeline battles, such as over Energy East, both showed short-term efforts by the proponent to change its technical features and was also caught up in the proponent's decision to suddenly cancel the project. Also involved in and sharpening the current pipeline battles are temporal predictions that the "fossil fuel era "is rapidly drawing to a close."

CONCLUSIONS

This chapter has examined the energy-environment-resources pipelines infrastructure regime through two basic but related policy and governance histories extending in total over a fifty-year period right up to the present. The first policy and governance history, on energy-environment-resource policy and institutional nexus dynamics and complexity, is necessarily broad, with its nexus having both policy and institutional features. But "nexus" as a conceptual underpinning was and is crucial, and nexus complexity has been cast as not a recent feature but rather one that we have shown was present from the beginning of the period being covered. Our second policy and governance history, on pipeline battles and survival for competing/colliding and threatened major pipelines, ultimately focused on the pipeline battles of the last decade. In a broader sense, however, because oil and gas pipelines as actual infrastructure are also being mapped, this history also weaves in the larger picture of de facto federal pipeline presence and growth in the provinces, but with a crucial focus on Alberta, as well as on Canada-US cross-border pipelines.

In our mapping of pipelines as infrastructure, we began with needed distinctions between oil versus natural gas pipelines, stressing that although both are coated steel pipe buried underground, natural gas transmission pipelines transport gas at higher pressures per square inch. Also important is the fact that natural gas pipelines service most major cities in Canada with connections to individual homes. Thus while citizens and voters may follow some of the broader pipeline battles, the pipelines they experience daily are the ones that are connected to their homes, seemingly in less controversial and more workable ways.

Both histories show how the meanings and content of the energy-environment-resource trilogy are never separately nor in combination a simple set of values and norms. They are complex and non-linear and also anchored by federal and provincial, and increasingly city-local, law and practice as well. We have seen, however, that even though multi-level policy and governance are a feature of this regime, it is also in key ways a realm of Alberta dominance and power, partly because of the province's initial oil and gas discoveries but even more via its oil sands-bitumen economy and society. This was oil and gas power in combination with the dominance in power for decades of Alberta's Progressive Conservative Party. This is also why there is so much interest in examining what the NDP Notley government did in power and how long it lasted as the first Alberta government to adopt an explicit climate change policy. As we have seen, the NDP premier also had to conduct a political battle to support and rescue two of the pipelines in particular, Trans Mountain Expansion and Energy East, the two piplines oriented to reach Canada's ocean coasts in the west and east, and thus enable increased oil and gas exports internationally to the US and beyond. The case is being made that these coastal pipelines' needs and extensions should be decided by a stronger sense of a pan-Canadian public interest. But this in turn, as we have seen, is occurring amidst some predictions that the oil sands face a globally declining future, potentially quite rapidly. These predictions included concerns about how to deal with issues of pipeline decisions such as those of the US on Keystone XL, in addition to the earlier Keystone development within the US that also promised economic benefits for Canadian oil interests centred on the oil sands.

The pipelines battle history shows the presence of the current Trudeau federal government's five decision principles now being operationalized for pipeline project reviews as a direct response to previous Harper-era summary dictums regarding "responsible resource development." In particular, these Trudeau Liberal substitutes relate to strengthened environmental assessment and also to strengthening and expanding the role and rights of Indigenous peoples, groups, and communities. Much of this has to be operationalized by new federal bodies, including the Impact Assessment Agency of Canada. However, our first policy history showed how many think tank and related commentaries and studies reveal that decision systems are already massively complex and still unable to deal with the needs of communities close to or separate from planned or expanding projects. The core politics and governance are changing following 2019–20 as a result of the United Conservative Party, led by Jason Kenney, coming to power and functioning in opposition to a weakened Trudeau minority government where Alberta is demanding a fair deal for Alberta in concert with other provinces in Western Canada. The economic crisis resulting from the pandemic has further intensified Western demands for Ottawa to revisit equalization payments and help Canada's energy sector as part of its plans for enabling economic recovery, with the federal Conservative Party amplifying the call. President Biden's 2021 decision to cancel the Keystone XL pipeline, allied to the fiscal pressures arising from the pandemic, will surely serve to fan the flames of east-west tensions for the foreseeable future.

9

The Science, Technology, and Innovation (STI) Infrastructure Policy and Governance Regime

INTRODUCTION

Our final regime analysis deals with the science, technology, and innovation (STI) infrastructure policy and governance regime. We begin with three policy and governance histories, namely those dealing with: 1) big science infrastructure policy and governance (from World War II to the present); 2) the Canada Foundation for Innovation as an STI infrastructure foundation (1997 to the present); and 3) the internet: from permissionless innovation STI infrastructure to regulated infrastructure media and threat to democracy (1990s to present). This allows us to see STI infrastructure in three of its own core home bases and locations and as it is revealed across the full STI spectrum of science, technology, and innovation. It should also be noted that science, technology, and innovation aspects have also been present in each of our previous regime chapters, 4 through 8, and also in chapter 1 as part of our preview of the nature of platforms.

We then provide an analysis across the three policy and governance histories, deploying the three elements in our analytical framework: ideas, discourse, and agendas; power structures, democracy, and governance; and temporal realities, cycles, conflicts, and technology. Conclusions then follow.

THREE STI INFRASTRUCTURE POLICY
AND GOVERNANCE REGIME HISTORIES

*1 Big Science Infrastructure Policy
and Governance, World War II to present*

In this brief history we trace "big science" as an infrastructure-related and defining concept in four basic stages: in an early US and Canadian World War II and postwar context; in relation to the structure and evolution of the National Research Council of Canada from the 1970s to the present; as influenced and changed by STI (as featured by reforms related more explicitly to the innovation economy and cast more in discourse and practice as networks of excellence, virtual-reality institutes, and conceptions of organization for government labs); and policies and governance debates more recently about handling "big science" versus "little science" and de facto "in-between" science and its infrastructure features and discourse. This journey overall feeds into the birth and evolution of the Canada Foundation for Innovation in the 1997 to 2017 period, the focus of our second policy history.

Part of the big-science infrastructure story federally is bound up in the work and organization of the National Research Council of Canada (NRC). The NRC was crucially involved in World War II in concert with the Department of National Defence, but also in relation to US and UK military technology development (Avery 1998). Avery's analysis used "big science" as a central theme and linked these developments to the national security state. This period included the development of radar, RDX explosives, proximity fuses, chemical and biological warfare, and the atomic bomb (6). NRC lab and related staff grew from 300 in 1939 to nearly 3,000 at the end of the war in 1945. Its wartime scientific research efforts also included subjects such as wartime food and experimental aircraft (Phillipson 1991; Thistle 1965). After the war, the NRC's laboratories moved away from military research, which was transferred to the newly created Defence Research Board in 1947.

The term "big science" as analytical discourse from World War II onwards carried with it the image of teams of researchers working in multi-million-dollar laboratories on grand projects (Doern 1972). In the US in particular, it typically involved the mobilization of various sectors of industry in support of the work via large purchases, subcontracts, and/or the establishment of facilities large enough for this work. US analyses of "big science" have also cast it in terms of the forging of the "military-industrial complex," both initially and in recent and earlier analyses of the history and evolution of US science and technology and its organization (Hilzik 2015; Galison and Hevly 1992; Panofsky 1968).

By the late 1960s, the federal government had already had to manage and involve itself in Canadian "big-science" infrastructures such as wind tunnels, atomic energy research facilities, and telescopes. Some universities, moreover, had to adopt some of the features of "big science" in their internal departmental organization as larger staffs were needed for them to become competitive in certain fields with other universities or laboratories in the world.

One of the "big science" debates to gain political attention in Canada was the late-1960s proposal by Atomic Energy of Canada Ltd (AECL) to construct an Intense Neutron Generator (Doern 1972). This facility was on a direct trajectory with the nature of high-energy physics as a basic science development in Canada, with research teams at several Canadian universities (105–15). Thus "big science" is immediately linked with infrastructure and high-cost projects. In such a two-category analytical world, "little science" is not associated with infrastructure and often is referred to as "everyday science," when in real terms infrastructure is needed here as well, even if only cast in terms of the office space needed for researchers to work in, along with the necessary laboratory equipment.

The National Research Council as a core science and research agency has since changed and reorganized on several occasions (Doern and Levesque 2002; Doern, Castle, and Phillips 2016) with various institutes and labs carrying out STI infrastructure tasks and mandates. At present, these include: Emerging Technologies-Platforms; National Infrastructure and Future Technologies; and a continuing lead research and regulatory role on Construction (NRC 2017a). An earlier NRC Strategy 2013–18 report had stressed that the NRC had three R&D divisions which covered twelve "portfolios" and "provided access to 37 *research infrastructure facilities*" (NRC 2013). At present, NRC Construction describes itself as being "active in the innovation of buildings – residential, commercial and institutional – as well as in civil engineering infrastructure" (NRC 2017c, 1).

When one looks beyond this NRC focus and into STI policy and institutional developments of the twenty-first century, the notion and discourse of "big science" certainly continue, but they are joined by other developments and discourse relating to the dynamics of the national and international emergence of the full STI spectrum. This includes the innovation economy and increasingly society, "clusters," and "networks," and also involves business, government departments and agencies, and universities in both competitive and cooperative dynamics relating to funding and research capacities and platforms, both new and established (Wolfe 2003; de la Mothe 2003; Atkinson-Grosjean 2006; Doern and Kinder 2007; Doern and Stoney 2009; Doern, Castle, and Phillips 2016). The funding dynamics were also pivotal, since there were serious deficits in both federal and provincial governments, a challenge compounded by the widely varying budgetary capacities of universities, all of whose student populations were growing at the undergraduate and graduate levels.

Many STI program and institutional experimentations were underway, but three in particular are noteworthy in the 1980s to mid-1990s period. One was the Networks of Centres of Excellence (NCE) established in 1989 (Doern, Castle, and Phillips 2016, 173–6). The notions of "networks" and "centres" do not evoke infrastructure as central discourse, but they do suggest partnerships in funding and work as developed by the then three main granting councils, and the two federal departments of Industry Canada and Health Canada. Various "centres" were also formed and involved as newer forms of levered co-funding were developed and encouraged. One key analysis saw the NCE system as being too strongly business- and private-sector-dominated in terms of actual STI impacts (Atkinson-Grosjean 2006). And though "virtual networks" were the norm, the centres involved were jointly deploying and creating platforms for their joint work, partly to ensure their survival in terms of funding.

A further STI institutional reform came with the establishment in 2000 of the Canadian Institutes of Health Research (CIHR). Its initial thirteen "virtual reality" institutes were established to facilitate improved links between researchers from all disciplines so as to focus resources on Canada's major health and well-being challenges (Canadian Institutes of Health Research 1999; Murphy 2007; Doern, Castle, and Phillips 2016, 176–83). The CIHR did well in garnering new funds for STI research and technology in the billion-dollar range, casting them effectively as *platforms*. Another key institutional indicator was that the CIHR functions through almost fifty peer review committees, compared to the tiny handful of discipline-based committees of the Medical Research Council that it replaced.

Also emerging in the STI nexus are research and innovation clusters as local or regional multi-organizational and stakeholder networks (Wolfe 2009). This also includes examples of universities creating spin-off companies, and, in the case of particular universities such as the University of Waterloo, branding themselves as newer and very much innovation-centred, company-creating universities. Also underway were explicit moves to co-locate federal labs on university campuses, such as the federal Wildlife Research lab at Carleton University. Kinder (2009) probes this kind of co-location model as an example of co-management arrangements for federal labs located on university campuses that stop short of full transfer but still provide many of the same quasi-infrastructure benefits.

Other examples of big-science analytical debates include one cast partly as "big science in a small country" in reference to Canada (Fazekas 2006). This analysis focused on Canada's role in research on astronomy, arguing that the key to Canada's success "is keeping a focus on particular research niches while maintaining a stake in some of the most important international astronomy projects" (1). On the other hand, at a Canadian Science Policy Conference (2015) on international perspectives on big science in Canada, the main panel discussion concluded that in Canada "there is no national policy framework considering, evaluating and overseeing large-scale research infrastructure" (2). This is despite the fact that "Canada is home to several 'big science' research facilities that cost upwards of $100 million, take years to build and operate on decade-long time scales" (2). The panel members were senior staff from international bodies, and included in their conclusions were recommendations that "Canada needs a vision and roadmap for big science" and "a big science model should be fair and flexible" (2).

Following another panel discussion, Ian Macdonald (2016), who heads the relatively small $2.6 million Banff International Research Station (BIRS), addressed initially what the definition of "big science infrastructure should be." His answer is that there are two types: first, "relatively small or medium-sized projects that are university-based and located on campuses mainly to benefit a local scientific community"; and second "and more challenging are the large, collaborative, multi-university projects. These have national and international scope with stakeholders crossing provincial or national boundaries" (2). The examples Macdonald gives here include: the Amundsen icebreaker, Canadian Light Source (CLS), SNOLAB, Compute Canada (CC), Ocean Networks Canada (ONC), Ocean Tracking Network (OTN), and the Vaccine and Infectious Disease Organization–International Vaccine Centre (VIDO–Intervac), which he notes "have all faced difficulties as they seek to secure adequate funding from a variety of sources" (1). Regarding "prioritization and advocacy" as crucial issues, he argues that projects "of this significance should not be funded based on who has better access to Ottawa. Lobbying is not a functional route for funding good science" (1).

The latter point is also featured in a US article (Hughes 2013) arguing that "Big Science efforts have big budgets, lists of participating institutions, big press coverage, and big pronouncements" (1) and as a result "we need to treat the process of Big Science as a science itself" (1). In the Canadian context, Fortin and Currie (2013) for different reasons also express caution in terms of giving further grants based on claimed impacts without assessing, in a big-science and little-science world, how scientific impact scales with funding.

2 The Canada Foundation for Innovation as an STI Infrastructure Foundation, 1997 to present

Now in its twenty-first year, the Canada Foundation for Innovation (CFI) describes itself as a foundation that is "[i]nvesting in *state-of-the-art infrastructure* that enables world-class research" (Canada Foundation for Innovation 2017, 1). It also draws immediate attention to how it provides "support through research infrastructure for the development of highly qualified personnel" (1). This term, HQP, evokes immediate notions of human capital. Its anniversary summary of notions and discourse regarding its core infrastructure mandate includes:

- "large research platforms" such as that which led to Canada's only dedicated research icebreaker, the CCGS Amundsen;
- "large-scale research-hospital-based infrastructure projects";
- "newer better labs and equipment";
- "cutting-edge labs, facilities and equipment";
- "research labs for cost-effective solutions to infrastructure renewal"; and

• "research infrastructure as state of the art equipment, laboratories, databases, specimens, scientific collections, computer hardware and software, communications linkages and buildings necessary to conduct leading-edge research" (1–4).

The CFI's annual report for 2015–16 (Canada Foundation for Innovation 2016) opens by drawing special attention immediately to its funding and distributive impacts by showing that to date the CFI has "committed more than $6.7 billion in support of 9,303 projects at 145 research institutions in 70 municipalities across Canada" (5). It states that its "smart funding model is how we do it" and that it is centred on "maximizing the funding it receives from the Government of Canada by contributing up to 40 percent of a projects research infrastructure costs" with institutions securing "the remaining 60 percent through partnerships with provincial governments and other public, private and non-profit organizations" (5).

The CFI was established in 1997 by the Chrétien government with strong influence from Paul Martin as minister of Finance and supported by strong prior lobbying by some key university presidents. It emerged at least partly because the federal fiscal coffers were overflowing after several years of federal deficits. It was among other early federal efforts to fund infrastructure more generally in the Canadian economy, including at the municipal level. Although the CFI drew attention to its presence in 66 Canadian communities and 138 research institutions, in reality the investments are concentrated in a much narrower set of major research universities. The CFI shows examples of its concentration as follows, drawn from the CFI website list under "our investments" (Canada Foundation for Innovation 2014). The six universities of British Columbia, Toronto, McGill, Alberta, Saskatchewan, and Dalhousie had garnered a total of $1.77 billion or 35 per cent of total CFI funding on 3,420 projects or 39.5 per cent of all CFI projects (Doern, Castle, and Phillips 2016, 185).

It is not surprising that such concentrations have occurred. It mostly reflects the roles these universities play as established major research universities, their internal capacities to organize and submit proposals, and their ability to raise the levered money from partners. In spite of this concentration, the other 60 per cent of the funding was distributed widely.

Lopreite and Murphy's analysis of the CFI from its birth to 2009 posits that the CFI acts as both a patron and regulator of Canada's research infrastructure (Lopreite and Murphy 2009). They show that the CFI is a *patron* based on its role as a funder and promoter. Although the CFI is an arm's-length foundation and is independent of politics in the partisan sense, it does have to deal, as all patrons do, with small-p politics among universities in the form of distributional disbursements, regionally or among different realms or disciplines of science, and the infrastructure each needs. These are, of course, not part of the CFI's terms of reference, but they are a part of how diverse research interests lobby the CFI and seek to change its program structure (124).

Lopreite and Murphy argue that the CFI also acts as a *regulator* because investments in research and development infrastructure must conform to certain "rules" set by the CFI, including requirements that universities submit *strategic research plans* and that funding be levered. In short, universities do not get infrastructure money unless they bring money in the form of commitments from other funders, public or private. Universities have widely different capacities to obtain these levered money commitments, which constitute 60 per cent of all CFI awards. Aspects of regulation also occur in the realm of defining what is eligible for funding, and hence in defining what in fact "infrastructure" is as capital spending rather than operational spending (CFI Eligibility). Such issues also inherently arise in the CFI's role of developing research "capacity" and in determining what "innovation" means in these funding choices and in addition to determining what kinds of research capacity-building might occur when CFI funds are allocated. Capacity building involves both complex physical-technical capacity and human capacity, in the form of Highly Qualified Manpower (HQM), and managerial and even entrepreneurial capacity (Lopriete and Murphy 2009, 124).

The CFI's initial strategy was to develop several types of programs. These included: a) the Innovation Fund to help institutions strengthen their research and training environment in priority areas that they themselves identify; b) the Infrastructure Operating Fund to help with the incremental operating and maintenance costs associated with infrastructure projects; c) the Research Hospital Fund to contribute to hospital-based projects that focus on innovative research and training; d) the New Opportunities Fund to provide infrastructure support to newly recruited academic staff; and e) the Canada Research Chairs Infrastructure Fund for infrastructure support to the Canada Research Chairs Program. Targeted international funds were established later.

Following a consultation process in 2007, a revised suite of programs emerged. As Lopreite and Murphy point out, some of the basis for the shift in the CFI suite of programs "can also be found in its program evaluation reports which were a part of its commitment to accountability" (133). An evaluation report by Bearing Point (2003) used a complex methodology to identify three strategic considerations facing the CFI:

1 Maintaining long-term sustainability will require institutions to convince their provincial partners to supply matching funds, and institutions to find O & M support for the long term. This is the most important long term strategic issue by far.
2 Additional opportunities for the CFI to act as a catalyst for pan-Canadian strategic planning related to research infrastructure should be investigated, possibly including opportunities to act as "the Canadian voice" in these matters internationally.
3 The CFI and the Social Sciences and Humanities Research Council should continue to investigate ways to encourage involvement in the CFI from researchers in the social sciences and the humanities. (4–5)

The CFI, like all federal agencies, has had to explain its role, with respect to science and research infrastructure, in the context of the knowledge and innovation economy and social innovation cast in terms of health research charities, the environment, and the local-regional economies that host the universities, community colleges, and polytechnics that operate the infrastructure.

As a foundation, the CFI has some implied independence, but its chief funder nonetheless remains the federal government. In its twenty-year-plus history there have been several funding infusions, each involving a funding agreement with the federal government. At present there are seven: the Innovation Fund; the Major Science Initiatives Fund; the John R. Evans Leaders Fund; the Cyberinfrastructure Fund; the College-Industry Innovation Fund; the Exceptional Opportunities Fund; and the Infrastructure Operating Fund (Canada Foundation for Innovation 2016, 11–13). These funding agreements allow the government to exercise some influence over the direction and scope of the infrastructure program areas. The government cannot direct the CFI to fund specific projects, due to the merit-review system, but it can push and nudge the CFI to move in some different directions or shift it by insisting on managerial reforms. Overall, three areas of the CFI's evolution warrant brief further mention: its merit-review process; boundary issues with the granting councils; and the impact on universities from the required research plans.

Standard peer review was not enough for infrastructure decisions for two reasons. The management of universities or research hospitals had to be involved and had to be assessed as to their merits and claims of merit on their own and/or in comparison with other competing project applications. This was also true, as we have seen, when Canadian research funding had to deal with so-called "big science" centred on large and politically visible research allocated according to classical distributional regional politics. Second, research partners in, and users of, a new facility or equipment were fundamentally involved because they brought much of the money needed to make the projects work. Project reviewers in the merit-review process had to judge (and rank) projects in relation to three main criteria: the quality of the research and the need for infrastructure; the project's contribution to strengthening the capacity for innovation; and the potential benefits for Canada (CFI 2012, 3). These are quite broad criteria and are imbued with the necessity for particular acts of judgment regarding "capacity" for innovation and "potential" for benefits. Evidence evaluation and judgment can be brought to bear by expert reviewers, but this sort of decision-making is art as much as science.

It would not be surprising if the merit-review system is under pressure internally, from applicants or from the government, all of whom might want it loosened or made more flexible. In research infrastructure, as in other kinds of infrastructure allocations and decisions, there is typically room for merit-based decisions and for distributive politics of the "small-p" or even occasionally "big-p" varieties. The boundary between the CFI and the other federal granting bodies is complicated; it is not difficult to see how pressures, overlaps, and gaps could arise. Given that the CFI is mandated to fund new infrastructure, who will fund the resulting projects' operations and renewal, and how they will do so, is less clear. The granting councils fund research, which can and often does cover some of the operational costs of the infrastructure, seldom covers all the costs, and seldom contributes much to renewal costs. In many universities, CFI infrastructure facilities are seen as drawing off resources that otherwise would cover other university priorities. It is also worth noting in this context that the birth of the CFI was accompanied in 1999 by a federal government agreement to pay universities' indirect overhead costs as a separate financial commitment (Morgan 2009).

Finally, we take note of the impact of CFI requirements that universities submit research plans as a part of their project applications. In this regard, Lopriete and Murphy (2009) looked briefly at two small universities, Saint Mary's University and Brock University, and at Canada's largest university, the University of Toronto. Their analysis concluded that Brock and Saint Mary's were able to use this process to improve their impact in CFI competitions and to transform their institutions into more focused research universities; nevertheless, and not surprisingly, the University of Toronto was able to garner an above-average share of the funding.

A recent effort at overall commentary on and assessment of the CFI is found in Canada's Fundamental Science Review report (Advisory Panel on Federal Support for Fundamental Science 2017). Some parts of its assessment are CFI-specific while others draw in its links with the earlier evolving networked and institutional array already traced above in our big-science policy and governance history. First, the study notes that the granting councils and the CFI "have made vital contributions to Canadian science," but then immediately says the "Panel could not find any broad external review of the federal agencies and research eco-system since the 1970s" (xvi). It then begins its own views of "Infrastructure" by saying that the "CFI confers distinct strategic advantages by depoliticizing research infrastructure decision-making" (xx). This is a curious summary claim, given the continuous lobbying on funding programs already noted above. But the Panel report then goes on to argue that the federal government mandate should be changed to "increase its share of the matching ratio for large scale MRFs (major research facilities) from 40 percent to 60 percent" (1). Much later in the report, in its discussion of "facilities and equipment" (167), the Panel argues that although the "CFI is effectively a permanent part of the funding environment, its relationship with the federal government does not reflect this reality. CFI is funded on an ad hoc basis instead of having an ongoing budget and it is mandated to create and manage specific funds for a set period of time ... In consequence, it is often impossible for CFI and researchers to know from one year to the next what the timing or the size of the next competition will be" (167). And finally, in a brief discussion on the subject of "platform technologies," it expresses concern about the need for a "depoliticized mechanism for ongoing review not only of the existing entities but also for any proposals for new contribution agreements" (199). The main example of this cited is digital research infrastructure (DRI), and the Panel notes that CANARIE and Compute Canada in some greater combined and coordinated way need "stable funding, greater coordination, and streamlined accountability to realize the full-potential of the investments being made by all parties" (1). CANARIE had been created in the early internet and Web era as a needed big S&T-infrastructure-linking entity, whereas Compute Canada was more recently created.

3 The Internet: From Permissionless Innovation STI Infrastructure to Regulated Infrastructure Media and Threat to Democracy, 1990s to present

The internet and its presence via the World Wide Web is transformational in the most utterly profound ways. If we continued the previous "big science" theme, it would not be in the least inaccurate to call the internet the ultimate "big-STI" infrastructure. It is both an infrastructure and a repository of new theories and practices, positive and negative alike, and covers almost all human information and knowledge and functions as a system of *permissionless innovation* (Thierer 2014; Floridi 2012) and with *no central control* because of the need for *internet neutrality.* The latter is a premise that the network should not be optimized for any particular use. This kind of unguided structure is continuously innovative and overall disruptive, because benign and subversive interactions alike can destabilize markets and society, often by intent. Social movements and NGOs have also connected with each other in ways that challenge industry, governments, and societies everywhere. Social media involves massive forms of social production by citizens, groups, and communities at the national, international, and local levels. The absence of gatekeepers has enabled people with malevolent goals to introduce malware, viruses, and spam, and to engage in cybercrime, cyberwarfare, and cyberterrorism (Schneier 2015).

As the World Wide Web reached its twenty-eighth anniversary in March 2017, the view regarding what kind of "platform" it was becoming became more explicit and seen as a threat rather than unambiguously positive. This centred in part on how it was now the "platform press" that had been created by the ways in which "Silicon Valley Reengineered Journalism" and was now itself a media deliberately manipulating information for profit and simultaneously a massive threat to regular media, especially press media struggling for revenue (Bell and Owen 2017; 2016; Bell 2017). This also became a growing threat to democracy, partly because of the above media transformation but also, even more dramatically, as previewed in chapter 1, after the revelations regarding the work and downfall of Cambridge Analytica and Allied Data Analytics, firms internationally complicit in direct election manipulation activities in the US and UK as well as in Canada (Solon and Graham-Harrison 2018).

It is necessary to focus here on our above-titled two-part "from-to" journey, which means events and pressures that especially emerged during the last decade, including recent and current data-analytics threats to democracy. But in the overall internet journey, existing accounts already have had to find ways to deal with, and take into account, discourse and international and national political-economic events. Thus, as we saw in chapter 1, from the 1970s to the early 1990s, Canadian responses were centred on recognizing and reacting to the internet as a new transformational technology (Doern, Castle, and Phillips 2016). From the mid-1990s to about 2002, the focus was on strategies for the Information Highway and broadband access (Tumin 2000; Turk 1998).

The period from about 1998 to 2015 saw the massive emergence of social media and social production in the US, globally, and in Canada (Keen 2015; Fox 2015; Carlson 2011). But in the last decade the internet has continued a cumulative era of national and global governance shocks and demands such as: the global impact of the Edward Snowden case and the invasive internet policies and actions by national security agencies; issues regarding the telecommunications and broadcasting industry and internet service providers; pressures to create "fast lanes" for web traffic that would clash with rules about internet neutrality, now being expressed in terms of the internet's key firms functioning as media infrastructure (Doern, Castle, and Phillips 2016, chap. 11; Keen 2015; Fox 2015).

Thus the internet as infrastructure has been cast as "search engines" such as those deployed by Google; as a "platform" in the case of Facebook; as the complex Internet of Things; as a "threat site" for terrorists and abusers; as a "threat to fair elections"; and overall as an arena for "social production" but also social abuse and disruption. In the last decade and at present, policies and instincts to control and regulate the internet and its companies and social media producers have included the use and invocation of: competition law and monopoly offences; tax policies to remedy international tax avoidance; privacy in general and for children in particular; offences and interventions by international and national security agencies; controls on the use of big data and analytical algorithms; and practices that have created combined forms of surveillance and monopoly capitalism.

Zuboff (2015) argues that "Google is to surveillance capitalism what General Motors was to managerial capitalism" (75). The new architecture she examines "produces a distributed and largely uncontested new expression of power ... It is constituted by unexpected and often illegible mechanisms of extraction, commodification, and control that effectively exile persons from their own behaviour while producing new markets of behavioural prediction and modifications" (76). Her thesis is that surveillance capitalism is both a threat to democracy and a major departure from regular historic market capitalism.

Naughton (2017a) agrees with the surveillance capitalism thesis. He comments on how the internet when it began "was a gloriously decentralized, creative, non-commercial system ... and in ... those heady days, only a few sceptics wondered how long it would take for capitalism to get a grip on it" (1). The answer for when the grip would close, he says, was twenty-one years later, because in 2004 "Google had its IPO, Facebook was launched and the business model that became known as 'surveillance capitalism' really got a grip on the network" (1). He concludes that "this is the model that provides supposedly free services in return for 'consent' to mine and exploit their personal data and digital trails in order to target adverts at them" (1). Authors such as Jonathan Taplin (2017b) have extended the key players from Google and Facebook to firms such as Amazon. He traces the reallocation of their money and profits as one that shifts power to "monopoly platforms" (1). He has also argued for the needed breakup of firms like Google by comparing them to previous eras when monopolies were broken up under US public utility and related competition law (Taplin 2017a). As we see in more detail below, Facebook's head, Mark Zuckerberg, is said to now acknowledge "the dangerous side of the social revolution he helped to start" (Manjoo 2017, 1).

A brief look at Canadian Harper-era digital policies and at the current Justin Trudeau Liberal agenda is needed in this broader context. The Harper government's plan, *Digital Canada 150* (Canada 2014), sought to provide a relatively comprehensive update and extension of internet-related policy geared to the content and discourse of the digital age. The "150" in the title was linked to Canada's 150th anniversary as a country in 2017. The strategy was anchored around five pillars: connecting Canadians; protecting Canadians; economic opportunities; digital government; and Canadian content. The strategy document is instructive, offering a vision of what Digital Canada aspires to look like and how its regulation and governance are changing and may yet need to change.

More than most past internet policies and strategies, the Digital Canada 150 plan spoke openly about the regulation of the internet in Canada. Shortly afterwards, Industry Canada announced new legislation: Bill S-4, the *Digital Privacy Act*, and Bill C-13, on cyberbullying. Geist's (2014a) initial assessment of the bills was that they are positive and required in some key respects, but also that they leave huge gaps that may encourage firms to engage in new anti-privacy practices. Geist argued that within Bill S-4 there is "a provision that threatens to massively expand warrantless disclosure of personal information," while he argues Bill C-13 "creates an incentive for companies to voluntarily disclose to law enforcement by granting them full immunity from any civil or criminal liability for doing so" (2). Although this is already done thousands of times each year, the concern among privacy advocates is that the immunity provisions will make this practice ubiquitous.

Privacy regulation, it is worth reiterating, predates the internet and the Web. The Privacy Commissioner of Canada was created in 1983 under the *Privacy Act* (Office of the Privacy Commissioner of Canada 2012). The commissioner acts as an independent Parliamentary officer to advocate for the privacy rights of Canadians as they relate to the federal public sector and to the private sector operating within federal jurisdiction. Diverse and changing views about privacy in a liberal political society, combined with rising concern about a growing surveillance society, make it difficult if not impossible to define and to deal with abuses effectively, efficiently, and equitably (Schneier 2015; Centre for Digital Democracy 2012).

In response to online behavioural advertising, the privacy commissioner expressed concerns about the massive growth in "the practice of tracking a consumer's online activities in order to deliver advertising geared to that consumer's inferred interests" (Office of the Privacy Commissioner of Canada 2012). She pointed to the regulatory challenges and gaps, arguing that "what it means in practice is that Internet ad networks follow you around online, watching what you do so that they can serve you targeted ads," and said that "we have specifically pointed out that organizations engaged in online behavioural advertising should avoid tracking children – or tracking on websites aimed at children – since meaningful consent may be difficult to obtain" (3).

Much more explicit concerns also emerged about the key internet-anchored firms as the issues of the new "platform press" also came up starkly in the politics and campaigns related to both the UK Brexit Referendum of 2016 and its aftermath, and the 2016 US election and the early decisions and style of debate by the elected Trump administration (Cadwalladr 2017; Flynn 2017). There also arose concerns by advertisers who have been "withdrawing from Google's digital ad exchange after discovering their ads alongside videos for, among other things, American white supremacists and violent extremists" (1–2). Google has had to take some steps to police its own ads and the EU Commission "is preparing to fine social networking sites up to $50 million if they fail to take down fake news, hate speech and defamatory content within 24 hours of it being posted" (Hutton 2017, 2).

For these cumulative reasons, the legendary web inventor Tim Berners-Lee issued a statement (2017) on the Web's twenty-eighth birthday. He stressed that in many ways, the Web has lived up to its initial open network vision, but noted that he had "become increasingly worried about three new trends which I believe we must tackle in order for the web to fulfill its true potential as a tool which serves all of humanity" (2). The three new trends he highlights are: 1) we've lost control of our personal data; 2) it is too easy for misinformation to spread on the web; and 3) political advertising online needs transparency and understanding (2–4).

Canada's response to Google and Facebook as media, and as a serious threat to regular news media, began to emerge under the Trudeau Liberals in 2016–17. It involved work by the Canadian Heritage Department but more broadly involved a study and consultation process the government commissioned the Public Policy Forum to lead (Beeby 2017). Its report, *The Shattered Mirror* (Public Policy Forum 2017), traced the decline of newspaper revenues and journalism staff, which began in earlier internet eras but worsened in combination with the above-noted Google and Facebook strategies to become media without calling themselves media companies, and also the early US Trump-era fake news dynamics (12–35). The report's recommendations included measures via tax changes (income tax and GST) to strengthen the economic sustainability of Canadian news media, but philosophically it was an effort to think comprehensively about "news, democracy and trust in the digital age" (3).

A further realm of internet infrastructure and broader governance came via competition policy. This had been examined in different national competition authorities as the social media giants got bigger and bigger, but concrete action was not the norm. The "prevailing wisdom, particularly in America, used to be that '*superplatforms*', despite their size, do not unfairly use their market power and thrive because of their unceasing innovation. The competition is just 'one click' away" (*Economist* 2017a, 61). But the EU's Competition Commissioner announced in June 2017 the imposition of a 2.4 billion Euro fine on Google on the grounds that it had abused its search dominance by promoting its own comparison-shopping service and demoting those of its competitors (Toplensky 2017, 1). Views also emerged that this would open the door to "damages cases from hundreds of businesses that lost revenues after they were demoted in Google's results" (1). More importantly in a larger sense, it was cast as a possible new era for other anti-monopoly action against the five massive big tech companies – Amazon, Apple, Facebook, Google, and Microsoft (Sherman 2017). As the *Economist* has argued, such firms own "the world's most valuable resource," namely vast flows of data, and, as in past eras of massive market power, "such dominance has prompted calls for the tech giants to be broken up" (*Economist* 2017f, 9). But Naughton (2017a, 1) argues that in reality "tech giants face no contest when it comes to competition law."

The nature of the challenge in managing regulatory-monitoring intervention, and who will do it, has raised serious practical dilemmas. Some of this has emerged regarding Facebook's early efforts to self-regulate via what Hopkins (2017) calls its "internal rulebook on sex, terrorism and violence" or policies guiding its "moderators on what content to allow." The moderating interpretive issues include "violence, hate speech, terrorism, pornography, racism, and self-harm." Hopkins observes "the challenges for moderators, who say they are overwhelmed by the volume of work, which means they often have 'just 10 seconds' to make a decision" (1). The initial team, then of about thirty moderators, were, not surprisingly, young people with the needed tech savvy, but not necessarily the policy/values savvy. But Naughton (2017c) is correct when he states that "with 1.3 million new posts every minute, it's impossible for the company's moderators to filter out all the nasty stuff" (1). Similar challenges would arise if, through some reform process, it were governmental teams of officials/ regulators who were the front-line moderator-regulators. As Gore (2017) argues, "as a consequence of the internet revolution, more material is now published than ever before. And yet never has it seemed so unfashionable to admit being a publisher. Google remains simply a search engine, helpfully directing internet users to a choice of destinations" (2). And of course, the use of algorithms is intended to favour some information over other content.

The efforts of Facebook to self-"moderate" coincided with appearances by its CEO, Mark Zuckerberg, before the US Senate and House of Representatives committees regarding his own firm's moderating behaviour and the demise of Cambridge Analytica and its digital tactics and behaviour. Zuckerberg faced questions about the need for Facebook to be regulated as opposed to just self-moderated. Facebook's first quarterly moderation report was released. As Frenkel (2018) reports, "Facebook has been under pressure for its failure to remove violence, nudity, hate speech and other inflammatory content from its site" (1), but in its eighty-six-page report, "Facebook revealed that it deleted 865.8 million posts in the first quarter of 2018, the vast majority of which were spam, with a minority of posts related to nudity, graphic violence, hate speech and terrorism" (1). Frenkel also argued that "Facebook attributed the increase in content removal ... to improved artificial intelligence programs that could detect and flag offensive content ... Zuckerberg has long highlighted A.I. as the main solution to helping Facebook sift through billions of pieces of content that people post to its cite every day" (4).

Other accounts of the Facebook report were similar in the nature of their criticisms of Facebook's efforts. Hern and Solon 2018 pointed out, however, that the Facebook figures came "a week after the release of the Santa Clara principles, an attempt to write a guidebook for how large platforms should moderate content" (3). They also point out how recently "YouTube revealed it removed 8.3 million videos" (3) for breaching its community guidelines. In the BBC's coverage Lee (2018) raised similar overall concerns but ended with his view that "Facebook remains coy about the make-up of its human moderation team. It said it did try to make sure US-based workers handled incidents where an understanding of American culture was beneficial – likewise for incidents in other countries" (4), but how the latter was done was not further discussed or revealed. And of course, as stressed above, these dynamics regarding infrastructure governance would also be present if the site were entirely or partly government regulated or jointly regulated/moderated.

Cambridge Analytica's role and demise only add further to the above infrastructure policy and governance complexity and challenges (Solon and Graham-Harrison 2018). Cambridge Analytica's role was exposed by newspaper revelations in the UK and US about how the core "software program at the heart of [the company] was created and how the company collected the data of tens of millions of Facebook users for commercial use, in violation of the social media giant's own rules" (1). But Facebook was itself slow to respond. Cambridge Analytica went on to "work for Donald Trump's election campaign" (2).

These initial exposés led to a storm of revelations that in a six-week period brought Cambridge Analytica down as it was investigated by US and UK authorities and was further exposed in media reports. One of these involved a Canadian firm, Aggregate IQ, that had worked with "leave campaigns" in the Brexit referendum. The Canadian firm denied any link with Cambridge Analytica, but it was involved in the Brexit campaign. On 2 May, Cambridge Analytica went into liquidation but "the team behind it has already set up a new company called Emerdata" (5). These kinds of threats to electoral and other aspects of democracy were also explored in conjunction with how Facebook and other Silicon Valley giants were in discussions, and participating in some initial experiments, with "tech humanists" and their hub of advocacy, the Centre for Humane Technology in San Francisco (*Guardian* 2018). The "tech humanists are making a bid to become tech's loyal opposition," claimed the *Guardian*, but in fact, the tech powerhouse players were benefiting because "they are starting to speak its idiom." This included Facebook's Mark Zuckerberg, who announced that Facebook had a new priority: maximizing "time well spent" on the platform, "rather than total time spent" (2). The *Guardian* analysis went on to argue that Silicon Valley could not fix itself because it was a world of billionaire owners and corporations, and that "anti-trust laws and tax policy offer useful ways to claw back the fortunes Big Tech has built on common resources" (10).

A key policy and governance development in 2018 was centred in the growing scope of European regulation of the technology giants and the internet's social networks. Germany, for example, introduced the enforcement processes and content to new online hate speech law (Bennhold 2018). Key features of it as criteria were to ensure that it severely policed activities that Nazi Germany under Hitler had deployed. Part of the apparatus of "enforcement" is Facebook's own operation in Berlin of a "deletion centre" staffed by more than 1,200 content moderators employed by Facebook. It was deployed by Richard Allan, Facebook's vice-president for public policy in Europe and "the leader of the company's lobbying effort against the German legislation" (5), because, as Allan put it, "We don't want to be the arbiters of free speech" (5).

However, far more crucial in the European setting was the enactment by the European Union of the General Data Protection Regulation (GDPR). The law (Satariano 2018) "lets people request their online data and restricts how businesses obtain and handle information" (1). In Satariano's view, "Europe is determined to cement its role as the world's foremost tech watchdog – and the region is only getting started. Authorities in Brussels and in the European Union's 28 member countries are also setting the bar for stricter enforcement of antitrust laws against the tech behemoths and are paving the way for tougher tax policies on the companies" (1–2).

The pace of pressure and mechanisms to review Facebook and its "fact-checkers" had by July 2018 led to Canada being "one of the countries where fact checkers hired by Facebook will review some of the links and news stories being shared on the platform" (Wherry 2018, 2). Indeed, Canada was the fifteenth country to have such reviews launched by Facebook. Wherry reports that "in Canada, Facebook is partnering with Agence France-Presse, the international news agency," and that AFP fact-checkers will review stories that are being shared on Facebook and rate the reports for accuracy. If a story is found to be "false," Facebook "will limit its distribution and notify all those who have shared the story" (3), and stresses that fact-checking "will always have to contend with human bias, partisanship, malicious actors and politicians who insist on their own versions of reality" (4). But even more critically, these processes will be propelled by the race to "regulate the use of Facebook and other online platforms before the 2019 federal election" (Boutilier 2018, 1). These will be centred on proposals to change Canada's elections laws.

Commenting on these types of changes globally, Bell (2018) shows how this kind of "[a]rchive of political content becomes a battleground between publishers and platforms" (1). This is because publishers "look to social platforms to question the labelling and representation of their work" (2). Thus Bell is correct when she states that the friction over regulation and monitoring "highlights a key tension within Facebook and all tech companies when it comes to dealing with cultural concepts. Should companies just rely far more heavily on human judgement or should they leave it to algorithms" (3). Bell concludes that "[n]ews and journalism are now dependent on Facebook, Google, Twitter, Apple and others for many aspects of their existence. What is clear is that these companies are not inherently suited to be custodians of our information ecosystem, and arguably never will be" (4).

Also of analytical interest is the work of Harris (2019), who traces fifteen years of Facebook back to its roots in 2004 and discusses how it has "changed the human condition" and how one of its key impacts is centred on the question "have we forgotten how to be alone?" (1). He links this question to social media users from children to teenagers, to the middle-aged and the elderly, and their various senses of the self, and how Facebook and related social media innovations have impacted on "the divide between our social and private lives" (3). He also links it to analysis and arguments about the so-called "surveillance capitalism" referred to in chapter 1 of this book.

While the content of Canada's elections law reform has to date not been made public, it is useful to see the example of the U K Electoral Commission, and what kind of reforms it is calling for in the even larger realm of regulating democracy (Waterson 2018, 2). These go well beyond fact-checking as discussed above, and include changes such as "a change in the law to require all digital political campaign material to state who paid for it ... and new legislation to make it clear that spending in U K elections and referendums by foreign organizations and individuals is not allowed" (2). As reported by Boutilier (2018), Canadian reforms are mooted to be those that would ensure "greater transparency by political actors" operating online, and "that foreign money doesn't fund domestic political advocacy" (2). Other Canadian authors such as Thomas (2018) stress that the current Trudeau government's belated commitment to electoral reform also relates to its earlier electoral reform pride that it had nicely dealt already with the sins of the previous Harper era. In short, it was ill-prepared to think through the new imperatives of dealing with and regulating social media platforms and the press as an internet platform. In 2020–21, closely linked and rapidly changing aspects of technology and power are being shaped by COVID-19 and related imperatives and uncertainties in global and Canadian terms. Harris (2020) stressed how Facebook, for example, "is still far too powerful," but it is "also how millions are coping with this crisis," since "the Covid moment demands a means of bringing people together while they largely stay in their homes and ensuring that whatever limited time they can spend in the real world is used as constructively as possible" (2). He argues that "in the UK alone, Facebook has facilitated the formation of an estimated 300 local Coronavirus support groups, whose combined membership totals more than a million people" (3).

In Canada, Grenier's (2020) analysis stresses how "pandemic-rattled Canadians" are "still cautious about everything from schools to 2nd lockdowns." He also draws attention to polls that "show the vast majority of Canadians expect to see a second wave in this country in the future," which would "hit the Canadian economy very hard due to people staying home and spending less" (3). Grenier cites polls that suggest "59 percent of Canadians fear contracting COVID-19." To address such concerns, in July 2020, Prime Minister Trudeau's government committed to provide the provinces and territories $19 billion to help enable a "safe start" of the economy. The money allocated responds to provincial needs and priorities that include testing and contact tracing, more childcare spaces, mental health services, and many other specific issues and problems (Cochrane and Jones 2020).

Internationally, a major 2020 study by the World Economic Forum, "Accelerating Digital Inclusion in the New Normal," argues that the new normal "will likely see an increase in speeds, devices and budgets required by households, and businesses, exacerbating existing divides" (2020b, 3). It argues that therefore "connectivity must become the top priority ... broadband internet user penetration should reach 75% worldwide and by 2025, broadband should cost no more than 2% of earnings" (3). A large follow-up section in the report stresses the urgency needed for the "digital inclusion agenda" and claims that the digital divide "has exacerbated the situation for far too many in vulnerable situations around the world" (2020a, 4). The current COVID-19 crisis, and preparation for future pandemics, will continue to accelerate the pace of technological change and our reliance upon new technology, underlining the importance of policies to effectively target the digital divide.

Analysis: The Three Regime Elements

With the aid of table 9.1 we now look across the three policy and governance histories presented above by examining the three elements featured in the book's overall analytical framework.

Regarding policy *ideas, discourse, and agendas*, the evidence across the three histories shows both differences and similarities depending in part on the time periods when STI infrastructure first emerged. Big science as infrastructure discourse emerged in the World War II and immediate post-war contexts, where multi-million-dollar labs and projects were big enough to evoke large infrastructure discourse, but always with some logical vagueness about when little science or smaller/medium-sized science might enter the definitional realm. Emerging and changing platforms at the NRC and at some universities were also noted. The language and reality of networks and virtual science institutes also emerged, including what they imply for Canada regarding "big science" in a small country, and their links to international big science projects and centres.

The CFI creation story is STI infrastructure-centred because the CFI was established to invest in state-of-the-art infrastructure that enables world-class research at Canada's universities. Forged in the late 1990s, the kinds of infrastructure supported included equipment, labs, databases, computer hardware, and buildings all intended to enable the creation and development of research institutes. The focus was on university research, and the scope quickly increased to 9,303 projects at 145 institutions in 70 universities across Canada.

Regarding the internet policy history, the notion of it being a huge pre-eminent and literal STI full-spectrum infrastructure emerges from the outset. The World Wide Web was unambiguously an information platform, cast as an information highway in early Canadian strategies. Because of the Web's place as a system of permissionless innovation driven by net neutrality, it yielded, especially in the early twenty-first century, a massive national and international array of social media and social production systems. But early on and in recent years at much greater speed, the internet became infrastructure of a much more questionable and criticized kind. It was an arena for advocates of "fast lanes" as a counter-pressure to internet neutrality. It was becoming a "threat site" for terrorists and abusers, and also a site for the immergence of big data and the growing use of algorithms as analytical weapons for online advantage. Above all, the internet was fast becoming a type of media itself that needed to be regulated and moderated, but there were great complexities involved in doing it or in sharing the almost impossible task.

Regarding *power structures, democracy, and governance*, in the STI infrastructure regime we have seen diverse features of change and

Table 9.1
The STI infrastructure regime and the three analytical elements: highlights

Policy and governance histories	Policy ideas, discourse, and agendas	Power structures, democracy, and governance	Temporal realities, cycles, conflicts, and Technology
Big science infrastructure policy and governance, World War II to present	• NRC and Department of National Defence World War II big science. • US war and post-war forging of the military-industrial complex. • Big Science as teams of researchers working in multi-million-dollar laboratories and projects. • Canadian related big science in wind tunnels, atomic energy, and telescopes. • Linked as well to high-energy physics and basic science at several Canadian universities in 1960s. • "Little science" also needs basic infrastructure (offices/buildings/ equipment). • Emerging technological platforms at NRC and at universities in STI spectrum era. • Infrastructure cast as being linked with networks and virtual networks. • Canadian Institutes of Health Research (CIHR) as virtual institutes. • Canada as "big science in a small country." • STI and infrastructure that are small and medium and are university-based versus large and collaborative multi-university projects, many linked with international big science.	• Defence Department and NRC wartime and post-war dominance as big science centre. • AECL's big science Intense Neutron Generator (ING) proposal rejected by government in late 1960s. • Reorganizations and reforms of NRC since but with continuing features of big science, recently described as containing "37 research infrastructure facilities." • STI funding cuts in 1980s to mid-1990s. • Networks of Centres of Excellence (NCE) as new institutional model. • CIHR as complex health and hospital virtual institutes, with fifty peer-review committees compared to five under former Medical Research Council (MRC). • Call for national policy for considering, evaluating, and overseeing large-scale research in Canada. • View that lobbying power is not itself a good criterion for funding.	• World War II big science surge as national and international infrastructure S&T. • Networks as fixed and changing in the medium term. • Cycles of international projects to join or not to join. • STI budget/funding cuts (1970s to 80s) and surges (late 1990s).

Table 9.1
The STI infrastructure regime and the three analytical elements: highlights (*Continued*)

Policy and governance histories	Policy ideas, discourse, and agendas	Power structures, democracy, and governance	Temporal realities, cycles, conflicts, and Technology
The Canada Foundation for Innovation as STI infrastructure foundation, 1997 to present	• Mandate expressed as CFI role in "investing in state-of-the art infrastructure that enables world-class research." • Centred on explicit demands that federal government pay for universities' "overhead expenses." • Large research infrastructure as "equipment, labs, databases, computer hardware and software, and buildings." • 9,303 projects at 145 research institutions in 70 universities across Canada. • Research hospital funds.	• Lobbying by key university presidents supported by Paul Martin as Finance minister to establish the CFI as "foundation" model. • CFI as both funding patron and regulator requiring universities to develop and submit research plans. • Big, small, and medium distributive politics at play for defining and changing competition programs/ purposes. • Federal government as main funder but matching leveraged funds required from provinces, charities, etc. • System centred on "merit review" system rather than normal peer review, because it was infrastructure- and facilities-centred.	• CFI caught late-1990s renewal of federal budget surpluses. • Periodically changing structure of funds and competitions. • Cycles of university's "research plans" to get fair share.
The internet: from Permissionless innovation STI infrastructure to regulated infrastructure media and threat to democracy, 1990s to present	• System of permissionless innovation. • No central control and internet neutrality. • World Wide Web as overarching platform. • Earlier conceptions in Canada as Information Highway. • Social media as driver of social production system.	• No power and control involved or seen to be involved in core internet and web functioning, but later contrary views of need for some kinds of control, due to lost control by individuals of their personal data. • Misinformation and "fake news" on the web highlighted in US Trump era and UK Brexit and post-Brexit dynamics.	• Disruptive nature of Google and Facebook. • Massive rapid high-volume creation of social media sites and social production in Canada and globally.

- Now increasingly seen as media/press platform.
- Ideas/advocacy of "fast lanes" and thus threat to internet neutrality.
- A growing "threat site" for terrorists and abusers.
- Privacy protection overall and especially regarding children.
- As "big data" source and fast-growing use of algorithms analytically; and as controlling strategy/instrument.
- Threat to newspaper industry over last twenty years and now by internet as media itself.
- Internet and web as "fake news" sources.
- Links to "superplatform" big tech companies and their "unceasing innovation" but also their monopoly power.

- Snowden case and growing internet incursions by national security agencies.
- Use and limits of competition law and policy vis-à-vis web platform.
- EU competition agency levies 2.4 billion Euro fine against Google for abusing its search dominance by promoting its own comparison shopping over others'.
- Emergence of "surveillance capitalism" and extended monopoly capitalism linked to Amazon and other big tech companies.
- Harper-era Digital Canada 150 strategy advocated some selected regulation re privacy but also loopholes therein.
- Privacy Commissioner of Canada's advocacy of internet controls regarding children in particular.
- Growing advertiser concerns about their ads showing alongside those of offensive groups.
- Public Policy Forum Study *Shattered Mirror* about threats to national press as industry and democratic fora in Canada.
- However, federal government's plans to fund selective media outlets met with scepticism by critics fearing a loss of independence.

- Facebook's self-monitoring temporal challenges by small team regarding having ten seconds to make its decisions and in relation to 1.3 million posts coming in every minute.
- Facebook's first Quarterly Moderation Report.
- Cambridge Analytica role in election advice and campaigns in US and the firm's sudden demise in early 2018.
- Canadian firms such as AggregateIQ involved in UK Brexit referendum but say they had no links with Cambridge Analytica.

inertia nationally and internationally with impacts on Canada. At its early stages in the big-science story, power during World War II and in the immediate post-war period was exercised by the NRC and the Department of National Defence. And the NRC was the locale of choice well into the 1970s. Even now, after considerable change, the NRC describes itself as an entity containing thirty-seven research infrastructure facilities. This policy history also shows that there were serious science budget cuts in the 1980s and 1990s. But also emerging in these two decades were the creation and funding of research networks such as the Networks of Centres of Excellence (NCE) program and, even more significantly, the formation and work of the Canadian Institutes of Health Research as virtual health and hospital-centred institutes. Also occurring were calls for better national policy for considering and evaluating and overseeing large-scale research in Canada, functioning with big science in a small country. As well, concerns emerged about whether lobbying power can ever itself be a "good" criterion for funding choices/approvals.

The CFI story politically was based on the lobbying power of key university presidents determined to garner support for any and all university research expenses and emerging and needed infrastructure. The CFI also emerged in a new period of budgetary surpluses. The CFI as a foundation was also an institutional experiment as an arm's-length entity intended to deal with different kinds of decision-making for infrastructure per se. In political and administrative power and governance terms, the CFI was both a patron and a regulator, and required universities to develop and submit public research plans. It also required funding decisions to be based on "merit review" of infrastructure as infrastructure and assets rather than on the normal peer-review system of the science being proposed or conducted. Levered funding was also the governing financial and funding norm. But the overall CFI twenty-year experience exhibited frequent concerns about big, small, and medium distributive politics regarding defining and changing research competition programs and purposes.

Regarding the internet STI infrastructure story (and indeed the Internet as "Big STI" incarnate) the internet as permissionless innovation succeeded in massive ways with its US impacts and its willing Canadian adoption – both early on and with the massive influx of social media and social production anchored in core firms and platforms such as Google and Facebook and functioning in the World Wide Web. Gradually but increasingly, governance and democratic

concerns began to emerge about the needs for regulation and monitoring. As examined earlier in this chapter, in Canada these concerns
came from privacy agencies and advocates, but also from within the
Harper government in its Digital Canada 150 reform strategy and
initial legislation. However, these concerns escalated enormously as
the politics of the "internet as media" advocacy and reality emerged,
including new direct threats to democracy, linked as they were to the
dubious business practices of the core Google and Facebook corporations, in addition to the emergence of firms such as Cambridge
Analytica and its numerous offspring and counterparts. In the current
Liberal Trudeau era, this has yielded more explicit concerns about
the impacts of the internet as media on traditional and threatened
print media and related journalism in a functioning democracy, including firms such as Aggregate IQ. The threats of power exercised through
"surveillance capitalism" were easily linked to other related tracks of
socio-economic pressure that needed to be dealt with because of the
actions of national security agencies and the need for greater competition policy actions analogous to that taken by the EU against Google.
Also emerging were concerns and pressures regarding how individuals
were losing control of their personal data in the increasingly complex
internet infrastructure.

Regarding *temporal realities, cycles, conflicts, and technology* as an
analytical element, the three policy histories reveal an array of separate
and related dynamics. In the big-science story, the fast imperatives of
World War II drove decisions and infrastructure focal points. These
impacts continued in the immediate decade after the war both within
the NRC and outside it in key federal science agencies. The cycles of
network formation (and discourse) emerged quite strongly but also
experimentally in the 1980s with new funding programs. Budget
cycles were also in operation, including the quite long presence of
science budget cuts in the 1980s to 1996 period. There were also
changes and uncertainty in the emergence of international big science
projects, and which ones, if any, Canada should join.

The CFI story and period were made possible initially by the emergence of federal budget surpluses and newly changed lobbying strategies by key university presidents to take advantage of this situation.
Also evident were the periodically changing structures of CFI funds
and competitions. Operating in different ways were the cycles and
impacts of universities' own "research plans" to garner various notions
of fair shares. And underpinning these short- and medium-term

dynamics was the emergence of new technologies as the focal point for some of the suggested funding changes.

The internet policy and governance history is woven with continuous and rapid forms of disruptive technology as revealed by the emergence of Google and later Facebook, the former with the core search engine driver of change. But it was the massive overall emergence and growth of social media sites and their social production that was continuously innovative and disruptive. The issue of speed and volume was shown in the example of Facebook's efforts to self-moderate and self-regulate, exposing concerns about various kinds of abusive and unfair practices, with a small team of reviewers forced to make decisions every ten seconds and facing the 1.3 million new posts every minute that needed review. The massive emergence of big data was also presenting both great opportunities for some and serious problems for others. These joined the fast emergence of the internet as a type of media itself and, crucially, in terms of modern infrastructure as well.

CONCLUSIONS

Our final regime chapter has mapped and analyzed the Science, Technology, and Innovation (STI) Infrastructure Policy and Governance Regime through three policy and governance histories in total spanning about six decades. This has been both a Canadian story and a US-Canada and international one, as science, technology, and innovation separately and together as an STI imperative changed the nature of what STI infrastructure is and has come to be: initially big science labs and projects that were big enough to evoke large infrastructure discourse but always with some logical vagueness about when little-science or smaller/medium-sized science might enter the definitional and practical operational realm.

Later STI infrastructure with a university focus is cast as being linked with networks and virtual networks and virtual institutes, but also with equipment, labs, databases, computer hardware, and buildings, and ultimately with the CFI as funding body geared explicitly to infrastructure and ways of assessing it via merit-based criteria rather than traditional peer review. With the emergence of the internet and the ubiquitous World Wide Web, STI became the sheer massive growth of Google and its search engines allied with tech giants such as Facebook as platforms. Social media emerged massively on and because of the permissionless nature of the internet. But the internet has also been transformed into infrastructure increasingly cast as a controlling medium by the commercial strategies and practices of its dominant firms, and itself now needs greater control along several policy dimensions. But this is emerging as we have seen in very tentative, complex, and imperfect ways, and now in 2021 urgent ways due to the many national and global imperatives of the COVID-19 pandemic.

The race for vaccines and the need for reliable and affordable connectivity during the pandemic have helped to put Canadian science and digital infrastructure at the front and centre of public and political scrutiny and debate. Canada's inability to develop its own domestic vaccine production and supply chain has been politically damaging for the federal government, especially given its early and doomed reliance on and faith in China (CanSino) to deliver the much-needed vaccines. Also damaging has been the protracted length of time taken to decide on Huawei's involvement in developing Canada's 5G telecommunications network. As the government plans to unleash billions of dollars to "build back better" it should be safe to assume that both types of infrastructure will be seen as funding priorities, along with Canadian science and research more generally.

10

Conclusions

This book has provided an in-depth academic analysis of Canadian infrastructure policy and governance regimes over five decades. We stressed from the outset the existence of core definitions of infrastructure, but also an appreciation of dozens of needed definitional types related both to the building of facilities and assets and to varied notions of their ongoing repair and refurbishment. Covering for the most part a fifty-year period, in addition to longer periods where needed, the analysis has centred on an account of our seventeen infrastructure policy and governance histories across six infrastructure policy and governance regimes. These policy and governance histories have been summarized in detail at the end of each of the six regime chapters (4 through 9).

Each regime analysis has also shed light on potential and real future infrastructure policy and governance challenges over the next two decades. We have shown that Canada's infrastructure story requires a multi-level governmental-political account embracing federal, provincial, and city-local jurisdictions and changing interactions. At the federal level we have explored actions and inactions across five prime ministerial eras: the current Justin Trudeau era, and the previous Stephen Harper, Jean Chrétien and Paul Martin, Brian Mulroney, and Pierre Trudeau eras.

The underpinning for our analysis was further supported in the first part of the book by a foundational literature review in chapter 1, an initial federal-provincial-urban-local infrastructure policy and governance mapping in chapter 2, and in chapter 3 a key changing international policy and institutional dynamics context. It begins with a particular focus on Canada-US relations, including in the Trump administration era, as well as other key changing international infra-structure policy and governance institutions. Furthermore, international dynamics and drivers have been shown to be present as well in all of the six regime chapters and policy histories, in addition to provincial, regional, and First Nation dynamics and tensions across Canada.

OUR SEVEN MAIN ARGUMENTS IN THE CONTEXT OF ANSWERING THE FIVE RESEARCH QUESTIONS

We now turn to a final discussion of our seven main arguments in the context of answering the five research questions posed in the book's Introduction. Necessarily and not surprisingly, the seven arguments can and should underpin more than one research question, given the evidence assembled in the six regimes and in the book as a whole, including chapters 1, 2, and 3.

Our *first research question* is:

"How has infrastructure policy emerged on the federal, provin-cial, and local policy and political agendas?"

We answer this in relation to our first two main arguments, namely:

1 Infrastructure policy has not ranked highly in federal agenda-setting Throne Speeches and Budget Speeches over the past fifty years. It has rarely been a standalone issue or discourse because it is typically embedded in and/or combined with numerous other socio-economic policy fields and buried in a myriad of lit-erally dozens of unmanageable and even unknowable funding programs.

2 Credible definitions and understandings of infrastructure are emerging, but, in a world of complex policy fields, traditional and fast-changing social media agendas, and descriptive dis-course, the politics of infrastructure discourse will always shift in unexpected directions and ways.

The support for these arguments is straightforward regarding federal government Throne Speeches and Budget Speeches, and emerges in chapters 1 and 2 as well as in chapter 3, where Canada-US cross-border infrastructure is ever more complex in terms of borders, bridges, and security/safety systems. As we saw also in chapter 4 on the business infrastructure policy and governance regime, its treatment of business self-funding infrastructure is also linked to the banking system. But the complexity and opaque nature of infrastructure definitions and discourse are evident in each of the regimes that are not necessarily at the centre of government (federal, provincial, city-local). This was apparent in each of the regimes for transport infrastructure, housing infrastructure, energy-environment-resources pipeline infrastructure, and science, technology, and innovation (STI) infrastructure, as shown in chapters 6, 7, 8, and 9.

Our *second research question* is:

"Is there a credible definition and understanding of what infrastructure is and of the implementation challenges and risks that it engenders in a federal multi-level system of governance and democracy?"

We answer this question in relation to our second, third, and fourth arguments, namely:

2 Credible definitions and understandings of infrastructure are emerging, but in a world of complex policy fields and traditional and fast-changing social media agendas and descriptive discourse, the politics of infrastructure discourse will always shift in unexpected directions and ways.
3 Canada, at all levels of government, needs to develop actual *capital budgets* so that funding captures and involves asset life cycles, is actually costed as a true investment activity, and is therefore funded in ways different from current normal operational distributive or retail public budgeting.
4 Most infrastructure is now built and fostered at the urban/city level of government because that is where 70 per cent of Canadians live and work. But cities have the weakest and most inadequate revenue sources, centred only or mainly on property taxes. Federal-provincial-city tax systems need major reform to give cities access to income tax revenue sources for some kinds of infrastructure repair in particular.

Once again, our second argument emerges in answering this research question because of evidence in chapters 1 and 3 in addition to the regime chapters already mentioned above in their specific policy fields.

Our analysis also shows both the absence of and advocacy for actual capital budgets in governments. Chapter 4's analysis of the business infrastructure policy and governance regime shows that only businesses have, and are allowed to have, capital budgets. In this context, several of our surveys of core or needed definitions in chapters 1 and 2, and in the regime chapters, make the case that infrastructure is above all about "capital" of various and diverse kinds.

Capital budgeting, also known as investment appraisal, is used by companies to evaluate major projects and investments, such as new plants or equipment. The process involves a detailed analysis of total project costs, lifetime cash flows, depreciation rates, asset maintenance costs, and net benefits and returns over the project's life cycle. In contrast to this, detailed public-sector evaluation of infrastructure investments is either absent, superficial, or not sufficiently transparent to enable political and public scrutiny. As we have argued in chapters 2 and 5 and elsewhere in the book, this omission is the product of several factors. First, infrastructure funding is usually undertaken at speed due to political and economic pressures to stimulate the economy and create jobs, reducing the time required to do due diligence on complex needs, costs, and benefits. This often results in a preference for 'shovel-ready products' that facilitate an expedited process of spending. In some cases, full environmental assessments have been streamlined to speed up the process further, as with the Harper government's stimulus programs following the financial crisis in 2008. Second, one of the key political attractions of infrastructure spending is that it is highly discretionary compared to other types of spending such as social programs for examples. Governments have little interest in reducing that discretion by using or making public evidence-based evaluations that may constrain their choice of project, particularly if the same information is also available to citizens, opposition parties, the media, and parliamentary watchdogs. A related factor is that governments have wider and legitimate criteria to weigh than the private sector when deciding which projects to invest in. For example, in addition to job creation, investment opportunities, and economic stimulus, regional, social, and political considerations come into play, in addition to equity, diversity, and urban vs. rural impacts. Finally, chapters 2 and 5 also illustrated the challenges presented by Canada's anachronistic system of governance and tax-raising powers that has resulted in a complex web of transfers and funding programs from both senior levels of government to municipalities. In addition to the

challenges this system has created for democratic and local accountability, it has also resulted in federal infrastructure funding being
highly skewed towards 'new build' projects as opposed to ongoing
maintenance and repair or associated operational costs. While this is
clearly desirable from a federal perspective, it presents enormous
challenges for municipalities, who are left to maintain infrastructure
projects over the duration of their life cycle. Moreover, it also helps
to further explain why the federal government is less inclined to be
concerned about the project life cycle evaluation that would normally
be included in capital budgeting and investment appraisal.

Our above fourth argument is relevant here. Both the transport
regime (chapter 6) and the housing regime (chapter 7) show in different ways how cities especially and systematically lack access to
even the minimum tax resources they need for complex infrastructure
demands and needs (new infrastructure and repairs to infrastructure).
These expanding needs ultimately arise in ever more pivotal ways
because they are now where the majority of Canadians live, vote, are
housed, and have to travel, illustrating the enormous economic and
social importance of infrastructure. We also saw this point further
underlined in chapter 3 regarding US infrastructure budgets and
funding and some of their increased links to Canada-US cross-border
trade and travel, requiring joint and therefore more complex funding
arrangements.

Our *third research question* is:

"Is corruption a growing or declining feature of infrastructure
policy, governance and democracy in Canada and to what extent
has there been change with respect to how it is defined, policed,
and regulated?"

We answer this again in relation to our second and third arguments:

2 Credible definitions and understandings of infrastructure are
   emerging, but in a world of complex policy fields and traditional
   and fast-changing social media agenda and descriptive discourse,
   the politics of infrastructure discourse will always shift in unexpected directions and ways.
3 Canada, at all levels of government, needs to develop actual
   capital budgets so that funding captures and involves asset life
   cycles, is actually costed as a true investment activity, and is

therefore funded in ways different from current normal operational distributive or retail public budgeting.

The analysis in chapter 5 of the paying for infrastructure policy and
governance regime necessarily weaves its way through the above kinds
of arguments about possible corruption but it also probes and scopes
out where possible related features and discourse exist. These include
notions of what political pressures, needs, political business cycles,
and contempt for taxpayers might empirically, rhetorically, and practi-
cally mean. As discussed in chapter 5, retail political notions and
discourse such as "shovel-ready" infrastructure projects, popular in
the Harper era and in earlier governments as well, can demonstrate
contempt for local priorities, value for money, and rigorous cost-
benefit analysis as just discussed in response to our second research
question. The Trudeau government's discursive preference for "shovel-
worthy" projects appears to have done little to introduce much-needed
rigour, planning, and objectivity into infrastructure funding decisions.
Chapter 4's discussion of SMEs versus "start-up" businesses and
public-private partnerships (P3s) are also relevant here and involve
analytical detective work both for ministers, officials, and key interests
(not to mention academics and think tanks). While it is clearly difficult
to quantify levels of corruption the potential for corruption and waste,
in its many forms, is heightened by the complexity of transfers and
the growing involvement of corporate interests, including commercial
confidentiality, that inevitably reduces transparency and opportunities
for public engagement and scrutiny. The massive scale and ambition
of the infrastructure spending being planned to help the economy
recover from the pandemic shutdown will provide a severe test of
Canadian governance and the measures currently in place to provide
scrutiny, oversight, and value for money.

Our *fourth research question* is:

"Is the funding of infrastructure characterized by the imperatives
of distributive retail politics or are other viable funding models
present or emerging?"

We answer this in relation to our third and fifth arguments:

3 Canada, at all levels of government, needs to develop actual
   capital budgets so that funding captures and involves asset life

cycles, is actually costed as a true investment activity, and is therefore funded in ways different from current normal operational distributive or retail public budgeting.

5 Some other funding models for infrastructure funding are emerging, such as infrastructure banks, but these at present seem too often to be simply timely reforms that can be announced. They tend not to be linked to the current role of the existing banking system in infrastructure funding and lending, nor to how reforms may play out in global banking and pension fund investment institutions.

All the issues already noted above about our third argument regarding capital budgets emerge again here. Argument five about infrastructure banks is necessarily discussed in different regime contexts, including P3s, but also infrastructure funding by the regular banking system in chapter 4, and the Canada Infrastructure Bank in chapters 1 and 5, as announced by the Justin Trudeau Liberals. Issues of trust and transparency for different players and interests are both extolled but also buried and shrouded in these kinds of choices. While it is still too early to tell if Canada's newly minted infrastructure bank will facilitate a more strategic and less politicized approach to investment, the Trudeau government's decision to establish political reach and influence over the Infrastructure Bank, allied with the 2019 appointment of a minister for Rural Infrastructure within Infrastructure Canada, suggests that retail politics will continue to thrive despite Liberal calls and promises in 2015 to 'do things differently' once in office. Moreover, after a stuttering start, the sudden replacement of senior management at the CIB in 2020 has still to show significant changes in direction or activity. With the post-pandemic stimulus rollout about to get underway, there is enormous potential for the CIB to play an important role in the recovery, but if not now, then when?

Our *fifth research question* is:

What are the main challenges for Canada's six infrastructure policy and governance regimes over the next ten to twenty years?

We answer this question in relation to our sixth, seventh, and fourth arguments:

6 The regulation of infrastructure is not normally or easily captured by existing regulatory theory or governance practice. Indeed, "rule-making" about infrastructure is far more likely to be carried out under tax and spending rules and rule-makers than via regulatory oversight institutions per se. Infrastructure decisions often involve corruption, both financially and regarding failures of democracy.

7 Other long-term related policy and governance needs for infrastructure also depend on a greater understanding of what kind of core expertise is needed to cope with and anticipate policy and governance in diverse infrastructure and related technological fields. These include expertise in logistics, national and international supply chains, and information-centred big data usefulness and abuses. Better underlying mappings are also needed of what the infrastructure socio-economic interest group structure is and how it is seeking to change how government works in Canadian multi-level federalism.

4 Most infrastructure is now built and fostered at the urban/city level of government because that is where 70 per cent of Canadians live and work. But cities have the weakest and most inadequate revenue sources, centred only or mainly on property tax sources. Federal-provincial-city tax systems need major reform to give cities access to income tax revenue sources for some kinds of infrastructure repair in particular.

The sixth argument emerged early on in chapter 1's foundational literature review, dealing with phases and layers of regulatory governance, including regulatory capitalism, and those tied to both rule complexity and systemic unruliness, means-ends ambiguity in addition to outsourced law systems cast as "all ends and no means." Budgetary and fiscal complexity also emerged, including the presence of demands for and features of macro structural fundamentalism as opposed to earlier Keynesian stimulus budgetary/spending and taxation concepts. The fourth argument has already been examined and is crucial for current and longer-term challenges concerning cities and tax-funding systems and capacities regarding infrastructure. Our seventh argument enters explicitly here for the first time because it raises crucial questions and ambiguities about long-term critical analytical capacities of various kinds regarding the coming two decades. These certainly emerge in chapter 8's regime analysis of the energy-environment-resources pipelines infrastructure regime, including its pipeline battles analysis, but also in chapter 9's discussion of the science, technology, and innovation (STI) regime, including its examination of the internet and social media as open versus regulated/moderated infrastructure and, as a medium itself, a growing threat to democracy. These emerge also quite explicitly in chapter 6's examination of the transport infrastructure policy and governance regime in relation to freight rail and complex international, cross-Canada, and Canada-US supply chain imperatives and with respect to transit infrastructure in cities and in Canada's many norths. Indeed, they also emerged in chapter 1 regarding what it means to define and plan for critical infrastructure, both domestically and with respect to crucial international links.

It is useful to remind the reader that our definitional starting point for infrastructure was also centred on public and private assets and their life cycles. It centred both on the building and construction of such assets in addition their repair and maintenance in complex settings, locations, and time frames. Our six regime analyses and the overall seventeen policy and governance histories have revealed dozens of infrastructure types and examples. In addition they have captured the specialized expertise and discourse involved with the assets in both the building and maintenance and repair phases, and in the context of complex multi-level federalism. In our discussion, we have attempted to illustrate the scope and importance of infrastructure policy and investment to the concept of Canada as a nation, to economic and urban competitiveness, and to social and community cohesion. We have also highlighted the challenges posed by accelerating technological change and an anachronistic Constitution that is increasingly out of step with the reality of Canada's urban growth and future. Despite federal promises to do things differently and to adopt a strategic approach to infrastructure financing, short-term horizons, political/partisan considerations, and corruption continue to pose seemingly intractable challenges to infrastructure policy. The willingness to engage private-sector and pension funds in the delivery and financing of infrastructure promises much in this respect, but unless there are meaningful governance reforms better able to limit political interference, then a more strategic approach to infrastructure investment seems unlikely to emerge. Moreover, unless measures are taken to incorporate local priorities and balance the need for transparency and public participation with growing trends in "commercial confidentiality," then infrastructure policy and governance will continue to produce sub-optimal outcomes and increase the risk of waste and corruption.

This is a necessarily complex book covering more than five decades of core content across many sectors via several policy lenses. Each chapter also provides an initial and necessarily brief analytical mention of the emergence of COVID-19 and the ensuing global pandemic in 2020 and heading into 2021. There is great complexity in the pandemic scenarios, emerging including potentially transformative economic, political, and social shifts. Although we have considered the impacts of the pandemic on each of the sectors covered, we do not claim or desire this to be a book about them.

By 2023–24 it may well be possible for us to weave together pandemic matters in more coherent ways that also incorporate changing Canadian and global affairs, in addition to important technological and social trends that are poised to transform infrastructure possibilities, needs, and thinking. In the meantime, as Canada (like the US and most developed countries) prepares to channel billions of dollars into "build back better" and "build back green"-inspired infrastructure projects, we sincerely hope and believe the historical analysis and lessons provided in this book will provide a valuable framework to both guide and inform future policies and programs.

References

Abbott, Kenneth W., David Levi-Faur, and Duncan Snidal. 2017.
"Regulatory Intermediaries in the Age of Governance." *The Annals of
the American Academy of Political and Social Science* 670, no. 1: 6–13.
Acemoglu, Daron, and Pascual Restrepo. 2017. *Robots and Jobs: Evidence
from US Labour Markets*. National Bureau of Economic Research.
NBER Working Paper No. 23285, March. http://www.nber.org/papers/
w23285.
Advisory Council on Economic Growth. 2016. *Unleashing Productivity
through Infrastructure*. Ottawa: Advisory Council on Economic
Growth.
Advisory Panel on Federal Support for Fundamental Science. 2017.
*Investing in Canada's Future: Strengthening the Foundations of
Canadian Research*. Ottawa: Canada's Fundamental Science Review.
Aiello, R. 2020. "Liberals to Back Off on Broad Spending Powers without
Oversight in Emergency Funding Bill." *CTV News*, 23 March.
Airbnb. 2017a. "About Us." https://www.airbnb.co.uk/about/about-us.
– 2017b. "Fast Facts." https://press.atairbnb.com/fast-facts.
Alberta Energy. 2017a. Office of the Minister. *Letter to Honourable James
Carr. Minister of Natural Resources, Government of Canada. Alberta's
feedback on NEB Modernization expert panel's report*. Calgary. https://
cepa.com/wp-content/uploads/2017/06/cepa-submimission-in-response-
to-neb-Modernization-Expert-Panel-Final.pdf.
– 2017b. "Oil." https://www.alberta.ca/oil.aspx.
Alberta Energy Regulator. 2017. "About AER Calgary." http://www.aer.ca/
about-aer.
Alberta Government. 2015. "Natural Gas Facts and Stats." https://open.
alberta.ca/dataset/3f1e7d53-798e-421d-8f09-dd0e493f62e8/

resource/9aa0a883-0f6d-44db-af98-79ab09f98b15/download/factsheet-ngfacts.pdf.

– 2017a. "About the Government of Alberta." Ministries and Departments. https://www.alberta.ca/about-government.aspx.

– 2017b. "Climate Leadership Plan." https://www.ccacoalition.org/en/resources/alberta-climate-leadership-plan.

– 2017c. *Making Life Better: Alberta's Provincial Affordable Housing Strategy*. June.

– 2017d. "Natural Gas Facts and Stats." https://open.alberta.ca/publications/natural-gas-prices-facts-and-stats.

– 2017e. "Oil Sands Facts and Stats." https://open.alberta.ca/publications/natural-gas-prices-facts-and-stats.

Alexander, J. 2009. *Pandora's Locks: The Opening of the Great Lakes–St. Lawrence Seaway*. Lansing, MI: Michigan State University Press.

Alexander, Nancy. 2015. *The World Bank: In the Vanguard of an Infrastructure Boom*. Bretton Woods Project. http://www.brettonwoodsproject.org/2015/02/world-bank-infrastructure.

Aliakbari, Elmira, and Ashley Stedman. 2018. "The Cost of Pipeline Constraints in Canada." *Fraser Research Bulletin*. Vancouver, BC: Fraser Institute, May.

Allan, John B., David L.A. Gordon, Kyle Hanniman, and Andre Juneau, eds. 2018. *Canada: The State of the Federation 2015: Canadian Federalism and Infrastructure*. Montreal, QC, and Kingston, ON: McGill-Queen's University Press.

Allan, Robyn. 2018. "Kinder Morgan Bailout to Cost North of $15 Billion." *National Observer*, 29 May. https://www.nationalobserver.com/2018/05/29/analysis/kinder-morgan-bailout-cost-north-15-billion.

Allen, Barbara. 2006. "How Ottawa Buys: Procurement Policy and Politics beyond Gomery." In *How Ottawa Spends 2006–2007: In from the Cold: The Tory Rise and the Liberal Demise*, edited by G. Bruce Doern, 95–115. Montreal, QC: McGill-Queen's University Press.

– 2007. "Putting the Squeeze on Procurement: Procurement Policy as Lever for Innovation, Science and Environment." In *Innovation, Science and Environment: Canadian Policies and Performance 2007–2008*, edited by G. Bruce Doern, 219–39. Montreal, QC: McGill-Queen's University Press.

Allen, Kate. 2017. "Uber Opening Toronto Research Hub for Driverless Car Technology." *Toronto Star*, 8 May. https://www.thestar.com/news/canada/2017/05/08/uber-opening-toronto-research-hub-for-driverless-car-technology.html.

American Society of Civil Engineers. 2017. *Failure to Act: Closing the Infrastructure Investment Gap for America's Economic Future.* Washington, DC: American Society of Civil Engineers.

Anderson, Drew. 2020. "Alberta Bets on Infrastructure Spending, Corporate Tax Cuts to Spur Recovery." *CBC News*, 29 June. https://www.cbc.ca/news/canada/calgary/kenney-economic-reboot-announcement-1.5631088.

Andrew, Caroline, and Jeff Morrison. 2001. "Infrastructure." In *Urban Policy Issues: Canadian Perspectives*, edited by David Siegel and Edmund P. Fowler, 237–52. Oxford, UK: Oxford University Press.

Andrew-Gee, Eric. 2019. "In Kingston, an Agonizing Question: What to Do about Sir John A. Macdonald?" *Globe and Mail*, 30 September.

Arctic Council. 2015. *Arctic Spatial Data Infrastructure.* Fairbanks, AK: Arctic Council.

– 2016. *Telecommunications Infrastructure in the Arctic.* Fairbanks, AK: Arctic Council.

Arctic Council Resilience Workshop. 2016. *Summary Report.* Fairbanks, AK: Arctic Council.

Arctic Maritime and Aviation Transportation Infrastructure Initiative. 2012. *Proceedings: Arctic Transportation Infrastructure: Response Capacity and Sustainable Development.* Reykjavik: Author.

Armstrong, Peter. 2019. "It's a Problem for Society: Climate Change Is Making Some Homes Uninsurable." *CBC News*, 17 June. https://www.cbc.ca/news/business/it-s-a-problem-for-society-climate-change-is-making-some-homes-uninsurable-1.5173697.

Arntz, M., T. Gregory, and U. Zierahn. 2016. *The Risk of Automation for Jobs in OECD Countries: A Comparative Analysis.* Paris: OECD Social, Employment and Migration Working Papers, No. 189.

Asach, R.L. 1999. *Politics and Public Debt: The Dominion, the Banks and Alberta Social Credit.* Edmonton: University of Alberta Press.

Aschauer, D.A. 1988. "Government Spending and the Falling Rate of Profit." *Economic Perspectives* 12: 11–17.

– 1990. *Public Investment and Private Sector Growth.* Washington, DC: Economic Policy Institute.

Atchison, Chris. 2016. "Do Your Bit for Canada's Economy – Renovate Your Home." *Globe and Mail*, 15 September. https://www.theglobeandmail.com/report-on-business/economy/growth/do-your-bit-for-canadas-economy-renovate-your-home/article31876788.

Atkins, Eric, and Verity Stevenson. 2015. "Six Former Railway Employees Charged in Lac-Megantic Disaster." *Globe and Mail*, 22 June.

Atkinson, M., D. Beland, G. Marchildon, K. McNutt, P. Phillips, and
K. Rasmussen. 2013. *Governance and Public Policy in Canada: A View
from the Provinces*. Toronto: University of Toronto Press.

Atkinson-Grosjean, Janet. 2006. *Public Science, Private Interests: Culture
and Commerce in Canada's Networks of Centres of Excellence*.
Toronto: University of Toronto Press.

Aucoin, Peter. 1997. *The New Public Management: Canada in
Comparative Perspective*. Montreal, QC, and Kingston, ON: McGill-
Queen's University Press.

– 2008. "New Public Management and New Public Governance: Finding
the Balance." In *Professionalism and Public Service: Essays in Honour
of Kenneth Kernaghan*, edited by David Siegel and Ken Rasmussen,
16–33. Toronto: University of Toronto Press.

Auditor General of Canada. 2010. *Fall Report of the Auditor General of
Canada*. Ottawa: Government of Canada. https://www.oag-bvg.gc.ca/
internet/English/parl_oag_201010_e_34282.htm.

– 2013. *Advance Funding – P3 Canada Fund*. 2013 Spring Report of
the Auditor General of Canada. Ottawa: Government of Canada.
https://www.oag-bvg.gc.ca/internet/English/parl_oag_201304_
10_e_38195.html.

– 2015. *PPP Canada Inc: Special Examination Report 2015*. 2016 Spring
Report of the Auditor General of Canada. Ottawa: Government
of Canada. https://www.oag-bvg.gc.ca/internet/English/parl_oag_
201602_06_e_41250.html.

– 2018. *Report of the Auditor General of Canada to the Board of
Directors of Ridley Terminals Inc*. Independent Auditors Report. Special
Examination – 2018. Ottawa: Government of Canada. https://www.
oag-bvg.gc.ca/internet/English/parl_oag_201805_11_e_43043.html.

Auld, Douglas. 1985. *Budget Reform: Should There Be a Capital Budget
for the Public Sector?* Toronto: C.D. Howe Institute.

Avery, Donald H. *The Science of War: Canadian Scientists and Allied
Military Technology During the Second World War*. Toronto: University
of Toronto Press.

Avery, Samuel. 2013. *The Pipeline and the Paradigm: Keystone XL, Tar
Sands, and the Battle to Diffuse the Carbon Bomb*. Washington, DC:
Ruka Press.

Bacher, John C. 1986. "Canadian Housing 'Policy' in Perspective." *Urban
History Review* XV, no. 1 (June): 3–18.

– 1993. *Keeping to the Marketplace: The Evolution of Canadian Housing
Policy*. Montreal, QC: McGill-Queen's University Press.

Bains, Camille. 2017. "B.C. Claims Approval of Trans Mountain Pipeline Expansion 'Lopsided' for Alberta." *Calgary Herald*, 6 October. https://calgaryherald.com/business/energy/b-c-claims-approval-of-trans-mountain-pipeline-expansion-lopsided-for-alberta.

Bakx, Kyle. 2020. "First Nations Worry They'll Lose Out on Cash to Clean Up Oil and Gas Wells in Western Canada." *CBC News*, 28 June. https://www.cbc.ca/news/business/irc-site-rehabilitation-orphan-inactive-well-1.5629036.

Bakx, Kyle, and Tony Seskus. 2018. "Oilpatch CEOs Blame High Costs, Red Tape for Erosion of Canada's Competitive Edge." *CBC News*, 7 May. http://www.cbc.ca/news/business/canada-oilpatch-investors-1.4649043.

Baldwin, Carliss Y., and C. Jason Woodward. 2009. "The Architecture of Platforms: A Unified View." In *Platforms, Markets and Innovation*, edited by Annabelle Gawer, 19–44. Cheltenham, UK: Edward Elgar.

Baldwin, Richard E. 2012. *Global Supply Chains: Why They Emerged, Why They Matter, and Where They Are Going*. Paper No. DP9103. London: Centre for Policy Research, National Bureau of Economic Research.

Balleisen, Edward J., Lori S. Bennear, Kimberly D. Krawiec, and Jonathan B. Wiener. 2017. *Policy Shock: Recalibrating Risk and Regulation After Oil Spills, Nuclear Accidents and Financial Crises*. Cambridge: Cambridge University Press.

Ballingall, Alex. 2017. "Mayor John Tory Wants Feds to Help." *Toronto Star*, 1 June. https://globalnews.ca/news/7327306/toronto-mayor-asks-feds-province-financial-help.

Banting, Keith G. 1990. "Social Housing in a Divided State." In *Housing the Homeless and the Poor: New Partnerships among the Private, Public and Third Sectors*, edited by George Fallis and Alex Murray, 115–63. Toronto: University of Toronto Press.

Barutciski, Milos. 2019. "Canada." In *Anti-Corruption Regulation – Getting the Deal Through*, edited by Homer E. Moyer Jr, 25–33. London: Law Business Research Unit.

BBC Business Matters. 2020. "US Economy Suffers Sharpest Contraction in Decades." 30 July. https://www.completeintel.com/2020/07/31/us-economy-contraction.

Bearing Point. 2003. *Evaluation of the CFI Innovation Fund, University Development Fund, and College Research Development Fund: Final Report*. http://www.innovation.ca/sites/defaults/default/files/pdf/2003_bearing2_e.pdf.

Beeby, Dean. 2017a. "Internal Document Raises Possibility of Taxing Netflix and Other Digital Services." *CBC News*, 17 January. https://www.cbc.ca/news/politics/sales-tax-netflix-bell-rogers-digital-melanie-joly-bill-morneau-internet-1.3937955.

– 2017b. "Squeeze Cash from Facebook, Google, Say Canadian News Media Readers." *CBC News*, 11 January. https://www.cbc.ca/news/politics/newspapers-news-media-digital-public-policy-forum-google-facebook-tax-1.3929356.

– 2018. "Federal Government Signs $500M Contract with IBM without Seeking Bids." *CBC News*, 13 May. http://cbc.ca/news/politics/ibm-shared-services-contract-1.4658682.

Beer, Mitchell. 2017. "TransCanada Dodged a Bullet by Cancelling Energy East." *Policy Options*, 11 October. https://policyoptions.irpp.org/magazines/october-2017/transcanada-dodged-a-bullet-by-cancelling-energy-east.

Bell, Emily. 2017. "Technology Company? Publisher? The Lines Can No Longer Be Blurred." *The Guardian*, 2 April. https://www.theguardian.com/media/2017/apr/02/facebook-google-youtube-inappropriate-advertising-fake-news.

– 2018. "Facebook Creates Orwellian Headache as News Is Labelled Politics." *The Guardian*, 24 June. https://www.theguardian.com/media/media-blog/2018/jun/24/facebook-journalism-publishers.

Bell, Emily, and T. Owen. 2016. *Journalism after Snowden: The Future of the Free Press in the Surveillance State*. New York: Columbia University Press.

– 2017. *The Platform Press: How Silicon Valley Reengineered Journalism*. New York: Tow Centre for Digital Journalism, Columbia Journalism School.

Bell, S., and Andrew Hindmoor. 2009. *Rethinking Governance: The Centrality of the State in Modern Society*. Cambridge: Cambridge University Press.

Bellefontaine, Michelle. 2018. "Alberta Passes Bill 'to Turn Off the Taps' to B.C. over Pipeline Delays." *CBC News*, 16 May. https://www.cbc.ca/news/canada/edmonton/alberta-rachel-notley-kinder-morgan-morneau-response-1.4665443.

Benjoe, Kerry. 2020. "Canada's History with Indigenous People Is Cruel and Unfair, but We Need to Own Up to It." *CBC News*, 1 July. https://www.cbc.ca/news/canada/saskatchewan/point-of-view-kerry-benjoe-racism-george-floyd-canada-indigenous-1.5632918.

Bennett, Dean. 2018a. "Alberta Premier Threatens to Turn Off Oil Taps in B.C. Pipeline Dispute." *Toronto Star*, 8 March. https://www.ctvnews.ca/

politics/alberta-premier-threatens-to-turn-off-oil-taps-in-b-c-dispute-1.3835009.

– 2018b. "Jason Kenney Declares War on Green Left." *Toronto Star*, 5 March. https://nationalpost.com/pmn/news-pmn/canada-news-pmn/jason-kenney-declares-war-on-green-left-in-speech-to-conservative-party.

Bennett, Nelson. 2017. "Appeal of Trans Mountain Pipeline Expansion Begins." *Law and Politics*, 2 October. https://biv.com/article/2017/10/appeal-trans-mountain-pipeline-expansion-begins.

Bennett, S.E. 2012. "Federal Infrastructure Program Impacts: Perceptions at the Community Level." In *How Ottawa Spends 2012–2013: The Harper Majority: Budget Cuts and the New Opposition*, edited by G. Bruce Doern and Christopher Stoney, 190–206. Montreal, QC, and Kingston, ON: McGill-Queen's University Press.

Bennhold, Katrin. 2018. "Germany Acts to Tame Facebook, Learning from Its Own History." *New York Times*, 5 May. https://www.nytimes.com/2018/05/19/technology/facebook-deletion-center-germany.html.

Benzie, Robert. 2017. "Kathleen Wynne Stopping John Tory's Plan for Tolls on DVP, Gardiner." https://www.thestar.com/news/queenspark/2017/01/26/kathleen-wynne-stopping-john-torys-plan-for-tolls-on-dvp-gardiner.html.

Berdahl, Loleen. 2004. "The Federal Urban Role and Federal-Municipal Relations in Canada." In *The State of the Federation: Municipal-Federal-Provincial Relations in Canada*, edited by Robert Young and Christian Leuprecht, 25–44. Montreal, QC, and Kingston, ON: McGill-Queen's University Press.

Berdahl, Loleen, and Roger Gibbins. 2014. *Regional Transformation and the Future of Canada*. Toronto: University of Toronto Press.

Berkman, Paul A. 2010. *Environmental Security in the Arctic Ocean: Promoting Co-operation and Preventing Conflict*. Whitehall Paper Series, vol 77. London: Royal United Services Institute for Defence and Security Services.

– 2013. "Preventing an Arctic Cold War." *New York Times*, 12 March. https://www.nytimes.com/2013/03/13/opinion/preventing-an-arctic-cold-war.html.

Bernhardt, Darren. 2019. *"There Has to Be Something Else": Winnipeg's Car Culture Is Unsustainable, Say Urban Planning Experts*. CBC News, 30 June.

Berners-Lee, Tim. 2017. "Three Challenges for the Web." Web Foundation, 12 March. http://webfoundation.org/2017/03/web-turns-28-letter.

Bilefsky, Dan, and Catherine Porter. 2018. "Trump's Bully Attack on Trudeau Outrages Canadians." *New York Times*, 10 June. https://www.nytimes.com/2018/06/10/world/canada/g-7-justin-trudeau-trump.html.

Bird, Richard M., and Enid Slack. 2017. *Financing Infrastructure: Who Should Pay?* Montreal, QC, and Kingston, ON: McGill-Queen's University Press.

Bird, Richard, Enid Slack, and Almos Tasronyi. 2012. *A Tale of Two Taxes: Property Tax Reform in Ontario*. Cambridge, MA: Lincoln Institute of Land Policy.

Bird, Richard M., and François Vaillancourt. 2006. "Changing with the Times: Success, Failure and Inertia in Canadian Federal Arrangements, 1945–2002." In *Federalism and Economic Reform-International Perspectives*, edited by Jessica S. Wallack and T.N. Srinivasan, 189–248. Cambridge: Cambridge University Press.

Bishop, Grant. 2013. "After Lac-Megantic, How Should We Regulate Risk?" *Globe and Mail*, 16 July.

Bloom, David. 2019. "Kenney Government's Bill 1 Will Roll Back Alberta Carbon Tax on Everyone but Large Emitters." *Ottawa Citizen*, 27 May.

Boasson, Vigdis, Joseph Chang, and Emil Boasson. 2012. "Applying Modern Portfolio Theory to Municipal Financial and Capital Budgeting Decisions." *Public and Municipal Finance* 1, no. 1: 58–65.

Boffey, Daniel. 2018. "Shape of Things to Come: Dutch to Build World's First 3D-Printed Housing Estate." *The Guardian*, 6 June. https://www.theguardian.com/artanddesign/2018/jun/06/netherlands-to-build-worlds-first-habitable-3d-printed-houses.

Bone, Heather Lynn. 2018. *Not in My Backyard: The Link between Demographic Characteristics and Anti-Development Sentiments*. Toronto: Social Economics, Department of Economics, University of Toronto, 30 March.

Bordeleau, Christian. 2012. "Public-Private Partnerships Canada and the P3 Fund: Shedding Light on a New Meso Institutional Arrangement." In *How Ottawa Spends 2012–2013: The Harper Majority, Budget Cuts and the New Opposition*, edited by G. Bruce Doern and Christopher Stoney, 145–60. Montreal, QC: McGill-Queen's University Press.

Borzykowski, Bryan. 2020. "Coronavirus Is Shaking Up Canada's Housing Market but Don't Expect a Crash." *Maclean's*, 26 May. https://www.macleans.ca/economy/realestateeconomy/coronavirus-is-shaking-up-canadas-housing-market-but-dont-expect-a-crash.

Botsman, Rachel, and Roo Rogers. 2011. *What's Mine Is Yours: How Collaborative Consumption Is Changing the Way We Live*. London: Collins.

Boudreau, S. 2005. "National Guide to Sustainable Municipal Infrastructure." http://nparc.nrc-cnrc.gc.ca/eng/view/accepted/?id=0fda9c0a-b047-45a1-b121-7248ea29aadb.

Boutilier, Alex. 2018. "Liberals Look to Election Law Changes after Facebook Scandal." *Toronto Star*, 27 April. https://www.thestar.com/news/canada/2018/04/27/liberals-look-to-election-law-changes-after-facebook-scandal.html.

Boylem, Jessica, Maxine Cunningham, and Julie Dekens. 2013. *Climate Change Adaptation and Canadian Infrastructure: A Review of the Literature*. Winnipeg: International Institute for Sustainable Development, November. https://www.iisd.org/publications/climate-change-adaptation-and-canadian-infrastructure-review-literature.

Bozikovic, Alex. 2017. "Lessons of the Grenfell Blaze: How Can Canada's Thousands of Aging Towers Be Kept Safe?" *Globe and Mail*, 23 June. https://www.theglobeandmail.com/life/home-and-garden/architecture/lessons-of-the-grenfell-blaze-how-can-canadas-thousands-of-aging-towers-be-kept-safe/article35445378.

Bracken, Amber, and Leyland Cecco. 2020. "Canada: Protests Go Mainstream as Support for Wet'suwet'en Pipeline Fight Widens." *The Guardian*, 20 June. https://www.theguardian.com/world/2020/feb/14/wetsuweten-coastal-gaslink-pipeline-allies.

Bradford, Neil, and Allison Bramwell. 2014. *Governing Urban Economies: Innovation and Inclusion in Canadian-City Regions*. Toronto: University of Toronto Press.

Braithwaite, John. 2008. *Regulatory Capitalism*. Cheltenham, UK: Edward Elgar.

Bratt, Duane. 2006. *Canada, the Provinces and the Global Nuclear Revival: Advocacy Coalitions in Action*. Montreal, QC, and Kingston, ON: McGill-Queen's University Press.

Breen, Sarah-Patricia. 2015. *Uncertain Foundation: Infrastructure in Rural Canada*. Report to the Rural Policy Learning Commons – Infrastructure and Services Theme Team. http://rplc-capr.ca/wp-content/uploads/2015/12/Infrastructure-in-Rural-Canada-Report.pdf.

Brooks, Richard. 2018a. *Bean Counters: The Triumph of the Accountants and How They Broke Capitalism*. Halifax: Atlantic Publishers.

– 2018b. "The Financial Scandal No One Is Talking About." *The Guardian*, 29 May. https://www.theguardian.com/news/2018/may/29/the-financial-scandal-no-one-is-talking-about-big-four-accountancy-firms.

Bruce Power. 2016. *The Role of Nuclear: Present and Future*. Submission to the House of Commons Standing Committee on Natural Resources.

Bruce Power and the Canadian Council for Public-Private Partnerships. 2017. *Bruce Power: Canada's Largest Public-Private Partnership: A Case Study on Delivering Clean, Affordable Electricity and Investment in Infrastructure – 2001–2016*.

Buckner, Dianne. 2017. "Canadian Startup Reebee Taking Retail Flyers into the Digital Age." *CBC News*, 6 May. http://www.cbc.ca/news/business/digital-flyers-booming-1.4099345.

Building Industry and Land Development Association. 2016. *Housing Prices Continue to Grow as Supply Trends Downwards.* https://bildgta.ca/news/newsreleases/housing-prices-continue-grow-supply-trends-downwards.

Bundale, Brett. 2018. "What B.C.'s LNG Megaproject Means for 2 Proposed Nova Scotia Facilities." *CBC News*, 5 October. https://www.cbc.ca/news/canada/nova-scotia/lng-bear-head-goldboro-nova-scotia-1.4851687.

Business Development Bank of Canada. 2016. *2016 Annual Report.* Montreal: Business Development Bank of Canada. https://www.bdc.ca/globalassets/digizuite/10187-bdc_ar2016_en_final.pdf.

Byers, Michael. 2009. *Who Owns the Arctic?* Madeira Park, BC: Douglas and McIntyre.

– 2014. "The North Pole Is a Distraction." *Globe and Mail*, 20 August.

Cadwalladr, Carole. 2017. "Cambridge Analytica Affair Raises Questions Vital to Our Democracy." *The Guardian*, 4 March. https://www.theguardian.com/politics/2017/mar/04/cambridge-analytica-democracy-digital-age.

– 2018. "A Withering Verdict: MPs Report on Zuckerberg, Russia and Cambridge Analytica." *The Guardian*, 28 July. https://www.theguardian.com/technology/2018/jul/28/dcms-report-fake-news-disinformation-brexit-facebook-russia.

Cain Miller, Clair. 2017. "Evidence that Robots Are Winning the Race for American Jobs." *New York Times*, 28 March. https://www.nytimes.com/2017/03/28/upshot/evidence-that-robots-are-winning-the-race-for-american-jobs.html.

Cairns, Malcolm. 2013. *Crude Oil by Rail: Parts I and II: Potential for the Movement of Alberta Oil Sands Crude Oil and Related Products by Canadian Railways.* Halifax: Canadian Transportation Research Forum, 11 June.

– 2015. *Staying on the Right Track: A Review of Canadian Freight Rail Policy.* Ottawa: Macdonald-Laurier Institute. https://www.ciltinternational.org/wp-content/uploads/2015/07/Malcolm-Cairns-N-America.pdf.

Cameron, Duncan, ed. 1988. *The Free Trade Deal.* Toronto: James Lorimer and Company.

Cameron, Maxwell A., and Brian W. Tomlin. 2000. *The Making of NAFTA: How the Deal Was Done.* Ithaca, NY: Cornell University Press,

Campbell, Thomas, C. Williams, Olga Ivanova, and B. Garrett. 2011. *Could 3D Printing Change the World? Technologies, Potential, and Implications of Additive Manufacturing*. Strategic Foresight Report. Washington, DC: Atlantic Council, October. https://www.researchgate. net/publication/257942754_Could_3D_Printing_Change_the_World_ Technologies_Potential_and_Implications_of_Additive_Manufacturing.

Campion-Smith, Bruce. 2016. "Ottawa Eyes Airport Sell-Off to Raise Infrastructure Cash." *Toronto Star*, 3 July. https://www.thestar.com/ news/canada/2016/07/03/ottawa-eyes-airport-sell-off-to-raise-infrastructure-cash.html.

Campion-Smith, Bruce, and Emily Matthieu. 2017. "Ottawa's Housing Plan Will Create 100,000 New Housing Units Nationally." *Toronto Star*, 22 November. https://www.thestar.com/news/gta/2017/11/22/ottawas-housing-plan-aims-to-help-530000-vulnerable-households.html.

Canada. 1985. *Freedom to Move: A Framework for Transportation Reform*. Ottawa: Minister of Transport.

– 2001. "Vision and Balance: Report of the *Canada Transportation Act* Review Panel." Ottawa: Minister of Public Works and Government Services, June.

– 2010. *National Policy Framework for Strategic Gateways and Trade Corridors*. Ottawa: Transport Canada. http://publications.gc.ca/pub? id=9.671105&sl=0.

– 2011. *Rail Freight Service Review: Final Report*. Ottawa: Transport Canada.

– 2013. *Standing Committee on Transportation, Infrastructure, and Communities*. Number 061, First Session, 41st Parliament. Evidence. 28 February.

– 2014a. *Asia-Pacific Gateway and Corridor Initiative*. Ottawa: Government of Canada, 10 March.

– 2014b. *Digital Canada 150*. Ottawa: Industry Canada.

– 2016a. "Governments of Canada and the Northwest Territories Invest in Transportation Infrastructure." http://news.gc.ca/web/article-en. do?nid=1095359.

– 2016b. *A Transformational Infrastructure Plan*. Ottawa: Government of Canada. https://www.budget.gc.ca/fes-eea/2016/docs/themes/ infrastructure-en.html.

– 2017a. *Backgrounder: Forty-Three New Infrastructure Projects Across Manitoba*. https://www.canada.ca/en/office-infrastructure/news/2017/03/ forty-three_new_infrastructureprojectsacrossmanitoba.html.

– 2017b. "Cabinet Directive on Improving the Performance of the Regulatory System for Major Resource Projects." https://www.ceaa. gc.ca/050/documents_staticpost/cearref_21799/83452/Vol1_-_Part03. pdf.

– 2017c. *Environmental and Regulatory Reviews: Discussion Paper*. June.

– 2017d. "Governments of Canada and Manitoba Support Public Transit Across Manitoba." https://www.canada.ca/en/office-infrastructure/ news/2017/03/governments_of_canadaandmanitobasupportpublic transitinfrastructu.html.

– 2017e. *Let's Talk Housing – What We Heard: Shaping Canada's National Housing Strategy*. Ottawa: Minister of Families, Children and Social Development.

– 2017f. *Major Crown Projects*. https://www.canada.ca/en/department-national-defence/corporate/reports-publications/departmental-plans/ departmental-plan-2019-20-index/supplementary-information-index/ report-crown-projects.html.

– 2017g. *Major Projects Management Office*. http://mpmo.gc.ca/12.

– 2018a. *Better Rules For Major Project Reviews: A Handbook*. http:// www.canada.ca/environmentalreviews.

– 2018b. *A Proposed New Impact Assessment System*. 23 August. https:// www.canada.ca/en/services/environment/conservation/assessments/ environmental-reviews/environmental-assessment-processes/a-technical-guide.html.

Canada and Manitoba. 2013. *Federal-Provincial Task Force on the Future of Churchill*. Final Report. January.

Canada Foundation for Innovation. 2012. *CFI Strategic Roadmap 2012– 17*. https://www.innovation.ca/sites/default/files/pdf/2011%20CFI%20 Strategic%20Roadmap%20final%20English%202012-04-04.pdf.

– 2014. "Our Investments." http://www.innovation.ca/en/OurInvestments.

– 2016. *Annual Report 2015–16*. https://www.innovation.ca/about/ governance/annual-corporate-reports.

– 2017. *Overview*. https://www.innovation.ca/about/overview/our-mandate.

Canada Infrastructure. 2016. *Canadian Infrastructure Report Card: Informing the Future*. https://www.pppcouncil.ca/web/News_Media/ 2016/2016_Canadian_Infrastructure_Report_Card__Informing_the_ Future.aspx.

Canada Infrastructure Bank. 2020. https://cib-bic.ca/en/ (accessed 2 February 2020).

Canada Infrastructure Bank Act, SC 2017, c 20, s.403. Assented to 22 June 2017.

Canada Mortgage and Housing Corporation. 2011. "History of CMHC." https://www.cmhc-schl.gc/en/corp/about/hi/index.cfm.

– 2012. *Renovation and Home Purchase Report.* Ottawa: Canada Mortgage and Housing Corporation. https://www.cbc.ca/bc/news/bc-120918-cmhc-renovation-and-home-purchase-report.pdf.

– 2015. *2015 Annual Report: Why Housing Matters.* Ottawa: Canada Mortgage and Housing Corporation. https://www.cmhc-schl.gc.ca/en/housing-observer-online/2019-housing-observer/why-housing-matters-national-housing-day-message-president-cmhc.

Canada Revenue Agency. 2017. *Classes of Depreciable Property: Capital Cost Allowance (CCA) Classes.* http://www.cra-arc.gc.ca/tx/bsnss/tpcs/slprtnr/rprtng/cptl/dprcbl-eng.

Canada Transport Act Review. 2014. *Discussion Paper: Canada Transportation Act Review.* https://tc.canada.ca/sites/default/files/migrated/ctar_discussion_paper_en.pdf.

Canada Transportation Act Review. 2015. *Pathways: Connecting Canada's Transportation System to the World.* Ottawa: Government of Canada.

Canada Transportation Act Review Panel. 2001. *Vision and Balance.* Report of the Canada Transportation Act Review Panel.

Canada West Foundation. 2013. *At the Intersection: The Case for Sustained and Strategic Public Infrastructure Investment.* Canada West Foundation Public Policy Brief, February. https://service.clearservice.com/constructionns/campaignimages/1/CCA_Report_At_The_Intersection.pdf.

– 2017. *Up Front: Modernizing the National Energy Board.* Canada West Foundation, April. https://cwf.ca/research/publications/up-front-modernizing-the-national-energy-board.

Canadian Academy of Engineering. 2016. *Canada's Challenge and Opportunity: Transformations for Major Reductions in GHG Emissions.* Full Technical Report and Modelling Results. Ottawa. Canadian Academy of Engineering. https://fr.davidsuzuki.org/publication-scientifique/executive-summary-canadas-challenge-opportunity-transformations-major-reductions-ghg-emissions.

Canadian Association for Community Living. 2017. *National Housing Strategy Makes Historic Investment: 2400 New Affordable Housing Units for People with Developmental Disabilities.* https://inclusionalberta.org/news/2017/11/24/media-releases/national-housing-strategy-makes-historic-investment-2400-new-affordable-housing-units-for-people-with-developmental-disabilities.

Canadian Association of Railway Suppliers. 2017. *Railway Infrastructure.* https://railwaysuppliers.ca//?lid=MHYDE-NEK9X-KXSGU&year=2017.

Canadian Bankers Association. 2016. *Bank Lending to Business*. https://www.cba.ca/Assets/CBA/Documents/Files/Article%20Category/PDF/bkg_banklending_en.pdf.

Canadian Centre for Economic Analysis. 2015. *Investing in Ontario's Public Infrastructure: Improved Economic Evaluation of Benefits and Risks*. CANCEA Bulletin #3, 2 December.

– 2016. *The Economic Impact of Canadian P3 Projects: Why Building Infrastructure "On Time" Matters*. A study funded by the Canadian Council for Public-Private Partnerships. November.

– 2017. *Understanding the Forces Driving the Shelter Affordability Issue: A Linked-Path Assessment of Housing Market Dynamics in Ontario and GTHA*. Canada: May. https://rccao.com/news/files/Affordability-Phase2-report.pdf.

– 2020. "Navigating the COVID-19 Socio-Economic Shock." https://rccao.com/research/files/How-Infrastructure-Investments-Will-Facilitate-Growth-June-2020.pdf.

Canadian Centre for Occupational Health and Safety. 2016. *Report of the Council: 2015–2016*. https://www.ccohs.ca/ccohs/reports/annual/2016/annual1617.html.

Canadian Chamber of Commerce. 2013. *The Foundations of a Competitive Canada: The Need for Strategic Infrastructure Investment*. 18 December. https://www.pppcouncil.ca/web/P3_Knowledge_Centre/Research/The_Foundations_of_a_Competitive_Canada__The_Need_for_Strategic_Infrastructure_Investment.aspx.

Canadian Construction Association. 2017. "About Canadian Construction Association." http://www.cca-acc.com/cca.

Canadian Council for Public-Private Partnerships. 2016. *CCPPP 2016 Federal Budget Submission*. https://www.ourcommons.ca/Content/Committee/421/FINA/Brief/BR8098409/br-external/CanadianCouncilForPublicPrivatePartnerships-e.pdf.

– 2017a. "About Us." https://www.pppcouncil.ca/web/About_Us/web/About_Us/About_Us.aspx.

– 2017b. "P3 Myths and Facts." https://www.pppcouncil.ca/web/P3_Knowledge_Centre/About_P3s/FAQs.aspx.

– 2018. "Canadian Council for Public-Private Partnerships." http://www.pppcouncil.ca (accessed 14 December 2018).

Canadian Energy Pipeline Association. 2015. *Committed to Safety. Committed to Canadians. 2015 Pipeline Industry Performance Report*. Canadian Energy Pipeline Association.

– 2018. *Submission to the Parliamentary Committee on Environment and Sustainable Development Bill C-69.*

Canadian Environmental Law Association. 2018. "The Federal Government's Proposed Impact Assessment Act: Some Forward Progress, but Changes Needed to Ensure Sustainability." 8 February. https://cela.ca/the-federal-governments-proposed-impact-assessment-act-some-forward-progress-but-changes-needed-to-ensure-sustainability.

Canadian Federation of Independent Business. 2017. "About Us." https://www.cfib-fcei.ca/en/about-us.

Canadian Federation of Municipalities. 2016a. "Big City Mayors Caucus." http://www.fcm.ca/home/about-us/big-city-mayors-caucus.htm.

– 2016b. "Our Members." http://www.fcm.ca/home/about-us/membership/our-members.

Canadian Home Builders Association. 2017. *Impact of the Housing Market on the Economy and the Challenges Surrounding Access to Homeownership.* https://www.chba.ca/CHBA/About/CHBA/The_National_Association.aspx (archived access available to members only).

Canadian Institutes of Health Research. 1999. *A New Approach to Health Research For the 21st Century: The Canadian Institutes of Health Research.* Ottawa: Canadian Institutes of Health Research.

Canadian Polar Commission. 2014. *Communications, Infrastructure and Transportation Systems in the Canadian North: Recent Advances and Remaining Knowledge Gaps and Research Opportunities.* Canadian Polar Commission, 31 March. http://www.polarcom.gc.ca/sites/default/files/e-communications_infrastructure_and_transportation_systems_summary_-_revised.pdf.

Canadian Public Works Association. 2017. "General Information." https://www.cpwa.net/CPWA/About/CPWA/About/About_landing_pg.aspx?hkey=a8d77519-cac7-42d2-99bb-ec9ddae8321b.

Canadian Science Policy Conference. 2015. *International Perspectives on Big Science in Canada: Where Should Canada Go?* (No longer accessible.)

Canadian Urban Transit Association. 2017. *Federal Budget 2017.* https://cutaactu.ca/sites/default/files/canadian_urban_transit_association_budget_analysis.pdf.

Carlson, Nicholas. 2011. "The Real History of Twitter." *Business Insider,* 13 April. https://www.lifewire.com/history-of-twitter-3288854.

Caron, Jacques. 2018. "Quebec's Management of Public Infrastructure." In *Canada: The State of the Federation 2015: Canadian Federalism and Infrastructure*, edited by John B. Allan, David L.A. Gordon, Kyle Hanniman, and Andre Juneau, 155–68. Montreal, QC, and Kingston, ON: McGill-Queen's University Press.

Carroll, Barbara Wake, and Ruth J.E. Jones. 2000. "The Road to Innovation, Convergence or Inertia: Devolution in Housing Policy in Canada." *Canadian Public Policy* XXVI, no. 3: 277–93.

Caselli, Stefano, Veronica Vecchi, and Guido Corbetta, eds. 2015. *Public Private Partnerships for Infrastructure and Business Development: Principles, Practices and Perspectives*. London: Palgrave MacMillan.

Cash, Martin. 2017. "Are Airships the Best Way to Replace Hudson's Bay Rail Line?" *Winnipeg Free Press*, 24 June. http://www.winnipegfreepress. com/business/are-airships-the-best-way-to-replace-hudson-bay-rail-line-430492263.html.

Cattaneo, Claudia. 2018. "'It's Not Just Oil': Vancouver Port's Expansion Delayed as NIMBYism Threatens Vital Projects." *Financial Post*, 21 May. https://financialpost.com/news/economy/its-not-just-oil-vancouver-ports-expansion-delayed-as-nimbyism-threatens-vital-projects.

CBC News. 2008. "PM: Dion's Carbon Tax Would 'Screw Everybody.'" 20 June. http://www.cbc.ca/news/canada/pm-dion-s-carbon-tax-would-screw-everybody-1.696762.

– 2013. "Lac-Mégantic Disaster Railway Gets Bankruptcy Protection – Montreal." 8 August. https://www.cbc.ca/news/canada/montreal/lac-m%C3%A9gantic-disaster-railway-gets-bankruptcy-protection-1.1341715.

– 2016. "Federal Transit Infrastructure Money: What Toronto Is Getting." 23 August. https://www.cbc.ca/news/canada/toronto/federal-transit-infrastructure-funds-1.3732283.

– 2017. "A Chronological History of Controversial Keystone XL Pipeline Project." https://www.cbc.ca/news/politics/keystone-xl-pipeline-timeline-1.3950156.

– 2018a. "Carillion Canada Gets Creditor Protection after Failure of U.K. Parent." 25 January. https://www.cbc.ca/news/business/carillion-canada-creditor-protection-1.4503849.

– 2018b. "Lac-Mégantic Residents Grapple with Verdict while Looking to Future." 20 January. https://www.cbc.ca/news/canada/montreal/lac-megantic-concerns-after-verdict-1.4497742.

Cecco, Leyland. 2018. "Prepare for the Worst: Souring Canada-US Relations Fuel Worries of Trade War." *The Guardian*, 11 June. https://

www.theguardian.com/world/2018/jun/11/trump-canada-latest-trade-war-trudeau-relationship-fears.

Center for Communication and Civic Engagement. 2017. *The Internet's Impact on New Media.* https://depts.washington.edu/ccce/digitalMedia/news/impact.html.

Centre for Digital Democracy. 2012. *Protecting Privacy, Promoting Consumer Rights and Ensuring Corporate Accountability.* Centre for Digital Democracy.

Champagne, Eric. 2014. "Tracking the Growth of the Federal Municipal Infrastructure Program Under Different Political Regimes." In *Canada in Cities: The Politics and Policy of Federal-Local Governance*, edited by Katherine Graham and Caroline Andrew, 164–92. Montreal, QC: McGill-Queen's University Press.

Champagne, Eric, and Charles-Etienne Beaudry. 2018. *The Influence of Federal Infrastructure Programs on Municipal Financial Planning in Ontario and Quebec.* University of Ottawa. March.

Charbonneau Commission. 2011. *Commission of Inquiry on the Awarding and Management of Public Contracts in the Construction Industry.* https://www.ceic.gouv.qc.ca/la-commission.html.

Chase, Steven. 2009. "Ottawa's Reporting on Stimulus Spending Gets Poor Grade from Watchdog." *Globe and Mail*, 10 October. https://www.theglobeandmail.com/news/politics/ottawas-stimulus-reporting-gets-poor-grade-from-watchdog/article1204078.

Chase, S., E. Anderson, and Bill Curry. 2009. "Stimulus Program Favours Tory Ridings." *Globe and Mail*, 21 October. https://www.theglobeandmail.com/news/politics/stimulus-program-favours-tory-ridings/article4295068.

Christopher, Martin. 2016. *Logistics and Supply Change Management*, 5th ed. London: FT Publishing International.

Chung, Emily. 2018. "Federal Scientists to Be Protected against Muzzling, Political Interference." *CBC News*, 30 July. http://www.cbc.ca/news/technology/scientific-integrity-1.4767227.

City of Toronto. 2017. *From Concept to Commercialization: A Startup Eco-system Strategy.* Toronto: Author.

City of Winnipeg. 2016. "Public Works." http://winnipeg.ca/publicworks/construction/majorProjects/default.stm.

Clark, C. Scott. 2018. "Fiscal Policy and Federal Infrastructure Financing." In *Canada: The State of the Federation 2015: Canadian Federalism and Infrastructure*, edited by John B. Allan, David L.A. Gordon, Kyle

Hanniman, and Andre Juneau, 197–206. Montreal, QC, and Kingston, ON: McGill-Queen's University Press.

Cleland, Michael, and Monica Gattinger. 2017. *System under Stress: Energy Decision-Making in Canada and the Need for Informed Reform*. Ottawa: University of Ottawa, March.

Coates, Ken S., P.W. Lackenbauer, William Morrison, and Greg Poelzer. 2008. *Arctic Front: Defending Canada in the Far North*. Toronto: Thomas Allen Publishers.

Cochrane, David, and Ryan Patrick Jones. 2020. "Federal Government to Provide Provinces and Territories with $19B for Safe Restart of Economy." *CTV News*, 17 July. https://www.CTVnews.ca/politics/feds-to-deliver-more-than-19b-to-provinces-and-territories-in-covid-19-support-1.5027090.

Coleman, John. 2015. *Understanding Interrelationships Among Capacity, Congestion, System Optimization, and Levels of Service in Canadian Freight Rail Transportation*. Paper prepared for the *Canada Transportation Act* Review Panel, July.

Coleman, John, and G. Bruce Doern. 2014. *Railway-Shipper Relations in a Networked Governance Model*. Regulatory Governance Initiative. Ottawa: School of Public Policy and Administration, Carleton University.

– 2015. *Submission to Canada Transportation Act Review Panel With a Focus on Canadian Transportation Policy, Governance, and Regulation*. 20 January.

Coleman, Stephen, and Jay G. Blumler. 2009. *The Internet and Democratic Citizenship*. New York: Cambridge University Press.

Combs, Jennifer, Danielle Kerrigan, and David Wachsmuth. 2019. *Short-Term Rentals in Canada: Uneven Growth, Uneven Impacts*. Montreal, QC: Upgo Lab. https://upgo.lab.mcgill.ca/publication/short-term-rentals-in-canada.

Commissioner of the Environment and Sustainable Development. 2016. *Federal Support for Sustainable Municipal Infrastructure*. Ottawa: Office of the Auditor General of Canada.

CompeteProsper. *Ontario's 2019 Budget: The Impact Is in the Details*. https://www.competeprosper.ca/blog/ontarios-2019-budget-the-impact-is-in-the-details.

Conference Board of Canada. 2015. *Transportation and Infrastructure Policy in Canada*. Ottawa: Centre for Transportation Infrastructure.

– 2017. *Rethinking Infrastructure Financing: Canada's Northern and Aboriginal Communities*. Ottawa: Conference Board of Canada.

Conley, Heather A., and Matthew Melino. 2016. *An Arctic Redesign: Recommendations to Rejuvenate the Arctic Council*. Washington, DC: Center for Strategic and International Studies.

– 2019. *The Implications of U.S. Policy Stagnation Toward the Arctic Region*. Washington, DC: Centre for Strategic Studies and International Studies, May.

Connor, Steve. 2013. "The $60 TRN Arctic Methane Time Bomb." *The Independent*, 25 July. https://www.iol.co.za/news/the-60-trillion-arctic-methane-time-bomb-1553430.

Council of the Federation. 2005. *Looking to the Future: A Plan for Investing in Canada's Transportation System*. Ottawa: Council of the Federation.

Council on Foreign Relations. 2017. *Rebuilding Trust Between Silicon Valley and Washington*. https://www.cfr.org/report/rebuilding-trust-between-silicon-valley-and-washington.

Coyne, Andrew. 2016. "Keep Tax Dollars and Public Pension Plans Away from Infrastructure Spending." *National Post*, 21 October. https://nationalpost.com/opinion/andrew-coyne-keep-scarce-tax-dollars-and-public-pension-plans-away-from-infrastructure-spending.

Craft, Jonathan, Michael Howlett, Mark Crawford, and Kathleen McNutt. 2013. "Assessing Policy for Climate Change Adaptation: Governance Arrangements, Resource Deployments, and Analytical Skills in Canadian Infrastructure Policy Making." *Review of Policy Research* 30, no. 1 (January): 42–65.

Crawford, Susan P. 2010. "Transporting Communications." *Boston University Law Review* 89: 871–925.

Creighton, D.G. 1932. *The Commercial Empire of the St. Lawrence 1760–1850*. Toronto: Ryerson Press.

– 1956. *The Empire of the St. Lawrence: A Study of Commerce and Politics*. Toronto: Macmillan of Canada.

Croce, Raffaela Della, and Stefano Gatti. 2015. "International Trends in Infrastructure Finance." In *Public Private Partnerships for Infrastructure and Business Development: Principles, Practices and Perspectives*, edited by Stefano Caselli, Veronica Vecchi, and Guido Corbetta, 81–100. London: Palgrave MacMillan.

Crowther, Sharon. 2017. "Proposed Calgary Tower Aims to Meet Student-Housing Demand." *Globe and Mail*, 23 June. https://www.theglobeandmail.com/real-estate/calgary-and-edmonton/proposed-calgary-tower-aims-to-meet-student-housing-demand/article35445658.

Cruickshank, Ainslie. 2019. "Trans Mountain Pipeline Expansion Faces New Setback as Indigenous Opponents Secure 'Huge Win in Court.'"

The Star, 4 September. https://www.thestar.com/politics/federal/2019/09/ 04/federal-court-to-rule-on-letting-trans-mountain-pipeline-challenges- proceed.html.

Cureton, Paul. 2020. "Drone Island." *The Independent*, 2 August. https:// www.independent.co.uk/topic/drones.

Curry, W. 2016. "The $125 Billion Question." *Globe and Mail*, 15 January. https://www.nationalnewswatch.com/2016/01/16/the-125-billion- question.

– 2017. "Cabinet to Have Final Word on Infrastructure Bank Projects." *Globe and Mail*, 16 May. https://www.theglobeandmail.com/news/ politics/cabinet-to-have-final-word-on-infrastructure-bank-projects- morneau-says/article35002677.

– 2020. "Infrastructure Bank Spent $3.8-Million on Termination Pay." *The Globe and Mail*, 15 October. https://www.theglobeandmail.com/ politics/article-canada-infrastructure-bank-paid-38-million-for- terminations-amid.

Dachis, Benjamin. 2017. *New and Improved: How Institutional Investment in Public Infrastructure Can Benefit Taxpayers and Consumers*. C.D. Howe Institute, Commentary No. 473, March. https:// www.cdhowe.org/sites/default/files/attachments/research_papers/mixed/ Commentary%20473.pdf.

Dahlgren, Peter. 2013. *The Political Web: Media, Participation and Alternative Democracy*. London: Palgrave MacMillan.

Dale, Daniel, Bruce Campion-Smith, and Tonda Maccharles. 2018. "Canada to Hit U.S. With Retaliatory Tariffs in Response to Trump's Steel Tariffs." *Toronto Star*, 31 May. https://www.cbc.ca/news/politics/ freeland-aluminum-imports-tariffs-trump-1.5677757.

Dalton, Melinda. 2015. "Charbonneau Commission Report: A Deeper Look at Recommendations." *CBC News*, 25 November. https://www. cbc.ca/news/canada/montreal/charbonneau-commission-report- recommendations-1.3335460.

Darryl, S., L. Jarvis, M. Ramesch, X. Wu, and E. Araral. 2011. *Infrastructure Regulation: What Works, Why and How Do We Know?* London: World Scientific.

Davies, Howard. 2010. *The Financial Crisis: Who Is to Blame?* Cambridge, UK: Polity Press.

Davies, Rob. 2018. "MP's Dole Out the Blame over Carillion's Collapse." *The Guardian*, 16 May. https://www.theguardian.com/business/2018/ may/16/mps-dole-out-the-blame-over-carillions-collapse.

deBellaigue, Christopher. 2020. "The End of Tourism?" *The Guardian*,
   18 June. https://www.theguardian.com/travel/2020/jun/18/end-of-
   tourism-coronavirus-pandemic-travel-industry.

de la Mothe, John. 2003. "Ottawa's Imaginary Innovation Strategy:
   Progress or Drift." In *How Ottawa Spends 2003–2004: Regime Change
   and Policy Shift*, edited by G. Bruce Doern, 172–86. Oxford, UK:
   Oxford University Press.

Demers, Fanny, and Michel Demers. 2016. "Infrastructure Policy and
   Spending: An Initial Look at the Trudeau Liberal Plan." In *How Ottawa
   Spends 2016–2017: The Trudeau Liberals in Power*, edited by G. Bruce
   Doern and Christopher Stoney, 30–84. Ottawa: School of Public Policy
   and Administration, Carleton University.

Dennis, Brady, and Steven Mufson. 2017. "As Trump Administration
   Grants Approval for Keystone XL Pipeline, an Old Fight Is Reignited."
   The Washington Post, 24 March. https://www.washingtonpost.com/
   news/energy-environment/wp/2017/03/24/trump-administration-grants-
   approval-for-keystone-xl-pipeline.

Denton, Jack O. 2019. "Doug Ford's 2019 Ontario Budget Promises
   Balance by 2023–2024 as Spending Climbs Higher." https://thevarsity.
   ca/2019/04/11/doug-fords-2019-ontario-budget-promises-balance-
   by-2023-2024-as-spending-climbs-higher.

Department of Finance. 1975. *Budget Highlights and Supplementary
   Information*. Ottawa: Department of Finance, 23 June.

– 2005. *Budget 2005*. Ottawa: Department of Finance.

– 2007. *Budget 2007: Aspire to a Stronger, Safer, Better Canada*. Ottawa:
   Department of Finance.

– 2008. *Budget Plan: Budget 2008*. Ottawa: Department of Finance Canada.

– 2018. "Agreement Reached to Create and Protect Jobs, Build Trans
   Mountain Expansion Project." https://www.canada.ca/en/department-
   finance/news/2018/05/agreement-reached-to-create-and-protect-jobs-
   build-trans-mountain-expansion-project.html.

DeSilva, Jan. 2017. "Four Measures that Will Create More Rental Units."
   Toronto Star, 4 May. https://www.thestar.com/opinion/commentary/
   2017/05/04/four-measures-that-will-create-more-rental-units.html.

Deveau, Scott. 2017. "Trump and Trudeau's Infrastructure Spends
   Unlikely to Be Lucrative Enough to Attract Big Global Investors, Fund
   Says." *Ottawa Citizen*, 27 March. https://nationalpost.com/news/
   economy/trump-and-trudeaus-infrastructure-spends-unlikely-to-be-
   lucrative-enough-to-attract-big-global-investors-fund-says.

Dewees, Donald N. 2005. "Electricity Restructuring in Canada." In *Canadian Energy Policy and the Struggle for Sustainable Development*, edited by G. Bruce Doern, 128–50. Toronto: University of Toronto Press.

Diebel, Linda. 2016. "Olive Branch Could End Detroit-Windsor Bridge Wars." *Toronto Star*, 13 February. https://www.thestar.com/news/canada/2016/02/13/olive-branch-could-end-detroit-windsor-bridge-wars.html.

Dinning, Jim. 2012. *Facilitator's Final Report: Service Agreement Template and Commercial Dispute Resolution Process*. 12 May.

Dodge, David. 2015. *Report to the Government of Alberta on the Development, Renewal and Financing of the Government's Plan for Spending on Capital Projects to 2019*. Bennett Jones LLP. https://www.bennettjones.com/Publications-Section/Articles/Report-to-the-Government-of-Alberta-on-the-Development-Renewal-and-Financing-of-the-Governments-plan-for-Spending-on-Capital-Projects-to-2019.

– 2016. "Don't Just Focus on 'Shovel-Readiness,' Says David Dodge." Interview with Chris Hall. *The House*. CBC Radio. 23 January.

Doern, G. Bruce. 1972. *Science and Politics in Canada*. Montreal, QC: McGill-Queen's University Press.

– 1977. "The Political Economy of Regulating Occupational Health: the Ham and Beaudry Reports." *Canadian Public Administration* 20, no. 1: 1–30.

– 1982. "Liberal Priorities 1982: The Limits of Scheming Virtuously." In *How Ottawa Spends Your Tax Dollars 1982: National Policy and Economic Development*, edited by G. Bruce Doern, 1–36. Toronto: James Lorimer and Company Ltd.

– 1994. "The Politics of Slow Progress." Paper prepared for the Royal Commission on Aboriginal Peoples. Ottawa.

– 1996. "Looking for the Core: Industry Canada and Program Review." In *How Ottawa Spends 1996–1997: Life Under the Knife*, edited by Gene Swimmer, 73–98. Ottawa: Carleton University Press.

– ed. 2002. *How Ottawa Spends 2002–2003: The Security Aftermath and National Priorities*. Toronto: Oxford University Press Canada.

– 2007. *Red-Tape, Red Flags: Regulation for the Innovation Age*. Ottawa: Conference Board of Canada.

– 2009. "Evolving Budgetary Policies and Experiments: 1980 to 2009–2010." In *How Ottawa Spends 2009–2010: Economic Upheaval and Political Dysfunction*, edited by Allan Maslove, 14–46. Montreal, QC: McGill-Queen's University Press.

– 2010. *The Relationships between Regulation and Innovation in the Transport Canada Context*. Paper prepared for Transport Canada.

– 2012. *Options on Alberta Energy Regulatory Governance: An Analysis and Commentary at the Pre-Legislative Stage*. Paper prepared for Alberta Energy. April. ·

– 2015. "The Relevance of Common Carrier Provision in the Context of 'Social Licence' and Social Regulation Concepts: Key Priorities, Complexity and Legitimacy in Long Term Canadian National Transportation Policy and Governance." Paper prepared for the Canada Transportation Act Review Secretariat. 15 July.

Doern, G. Bruce, Graeme Auld, and Christopher Stoney. 2015. *Green-lite: Complexity in Fifty Years of Canadian Environmental Policy, Governance and Democracy*. Montreal, QC, and Kingston, ON: McGill-Queen's University Press.

Doern, G. Bruce, David Castle, and Peter Phillips. 2016. *Canadian Science, Technology and Innovation Policy: The Innovation Economy and Society Nexus*. Montreal, QC, and Kingston, ON: McGill-Queen's University Press.

Doern, G. Bruce, John Coleman, and Barry Prentice. 2019. *Canadian Multi-Modal Transport Policy and Governance*. Montreal, QC: McGill-Queen's University Press.

Doern, G. Bruce, and Tom Conway. 1994. *The Greening of Canada*. Toronto: University of Toronto Press.

Doern, G. Bruce, and Monica Gattinger. 2003. *Power Switch: Energy Regulatory Governance in the Twenty-First Century*. Toronto: University of Toronto Press.

Doern, G. Bruce, and Jeffrey S. Kinder, eds. 2007. *Strategic Science in the Public Interest: Canada's Government Laboratories and Science-Based Agencies*. Toronto: University of Toronto Press.

Doern, G. Bruce, and Richard Levesque. 2002. *The National Research Council in the Innovation Policy Era: Changing Hierarchies, Networks and Markets*. Toronto: University of Toronto Press.

Doern, G. Bruce, and Mark MacDonald. 1999. *Free Trade Federalism*. Toronto: University of Toronto Press.

Doern, G. Bruce, Allan Maslove, and Michael J. Prince. 2013. *Canadian Public Budgeting in the Age of Crises: Shifting Budgetary Domains and Temporal Budgeting*. Montreal, QC, and Kingston, ON: McGill-Queen's University Press.

Doern, G. Bruce, and Robert Morrison. 2009. *Canadian Nuclear Crossroads: Steps to a Viable Nuclear Energy Industry*. C.D. Howe Institute, Commentary No. 290. June.

Doern, G. Bruce, and Richard Phidd. 1983. *Canadian Public Policy: Ideas, Structure, Process*. Toronto: Methuen.

– 1992. *Canadian Public Policy: Ideas, Structure, Process*, 2nd ed. Toronto: Nelson Canada.

Doern, G. Bruce, and Michael J. Prince. 2012. *Three Bio-Realms: Biotechnology and the Governance of Food, Health and Life in Canada*. Toronto: University of Toronto Press.

Doern, G. Bruce, Michael Prince, and Garth McNaughton. 1982. *Living With Contradictions: Health and Safety Regulation and Implementation in Canada*. Ottawa: Queen's Printer.

Doern, G. Bruce, Michael J. Prince, and Richard J. Schultz. 2014. *Rules and Unruliness: Canadian Regulatory Democracy, Governance, Capitalism and Welfarism*. Montreal, QC, and Kingston, ON: McGill-Queen's University Press.

Doern, G. Bruce, and Christopher Stoney, eds. 2009. *Research and Innovation Policy: Changing Federal Government-University Relations*. Toronto: University of Toronto Press.

Doern, G. Bruce, and Brian W. Tomlin. 1991. *Faith and Fear: The Free Trade Story*. Toronto: Stoddart.

Doern, G. Bruce, and Glen Toner. 1985. *The Politics of Energy*. Toronto: Methuen.

Donnan, Shawn. 2018. "Trump Takes Aim at Canada over Trade Frustrations." *Financial Times*, 25 January. https://www.ft.com/content 7c842d76-01f7-11e8-9650-9c0ad2d7c5b5.

Dourade, Eli. 2016. *Airport Noise Nimbyism: An Empirical Investigation*. Technology Policy Mercatus on Policy Series, 17 October. https://www.mercatus.org/system/files/dourado-airport-noise-mop-v1.pdf.

Drazen, Allan. 2001. "The Political Business Cycle after 25 Years." *NBER Macroeconomics Annual 2000* 15: 75–138.

Duclos, Jean-Yves. 2017. "Minister Duclos Meets Housing Experts in Final Stage of National Housing Strategy Design." 5 October. Ottawa: Canada Mortgage and Housing Corporation. https://www.newswire.ca/news-releases/minister-duclos-meets-housing-experts-in-final-stage-of-national-housing-strategy-design-649623343.html.

Duke, Laura E. 2018. *Impact Assessment Agency – An Overview*. Project Law Blog. https://www.lawsonlundell.com/project-law-blog/the-impact-assessment-agency-an-overview.

Dunlop, Tim. 2016a. "Humans Are Going to Have the Edge over Robots where Work Demands Creativity." *The Guardian*, 26 September. https://

www.theguardian.com/sustainable-business/2016/sep/26/humans-are-going-to-have-the-edge-over-robots-where-work-demands-creativity.

– 2016b. *Why the Future Is Workless*. NewSouth. https://www.amazon.com/Why-Future-Workless-Tim-Dunlop/dp/1742234828.

– 2017. "The Robot Debate Is Over: The Jobs are Gone and They Aren't Coming Back." *The Guardian*, 31 March. https://www.theguardian.com/sustainable-business/2017/mar/31/the-robot-debate-is-over-the-jobs-are-gone-and-they-arent-coming-back.

Dunn, Christopher. 2005. "Fed Funding of Cities: That's All There Is." *Policy Options* 26, no. 8 (October): 58–62.

Dutil, P., and B. Park. 2012. "How Ontario Was Won: The Harper Economic Action Plan in Ontario, 2009–2011." In *How Ottawa Spends 2012–2013: The Harper Majority: Budget Cuts and the New Opposition*, edited by G. Bruce Doern and Christopher Stoney, 207–26. Montreal, QC, and Kingston, ON: McGill-Queen's University Press.

Dyer, Evan. 2020. "Timing Is Everything: How Canada Got into a Pandemic Economy and How It Might Get Out." *CBC News*, 24 June. https://www.cbc.ca/news/politics/pandemic-covid-coronavirus-economy-debt-canada-1.5622374.

Economist. 2013. "Internet Security: Besieged." *Economist*, 9 November, 93–4.

– 2014. "Infrastructure Funding: A Long and Winding Road." *Economist*, 22 March. http://www.economist.com/news/finance-and-economics/21599394.

– 2017a. "Europe versus Google: Not So Froogle." *Economist*, 1 July, 61–2.

– 2017b. "An Insurgent in the Whitehouse" and "America First and Last." *Economist*, 4 February, 7, 17–19.

– 2017c. "Maple Grief: The Lessons from Canada's Attempts to Curb Its House-Price Boom." *Economist*, 17 June, 16–17.

– 2017d. "Sucking Up Carbon." Briefing: Combatting Climate Change. *Economist*, 18 November, 21–4.

– 2017e. "Why Everything Is Hackable." *Economist*, 8 April, 73–4.

– 2017f. "The World's Most Valuable Resource Is No Longer Oil, but Data." *Economist*, 6 May, 9-12.

– 2018a. "Briefing: The World Trading System." *Economist*, 21 July, 17–19.

– 2018b. "*NAFTA* Rule Breakers." *Economist*, 3 February, 68.

– 2018c. "Special Report: Fixing the Internet: The Ins and Outs." *Economist*, 30 June, 1–12.

– 2018d. "Special Report: The Geopolitics of Energy." *Economist*, 17 March, 3–11.

– 2019a. "Combatting Drones: A New Dogfight." *Economist*, 26 January, 79–80.

– 2019b. "A Slow Unravelling." Special Report on Global Supply Chains. *Economist*, 13 July, 3–12.

– 2019c. "The Splinternet: Net Loss." *Economist*, 9 November, 57–8.

– 2020. "Briefing: Covid-19 and College." *Economist*, 8 August, 15–17.

Edgerton, David. 2019. "Brexit Is a Necessary Crisis – It Reveals Britain's True Place in the World." *The Guardian*, 9 October.

Edwards, M., ed. 2014. *Critical Infrastructure Protection*. Amsterdam: IOS Press.

Elgie, Stewart. 2020. "What Canada's COVID-19 Economic Stimulus Plan Should Look Like When It Comes." *Maclean's*, 14 April. https://www.macleans.ca/economy/economicanalysis/what-canadas-covid-19-economic-stimulus-plan-should-look-like-when-it-comes.

Emery, Herb. 2015. *A Brief History of Infrastructure in Canada, 1870–2015*. Calgary: School of Public Policy, University of Calgary.

Emmerson, Charles. 2011. *Future History of the Arctic*. New York: Vintage Publishing.

English, John. 2013. *Ice and Water: Politics, Peoples and the Arctic Council*. Toronto: Penguin Canada.

Estache, Antonio, and Marianne Fay. 2007. *Current Debates on Infrastructure Policy*. Washington, DC: The World Bank, Poverty Reduction and Economic Management Vice-Presidency, November.

Etzioni, Amitai. 2012. "The Privacy Merchants: What Is to Be Done?" *University of Pennsylvania Journal of Constitutional Law* 14, no. 4: 929–51.

European Commission. 2014. *New EU Infrastructure Policy*. Brussels: European Commission. https://ec.europa.eu/commission/presscorner/detail/en/IP_13_948.

– 2016a. *Strategic Plan 2016–2020: Office for Infrastructure and Logistics in Brussels*. Brussels: European Commission.

– 2016b. *Strategic Plan Digit 2016–2020 Directorate General Informatics*. Brussels: European Commission.

– 2017. *White Paper on the Future of Europe: Reflections and Scenarios for the EU 27 by 2025*. Brussels: European Commission.

Fairbnb. 2017. *Squeezed Out: Airbnb's Commercialization of Home-Sharing in Toronto*. https://fairbnb.ca/Fairbnb_Report_Feb_29.pdf.

Falvo, Nick. 2017. *Calgary Homeless Foundation's Initial Reflections on the National Housing Strategy*. Calgary Homeless Foundation, 22 November. http://calgaryhomeless.com/blog/initial-reflections-national-housing-strategy.

Fast, Stewart. 2014. "NIMBY's Are Not the Problem." *Policy Options*, 2 September. https://policyoptions.irpp.org/magazines/beautiful-data/fast.

Fazekas, Andrew. 2006. "Big Science in a Small Country." *Science Magazine*. https://www.nature.com/articles/550S49a.

Fearn, Hannah. 2014. "If Housing Were Seen as Infrastructure There Would Be a Lot More of It." *The Guardian*, 31 January. https://www.theguardian.com/housing-network/editors-blog/2014/jan/31/affordable-housing-infrastructure-investment.

Federation of Canadian Municipalities. 1985. "Municipal Infrastructure in Canada: Physical Condition and Funding Adequacy." 4, no. 1. Backgrounder. Ottawa.

– 2006. *Building Prosperity from the Ground Up: Restoring Municipal Fiscal Balance*. Ottawa: Federation of Canadian Muncipalities.

– 2009a. "Move Infrastructure Funds Fast to Fight Recession, Say FCM Big City Mayors." 15 January. https://www.canadianconsultingengineer.com/engineering/municipalities-push-for-money-for-infrastructure/1000088729.

– 2009b. "Statement by FCM President on Today's Infrastructure Announcement by Minister Baird." 26 January.

– 2016. *Canada's Housing Opportunity: Urgent Solutions for National Housing Strategy*. Federation of Canadian Municipalities, October.

– 2019. *Election 2019: Housing Affordability-Backgrounder*. 28 August. https://fcm.ca/en/news-media/news-release/election-2019-make-housing-more-affordable/backgrounder.

Filion, P., M. Moos, Ryan Walker, and Tara Vinodrai, eds. 2015. *Canadian Cities in Transition*, 5th ed. Oxford, UK: Oxford University Press.

Finance Canada. 2005. *Budget 2005, Moving Towards a Green Economy*. 23 February. https://www.cbc.ca/news2/background/budget2005/documents/budget05/pdf/pagree.pdf.

– 2018. "Agreement in Principle Reached to Restart Construction in 2018 and Ensure Completion of Transmountain Expansion." Backgrounder, 29 May.

Financial Post. 2017. "Residents Rail against U.S. Company as Port Churchill's Future Is on the Line." *Financial Post*, 15 May. https://financialpost.com/transportation/residents-rail-against-u-s-company-as-port-churchills-future-is-on-the-line.

Findlay, Martha Hall, Maria Orenstein, Colleen Collins, and Naomi
Christensen. 2018. *Unstuck: Recommendations for Reforming Canada's
Regulatory Process for Energy Projects*. Calgary: Canada West
Foundation, Natural Resources Centre, May.

Flemming, Brian. 2012. "A White Paper on Reforming Canada's
Transportation Policies for the 21st Century." *University of Calgary,
School of Public Policy* 5, no. 18 (June): 1–20.

– 2014a. *The 2014–2015 Canada Transport Act Review: Once More
unto the Breach, Dear Friends*. Ottawa: Conference Board of Canada,
25 November.

– 2014b. "Catching Up: The Case for Infrastructure Banks in Canada."
Ottawa: The Van Horne Institute, February.

– 2015. "The Political Economy of Canada's Transportation Policies in
2015: The 'What' Is Easy; the 'How' Is Hard." Keynote address to the
Atlantic Provinces Transportation Forum 2015, St John's, 20 May.

– 2016. "The Automated Vehicle: The Coming of the Next Disruptive
Technology." Address to the Association of Canadian Engineering
Companies, Vancouver, BC, 28 January.

Fletcher, Robson. 2017. "Starting With Eastern Bastards Remark, Notley
Wins Over Calgary Business Crowd." *CBC News*, 24 November. https://
www.cbc.ca/news/canada/calgary/rachel-notley-calgary-chamber-2017-
speech-1.4418632.

Florida, Richard. 2017a. *The New Urban Crisis*. New York: Basic Books.

– 2017b. "Lost in Housing Hysteria, Middle-Class Neighbourhoods Have
Gone Extinct." *Globe and Mail*, 24 April. https://www.theglobeandmail.
com/opinion/lost-in-housing-hysteria-middle-class-neighbourhoods-
have-gone-extinct/article34793060.

Floridi, Luciano. 2014. *The 4th Revolution: How the InfoSphere Is
Reshaping Human Reality*. Oxford, UK: Oxford University Press.

Flynn, Paul. 2017. "What Brexit Should Have Taught Us about Voter
Manipulation." *The Guardian*, 17 April. https://www.theguardian.com/
commentisfree/2017/apr/17/brexit-voter-manipulation-eu-referendum-
social-media.

Fortin, Jean-Michel, and David J. Currie. 2013. "Big Science vs. Little
Science: How Scientific Impact Scales with Funding." *PLOS One*. https://
journals.plos.org/plosone/article?id=10.1371/journal.pone.0065263.

Found, Adam. 2016. *Tapping the Land Tax: Tax Increment Financing
of Infrastructure*. C.D. Howe Institute, Essential Policy Intelligence.

Fox, Martha Lane. 2015. "Tech Giants Have Too Much Power: Let's Reclaim the Internet." *Guardian*, 30 March.

Fragomeni, Carmela. 2019. "North America's First Smart-Tech Care Home for Patients With Dementia and Alzheimer's Being Built in Hamilton." *Toronto Star*, 16 June. https://www.thestar.com/news/gta/2019/06/16/north-americas-first-smart-tech-care-home-for-patients-with-dementia-and-alzhemiers-being-built-in-hamilton.html.

Franson, Jason. 2019. "Jason Kenney's First Throne Speech Promises to Undo Much of Notley Government's Work." *Ottawa Citizen*, 23 May. https://nationalpost.com/news/politics/jason-kenneys-first-throne-speech-promises-to-undo-much-of-notley-governments-work.

Fraser, Laura. 2016. "Toronto Council Approves Road Tolls for Gardiner Expressway and Don Valley Parkway." CBC News, 13 December. http://www.cbc.ca/news/canada/toronto/city-council-meeting-road-tolls-1.3893884.

Frenkel, Sheera. 2018. "Facebook Says It Deleted 865 Million Posts, Mostly Spam." *New York Times*, 15 May. https://www.todayonline.com/world/facebook-says-it-deleted-865-million-posts-mostly-spam.

Furth, Peter G. 2012. "Bicycling Infrastructure for Mass Cycling." In *City Cycling*, edited by John Pucher and Ralph Buehler, 105–40. Cambridge, MA: MIT Press.

Galison, Peter, and Bruce W. Hevly. 1992. *Big Science: The Growth of Large-Scale Research*. Palo Alto, CA: Stanford University Press.

Galloway, Gloria. 2017. "Globe and Mail Census 2016: More Canadians than Ever Are Living Alone and Other Takeaways." https://www.mcgill.ca/channels/channels/news/more-canadians-ever-are-living-alone-and-other-takeaways-269222.

Galvin, Patrick. 2012. *Local Government and Cluster-Related Innovation Policy: Two Industry Clusters in the City of Toronto*. Doctoral dissertation. Exeter, UK: University of Exeter.

Gattinger, Monica, and Geoffrey Hale, eds. 2010. *Borders and Bridges: Canada's Policy Relations in North America*. Toronto: Oxford University Press Canada.

Gaudreault, Valerie, and Patrick Lemire. 2003. *The Age of Public Infrastructure in Canada*. Statistics Canada. https://www150.statcan.gc.ca/n1/pub/11-621-m/11-621-m2006035-eng.htm.

Gawer, Annabelle, ed. 2009. *Platforms, Markets and Innovation*. Cheltenham, UK: Edward Elgar.

Geist, Michael. 2014a. "Digital Canada 150: The Digital Strategy without a Strategy." *Toronto Star*, 4 April. https://www.michaelgeist.ca/2014/04/digital-canada-150-2.

– 2014b. "Why the Government's New Digital Privacy Act Puts Your Privacy at Risk." *Toronto Star*, 11 April. https://www.thestar.com/business/2014/04/11/why_the_governments_new_digital_privacy_act_puts_your_privacy_at_risk.html.

– 2017a. "Net Neutrality Alive and Well in Canada: CRTC Crafts Full Code With Zero Rating Decision." https://www.michaelgeist.ca/2017/04/net-neutrality-alive-well-canada-crtc-crafts-full-code-zero-rating-decision.

– 2017b. "The Trouble for Canadian Digital Policy in an 'America First' World." *Globe and Mail*, 24 January. https://www.theglobeandmail.com/report-on-business/rob-commentary/the-trouble-for-canadian-digital-policy-in-an-america-first-world/article33729352.

Gendron, Angela. 2010. *Critical Energy Infrastructure Protection in Canada*. Ottawa: Defence R&D Canada, National Defence Canada, December.

Gertz, Geoffrey. 2018. *5 Things to Know About USMCA, the New NAFTA*. Brookings Institution, 2 October. https://www.brookings.edu/blog/up-front/2018/10/02/5-things-to-know-about-usmca-the-new-nafta.

Georges, Patrick. 2017. *Canada's Trade Policy Options Under Donald Trump: NAFTA's Rules of Origin, Canada-U.S. Security Perimeter and Canada's Geographic Trade Diversitifaction Opportunities*. Working Paper #1707E. Ottawa: Department of Economics, Faculty of Social Sciences, University of Ottawa. https://ruor.uottawa.ca/handle/10393/40361.

Georgopoulos, Aris, Bernard Hoekman, and Petros C. Mavroidis, eds. 2017. *The Internationalization of Government Procurement Regulation*. Oxford, UK: Oxford University Press.

Geyer, Robert, and Samie Rihani. 2010. *Complexity and Public Policy*. London: Routledge.

Gibbins, Roger, Antonia Maioni, and Janice Gross Stein. 2006. *Canada by Picasso: The Faces of Federalism*. Ottawa: Conference Board of Canada.

Gidengil, Elisabeth, and Heather Bastedo, eds. 2014. *Canadian Democracy from the Ground Up: Perceptions and Performance*. Vancouver, BC: UBC Press.

Gill, Vijay. 2014. *Defining a New National Transportation Policy*. Ottawa: Conference Board of Canada, 13 March.

Gilmore, Scott. 2016. "The North and the Great Canadian Lie." *Maclean's*, 11 September.

Global Affairs Canada. 2019. *Canada Marks Major Milestone in Defining Its Continental Shelf in Arctic Ocean.* Ottawa: Global Affairs Canada.

Globerman, Steven, and Jason Clements, eds. 2018. *Demographics and Entrepreneurship: Mitigating the Effects of an Aging Popultaion.* Vancouver, BC: Fraser Institute.

Golden, Anna, and Alan Broadbent. 2019. "Five Things to Know about the Sidewalk Toronto Project." *Sidewalk Toronto,* 30 August. https://www.sidewalktoronto.ca/five-things-to-know.

Goldratt, Eliyahu. 1984. *The Goal.* Great Barrington, MA: North River Press.

Gonzales-Rodriguez, Angela. 2019. "HBC Confirms Is Fully Exiting the Netherlands." *FashionUnited,* 23 September. https://fashionunited.com/executive/management/hudson-s-bay-co-confirms-is-fully-exiting-the-the-netherlands/2019092330071.

Gordon, Josh. 2017. *In High Demand: Addressing the Demand Factors behind Toronto's Housing Affordability Problem.* City Building Institute Policy Paper. Toronto: Ryerson City Building Institute, 13 March.

Gore, Will. 2017. "Facebook and Google Are Cannibalizing Journalistic Content while Pretending Not to Be Publishers." *Independent,* 23 May. https://www.independent.co.uk/voices/facebook-google-fake-news-cannibalise-journalism-content-ethical-standards-a7749976.html.

Goss Gilroy Inc. 2012. *Evaluation of the NRC Industrial Research Assistance Program (NRC-IRAP). Final Report.* Ottawa: National Research Council. https://nrc.canada.ca/en/corporate/planning-reporting/evaluation-industrial-research-assistance-program-irap.

Gourley, Julie. 2016. *The Arctic Council and the Paris Agreement.* Washington, DC: Office of Ocean and Polar Affairs, US Department of State.

Government of Canada. 2009. *Building Canada* website. https://budget.gc.ca/2009/pdf/budget-planbugetaire-eng.pdf.

– 2015. *Crown-Indigenous Relations and Northern Affairs Canada.* Ottawa: Author, 15 July. Graham, Andrew. 2011. *Canada's Critical Infrastructure: When Safe Enough Is Safe Enough?* Ottawa: Macdonald-Laurier Institute.

– 2019. *Canadian Public Sector Financial Management,* 3rd ed. Montreal, QC: McGill-Queen's University Press.

Graham, Katherine, and Caroline Andrew, eds. 2014. *Canada in Cities: The Politics and Policy of Federal-Local Governance.* Montreal, QC: McGill-Queen's University Press.

Graney, Emma. 2017. "Energy East Pipeline Cancellation an 'Attack on Alberta.'" *Edmonton Journal,* 5 October. https://edmontonjournal.com/

news/politics/energy-east-pipeline-cancellation-leaves-rachel-notley-deeply-disappointed.

Great Lakes St Lawrence Seaway System. 2016. "The Seaway." https://greatlakes-seaway.com/en/the-seaway.

Great-West Life. 2016. *Annual Report 2016.* https://www.greatwestlife.com/content/dam/gwl/documents/2016-GWLEnglishARCompleteBook E987-FINAL.pdf.

Green, Melanie. 2019. "Most British Columbians Now Support Trans Mountain Pipeline, Poll Shows." *The Star*, 4 July.

Grenier, Eric. 2020. "Pandemic-Rattled Canadians Still Cautious about Everything from Schools to 2nd Lockdowns, Polls Say." *CBC News*, 17 July. https://www.cbc.ca/news/politics/grenier-covid-caution-pandemic-polling-1.5652609.

Griggs, Troy, Gregor Aisch, and Sarah Almukhtar. 2017. "America's Aging Dams Are in Need of Repair." *New York Times*, 23 February. https://www.ussdams.org/our-news/americas-aging-dams-in-need-of-repair.

Griwkowsky, Catherine. 2018. "Fort McMurray Rebuild Continues Two Years after 'The Beast.'" *Toronto Star*, 3 May. https://www.thestar.com/edmonton/2018/05/02/fort-mcmurray-rebuild-continues-two-years-after-the-beast.html.

Guardian. 2018. "Why Silicon Valley Can't Fix Itself." *The Guardian*, 3 May. https://www.theguardian.com/news/2018/may/03/why-silicon-valley-cant-fix-itself-tech-humanism.

Gustin, Georgina. 2017. "World Bank Favors Fossil Fuel Projects in Developing Countries, Report Says." *Inside Climate News*, 26 January. https://insideclimatenews.org/news/26012017/world-bank-global-warming-coal-gas-developing-countries.

Gwyn, Richard. 2011. *Nation Maker – Sir John A. Macdonald: His Life, Our Times.* Toronto: Random House Canada.

Haavardsrud, Paul. 2017. "Keystone XL Clears Final Hurdle Only to See More Hurdles." *CBC News*, 21 November. https://www.cbc.ca/news/business/keystone-nebraska-regulatory-approval-1.4411452.

Hagiu, Andrei. 2014. "Strategic Decisions for Multisided Platforms." *MIT Sloan Management Review* 55, no. 2 (Winter): 71–80.

– 2015. "Companies Need an Option between Contractor and Employee." *Harvard Business Review* (21 August): 1–6. http://www.bollettinoadapt.it/wp-content/uploads/2015/08/Companies-Need-an-Option-Between-Contractor-and-Employee.pdf.

Hale, Geoffrey. 2012. "Toward a Perimeter: Incremental Adaptation or a
    New Paradigm for Canada–US Security and Trade Relations?" In *How
    Ottawa Spends 2012–2013: The Harper Majority, Budget Cuts and the
    New Opposition*, edited by G. Bruce Doern and Christopher Stoney, 106–
    26. Montreal, QC, and Kingston, ON: McGill-Queen's University Press.
– 2017. *Uneasy Partnership: The Politics of Business and Government
    in Canada*, 2nd ed. Toronto: University of Toronto Press.
Hamelin, Louis-Edmond. 2003. "An Attempt to Regionalize the Canadian
    North." In *Canada's Changing North*, rev. ed., edited by William C.
    Wonders, 8–14. Montreal, QC, and Kingston, ON: McGill-Queen's
    University Press.
Hanniman, Kyle. 2018. "In Defence of Borrowing." In *Canada: The State
    of the Federation 2015: Canadian Federalism and Infrastructure*, edited
    by John B. Allan, David L.A. Gordon, Kyle Hanniman, and Andre
    Juneau, 169–84. Montreal, QC, and Kingston, ON: McGill-Queen's
    University Press.
Harchaoui, Tarek M., F. Tarkhani, and Paul Warren. 2004. "Public
    Infrastructure in Canada, 1961–2002." *Canadian Public Policy* 30,
    no. 3: 303–18.
Harms, Adam. 2019. *The Politics of Fiscal Federalism*. Montreal, QC:
    McGill-Queen's University Press.
Harris, John. 2019. "Death of the Private Self: How Fifteen Years of
    Facebook Changed the Human Condition." *The Guardian*, 31 January.
    https://www.theguardian.com/technology/2019/jan/31/how-facebook-
    robbed-us-of-our-sense-of-self.
– 2020. "Facebook Is Still Far Too Powerful. It's Also How Millions Are
    Coping with This Crisis." *The Guardian*, 23 March. https://www.
    theguardian.com/commentisfree/2020/mar/22/facebook-powerful-crisis-
    coronavirus-communities-online.
Harris, Michael. 2018. "Why Trudeau Best Not Buy a Bricklin." *ipolitics*,
    27 May. https://ipolitics.ca/2018/05/27/why-trudeau-best-not-buy-
    a-bricklin.
Harris, Sophia. 2020. "The Canada-U.S. Border Could Be Closed for
    Months. Here's What You Need to Know Now." *CBC News*, August.
    https://www.cbc.ca/news/business/canada-u-s-border-travel-couples-
    alaska-1.5670867.
Harrison, Kathryn. 2017. "A Historic Moment for B.C. Politics – and Our
    Environment." *Reflections on Public Affairs* (blog). https://blogs.ubc.ca/

kathrynharrison/2017/06/06/a-historic-moment-for-b-c-politics-and-our-environment.

Heaver, Trevor D. 2009. *Canadian Railway Service Issues in 2009*. Presentation to Canada Transportation Research Forum Conference, Victoria, 24–27 May.

– 2013. *Submission to the Standing Committee on Transport, Infrastructure and Communities*. Parliament of Canada, 15 February.

Hebert, Chantal. 2017. "The End of the Energy East Pipeline Could Mark the Start of Federal-Provincial Turmoil." *Toronto Star*, 6 October. https://www.thestar.com/news/canada/2017/10/06/the-end-of-the-energy-east-pipeline-could-mark-the-start-of-federal-provincial-turmoil-hbert.html.

Helm, Dieter. 2012. *Carbon Crunch*. New Haven, CT: Yale University Press.

Hemery, H. *A Brief History of Infrastructure in Canada, 1870–2015*. Calgary: Department of Economics, School of Public Policy, University of Calgary. http://www.queensu.ca/iigr/sites/webpublish.queensu.ca. iigrwww/files/files/conf/SOTF/2015SOTF/EmeryHerbSOTF2015.pdf (accessed 27 October 2017).

Hern, Alex. 2019. "Google and Facebook Considering Ban on Micro-Targeted Political Ads." *The Guardian*, 7 November. https://www.theguardian.com/media/2019/nov/07/google-facebook-considering-ban-micro-targeted-political-ads.

Hern, Alex, and Olivia Solon. 2018. "Facebook Closed 583 Fake Accounts in First Three Months of 2018." *The Guardian*, 15 May. https://www.theguardian.com/technology/2018/may/15/facebook-closed-583m-fake-accounts-in-first-three-months-of-2018.

Herrman, John. 2018. "Want to Understand What Ails the Modern Internet? Look at eBay." *New York Times*, 20 June. https://www.nytimes.com/2018/06/20/magazine/want-to-understand-what-ails-the-modern-internet-look-at-ebay.html.

Hesketh, B. 1997. *Major Douglas and Alberta Social Credit*. Toronto: University of Toronto Press.

Hill, Margaret M. 1988. *Freedom to Move: Explaining the Decision to Deregulate Canadian Air and Rail Transportation*. Unpublished research paper. Ottawa: School of Public Administration, Carleton University.

– 1999. "Recasting the Federal Transport Regulator: The Thirty Year's War." In *Changing the Rules: Canadian Regulatory Regimes and Institutions*, edited by Bruce Doern, Margaret Hill, Michael J. Prince, and Richard J. Schultz, 57–81. Toronto: University of Toronto Press.

Hill, Stephen. 2015. *Raw Deal: How the Uber Economy and Runaway Capitalism Are Screwing American Workers*. New York: St Martin's Press.

Hilton, Robert. 2006. *Building Political Capital: The Politics of "Need" in the Federal Government's Municipal Infrastructure Programs, 1993–2006*. Unpublished MA thesis. Ottawa: School of Public Policy and Administration, Carleton University.

Hilton, Robert N., and Christopher Stoney. 2009a. "Federal Gas Tax Transfers: Politics and Perverse Policy." In *How Ottawa Spends 2009–2010: Economic Upheaval and Political Dysfunction*, edited by Allan M. Maslove, 175–93. Montreal, QC, and Kingston, ON: McGill-Queen's University Press.

– 2009b. "Sustainable Cities: Canadian Reality or Urban Myth?" *Commonwealth Journal of Local Governance* 4 (November 2009): 46–76.

Hiltzik, Michael. 2015. *Ernest Lawrence and the Invention that Launched the Military-Industrial Complex*. Simon and Schuster.

Hinkson, Kamila. 2019. "SNC-Lavalin Pleads Guilty to Fraud during Its 2001–2011 Activities in Libya." *CBC News*, 18 December. https://www.cbc.ca/news/canada/montreal/snc-lavalin-trading-court-libya-charges-1.5400542.

Hobbs, Steven. 2016. *An Overview of Public-Private Partnerships in Canada*. Presentation to the Economic Developers Council of Ontario Spring Symposium, Sault-Ste-Marie, ON, 19 May. https://myfreedom2017.com/wp-content/uploads/mdocs-ftp/online%20ppp%20course/Steve%20Hobbs-20Public%20Private%20Partnerships.pdf.

Hoberg, George. 2013. "The Battle over Oil Sands Access to Tidewater: A Political Risk Analysis of Pipeline Alternatives." *Canadian Public Policy* 39, no. 3: 371–91. https://www.jstor.org/stable/23594717?seq=1.

– 2016. *Pipelines and the Politics of Structure: A Case Study of the TransMountain Pipeline*. Paper presented at the Annual Meeting of the Canadian Political Science Association, Calgary, 31 May–2 June. https://sppga.ubc.ca/news/pipelines-politics-structure.

Hodson, Hal. 2013. "Stopping the Spooks." *New Scientist* (23 November): 24.

Hopkins, Nick. 2017. "Revealed: Facebook's Internal Rulebook on Sex, Terrorism and Violence." *The Guardian*, 21 May. https://www.theguardian.com/news/2017/may/21/revealed-facebook-internal-rulebook-sex-terrorism-violence.

Horack, Martin, and Robert Young, eds. 2012. *Sites of Governance: Multilevel Governance and Policy Making in Canada's Big Cities*. Montreal, QC: McGill-Queen's University Press.

Howlett, Michael. 2011. *Designing Public Policies: Principles and Instruments*. London: Routledge.

Howlett, Michael, and Jeremy Rayner. 2013. "Patching vs. Packaging in Policy Formulation: Assessing Portfolio Design." *Politics and Governance* 1, no. 2: 170–82.

Hudson's Bay Company. 2017. *Annual Information Form: Fiscal Year Ended January 28, 2017*.

Hughes, Nicolas. 2016. "Contaminated Site Update: Rough and Ready Allocation of Liability." *Canadian ERA Perspectives*, 23 June. https://www.mccarthy.ca/en/insights/blogs/canadian-era-perspectives/contaminated-site-update-rough-and-ready-allocation-liability.

Hughes, Virginia. 2013. "The Science of Big Science." *National Geographic*, 9 April. https://www.nationalgeographic.com/science/phenomena/2013/09/04/the-science-of-big-science.

Hulchanski, J. David. 2004. "What Factors Shape Canadian Housing Policy? The Intergovernmental Role in Canada's Housing System." In *Canada: The State of the Federation: Federal-Provincial Relations in Canada*, edited by Robert Young and Christian Leuprecht, 221–47. Montreal, QC: McGill-Queen's University Press.

Hunt, Stephen. 2019. "Scheer Outlines 'Vision for Canada that Includes National Corridor for Energy, Telecommunications.'" *CBC News*, 25 May. https://www.cbc.ca/news/canada/calgary/national-northern-corridor-1.5150036.

Hunter, Chantal. 2013. *Sustaining Infrastructure in Canada's North*. https://www.nrcan.gc.ca/home (now removed from site).

Hutton, Will. 2016. "The Gig Economy Is Here to Stay. So Making It Fairer Must Be a Priority." *The Guardian*, 3 September. https://www.theguardian.com/commentisfree/2016/sep/03/gig-economy-zero-hours-contracts-ethics.

– 2017. "Are We Finally Reacting to the Disruptive Supremacy of Facebook and Google?" *The Guardian*, 3 April. https://www.theguardian.com/commentisfree/2017/mar/26/finally-reacting-disruptive-supremacy-of-facebook-and-google.

Iacobacci, Mario. 2017. *Business Cases for Major Public Infrastructure Projects in Canada*. University of Calgary School of Public Policy. Research Paper. Volume 10 (November): 28.

Iacobucci, E., Michael Trebilcock, and Ralph Winter. 2006. *The Political Economy of Deregulation in Canada*. Working Paper 2006-05. Vancouver, BC: Phelps Centre for the Study of Government and Business, Sauder School of Business, University of British Columbia.

Independent Evaluation Group and World Bank Group. 2012. *World Bank Group Support to Public-Private Partnerships: Lessons From Experience in Client Countries*. FT02-12. https://openknowledge. worldbank.org/handle/10986/22908.

Inderst, Georg, and Raffaele Della Croce. 2013. *Pension Fund Investment in Infrastructure: A Comparison between Australia and Canada*. Paris: OECD. July. https://www.oecd.org/pensions/pensionfundinfrastructure australiacanada2013.pdf.

Indigenous and Northern Affairs Canada. 2017. "About Indigenous and Northern Affairs Canada." https://www.aadnc-aandc.gc.ca/eng/ 1100100010023/1100100010027.

Industry Canada. 2015. *Logistics and Supply Chain Management*. Industry Canada. (No longer accessible.)

Infrastructure Canada. 2003. "Canada's Municipal Development and Loan Fund (1963–1966)." (No longer accessible.)

– 2007. Cities and Communities Branch, "Tracing the Development of the Gas Tax Fund," Revised Final Version. 17 January. (No longer accessible.)

– 2008. *Building Canada Plan 2008*. http://www.infrastructure.gc.ca/ media/presentations/20080601fcm-eng.html.

– 2010. *The Gasoline Tax and Infrastructure Funding: An Examination of Governance Structures and Spending Patterns*. (No longer accessible.)

– 2011. "Border Infrastructure Fund Projects." 26 October. https://www. infrastructure.gc.ca/prog/bif-fif-eng.html.

– 2014a. *Building Canada Plan 2014*. https://www.infrastructure.gc.ca/ plan/nbcp-npcc-eng.html.

– 2014b. "The Federal Gas Tax Fund." 31 March. https://www. infrastructure.gc.ca/plan/gtf-fte-eng.html.

– 2014c. "Final Report: Evaluation of the Gas Tax Fund." https://www. infrastructure.gc.ca/pd-dp/eval/2015-gtf-fte-eng.html.

– 2015a. "Other Programs." List of funding programs being wound down. https://www.infrastructure.gc.ca/prog/programs-infc-summary-eng.html.

– 2015b. "Report on Plans and Priorities 2015–16." 31 March. https:// www.infrastructure.gc.ca/alt-format/pdf/RPP-2015-2016-eng.pdf.

– 2016a. "The 2014 New Building Canada Fund." 17 May. https://www. infrastructure.gc.ca/plan/nbcf-nfcc-eng.html.

– 2016b. "Building Strong Cities through Investments in Public Transit." 22 November. http://www.infrastructure.gc.ca/plan/ptif-fitc-eng.php.

– 2016c. "Gas Tax Fund: National GTF Investments." 31 May. http:// www.infrastructure.gc.ca/plan/gtf-fte/gtf-fte-04-eng.html#cb.

– 2016d. "New Building Canada Fund: National Infrastructure Component. Project Business Case Guide." http://www.infrastructure. gc.ca/plan/nic-vin/bc-ar03-eng.html.

– 2016e. "Public Transit Infrastructure Fund: Program Overview." 16 May. https://www.infrastructure.gc.ca/plan/ptif-fitc/ptif-program-programme-eng.html.

– 2017a. "Canada Launches Negotiations with Provinces and Territories for Long Term Infrastructure Investments." News release, 6 July. https://www.canada.ca/en/office-infrastructure/news/2017/07/canada_launches_negotiationswithprovincesandterritoriesforlongte.html.

– 2017b. "Government of Canada Announces Wind-Down of PPP Canada Crown Corporation." https://www.canada.ca/en/office-infrastructure/news/2017/11/government_of_canadaannounceswind-downofppcanadacrowncorporatio.html.

– 2019. "Infrastructure Canada Projects and Programs (since 2002) National." https://www.infrastructure.gc.ca/investments-2002-investissements/on-eng.html.

– 2021. "Canada Infrastructure Bank." https://www.infrastructure.gc.ca/ CIB-BIC/index-eng.html.

Infrastructure Ontario. 2017. *Enhancing the Economic Framework of Canada's Largest Province.* http://www.cbj.ca/infrastructure-ontario.

Ingram, Gregory K., and Karin L. Brandt, eds. 2013. *Infrastructure and Land Policies.* Cambridge, MA: Lincoln Institute of Land Policy, May. https://www.lincolninst.edu/publications/books/infrastructure-land-policies.

Institute for Governance of Private and Public Organizations. 2014. *The Governance of Canadian Airports: Issues and Recommendations.* Montreal, QC: Institute for Governance of Private and Public Organizations. http://igopp.org/wp-content/uploads/2014/04/igopp_gouvernanceaeroport_en_web_lowres.pdf.

International Atomic Energy Agency. 2016. *Country Nuclear Profiles – Canada.* Vienna: International Atomic Energy Agency. https://cnpp.iaea. org/countryprofiles/Canada/Canada.htm.

International Energy Agency. 2020. "Changes in Transport Behaviour during the Covid-19 Crisis." 15 August. https://www.iea.org/articles/ changes-in-transport-behaviour-during-the-covid-19-crisis.

International Federation of Robotics. 2016. *Executive Summary World Robotics 2016 Industrial Robots.* https://ifr.org/img/uploads/Executive_Summary_WR_Industrial_Robots_20161.pdf.

International Financial Consulting Ltd. 2008. *The Legislative Review of Export Development Canada*. Ottawa: Author, December. https://www.edc.ca/content/dam/edc/en/non-premium/final_report_jun_09_e.pdf.

– 2019. *Study for Global Affairs Canada on Export Development Canada*. Tabled in Parliament, 20 June. (No longer accessible.)

Investment Industry Regulatory Organization of Canada. 2018. "About HROC." http://www.iiroc.ca/about/Pages/default.aspx.

Irwin, Neil. 2018. "The Trump Trade Strategy Is Coming into Focus. That Doesn't Necessarily Mean It Will Work." *New York Times*, 6 October. https://www.nytimes.com/2018/10/06/upshot/trump-trade-strategy-coming-into-focus.html.

Israel, Solomon. 2017. "Canada's Biggest Cities Move to Regulate Airbnb, but It's No Easy Task." *CBC News*, 17 June. https://www.cbc.ca/news/business/airbnb-municipal-regulations-canada-1.4164056.

Ivison, John. 2017. "Spat between Toronto Mayor and Wynne Government Highlights Infrastructure Spending Logjam." *National Post*, 1 June. https://nationalpost.com/opinion/john-ivison-tory-blames-wynne-for-transit-woes.

Jacobs, Jane. 1994. *Systems of Survival: A Dialog on the Moral Foundations of Commerce and Politics*. Toronto: Vintage Books.

Jamasi, Zohra, and Trish Hennessy. 2016. *Nobody's Business: Airbnb in Toronto*. Canadian Centre for Policy Alternatives. Ontario, September. https://www.policyalternatives.ca/sites/default/files/uploads/publications/Ontario%20Office/2016/09/CCPA%20ON%20Nobodys%20Business%20FINAL%203.pdf.

James, Royson. 2017. "Our Politician's Transit Shenanigans." *Toronto Star*, 3 April. https://www.thestar.com/news/city_hall/2017/04/03/our-politicians-transit-shenanigans-are-causing-civic-suicide-james.html.

Jaremco, Gordon. 2010. "Canada's Top 25 Energy Infrastructure Projects." *Alberta Oil*. 7 April. (No longer accessible.)

Jeffrey, Anja, Adam Fiser, Natalie Brender, and Brent Dowdall. 2015. *Building a Resilient and Prosperous North: Centre for the North Five-Year Compendium Report*. Ottawa: Conference Board of Canada. https://www.conferenceboard.ca/networks/cfn/default.aspx.

Jenish, D'Arcy. 2009. *The St. Lawrence Seaway: Fifty Years and Counting*. Oshawa, ON: Penumbra Press.

Johal, Sunil, and Michael Crawford Urban. 2017. *Regulating Disruption: Governing in an Era of Rapid Technological Change*. Mowat Research #147. Toronto: Mowat Centre, University of Toronto. https://

munkschool.utoronto.ca/mowatcentre/wp-content/uploads/publications/
147_regulating_disruption.pdf.

Johal, Sunil, Jordan Thirgood, and Michael Crawford (with Kiran Alwani and
Mati Dubrobinsky). 2018. *Robots, Revenues and Responses: Ontario and
the Future of Work*. Toronto: Mowat Centre, University of Toronto. https://
munkschool.utoronto.ca/mowatcentre/robots-revenues-responses.

Jones, Braeden. 2017. "Palister Not Displeased." *Metro News* 23 March.
https://www.readmetro.com/en/canada/winnipeg/20170323/1/#book/5.

Jones, Bryan D., and Frank R. Baumgartner. 2005. *The Politics of
Attention: How Government Prioritizes Problems*. Chicago: University
of Chicago Press.

– 2012. "From There to Here: Punctuated Equilibrium to the General
Punctuation Thesis to a Theory of Government Information Processing."
Policy Studies Journal 40: 1–20.

Jones, David P., and Anne S. de Villars. 2014. *Principles of Administrative
Law*, 6th ed. Toronto: Carswell.

Jones, Jeffrey. 2013. "Oil's New Arctic Passage to Europe." *Globe and
Mail*, 15 August. https://www.theglobeandmail.com/report-on-business/
oils-new-arctic-passage-to-europe/article13803628.

– 2019a. "Alberta Energy Regulator Faces Cuts up to $147-Million in
Jason Kenney's First Budget." *Globe and Mail*, 25 October. https://www.
theglobeandmail.com/business/article-alberta-energy-regulator-faces-
cuts-of-up-to-58-per-cent-in-jason.

– 2019b. "Senior Staff at Alberta Energy Regulator Exit, Reorganization
on Hold amid Scandal." *Globe and Mail*, 23 October. https://www.
theglobeandmail.com/business/article-senior-staff-at-alberta-energy-
regulator-exit-restructuring-on-hold.

Jones, John. 2017. *Depreciation and Taxes*. Lecture Material. Vancouver,
BC: Simon Fraser University. http://www.sfu.ca/-jones/ENSC201/Unit11/
lecture11.html. (No longer accessible.)

Jones, Owen. 2018. "Carillion Is No One-Off Scandal. Neoliberalism Will
Bring Many More." *The Guardian*, 18 May. https://www.theguardian.
com/commentisfree/2018/may/16/
carillion-scandal-neoliberalism-public-services-profit.

Journal of Unmanned Vehicle Systems. 2016. "About the Journal." https://
cdnsciencepub.com/doi/abs/10.1139/juvs-2016-0033.

Jozic, Jennifer. 2006. *Northern Transportation Today: Snowmobiles,
Airplanes and the Occasional Train*. Saskatoon, SK: Northern Research
Portal, University of Saskatchewan. http://scaa.usask.ca/gallery/northern/
content.php.

Juneau, Andre. 2018. "Infrastructure and Intergovernmental Relations:
A Policy Framework, Roles, and Relationships, and a Case Study." In
*Canada: The State of the Federation 2015: Canadian Federalism and
Infrastructure*, edited by John B. Allan, David L.A. Gordon, Kyle
Hanniman, and Andre Juneau, 141–54. Montreal, QC, and Kingston,
ON: McGill-Queen's University Press 2018.

Justice Canada. 2013. *An Act to Amend the Canada Transportation Act.*
Bill C-52. Assented to, 26 June 2013.

– 2016a. *Aeronautics Act.*

– 2016b. *Aeronautics Act. Regulations Made Under This Act.*

– 2016c. *Transportation of Dangerous Goods Act.*

– 2017. *Canada Occupational Health and Safety Regulations.*

Kaiser, Ed. 2019. "Nowhere across the Country Will Be Free to Pollute.
Trudeau Says Replacement for Alberta Carbon Tax under Discussion."
Edmonton Journal, 11 May.

Kalinowski, Tess. 2015. "Driverless Cars Shaking up Ontario's Auto
Industry, Warns Minister." *Toronto Star*, 17 September. https://www.the-
star.com/news/gta/transportation/2015/09/17/driver-less-cars-shaking-
up-ontarios-auto-industry-warns-minister.html.

– 2017. "Toronto Should Require Airbnb Permits, Says Report." *Toronto
Star*, 3 March. https://www.thestar.com/business/2017/03/03/toronto-
should-require-airbnb-permits-says-report.html.

Kang, Celia. 2016a. "U.S. Signals Backing for Self-Driving Cars." *Boston
Globe*, 19 September. https://www.bostonglobe.com/business/2016/09/
19/feds-want-regulate-self-driving-cars/kdTGfHRaG8KV2XJTNInKxI/
story.html.

– 2016b. "U.S. Signals Backing for Self-Driving Cars." *New York Times*,
20 September. https://www.nytimes.com/2016/09/20/technology/self-
driving-cars-guidelines.html.

Kassam, Ashifa. 2018. "'…Our Land Is Our Home': Canadians Build Tiny
Homes in Bid to Thwart Pipeline." https://www.theguardian.com/world/
2018/may/08/canadian-activists-pipeline-tiny-homes-british-columbia.

Kavanagh, Sean. 2019. "New Rapid Bus Lines Could Mean Massive
Changes for Winnipeg Transit." *CBC News*. https://www.cbc.ca/news/
canada/manitoba/transit-winnipeg-rapid-line-route-changes-1.5339364.

Keen, Andrew. 2015. *The Internet Is Not the Answer*. London: Atlantic
Books.

Keesmaat, Jennifer. 2017. *Big Cities Need New Governance*. Toronto:
Mowat Centre, 9 May. https://munkschool.utoronto.ca/mowatcentre/
big-cities-need-new-governance.

Kernaghan, Kenneth, Brian Marson, and Sandford F. Borins. 2000. *The New Public Organization.* Toronto: Institute of Public Administration of Canada.

Kinder, Jeffrey S. 2009. "The Co-Location of Public Science: Government Laboratories on University Campuses." In *Research and Innovation Policy: Changing Federal Government-University Relations,* edited by G. Bruce Doern and Christopher Stoney, 215–41. Toronto: University of Toronto Press.

Kirby, J. 2020. "Canada Needs a Plan to Rebuild Itself. Let the Transformation Begin." *Maclean's,* 23 June. https://www.macleans.ca/economy/canada-needs-a-plan-to-rebuild-itself-let-the-transformation-begin.

Kitchen, Harry. 1982. "Municipal Income Taxation – A Revenue Alternative." *Canadian Tax Journal* 30, no. 5 (September–October): 781–6.

– 2002. "Canadian Municipalities: Fiscal Trends and Sustainability." *Canadian Tax Journal* 50, no. 1: 156–80.

– 2004. "Financing Local Government Capital Investment." Paper prepared for a workshop on Strengthening Responsive and Accountable Local Government in China. Dali, Yunnan Province, China, 9–12 August 2004, 1–31. https://carleton.ca/cure/wp-content/uploads/Financing_Capital_Investment.pdf.

Kitchen, Harry, and Enid Slack. 2016. "New Tax Sources for Canada's Largest Cities: What Are the Options?" *Institute on Municipal Finance and Governance Perspectives* no. 15.

Klein, Naomi. 2014. *This Changes Everything: Capitalism vs The Climate.* New York: Simon & Schuster.

Koenig, Christian, and Bernhard von Wendland. 2017. *The Art of Regulation: Competition in Europe – Wealth and Wariness.* Cheltenham, UK: Edward Elgar.

Kovachevska, Marija. 2020. "22 Astonishing Airbnb Statistics for All New Hosts in 2020." *Capital Counselor,* 14 June. https://capitalcounselor.com/airbnb-statistics.

KPMG. 2016. *PPP Canada: P3 Canada Fund Summative Evaluation.* Final Report. KPMG. https://www.oag-bvg.gc.ca/internet/English/parl_oag_201602_06_e_41250.html.

Krugel, Lauren. 2014. "Canada's Oil-by-Rail Liability Rules Pit Regulators against Energy Players." *Huffington Post,* 24 May.

Krugman, Paul. 2018. "Debacle in Quebec." *New York Times*, 9 June. https://www.nytimes.com/2018/06/09/opinion/debacle-in-quebec.html.

Kucerak, Ian. 2019. "Alberta Alters Rules on Oil Production Limits to Spur More Conventional Drilling." *Edmonton Journal*, 9 November. https://edmontonjournal.com/news/local-news/alberta-alters-rules-on-oil-production-limits-to-spur-more-conventional-drilling.

Laanela, Mike. 2018. "The B.C. Pipeline Project You've Never Heard of – and Why It May Succeed." *CBC News*, 5 May. https://www.cbc.ca/news/canada/british-columbia/the-b-c-pipeline-project-you-ve-never-heard-of-and-why-it-may-succeed-1.4646892.

LaForest, Gerald Vincent. 1981. *The Allocation of Taxing Power under the Canadian Constitution.* 2nd ed. Canadian Tax Paper No. 65. Toronto: Canadian Tax Foundation, May.

Laframboise, Kaline, and Alison Brunette. 2018. "All 3 MMA Rail Workers Acquitted at Lac Megantic Disaster Trial." *CBC News*, 19 January. https://www.cbc.ca/news/canada/montreal/lac-megantic-criminal-negligence-verdict-1.4474848.

Lalami, Laila. 2017. "The Border Is All Around Us, and It's Growing." *New York Times Magazine*, 25 April. https://www.nytimes.com/2017/04/25/magazine/the-border-is-all-around-us-and-its-growing.html.

Lalancette, Mireille, Vincent Raynauld, and Erin Crandall, eds. 2019. *What's Trending in Canadian Politics?* Vancouver, BC: UBC Press.

Lalonde, Paul. 2017. "The Internationalization of Canada's Procurement." In *The Internationalization of Government Procurement Regulation*, edited by Aris Georgopoulos, Bernard Hoekman, and Petros C. Mavroidis, 300–18. Oxford, UK: Oxford University Press.

Lamb, Creig. 2016. *The Talented Mr. Robot: The Impact of Automation on Canada's Workforce.* Toronto: Brookfield Institute, Ryerson University, June.

Lambert, Steve. 2009. "Opponents to 'Duff's Folly' Hard to Find Today." *Globe and Mail*, 31 March.

Lammam, C., and H. MacIntyre. 2017. *Myths of Infrastructure Spending in Canada.* Vancouver, BC: Fraser Institute.

Langford, John. 1976. *Transport in Transition: The Reorganization of the Federal Transport Portfolio.* Montreal, QC, and Kingston, ON: McGill-Queen's University Press.

– 1982. "Transport Canada and the Transport Ministry: The Attempt to Retreat to Basics." In *How Ottawa Spends Your Tax Dollars: National*

Policy and Economic Development 1982, edited by G. Bruce Doern, 147–72. Toronto: James Lorimer Publishers.

Laxer, Gordon. 2015. *After the Sands: Energy and Ecological Security for Canadians*. Vancouver, BC: Douglas and McIntyre.

Layne, Donald. 2016. *History of the Business Development Bank of Canada: The FBDB Period (1975–1995)*. Montreal, QC: Business Development Bank of Canada.

Lee, Dave. 2018. "Facebook Details Scale of Abuse on Its Site." *BBC News*, 15 May. http://www.bbc.co.uk/news/technology-44122967.

Lee, Dwight R. 1994. "Reverse Revenue Sharing: A Return to Fiscal Federalism." *The Cato Journal* 14, no. 1 (Spring/Summer). https://citeseerx.ist.psu.edu/viewdoc/download?doi=10.1.1.552.1073&rep=rep1&type=pdf.

LeGrande, Julian. 2004. *Motivation, Agency and Public Policy*. Oxford, UK: Oxford University Press.

Lester, John. 2016. "Canada Needs an Entrepreneurship Policy, Not a Small Business Policy." In *How Ottawa Spends 2016–2017: The Trudeau Liberals in Power*, edited by G. Bruce Doern and Christopher Stoney, 85–110. Ottawa: School of Public Policy and Administration, Carleton University.

Levinson-King, Robin. 2019. "The Superpower Fight for Internet Near the Arctic." *BBC News*, 9 October. https://www.bbc.com/news/world-us-canada-49415867.

Lewis, Ted G. 2015. *Critical Infrastructure Protection in Homeland Security: Defending a Networked Nation*. Hoboken, NJ: John Wiley and Sons.

Liberal Party of Canada. 1993. "Creating Opportunity: The Liberal Plan for Canada" (Red Book 1), 6.

Library of Parliament. 2017. Legislative Summary. Bill C-48: *An Act Respecting the Regulation of Vessels That Transport Crude Oil or Persistent Oil to or From Ports or Marine Installations along British Columbia's North Coast*. Jed Chong and Nicole Sweeney. Publication No. 42-1-C48-E, 19 May.

Lipton, Eric, and B. Appelbaum. 2017. "Leashes Come Off Wall Street, Gun Sellers, Polluters and More." *New York Times*, 5 March. https://www.nytimes.com/2017/03/05/us/politics/trump-deregulation.

Lithwick, N. Harvey. 1970. *Urban Canada: Problems and Prospects*. Ottawa: Canada Mortgage and Housing Corporation.

Lo, Lucia, V. Preston, Paul Anisef, Ranu Basu, and Shuguang Wang. 2015. *Social Infrastructure and Vulnerability in the Suburbs*. Toronto: University of Toronto Press.

Locatelli, Giogio, G. Marianni, T. Sainati, and M. Greco. 2017. "Corruption in Public Projects and Mega Projects: There Is an Elephant in the Room." *International Journal of Project Management* 35, no. 3: 241–51.

Logistics Institute. 2016. "History." https://loginstitute.ca/about-cpli/history.

Lohr, Steve. 2015. "FCC Plans Strong Hand to Regulate the Internet." *New York Times*, 4 February. https://www.nytimes.com/2015/02/05/technology/fcc-wheeler-net-neutrality.html.

– 2017. "Canada Tries to Turn Its A.I. Ideas into Dollars." *New York Times*, 9 April. https://www.nytimes.com/2017/04/09/technology/canada-artificial-intelligence.html.

Lopreite, Debora, and Joan Murphy. 2009. "The Canada Foundation for Innovation as Patron and Regulator." In *Research and Innovation Policy: Changing Federal Government-University Relations*, edited by G. Bruce Doern and Christopher Stoney, 123–47. Toronto: University of Toronto Press.

Lorimer, James. 1978. *The Developers*. Toronto: James Lorimer.

Lund, Susan, and Laura Tyson. 2018. "Globalization Is Not in Retreat: Digital Technology and the Future of Trade." *Foreign Affairs* 97, no. 3: 130–40.

MacCharles, Tonda, and Alex Ballinggall. 2019. "SNC-Lavalin: What Happened and When?" *The Star*, 15 February. https://www.thestar.com/politics/federal/2019/02/15/snc-lavalin-what-happened-and-when.html.

MacDonald, Art. 2016. "About Naylor's Panel Roundtable Regarding Big Science in a Canadian Context." https://nghoussoub.com/2016/10/04/about-naylors-panel-roundtable-regarding-big-science-in-a-canadian-context.

Macfarlane, D. 2014. *Negotiating a River: Canada and the U.S. and the Creation of the St. Laurence Seaway*. Vancouver, BC: UBC Press.

Mackenzie, H. 2013. *Canada's Infrastructure Gap: Where It Came From and Why Will It Cost So Much to Close*. Ottawa: Centre for Policy Alternatives. https://www.policyalternatives.ca/publications/reports/canadas-infrastructure-gap.

Mackrael, Kim. 2013. "Safety Board Warns against Blaming One Person for Lac-Megantic Disaster." *Globe and Mail*, 13 July. https://www.theglobeandmail.com/news/national/tsb-says-several-things-led-to-derailment/article13207255.

MacLean, Cameron. 2017. "It's About Time to Build a Road to Churchill: Engineer Says It Is Possible." *CBC News*, 24 June. https://www.cbc.ca/news/canada/manitoba/churchill-build-road-engineer-1.4174034.

MacLean, Jason. 2016. "Striking at the Root Problem of Canadian Environmental Law: Identifying and Escaping Regulatory Capture." *Journal of Environmental Law and Practice* 29: 111–23.

MacMillan, Margaret. 2018. "Canada and America Are Cousins. We Don't Stab Each Other in the Back." *The Guardian*, 11 June. https://www.theguardian.com/commentisfree/2018/jun/11/trump-canada-relationship-us.

Major Projects Management Office. 2017. *Energy East Pipeline Project*. http://mpmo.gc.ca/measures/257. (No longer accessible.)

Major Projects Task Force. 1981. *Major Canadian Projects: Major Canadian Opportunities*. Ottawa: Supply and Services Canada.

Manjoo, Farhad. 2017. "Can Facebook Fix Its Own Worst Bug." *New York Times Magazine*, 25 April. https://www.nytimes.com/2017/04/25/magazine/can-facebook-fix-its-own-worst-bug.html.

Markusoff, Jason. 2019. "Greta Thunberg's Visit to Alberta Was No Ordinary Celebrity Drop-in." *Maclean's*, 12 November. https://www.macleans.ca/society/environment/greta-thunbergs-visit-to-alberta-was-no-ordinary-celebrity-drop-in.

Marowits, Ross. 2017. "After Worst Cargo Season in Years, St. Lawrence Seaway Opens for Shipping." *CTV News*, 20 March. https://www.CTVnews.ca/business/after-worst-cargo-season-in-years-st-lawrence-seaway-opens-for-shipping-1.3332519.

– 2018. "Growth of Low-Cost Airlines Giving Boost to Secondary Airports in Canada." *Toronto Star*, 25 June. https://www.thestar.com/business/2018/06/25/growth-of-low-cost-airlines-giving-boost-to-secondary-airports-in-canada.html.

Massey, Andrew. 2018. "Persistent Public Management Reform: An Egregore of Liberal Authoritarianism?" *Public Money and Management*. https://www.tandfonline.com/doi/full/10.1080/09540962.2018.1448160.

Mathieu, Emily. 2018. "Report Outlines Ambitious Housing Strategy for Ontario." *Toronto Star*, 17 May. https://www.thestar.com/news/gta/2018/05/17/report-outlines-ambitious-housing-strategy-for-ontario.html.

Mayer, Andre. 2020. "From Calgary to Milan to Bogata, Covid-19 Is Changing How Cities Look and Operate." *CBC News*, 1 May. https://flipboard.com/topic/calgarycoronavirus/from-calgary-to-milan-to-bogota-covid-19-is-changing-how-cities-look-and-operat/a-h8sJtOu3RBiRbkGuQqjRQA%3Aa%3A107108217-345d32b412%2Fcbc.ca.

Mazzacato, Mariana. 2013. *The Entrepreneurial State*. London: Anthern Press.

McClearn, Matthew. 2019. "Federal Review of Export Development Canada Finds Inadequate Disclosure Practices." *Globe and Mail*, 1 July. https://www.theglobeandmail.com/canada/article-morning-update-federal-review-of-export-development-canada-finds.

McConaghy, Dennis. 2017. *Dysfunction: Canada After Keystone XL*. Toronto: Dundurn.

McGrane, David. 2013. "National Unity through Disengagement: The Harper Government's One-Off Federalism." In *How Ottawa Spends 2013–2014: The Harper Government: Mid-Term Blues and Long-Term Plans*, edited by Christopher Stoney and G. Bruce Doern, 114–26. Montreal, QC: McGill-Queen's University Press.

McGregor, Janyce. 2018. "Auto Industry Relieved by NAFTA 2.0, But Results May Be Mixed." *CBC News*, 4 October. https://www.cbc.ca/news/politics/auto-impact-usmca-wednesday-1.4848589.

McGuire, Cecelia. 2004. *100 Years at the Heart of Transportation: An Historical Perspective*. Ottawa: Canadian Transportation Agency.

McIntosh, Emma. 2019. "Supreme Court of Canada Says Bankrupt Energy Companies Must Clean Up Old Oil, Gas Wells before Paying Off Creditors." *Star Metro Calgary*, 31 https://www.thestar.com/calgary/2019/01/31/supreme-court-of-canada-says-bankrupt-energy-companies-must-clean-up-old-oil-and-gas-wells-before-paying-off-creditors.html.

McKenna, Barry. 2012 [2017]. "The Hidden Price of Public-Private Partnerships." *Globe and Mail*, published 14 October 2012, updated 26 March 2017. https://www.theglobeandmail.com/report-on-business/economy/the-hidden-price-of-public-private-partnerships/article4611798.

McKeown, Robert J. 2016. *An Overview of the Canadian Banking System: 1996 to 2015*. Toronto: University of Toronto. https://ideas.repec.org/p/qed/wpaper/1379.html.

McMillan, Melville L. 2003. "Municipal Relations with the Federal and Provincial Governments: A Fiscal Perspective." Prepared for the Municipal-Provincial-Federal Relations Conference, Kingston, ON, Queen's University, 9–10 May 2003. http://citeseerx.ist.psu.edu/viewdoc/download?doi=10.1.1.487.9221&rep=rep1&type=pdf.

McNally, Chris, Bill Ferreira, and David L.A. Gordon. 2018. "The Canadian Infrastructure Report Card." In *Canada: The State of the Federation 2015: Canadian Federalism and Infrastructure*, edited by John B. Allan, David L.A. Gordon, Kyle Hanniman, and Andre

Juneau, 27–44. Montreal, QC, and Kingston, ON: McGill-Queen's University Press.

McNeill, Jodi. 2017. *Will Alberta's Oilsands Tailings Finally Be Cleaned Up?* Calgary: Pembina Institute. https://www.pembina.org/blog/will-alberta-s-oilsands-tailings-finally-be-cleaned-up.

McQuaig, Linda. 2018. "Trudeau's Pipeline Gambit Puts Him on the Wrong Side of History." *Toronto Star*, 6 June. https://www.thestar.com/opinion/star-columnists/2018/06/06/trudeaus-pipeline-gambit-puts-him-on-wrong-side-of-history.html.

McQuarrie, Jonathan. 2016. "Bombardier Inc." https://www.thecanadianencyclopedia.ca/en/article/bombardier-inc.

McSheffrey, Elizabeth. 2017. "Big Business and Big Oil Lose Climate Battle in Pipeline Review." *National Observer*, 23 August. https://www.nationalobserver.com/2017/08/23/news/big-business-and-big-oil-lose-climate-battle-pipeline-review.

Meadowcroft, James, and Matthew Hellin. 2010. "Policy Making in the Indeterminate World of Energy Transitions: Carbon Capture and Storage as Technological Transition or Enhanced 'Carbon Lock In.'" In *Policy: From Ideas to Implementation*, edited by Glen Toner, Leslie A. Pal, and Michael J. Prince, 232–56. Montreal, QC, and Kingston, ON: McGill-Queen's University Press.

Mendoza, M.R., Patrick Low, and B. Kotschwar, eds. 1999. *Trade Rules in the Making*. Organization of American States. Washington, DC: Brookings Institution Press.

Metrolinx. 2017. "Metrolinx Overview." http://www.metrolinx.com/en/aboutus/metrolinxoverview/metrolinx_overview.aspx.

Miller, Glenn. 2017. "No Place to Grow Old: How Canadian Suburbs Can Become Age-Friendly." *IRPP Insight* no. 14 (March): 1–25. Institute for Research on Public Policy.

Minister of Infrastructure and Communities. 2015. "Mandate Letter (November 12, 2015), PMO." https://pm.gc.ca/eng/minister-infrastructure-and-communities-mandate-letter.

Mintz, Jack M., and Tom Roberts. 2006. "Running on Empty: A Proposal to Improve City Finances." C.D. Howe, The Urban Papers, No. 226, February. http://www.cdhowe.org/pdf/commentary_226.pdf. (No longer accessible.)

Mintz, Jack M., and Michael Smart. 2006. *Incentives for Public Investment Under Fiscal Rules*. World Bank Policy Research Working Paper 3860. March. https://openknowledge.worldbank.org/handle/10986/8346.

Moody's Investor Service. 2018. "Credit Overview: Rating Agency Process, Municipal Financial Health, and MFABC." https://mfa.bc.ca/sites.default/files/About%20Usmfa_2018_ff1-%20_moodies_municipal_financial_health_and_mfabc-ahardi.pdf. (No longer accessible.)

Monbiot, George. 2016. "Our Roads Are Choked. We're on the Verge of Carmageddon." *The Guardian*, 20 September. https://www.theguardian.com/commentisfree/2016/sep/20/roads-car-use-health-driving.

– 2018. "Donald Trump Was Right: The Rest of the G7 Were Wrong." *The Guardian*, 13 June. https://www.theguardian.com/commentisfree/2018/jun/13/trump-nafta-g7-sunset-clause-trade-agreement.

Montsion, Jean Michel. 2015. "Churchill, Manitoba and the Arctic Gateway: A Historical Contextualization." *The Canadian Geographer* 59, no. 3 (Fall): 304–16.

Moore, Rowan. 2018. "An Inversion of Nature: How Air Conditioning Created the Modern City." *The Guardian*, 14 August. https://www.theguardian.com/cities/2018/aug/14/how-air-conditioning-created-modern-city.

Morgan, Clara. 2009. "Higher Education Funding and Policy Trade-offs: The AUCC and Federal Research in the Chretien-Martin Era." In *Research and Innovation Policy: Changing Federal Government-University Relations*, edited by G. Bruce Doern and Christopher Stoney, 59–88. Toronto: University of Toronto Press.

Morgan, Geoffrey. 2018. "First of Many: $40B LNG Canada Signals Revival of Mega Projects." *Financial Post*, 2 October. https://financialpost.com/commodities/first-of-many-40b-lng-canada-signals-revival-of-mega-projects.

Moscrop, David. 2018. "The USMCA Keeps Canada in America's Thrall." *Maclean's*, 1 October. https://www.macleans.ca/opinion/the-usmca-keeps-canada-in-americas-thrall.

Moteff, John D. 2015. *Critical Infrastructures: Background, Policy and Implementation*. Washington, DC: Congressional Research Service.

Mufson, Steven. 2017. "Economists Pan Infrastructure Plan Championed by Trump Nominees." *Washington Post*, 17 January. https://www.washingtonpost.com/business/economy/economists-pan-infrastructure-plan-championed-by-trump-nominees/2017/01/17/0ed1ad5e-dc5e-11e6-918c-99ede3c8cafa_story.html.

Murphy, Joan. 2007. "Transforming Health Sciences Research: From the Medical Research Council to the Canadian Institutes of Health Research." In *Innovation, Science, Environment: Canadian Policies and*

Performance 2007–2008, edited by G. Bruce Doern, 240–61. Montreal, QC, and Kingston, ON: McGill-Queen's University Press.

Murray, Tom. 2011. *Rails Across Canada: The History of Canadian Pacific and Canadian National Railways*. St Paul: MBI Publishing.

National Energy Board. 2008. *2007 Annual Report to Parliament*. Ottawa: National Energy Board.

– 2011. *The National Energy Board Filing Requirements for Offshore Drilling in the Canadian Arctic*. Ottawa: National Energy Board.

– 2012. *Annual Report 2011 to Parliament*. Ottawa: National Energy Board.

– 2017a. *2016–17 Annual Report*. Ottawa: National Energy Board.

– 2017b. *Energy East and Eastern Mainline Projects: TransCanada Termination of Hearing*. https://www.cer-rec.gc.ca/en/applications-hearings/view-applications-projects/energy-east/index.html?=undefined&wbdisable=true.

National Research Council of Canada (NRC). 2013. *Strategy: 2013–2018*. http://www.nrc-cnrc.gc.ca/obj/doc/reports-rapports/NRC_Strategy_2013_2018_e.pdf.

– 2016. *Corporate Overview*. http://www.nrc-cnrc.gc.ca/eng/about/corporate_overview/index.html.

– 2017a. *Construction*. http://www.nrc-cnrc.gc.ca/eng/rd/construction/index.html.

– 2017b. *Industrial Research Assistance Program (IRAP)*. "About." http://www.nrc-cnrc.gc.ca/eng/irap/about/mandate.html.

– 2017c. *Industrial Research Assistance Program (IRAP)*. "Benefits to Canadians." http://www.nrc-cnrc.gc.ca/eng/irap/about/benefits.html.

– 2017d. *Industrial Research Assistance Program (IRAP)*. "Ideal Products." http://www.nrc-cnrc.gc.ca/eng/irap/success/2017/ideal_products.html.

– 2017e. *Industrial Research Assistance Program (IRAP)*. "Math Game." http://www.nrc-cnrc.gc.ca/eng/irap/success/2017/smartteacher.html.

– 2019. "NRC Research Centres." https://nrc.canada.ca/en/research-development/research-collaboration/research-centres.

National Round Table on the Environment and the Economy. 2009. *True North: Adapting Infrastructure to Climate Change in Northern Canada*. http://nrt-trn.ca/climate/true-north.

Natural Gas Association. 2018. *Driving Productivity and Competitiveness with Natural Gas: Canadian Gas Association 2018 Pre-Budget Submission*.

Natural Resources Canada (NRCan). 2016. *Pipelines across Canada*. http://www.nrcan.gc.ca/energy/infrastructure/18856.

– 2017a. *2017 NGTL System Expansion Project*. https://www.nrcan.gc.ca/energy/resources/19124.

- 2017b. *2017 Transmountain Expansion Project.* https://www.nrcan. gc.ca/energy/resources/19142.
- 2017c. *Energy Pipeline Projects.* https://www.nrcan.gc.ca/energy/ resources/19120.
- 2017d. *General Information on Pipelines.* Section 1.4. https://www. nrcan.gc.ca/energy/infrastructure/5893.
- 2017e. *Line 3 Replacement.Project.* https://www.nrcan.gc.ca/energy/ resources/19188.
- 2017f. *Towerbirch Expansion Project.* https://www.nrcan.gc.ca/energy/ resources/19424.
- 2019. *Natural Resources Canada.* https://www.nrcan.gc.ca/home.

Naughton, John. 2012. *From Guttenberg to Zuckerberg: What You Really Need to Know about the Internet.* Toronto: Quercus.
- 2017a. "Move Fast and Break Things Review – Google, Facebook and Amazon Exposed." *The Guardian,* 17 April. https://www.theguardian. com/books/2017/apr/17/move-fast-and-break-things-review-google-facebook-amazon-exposed.
- 2017b. "Move Fast Zuckerberg, or It Will Kill Facebook." *The Guardian,* 28 May. https://www.theguardian.com/commentisfree/2017/ may/28/hate-speech-facebook-zuckerberg-content-moderators.
- 2017c. "Tech Giants Face No Contest When It Comes to Competition Law." *The Guardian,* 25 June. https://www.theguardian.com/ commentisfree/2017/jun/25/tech-giants-no-contest-on-competition-law-amazon-whole-foods.
- 2018a. "Has Zuckerberg, like Frankenstein, Lost Control of the Monster He Created?" *The Guardian,* 29 July. https://goldsteinreport.com/ has-zuckerberg-like-frankenstein-lost-control-of-the-monster-he-created.
- 2018b. "Magical Thinking about Machine Learning Won't Bring the Reality of AI Any Closer." *The Guardian,* 5 August. https://www. youtobia.com/book/pages/magical-thinking-about-machine-learning-wont--2226329761.
- 2019. "The White Paper on Online Harms Is a Global First. It Has Never Been More Needed." *The Guardian,* 4 April. https://www. theguardian.com/commentisfree/2019/apr/14/white-paper-online-harms-global-first-needed-tech-industry-dcms-google-facebook.

Nav Canada. 2014. *Annual Report 2014: Pushing Boundaries.* https://www.navcanada.ca/EN/media/Publications/AnnualReport-2014-EN.pdf.
- 2015a. *Annual Report 2015: Connections.* https://www.navcanada.ca/ EN/media/Publications/AnnualReport-2015-EN.pdf.

– 2015b. *The Test of Time. Nav Canada: How Nav Canada Really Works*. https://www.navcanada.ca/EN/media/Publications/Test%20of%20 Time-EN.pdf.

Noble, Bram. 2016. *Learning to Listen: Snapshots of Aboriginal Participation in Environmental Assessment*. Ottawa: MacDonald-Laurier Institute, July.

Northern Development Ministers Forum. 2010. *Northern Infrastructure*. Thunder Bay, ON: Northern Development Ministers Forum.

O'Doherty, Kieran, and Edna Einsiedel, eds. 2013. *Public Engagement and Emerging Technologies*. Vancouver, BC: UBC Press 2013.

OECD. 2008. *Protection of 'Critical Infrastructure' and the Role of Investment Policies Relating to National Security*. Paris: Organization for Economic Cooperation and Development, May.

– 2014. *The Impacts of Large Research Infrastructures on Economic Innovation and Society: Case Studies at CERN*. Paris: Organization for Economic Cooperation and Development.

– 2015a. *Fostering Investment Infrastructure*. Paris: Organization for Economic Cooperation and Development, January.

– 2015b. *Infrastructure Financing Instruments and Incentives*. Paris: Organization for Economic Cooperation and Development.

– 2015c. *Towards a Framework for the Governance of Infrastructure*. Paris: Organization for Economic Cooperation and Development, September.

– 2019. *Good Governance for Critical Infrastructure Resilience*. Paris: Organization for Economic Cooperation and Development, April.

Office of the Auditor General of Canada. 1996. Exhibit 26.1 http://publications.gc.ca/collections/collection_2015/bvg-oag/FA1-1-1996=eng.pdf (accessed 14 December 2018).

– 2010. *Report of the Auditor General of Canada*. Office of the Auditor General 2010: 1. p. 63–4. https://www.oag-bvg.gc.ca/internet/English/parl_oag_201010_e_34282.html.

– 2015. *PPP Canada Inc. – Special Examination Report*. http://www.oag-bvg.gc.ca/internet/English/parl_oag_201602_06_e_41250.html.

– 2017. *Independent Audit Report 6 – Civil Aviation Infrastructure in the North – Transport Canada*. https://www.oag-bvg.gc.ca/internet/English/parl_oag_201705_06_e_42228.html.

Office of the Auditor General for the Province of British Columbia. 2011. https://www.bcauditor.com/sites/default/files/publications/2011/report2/files/oagbc-understanding-p3-public-private-partnerships.pdf.

Office of the Chief Science Advisor. 2018. *Model Policy on Scientific Integrity*. Government of Canada. https://www.ic.gc.ca/eic/site/052.nsf/eng/00010.html.

Office of the Privacy Commissioner of Canada. 2012. *Annual Report to Parliament*. Ottawa: Office of the Privacy Commissioner of Canada.

Office of the Superintendent of Financial Institutions. 2017. *Our History*. https://www.osfi-bsif.gc.ca/Eng/osfi-bsif/Pages/hst.aspx.

O'Hara, Kathryn, and Paul Dufour. 2014. "How Accurate Is the Harper Government's Misinformation: Scientific Evidence and Scientists in Federal Policy Making." In *How Ottawa Spends 2014–2015: The Harper Government – Good to Go*, edited by G. Bruce Doern and Christopher Stoney, 178–91. Montreal, QC, and Kingston, ON: McGill-Queen's University Press.

O'Kane, Josh. 2019. "Indigenous Group Speaks Out over Grossly Misleading Sidewalk Labs Consultation." *Globe and Mail*, 26 October. https://www.theglobeandmail.com/business/article-indigenous-leaders-speak-out-over-grossly-misleading-sidewalk-labs.

Ontario Ministry of Finance. 2000. *Building Ontario's Future A SuperBuild Progress Report*. https://www.fin.gov.on.ca/en/publications/2000/sbfine00.html.

– 2017. *Ontario's Fair Housing Plan*. 20 April. https://news.ontario.ca/en/backgrounder/44468/ontarios-fair-housing-plan.

Ontario Ministry of Municipal Affairs and Ministry of Housing. 2016. *Ontario's Long-Term Affordable Housing Strategy Update*. March.

Ostrom, Elinor. 1990. *Governing the Commons: The Evolution of Institutions for Collective Action.* New York: Cambridge University Press.

– 2012. *The Future of the Commons: Beyond Market Failure and Government Regulation*. London: Institute of Economic Affairs.

Ostry, Sylvia. 1997. *The Post-Cold War Trading System: Who's on First?* Chicago, IL: University of Chicago Press.

Oved, Marco Chown. 2019. "How Waterfront Toronto's Stephen Diamond Went Up against Sidewalk Labs and Won." *Toronto Star*, 31 October.

Pagliaro, Jennifer, and Betsy Powell. 2017. "Unlicensed Group Home Operators Face New Health and Safety Violations." *Toronto Star*, 21 July. https://www.thestar.com/news/city_hall/2017/07/21/unlicensed-group-home-operators-face-new-health-and-safety-violations.html.

Pal, Leslie A. 2011. "Into the Wild: The Politics of Economic Stimulus." In *How Ottawa Spends 2011–2012: Trimming Fat or Slicing Pork,* edited by Christopher Stoney and G. Bruce Doern, 39–59. Montreal, QC: McQueen's University Press.

– 2014. *Beyond Policy Analysis: Public Issue Management in Turbulent Times*. Fifth Edition. Toronto: Nelson.

Pal, Leslie, and Judith Maxwell. 2003. *Assessing the Public Interest in the 21st Century: A Framework*. Paper prepared for the External Advisory Committee on Smart Regulation, Ottawa.

Panofsky, W.K.H. 1968. "Big Science and Graduate Education." In *Science Policy and the University*, edited by H. Orlans, 189–206. Washington, DC: The Brookings Institution.

Parent, Louis-Martin, and Emile Poitevin. 2016. *Beyond the Big Idea: Redefining and Rethinking the Innovation Agenda*. Canadian Federation of Independent Business, Ottawa: October.

Parliamentary Budget Officer. 2010. *Report: Economic and Fiscal Assessment*. Office of the Parliamentary Budget Officer, 3 November. https://www.pbo-dpb.gc.ca/web/default/files/files/files/Publications/ EFA_2010.pdf.

Patenaude, Jean. 2016. "Recent Public Policy Initiatives in Respect of Railway Services." 51st Annual Conference, Canadian Transportation Research Forum, 1–4 May. https://ctrf.ca/wp-content/uploads/2016/05/ CTRF2016PatenaudeRailTransport.pdf.

Pedwell, Terry. 2016. "CRTC Declares Broadband Internet a Basic Service." *Toronto Star*, 21 December. https://www.thestar.com/news/canada/ 2016/12/21/crtc-declares-broadband-internet-a-basic-service-like -telephone.html.

Pembina Institute. 2014. *Fast Cities: A Comparison of Rapid Transit in Major Canadian Cities*. Toronto: Pembina Institute. https://www. pembina.org/reports/fast-cities-summary.pdf.

Penn, Ivan. 2018. "The $3 Billion Plan to Turn Hoover Dam into a Giant Battery." *New York Times*, 24 July. https://www.nytimes.com/interactive/ 2018/07/24/business/energy-environment/hoover-dam-renewable- energy.html.

Penner, Derrick. 2017. "B.C. Joins Legal Battles Against Trans Mountain Pipeline Expension." *Vancouver Sun*, 10 August. https://vancouversun. com/news/local-news/ live-b-c-government-to-announce-steps-against-trans-mountain-pipeline.

Perry, David. 2018. *Following the Funding in Strong, Secure, Engaged*. Prepared for the Canadian Global Affairs Institute, Calgary. https:// www.cgai.ca/following_the_funding_in_strong_secure_engaged.

Peterborough.ca. 2020. "Support for 24/7 Intake for Housing and Homelessness Services." 17 August. https://www.peterborough.ca/en/news/support-for-24-7-intake-for-housing-and-homelessness-services.aspx.

Petroski, Henry. 2016. *The Road Taken: The History and Future of America's Infrastructure*. New York. Bloomsbury.

Petty, Kathleen. 2019. "Does West Want Out? Not Really but the Rallying Cry Needs to Be Heard." *CBC News*, 4 October. https://www.cbc.ca/news/canada/calgary/west-of-centre-alienation-kathleen-petty-1.5306529.

Phillips, Peter W.B. 2007. *Governing Transformative Technological Innovation: Who's in Charge?* London: Edward Elgar.

Phillips, Peter W.B., and James Nolan. 2007. *Strategic Options in Canadian Transportation Policy: The Interface Between Trade Pressures and Domestic Policy*. Paper presented at International Conference on Transport Gateways. Winnipeg, 24–27 April 2007. https://www.academia.edu/24633498/Strategic_Options_in_Canadian_Transport_Policy_The_Interface_between_Trade_Pressures_and_Domestic_Policy.

Phillips, R.A.J. 1967. *Canada's North*. New York: St Martin's Press.

Phillipson, Donald J.C. 1991. "The National Research Council of Canada: Its Historiography, Its Chronology, Its Bibliography." *Scientia Canadensis* 15, no. 2: 177–97.

Pittis, Don. 2017. "Don't Expect Government Meddling in the Housing Market to Fix It." *CBC News*, 22 November. https://www.cbc.ca/news/business/housing-canada-policy-market-1.4413882.

Plamondon, Aaron. 2010. *The Politics of Procurement*. Vancouver, BC: UBC Press.

Poschmann, Finn. 2020. *Fiscal Policy and Recessions: The Role of Public Infrastructure Spending*. Vancouver, BC: Fraser Institute. https://www.fraserinstitute.org/studies/fiscal-policy-and-recessions.

PPP Canada. 2009a. "Public Private Partnerships: Building Infrastructure." 2008–09 Annual Report.

– 2009b. "Summary Amended Corporate Plan 2008 to 2012, Summary Amended Operating And Capital Budgets 2008."

– 2015–16. "Summary Corporate Plan for the 2015–16 to 2019–20 Planning Period."

– 2016. "Public Private Partnerships: Transforming Infrastructure Delivery." Annual Report 2015–16.

Pratte, Steve. 2016. "Government Hopper Cars and the Canadian Grain Handling and Transportation System." *Canadian Transportation*

Research Forum, Proceedings Issue, 51st Annual Meeting: 464–71.
https://www.ccga.ca/policy/Documents/hopper_cars_grain_handling_
transport.pdf.

Prentice, Barry E. 2010. *Transport Challenges and Opportunities in the
North*. Presentation to Supply Chain Connections 2010: Northern
Exposure Conference, Supply Chain Management, Winnipeg, School of
Business, University of Manitoba, 29–30 September. https://umanitoba.
ca/faculties/management/ti/media/docs/barry_prentice.pdf.

– 2015a. "Canadian Airport Security: The Privatization of a Public
Good." *Journal of Air Transport Management* 48: 52–9.

– 2015b. "Peak-Load Management and Surge Capacity in Western Grain
Transportation." *Canadian Transportation Research Forum, Proceedings
Issue, 50th Annual Meeting*: 382–96. https://www.researchgate.net/
publication/281100470_PEAK-LOAD_MANAGEMENT_AND_SURGE_
CAPACITY_IN_WESTERN_CANADIAN_GRAIN_TRANSPORTATION.

– 2016. *Transport Airships for Northern Logistics: Technology for the
21st Century*. Supply Chain Management, Winnipeg, School of Business,
University of Manitoba. https://www.academia.edu/14632489/Transport_
Airships_for_Northern_Logistics_Technology_for_the_21st_Century.

Prentice, Barry E., Jake Kosior, and Bob McLeod. 1996. *Agriculture
Trucking in Manitoba*. Winnipeg, University of Manitoba, Transport
Institute, Research Bulletin #16. https://www.umanitoba.ca/faculties/
management/ti/media/docs/Agriculture_Trucking_MB_1996.pdf.

Press, Jordan. 2017. "Canadian Census 2016: Big Cities Getting Bigger
as Smaller Cities Getting Smaller." *National Post*, 6 February. https://
nationalpost.com/news/canada/canadian-census-2016-big-cities-getting-
bigger-as-smaller-cities-getting-smaller.

Preston, Benjamin. 2017. "Fixing America's Failing Infrastructure Won't
Be Easy, Despite Trump's Pledge." *The Guardian*, 4 March. https://www.
theguardian.com/us-news/2017/mar/04/donald-trump-infrastructure-plan-
roads-highway-trust-fund.

Pretto, Andre, and Joseph F. Schulman. 2015. *Canada-United States
Freight Rail Economic Regulation Comparison*. Paper presented to the
Canadian Transport Research Forum, Toronto, 10 May.

Prime Minister of Canada. 2016. *Minister of Transport Mandate Letter*.
http://pm.gc.ca/eng/minister-transport-mandate-letter.

– 2019. Minister of Infrastructure and Communities Mandate Letter.
https://pm.gc.ca/en/mandate-letters/2019/12/13/minister-infrastructure-
and-communities-mandate-letter (accessed 20 December 2019).

Prince, Michael J. 1995. "The Canadian Housing Policy Context."
    Housing Policy Debate 6, no. 3: 721–58.
– 1999. "Civic Regulation: Regulating Citizenship, Morality, Social Order
    and the Welfare State." In *Changing the Rules: Canadian Regulatory
    Regimes and Institutions*, edited by Bruce Doern, Margaret Hill, Michael
    Prince, and Richard Schultz, 201–27. Toronto: University of Toronto Press.
– 2003. "Taking Stock: Governance Practices and Portfolio Performance
    of the Canada Pension Plan Investment Board." In *How Ottawa Spends
    2003–2004: Regime Change and Policy Shift*, edited by G. Bruce Doern,
    134–54. Oxford, UK: Oxford University Press.
Proctor, Jason. 2018. "High Noon at the Oasis: BC Airbnb Hostel Battle
    Erupts into the Open." *CBC News*, 28 July. https://www.cbc.ca/news/
    canada/british-columbia/airbnb-strata-fight-emily-yu-1.4765183.
Prud'Homme, Alex. 2014. *Hydrofracking*. Oxford, UK: Oxford University
    Press.
Public Policy Forum. 2016. *Building the Future: Strategic Infrastructure
    for Long-Term Growth in Canada*. 13 October. https://www.
    infrastructureontario.ca/uploadedFiles/_PAGES/News_and_Media/
    Third_Party_Reports/PPF_Building_Future_INTERIM_Report.pdf.
– 2017. *The Shattered Mirror: News, Democracy and Trust in the Digital
    Age*. January. https://shatteredmirror.ca.
– 2018a. *Independent and Accountable: Modernizing the Role of Agents
    of Parliament and Legislatures*. April. https://ppforum.ca/publications/
    independent-accountable.
– 2018b. *The Next-Level Border: Advancing Technology and Expanding
    Trade*. Summary Report, July 30. https://ppforum.ca/publications/
    the-next-level-border-advancing-technology-expanding-trade.
– 2018c. *Ontario Digital Inclusion Summit: Summary Report*. May.
    https://ppforum.ca/publications/ontario-digital-inclusion-summit-
    summary-report.
Public Safety Canada. 2014[–17]. *Action Plan for Critical Infrastructure*.
    https://www.publicsafety.gc.ca/cnt/rsrcs/pblctns/pln-crtcl-nfrstrctr-2014-
    17/index-en.aspx.
– 2019. *National Cyber Security Action Plan (2019–2024)*. https://
    www.publicsafety.gc.ca/cnt/rsrcs/pblctns/ntnl-cbr-scrt-strtg-2019/index-
    en.aspx.
Public Services and Procurement Canada. 2017. *Buying and Selling*.
Purdon, Nick, and Leonardo Palleja. 2019. "'I wanna own this thing.'
    Meet the Indigenous Groups Trying to Buy the Trans Mountain

Pipeline." *CBC News*, 5 October. https://www.cbc.ca/news/canada/
trans-mountain-pipeline-first-nations-purchase-1.5279387.

Pursaga, Joyanne. 2017. "Lodges Cry Foul over Regulations Imbalance:
Association Plans One-Day Strike in Protest." *Winnipeg Sun*, 27 July.
https://triblive.com/news/world/protesters-crying-foul-over-vote-counts-
stir-safety-concerns.

Quigley, Kevin, Ben Bisset, and Bryan Mills. 2017. *Too Critical to Fail:
How Canada Manages Threats to Critical Infrastructure*. Montreal,
QC, and Kingston, ON: McGill-Queen's University Press.

Rainie, Lee, and Barry Wellman. 2012. *Networked: The New Social
Operating System*. Cambridge, MA: MIT Press.

Raj, Althia. 2009a. "Baird: Not My Job to Track Cash." *Calgary Sun*,
30 July.

– 2009b. "Job Creation Numbers Remain a Mystery." *Ottawa Sun*,
1 September.

Ratner, J.B. 1983. "Government Capital and the Production Function
for U.S. Private Output." *Economics Letters* 13: 213–17.

Raworth, Kate. 2017. *Doughnut Economics*. London: Penguin Random
House.

Reich, Robert. 2020. "Donald Trump Rushed to Reopen America –
Now Covid Is Closing in on Him." *The Guardian*, 5 July. https://www.
theguardian.com/commentisfree/2020/jul/05/donald-trump-reopen-
america-covid-19-coronavirus.

Revie, R. Winston, ed. 2015. *Oil and Gas Pipelines: Integrity and Safety
Handbook*. New York: John Wiley and Sons.

Rice, James J., and Michael J. Prince. 2000. *Changing Politics of Canadian
Social Policy*. Toronto: University of Toronto Press.

Rieger, Sarah. 2019. "'It's Time for Ottawa to Start Working for Us': Alberta
Looks to Gain More Provincial Autonomy." *CBC News*, 9 November.

– 2020. "WestJet Lays Off 3,333 Workers as Pandemic Continues to Wipe
Out Demand for Air Travel." *CBC News*, 24 June. https://calgaryherald.
com/business/local-business/westjet-lays-off-3333-employees-as-the-
calgary-based-airline-continues-to-struggle-in-face-of-covid-19.

Robins, Steven. 2017. *A Better Flight Plan: How Ottawa Can Cash in on
Airports and Benefit Travellers*. Toronto: C.D. Howe Institute, Essential
Policy Intelligence, 7 February. https://www.cdhowe.org/public-policy-
research/better-flight-path-how-ottawa-can-cash-airports-and-
benefit-travellers.

Rocha, Roberto. 2019. "As the Popularity of Drones Explodes, So Do the Risks to Airplanes." CBC News, 12 January. https://www.cbc.ca/news/canada/drone-airline-airport-incidents-data-canada-1.4973888.

Rohmer, R. 1970. *Essays on Mid-Canada*. Toronto: Mid-Canada Development Foundation.

Rose, Albert. 1983. *Canadian Housing Policies 1935–1980*. Toronto: Butterfield and Co.

Rotman School of Management. 2017. *U of T's Creative Destruction Lab Announces National Expansion*. Toronto: University of Toronto, 18 May. https://www.creativedestructionlab.com/2017/05/cdl-announces-national-expansion-3-new-sites.

Rousseau, Marie-Helene, and Claude Rivest. 2018. "What the Jury in the Lac-Megantic Trial Didn't Hear." CBC News, 11 January. https://www.cbc.ca/news/canada/montreal/lac-m%C3%A9gantic-rail-disaster-1.4481968.

Royal Commission on Aboriginal Peoples. 1996. *Report of the Royal Commission on Aboriginal Peoples*. https://www.bac-lac.gc.ca/eng/discover/aboriginal-heritage/royal-commission-aboriginal-peoples/Pages/final-report.aspx.

Ruffilli, Dean. 2011. *Arctic Marine and Intermodal Infrastructure: Challenges and the Government of Canada's Response*. Library of Parliament. In Brief publication No. 2011-77-E, 21 July.

Rushowy, Kristin, and Ben Spurr. 2018. "Subway Lines to Pickering, Markham, in the Long-Term, Says Doug Ford." *Toronto Star*, 21 June. https://www.thestar.com/news/queenspark/2018/06/21/subway-lines-to-pickering-markham-in-the-long-term-says-doug-ford.html.

Saskatchewan Housing Corporation. 2016. *Annual Report for 2016*. Regina: Government of Saskatchewan.

Satariano, Adam. 2018. "G.D.P.R., a Privacy Law Europe World's Leading Tech Watchdog." *New York Times*, 24 May. https://www.nytimes.com/2018/05/24/technology/europe-gdpr-privacy.html.

Savage, Luiza Ch. 2015. "Land of the Freeloaders: The Battle for a New Cross-Border Bridge." *Maclean's*, 21 May. http://www.macleans.ca/news/canada/land-of-the-freeloaders.

Scaffold Industry Association of Canada. 2019. *Types of Scaffolding*. http://www.siac-ontario.com/types-of-scaffolding (accessed 23 March 2019).

Schabas, Michael. 2019. *Transit Governance that Works: Who Plans? Who Pays? Who Delivers? Why Does It Matter?* Toronto: Institute on

Municipal Finance and Governance, Munk School–University of Toronto, 21 February. https://munkschool.utoronto.ca/imfg/event/governance-models-for-successful-regional-transit-who-owns-it-who-pays-for-it-who-delivers-it.

Schmunk, Rhianna. 2018. "$40B LNG Project in Northern B.C. Gets Go-Ahead." *CBC News*, 2 October. https://www.cbc.ca/news/canada/british-columbia/kitimat-lng-canada-1.4845831.

Schneier, Bruce. 2015. *Data and Goliath: The Hidden Battles to Collect Your Data and Control Your World*. New York: W.W. Norton.

Schultz, Kenneth A. 1995. "The Politics of the Political Business Cycle." *British Journal of Political Science* 25: 79–99.

Schumpeter, Joseph A. 1934. *The Theory of Economic Development*. Cambridge, MA: Harvard Economic Studies.

– 1942. *Capitalism, Socialism and Democracy*. New York: Harper and Brothers.

– 1954. *History of Economic Analysis*. London: Allen and Unwin.

Scoffield, Heather. 2010. "Stimulus a Job Flop, Survey Suggests Economic Action Plan Didn't Create Much Employment, Poorly Tracked." *The Canadian Press*, 2 December.

Scotiabank. 2016. *2016 Annual Report: Banking the Real Economy*.

– 2017. *Corporate Profile*. https://www.scotiabank.com/ca/en/about/our-company/corporate-profile.html.

Seskus, Tony. 2019. "Why Alberta's Review of Its Energy Watchdog Is Vital to Get Right – and Difficult to Do." *CBC News*, 9 November. https://www.cbc.ca/news/business/alberta-energy-regulator-review-1.5329044.

Sell, Susan. 1998. *Power and Ideas: North-South Politics of Intellectual Property and Antitrust*. New York: State University of New York Press.

Selley, Chris. 2017. "Toronto's Transit Remains at the Mercy of Queen's Park's Whims." *National Post*, 8 March.

Senate of Canada. 2017. "Smarter Planning, Smarter Spending: Achieving Infrastructure Success." Ottawa: Report of the National Standing Senate Committee on National Finance, February.

Sengupta, Kim. 2020. "A Decision with Global Intelligence Repercussions." *The Independent*, 21 January. https://www.independent.co.uk/news/science/artificial-intelligence-diversity-problem-data-reliance-a9161351.html.

Shecter, Barbara, and Drew Hasselback. 2016. "Trudeau's Investment Pitch Wins Praise as Ottawa Courts World's Most Powerful Investors." *Financial Post*, 14 November. https://financialpost.com/news/economy/

trudeaus-investment-pitch-wins-praise-as-ottawa-courts-worlds-most-powerful-investors.

Sherman, Natalie. 2017. "Are Google, Amazon and Others Getting Too Big." *BBC News*, 9 June. http://www.bbc.co.uk/news/business-39875417.

Sherwood, Harriet. 2019. "How Airbnb Took Over the World." *The Guardian*, 5 May. https://www.theguardian.com/technology/2019/may/05/airbnb-homelessness-renting-housing-accommodation-social-policy-cities-travel-leisure.

Shingler, Benjamin, and Kate McKenna. 2016. "Quebec Fails to Follow Through on Charbonneau Recommendations, Watchdog Group Says." *CBC News*, 23 November. https://www.cbc.ca/news/canada/montreal/charbonneau-report-independent-committee-corruption-1.3862914.

Shore, Jacques J.M. 2008. *The Legal Imperative to Protect Critical Energy Infrastructure*. Ottawa: Canadian Centre of Intelligence and Security Studies, Carleton University, March. http://cip.management.dal.ca/publications/The%20Legal%20Imperative%20to%20Protect%20critical%20energy%20infrastructure.pdf.

Shrivastava, M., and Lorna Stefanick, eds. 2016. *Alberta Oil and the Decline of Democracy in Canada*. Athabasca, AB: Athabasca University Press.

Shull, Aaron. 2019. "Canada and Cyber Governance." 17 November. https://www.cigionline.org/articles/canada-and-cyber-governance.

Siddall, Evan. 2017. *No Solitudes: A Canadian National Housing Strategy*. Presentation to Canadian Club of Toronto, Toronto, 1 June. https://www.cmhc-schl.gc.ca/en/corp/nero/sp/2017/2017=05-01-1245-cfm.

Siemiatycki, Matti. 2012. *Is There a Distinct Canadian PPP Model? Reflections on Twenty Years of Practice*. CBS-Sauder-Monash Public-Private Partnership Conference Series. Vancouver, BC: University of British Columbia. http://www.bahamasengineers.org/cms/wp-content/uploads/Dr.-Siemiatycki_UniversityofToronto_BSE-2014-Presentation.pdf.

– 2016. *Implementing a Canadian Infrastructure Investment Agency*. Paper prepared for the Residential and Civil Construction Alliance of Ontario. https://www.tarba.org/wp-content/uploads/2017/09/2016-implementing-a-canadian-infrastructure-investment-agency.pdf.

– 2018. "Cost Overruns on Infrastructure Projects: Patterns, Causes, and Cures." In *Canada: The State of the Federation 2015: Canadian Federalism and Infrastructure*, edited by John B. Allan, David L.A. Gordon, Kyle Hanniman, and Andre Juneau, 125–40. Montreal, QC, and Kingston, ON: McGill-Queen's University Press 2018.

Silver, Sheldon. 1968. "The Feasibility of a Municipal Income Tax in Canada." *Canadian Tax Journal* XVI, no. 5 (September–October): 398–407.

Slack, Enid, and Richard Bird. 2018. "Financing Regional Public Transit in Ontario: The Case for Strengthening the Wickscellian Connection." In *Canada: The State of the Federation 2015: Canadian Federalism and Infrastructure*, edited by John B. Allan, David L.A. Gordon, Kyle Hanniman, and Andre Juneau, 45–74. Montreal, QC, and Kingston, ON: McGill-Queen's University Press 2018.

Slack, Enid, Larry S. Bourne, and Merc S. Gertler. 2003. "Vibrant Cities and City-Regions: Responding to Emerging Challenges." Paper prepared for the Panel on the Role of Government, Kingston, ON, 13 August. http://www.probeinternational.org/old_drupal/UrbanNewSite/rural2.pdf.

Slee, Tom. 2016. *What's Yours Is Mine: Against the Sharing Economy*. New York: OR Books.

Smith, Mitch. 2017. "Nebraska Regulators Approve Alternative Route for Keystone XL Pipeline." *New York Times*, 20 November. https://www.cbc.ca/news/business/nebraska-keystone-1.4409960.

Snyder, J. 2020a. "Canada's Fiscal Snapshot Predicts $343 Billion Deficit as Liberals Offer Little Intention to Curb Spending." https://nationalpost.com/news/politics/liberals-fiscal-snapshot-predicts-343-billion-deficit-as-bill-morneau-offers-little-intention-to-curb-spending.

– 2020b. "A Public Relations Campaign: Some Provinces at Odds with Trudeau Government over COVID-19 Infrastructure Plans." *National Post*, 18 June.

Solon, Olivia, and Emma Graham-Harrison. 2018. "The Six Weeks that Brought Cambridge Analytica Down." *The Guardian*, 3 May. https://www.theguardian.com/uk-news/2018/may/03/cambridge-analytica-closing-what-happened-trump-brexit.

Sorensen, Chris, and Jason Kirby. 2011. "The CMHC: Canada's Mortgage Monster." *Maclean's*, 23 March. http://www.macleans.ca/economy/business/a-mortgage-monster.

Soroka, Stuart N. 2002. *Agenda-Setting Dynamics in Canada*. Vancouver, BC: UBC Press.

Spacey, Mason. 2017. "11 Types of Economic Infrastructure." *Simplicable*. https://simplicable.com/new/economic-infrastructure.

Spence, Jennifer. 2014. "The National Shipbuilding Model for Government Procurement: Separating the Wheat from the Chaff." In *How Ottawa Spends 2014–2015: The Harper Government – Good to Go*, edited by G. Bruce Doern and Christopher Stoney, 165–77. Montreal, QC: McGill-Queen's University Press.

Spurr, Ben. 2017. "How Do TTC's Streetcar Options Compare? It's Bombardier versus Alstom." *Toronto Star*, 13 May. https://www.thestar.com/news/gta/2017/05/13/how-do-ttcs-streetcar-options-compare-its-bombardier-versus-alstom.html.

Spurr, Ben, E. Keenan, Marco Chown Oved, Jayme Poisson, Marina Jimenez, and D. Rider. 2017. *Inside Bombardier's Delayed Streetcar Deliveries: Not in Service*. https://projects.thestar.com/bombardier-ttc.

St Lawrence Seaway Development Corporation. 2015a. *Annual Corporate Summary 2014–2015*. Massena, NY: St Lawrence Seaway Management Corporation.

– 2015b. *Corporate Social Responsibility*. Massena, NY: St Lawrence Seaway Management Corporation.

– 2015c. *Fiscal Year 2015 Annual Report*. Massena, NY: Author.

Standing Committee on Public Accounts. 1998. *Transport Canada: The Commercialization of the Air Navigation System*. Fourth Report. Ottawa: House of Commons.

Standing Committee on Transport, Infrastructure and Communities. 2013. *Innovative Transportation Technologies*. Ottawa: House of Commons, 41st Parliament, 1st Session, February.

– 2015. *Review of the Canadian Transportation Safety Regime: Transportation of Dangerous Goods and Safety Management* Systems. Ottawa: House of Commons, 41st Parliament, 2nd Session, March.

Standing Senate Committee on Transport and Communications. 2013. *One Size Doesn't Fit All: The Future Growth and Competitiveness of Canadian Air Travel*. Ottawa: April.

Stanford Global Projects Center. 2017. *US Federal Infrastructure Policy: Opportunities For Change*. Palo Alto, CA: Stanford University.

Staples, David. 2019. "Greta Thunberg Gracious and Articulate in Alberta But Needs to Do More Homework on Climate Change." *Edmonton Journal*, 12 November. https://edmontonjournal.com/news/politics/election-2019/david-staples-a-gracious-greta-thunberg-thanked-alberta-for-warm-welcome-but-was-short-on-answers-for-climate-change.

Startup Canada. 2017. *About*. https://www.startupcan.ca/2017/10/2017-national-startup-canada-award-winners-celebrated-ottawa.

Statistics Canada. 2016. *Investment in Non-Residential Building Construction*. Statistics Canada: The Daily. 14 October. https://www150.statcan.gc.ca/t1/tbl1/en/tv.action?pid=3410001101.

– 2017a. *Building Permits: Chart 1*. https://www150.statcan.gc.ca/t1/tbl1/en/tv.action?pid=3410006601.

– 2017b. *Building Permits: Chart 5.* https://www150.statcan.gc.ca/t1/tbl1/en/tv.action?pid=3410006601.

– 2017c. *Construction.* Statistics Canada. https://www150.statcan.gc.ca/n1/en/subjects/Construction.

Stephenson, Amanda. 2017. "Alberta Hotel Association Argues for Regulation of Airbnb and Other Vacation Rentals." *Calgary Herald,* 9 January. https://calgaryherald.com/business/local-business/hotels-association-urging-regulation-of-airbnb-and-other-vacation-rentals-in-alberta.

Stevenson, Don, and Richard Gilbert. 2005. "Coping with Canadian Federalism: The Case of the Federation of Canadian Municipalities." *Canadian Public Administration* 48, no. 4 (Winter): 528–51.

Stoney, Chris. 2016. "Challenges for Smart Growth: Governing from the Periphery." Presentation to joint meeting of the Chartered Institute of Logistics and Transport in North America and Carleton University School of Public Policy and Administration. Ottawa, 5 October.

Stoney, Christopher, and K. Graham. 2009. "Federal-Municipal Relations in Canada: The Changing Organizational Landscape." *Canadian Public Administration* 3, no. 52: 371–94.

Stoney, Chris, and T. Krawchenko. 2012. "Transparency and Accountability in Infrastructure Stimulus Spending: A Comparison of Canadian, Australian and US Programs." *Canadian Public Administration* 55, no. 4 (December): 481–503.

Stopher, Peter, and John Stanley. 2014. *Introduction to Transport Policy: A Public Policy View.* Cheltenham, UK: Edward Elgar.

Struzik, Ed. 2016. "Once Unstoppable, Tar Sands Now Battered from All Sides." *Yale Environment 150,* 1 February. https://e360.yale.edu/features/once-unstoppable_tar_sands_now_battered_from_all_sides.

Sulzenko, Andrei, and G. Kent Fellows. 2016. "Planning for Infrastructure to Realize Canada's Potential: The Corridor Concept." *University of Calgary, School of Public Policy, SPP Research Papers* 9, no. 22 (May): 1–43.

Sundararajan, Arun. 2016. *The Sharing Economy.* Cambridge, MA: MIT Press.

Sussman, G. 1978. *The St. Lawrence Seaway: History and Analysis of a Joint Water Highway.* Toronto: C.D. Howe Research Institute.

Suttor, Greg. 2016. *Still Renovating: A History of Canadian Social Housing.* Montreal, QC, and Kingston, ON: McGill-Queen's University Press.

Swanson, Ana. 2018. "Boeing Denied Bid for Tariffs on Canadian Jets." *New York Times,* 26 January. https://www.nytimes.com/2018/01/26/us/politics/boeing-bombardier-tariffs.html.

Swift, Catherine. 2016. "The Big Infrastructure Ripoff." *Financial Post,* 15 January. https://financialpost.com/opinion/the-big-infrastructure-ripoff.

Taplin, Jonathan. 2017a. "Is It Time to Break-up Google?" *New York Times,* 22 April. https://www.nytimes.com/2017/04/22/opinion/sunday/is-it-time-to-break-up-google.html.

– 2017b. *Move Fast and Break Things: How Facebook, Google and Amazon Cornered Culture and Undermined Democracy.* New York: Little Brown and Company.

Taylor, Matthew, Nick Hopkins, and Jenima Kiss. 2013. "NSA Surveillance May Cause Break-up of the Internet, Warn Experts." *The Guardian,* 1 November. https://www.theguardian.com/world/2013/nov/01/nsa-surveillance-cause-internet-breakup-edward-snowden.

TD Economics. 2002. "Special Report: A Choice between Investing in Canada's Cities and Disinvesting in Canada's Future." https://www.torontopubliclibrary.ca/detail.jsp?Entt=RDM566069&R=566069.

– 2015. *Canada's Non-Residential Construction Outlook: Weaknesses in Oil Patch Will Conceal Pockets of Solid Growth.* Toronto: TD Economics, 27 May. https://www.td.com/document/PDF/economics/special/Non_Residential_Construction_Outlook.pdf.

– 2017a. *Canadian Regional Housing Outlook: Navigating a Soft Landing.* Toronto: TD Economics, 28 August. https://economics.td.com/canadian-regional-housing-outlook-aug-2017.

– 2017b. *Toronto Housing: The Heat Is on Buyers Caught up in the Action.* Toronto: TD Economics, 20 March. https://economics.td.com/toronto-housing-heat-is-on.

Telford, Rachel. 2015. *The St. Lawrence Seaway: Investments and Changing Regulations.* Ontario Grain Farmer. https://ontariograinfarmer.ca/2015/09/01/the-st-lawrence-seaway.

Thierer, Adam. 2014. *Permissionless Innovation: The Continuing Case for Comprehensive Technological Freedom.* Arlington, VA: Mercatus Center, George Mason University.

Thistle, Mel. 1965. *The Inner Ring.* Toronto: University of Toronto Press.

Thomasson, Scott. 2012. *Encouraging U.S. Infrastructure Investment.* Council on Foreign Relations. Policy Innovation Memorandum No. 17. April.

Thompson, G., J. Frances, R. Levacic, and J. Mitchell, eds. 1991. *Markets, Hierarchies and Networks: The Coordination of Social Life.* Thousand Oaks, CA: Sage Publishers.

Thrush, Glenn, and Maggie Haberman. 2017. "Trump Weighs Infrastructure Bill but Keeps New York Up in the Air." *New York Times,* 5 April. https://www.nytimes.com/2017/04/05/us/politics/donald-trump-infrastructure-bill.html.

Tindal, Richard C., and Susan N. Tindal. 2000. *Local Government in Canada,* 5th ed. Scarborough, ON: Thomson Nelson.

– 2004. *Local Government in Canada,* 6th ed. Scarborough, ON: Nelson.

Toner, Glen, David Cherniak, and Kevin Force. 2016. "Liberal Energy and Climate Change Governance: The Energy/Environment Domain Post-Harper." In *How Ottawa Spends 2016–2017: The Trudeau Liberals in Power,* edited by G. Bruce Doern and Christopher Stoney, 167–90. Ottawa: School of Public Policy and Administration, Carleton University.

Toplensky, Rochelle. 2017. "Brussels' 2.4 bn Euro Fine for Goggle Raises Stakes in Transatlantic Tussle." *Financial Times,* 28 June. https://www.cnbc.com/2017/06/27/eu-hits-google-with-a-record-antitrust-fine-of-2-point-7-billion.html.

Toronto Star Editorial Board. 2017. "On Housing, Ottawa Must Follow Through on Its Fine Words: Editorial." *Toronto Star,* 22 November. https://www.thestar.com/opinion/editorials/2017/11/22/on-housing-ottawa-must-follow-through-on-its-fine-words-editorial.html.

Transit Toronto. 2015. *A Brief History of Transit in Toronto.* http://transit.toronto.on.ca/spare/0012.shtml.

Transport Canada. 2016a. *Transportation of Dangerous Goods. Who We Are.* http://www.tc.gc.ca/eng/tdg/who-233.htm.

– 2016b. *Transportation of Dangerous Goods General Policy Advisory Council.* http://www.tc.gc.ca/eng/tdg/consult-advisorycouncil-488.htm.

Transport Canada, US Army Corps of Engineers, US Department of Transportation, St Lawrence Seaway Management Corporation, Saint Lawrence Seaway Development Corporation, Environment Canada, and US Fish and Wildlife Service. 2007. *The Great Lakes St. Lawrence Seaway Study.* Final Report. Ottawa and Washington.

Transportation Safety Board of Canada. 2016. *Lac-Megantic Runaway Train and Derailment Investigation Summary.* https://www.tsb.gc.ca/eng/rapports-reports/rail.

Treasury Board Secretariat. 2008. "Accounting Standard 3.2 - Transfer Payments (Grants and Contributions)." https://www.tbs-sct.gc.ca/pol/doc-eng.aspx?id=12257&section=html.

– 2013. *Cabinet Directive on Regulatory Management*. Ottawa. https://www.
canada.ca/en/government/system/laws/developing-improving-federal-
regulations/requirements-developing-managing-reviewing-regulations/
guidelines-tools/cabinet-directive-regulatory-management.html.

– 2015. "Border Infrastructure Fund. Performance Highlights."
30 November. https://www.infrastructure.gc.ca/pd-dp/eval/2014-
csif-bif-fcis-fif-eng.html.

Trebilcock, Michael J. 2011. *Understanding Trade Law*. London:
Edward Elgar.

Trebilcock, Michael J., and Robert House. 1995. *The Regulation
of International Trade*, 2nd ed. London: Routledge.

Trebilcock, Michael, Robert House, and Antonia Eliason. 2013.
International Trade, 4th ed. London: Routledge.

Truth and Reconciliation Commission of Canada (TRC). 2015. *TRC
Recommendations* http://trc.ca/assets/pdf/Calls_to_Action_English2.pdf.

Tumin, Zachary. 1998. *Connecting Canadians: Canada's Community
Access Program*. Boston, MA: Harvard Information Infrastructure
Project. John F. Kennedy School of Government. http://nshdpi.ca/is/
connect-canadians.html.

Turk, Eli. 1998. *Canada's Strategy for the Information Highway*.
Harvard Information Infrastructure Project. John F. Kennedy School
of Government.

Urquhart, Ian. 2018. *Costly Fix: Power, Politics and Nature in the Tar
Sands*. Toronto: University of Toronto Press.

US Committee on the Marine Transportation System. 2016. *A Ten-Year
Prioritization of Infrastructure Needs in the U. S. Arctic*. Prepared for
the US Department of Transportation.

Valverde, Marianna. 2019. "Safe As Houses." *The Independent*,
27 January. https://www.independent.co.uk/property/house-and-home/
safe-as-houses-if-you-want-a-really-secure-home-its-all-about-the-
hardware-2211228.html.

Van der Heijden, Jeroen. 2017. "Brighter and Darker Sides of
Intermediation: Target-Oriented and Self-Interested Intermediaries in
the Regulatory Governance of Buildings." In *Regulatory Intermediaries
in the Age of Governance*, edited by Abbott, Kenneth W., David Levi-
Faur, and Duncan Snidal, ch. 11. The Annals of the American Academy
of Political and Social Science. Vol. 670, Issue 1.

Van Harten, Gus, Geraild Heckman, and David Mullan. 2010.
Administrative Law: Cases, Text and Materials, 6th ed. Toronto:
Edmond Montgomery.

Van Praet, N. 2020. "SNC Eyes Infrastructure Spending in New Push to Governments." *Globe and Mail*, 14 May. https://www.theglobeandmail.com/business/article-snc-lavalin-offers-to-help-governments-speed-infrastructure-spending.

Van Wee, Bert, Jan Anne Annema, and David Banister, eds. 2013. *The Transport System and Transport Policy*. Cheltenham, UK: Edward Elgar.

Von Scheel, Elise. 2018. "Saskatchewan Would Support Alberta's Decision to Turn Off Oil Taps." *CBC News*, 17 March. https://www.cbc.ca/news/politics/saskatchewan-alberta-bc-pipeline-trans-mountain-expansion-1.4580650.

Wachsmuth, David, Dannielle Kerrigan, David Chaney, and Andrea Shillolo. 2017. *Short-Term Cities: Airbnb's Impact on Canadian Housing Markets*. A report from the Urban Politics and Urban Politics and Governance research group. Montreal, QC: School of Urban Planning, McGill University, 10 August. https://upgo.lab.mcgill.ca/publication/short-term-cities.

Walby, Sylvia. 2007. "Complexity Theory, Systems Theory, and Multiple Intersecting Social Inequalities." *Philosophy of the Social Sciences* 37, no. 4: 449–70.

Walkom, Thomas. 2018. "Nationalizing Trans Mountain Pipeline a Big Mistake." *Toronto Star*, 29 May. https://www.thestar.com/opinion/star-columnists/2018/05/29/nationalizing-trans-mountain-pipeline-a-big-mistake.html.

– 2019. "B.C. Pipeline Unable to Navigate Maze of Indigenous Politics." *Toronto Star*, 10 January. https://www.thestar.com/opinion/star-columnists/2019/01/10/bc-pipeline-unable-to-navigate-maze-of-indigenous-politics.html.

Walpole, Ben. 2017. *ASCE's New Infrastructure Report Card: Another D+, but Solutions Available*. https://source.asce.org/asces-new-infrastructure-report-card-another-d-but-solutions-available.

Warf, Barney, ed. 2017. *Handbook on Geographies of Technology*. Cheltenham, UK: Edward Elgar.

Warrack, Allan. 1982. *The Alberta Heritage Savings Trust Fund: An Historical Evaluation*. Ottawa: Economic Council of Canada.

Warren, May. 2019. "A Third of Toronto's Young Adults Live with Their Parents. Here's How Bloor West Compares to the Bridle Path, and More." *Toronto Star*, 11 January. https://www.thestar.com/news/gta/2019/01/11/living-with-your-parents-in-toronto-youre-lucky-not-lazy-experts-say.html.

Waterson, Jim. 2018. "UK Democracy Under Threat and Need for Reform Is Urgent, Says Regulator." *The Guardian*, 26 June. https://www. theguardian.com/politics/2018/jun/26/uk-democracy-under-threat-and-reform-is-urgent-says-electoral-regulator.

Watson, Peter. 2017. *Safety Culture Summit, NEB Chair and CEO Peter Watson Remarks*. Halifax, 12 October. https://www.cer-rec.gc.ca/en/about/publications-reports/performance-summary/2017-18/prfrmncsmmr2017-eng.pdf.

Wells, Jennifer. 2018. "Hydro One's Takeover of U.S. Utility Sparks Customer Backlash: 'This Is an Incredibly Bad Idea.'" *Toronto Star*, 9 May. https://www.thestar.com/business/opinion/2018/05/09/hydro-ones-takeover-of-us-utility-sparks-customer-backlash-this-is-an-incredibly-bad-idea.html.

Wells, P. 2016. "Risks Abound as Trudeau Makes Big Pitch to Giant Investors." *Toronto Star*, 13 November. https://www.thestar.com/news/canada/2016/11/13/trudeau-aims-to-attract-billions-in-private-sector-capital-for-infrastructure-projects.html.

– 2020. "Farewell, Then, Canada Infrastructure Bank." *Maclean's*, 1 October. https://www.macleans.ca/politics/ottawa/farewell-then-canada-infrastructure-bank.

Welsh, Moira. 2018. "The Fix." *The Star*, 20 June. https://projects.thestar.com/dementia-program.

Westerman, Pauline. 2018. *Outsourcing the Law: A Philosophical Perspective on Regulation*. Cheltenham, UK: Edward Elgar Publishing.

Western Canada Roadbuilders & Heavy Construction Association. 2016. *A Look at Past, Present and Future: 2016 Priorities and Beyond*. http://wcrhca.com/PDFs/AGM_Reports/2015/committed-advocate-for-economic-and-industry-growth-as-adotped-march-2016.pdf.

Wheeler, Scott. 2017. "Embark Technology's Young Team Making Inroads in Autonomous Trucking." *Globe and Mail*, 3 May. https://www.theglobeandmail.com/globe-drive/news/industry-news/embarks-young-team-making-inroads-in-autonomous-trucking/article34871995.

Wherry, Aaron. "Facebook's Fake News Squad Comes to Canada – Just in Time for 2019." *CBC News*, 27 June. http://www.cbc.ca/news/politics/facebook-fact-check-canada-1.4722349.

White, Adam J. 2012. "Infrastructure Policy: Lessons From American History." *The New Atlantis* (Spring): 3–31. https://www.thenewatlantis.com/publications/infrastructure-policy-lessons-from-american-history.

White, Richard. 2018. "Why a Whopping 6,500 Condo Units Are Being Built in Calgary Right Now." *CBC News*, 13 May. https://www.cbc.ca/

news/canada/calgary/calgary-condo-boom-downtown-to-suburbs-1.4655325.

Whiteman, Gail, Chris Hope, and Peter Wadhams. 2013. "Climate Science: Vast Costs of Arctic Change." *Nature* 499: 401–3.

Whiteside, Heather. 2015a. "How Ottawa Shifts Spending: Private Financing and the Municipal Infrastructure Gap." In *How Ottawa Spends 2015–2016: The Liberal Rise and the Tory Demise*, edited by Christopher Stoney and G. Bruce Doern, 90–131. Ottawa: School of Public Policy and Administration, Carleton University.

– 2015b. *Purchase for Profit: Public-Private Partnerships and Canada's Public Health Care System*. Toronto: University of Toronto Press.

– 2016. "The Canada Infrastructure Bank: Theft by Deception." *Canadian Dimension*, 4 December. https://canadiandimension.com/articles/view/the-canada-infrastructure-bank-theft-by-deception.

Whittington, L. 2009. "Dion's Carbon Tax Plan Was a Vote Loser, Ignatieff Says." *Toronto Star*, 28 February. http://www.thestar.com/news/canada/2009/02/28/dions_carbon_tax_plan_was_a_vote_loser_ignatieff_says.print.html.

Windsor-Detroit Bridge Authority. 2016. "About the WDBA." https://www.wdbridge.com/en.

Winnipeg. 2011. *Winnipeg Transportation Master Plan*. Executive Summary. City of Winnipeg. https://winnipeg.ca/publicworks/transportation/pdf/transportationMasterPlan/2011-11-01-TTR WinnipegTMP-Final-Report.pdf.

Winnipeg Transit. 2017. "About Rapid Transit." http://winnipegtransit.com/en/major-projects/rapid-transit.

Winston, Clifford. 2010. *Last Exit: Privatization and Deregulation of the US Tranportation System*. Washington, DC: Brookings Institution.

Wise, Lindsay. 2017. "Trump's Infrastructure Plan Caught in a White House Turf War." 29 March. https://www.mcclatchydc.com/news/politics-government/white-house/article141333648.html.

Wolfe, David, ed. 2003. *Clusters Old and New: The Transition to a Knowledge Economy in Canada's Regions*. Kingston, ON: School of Policy Studies, Queen's University.

– 2009. "Universities and Knowledge Transfer: Powering Local Economic and Cluster Development." In *Research and Innovation Policy: Changing Federal Government-University Relations*, edited by G. Bruce Doern and Christopher Stoney, 265–87. Toronto: University of Toronto Press.

Wolfe, Jeanne. 2003. "A National Urban Policy for Canada? Prospects and Challenges." *Canadian Journal of Urban Research* 12, no. 1 (Summer): 1–21.

Wolfe, Michelle, Bryan D. Jones, and Frank R. Baumgartner. 2013. "A Failure to Communicate: Agenda Setting in Media and Policy." *Political Communication* 30, no. 2: 175–92.

Wonders, William C., ed. 2003. *Canada's Changing North*, rev. ed. Montreal, QC, and Kingston, ON: McGill-Queen's University Press.

World Bank. 2016a. *Annual Report 2016*. World Bank. https://openknowledge.worldbank.org/handle/10986/24985.

– 2016b. *The World Bank in Canada*. World Bank. https://www.worldbank.org/en/country/canada/overview.

– 2019. *Ending Poverty, Investing in Opportunity. Annual Report 2019*. https://openknowledge.worldbank.org/handle/10986/32333.

World Bank Group. 2011. *Transformation Through Infrastructure*. Infrastructure Strategy Update FY 2012–2015. World Bank Group. https://openknowledge.worldbank.org/handle/10986/26768.

– 2017. *Main Financing Mechanisms for Infrastructure Projects*. World Bank. https://ppp.worldbank.org/public-private-partnership/financing/mechanisms.

World Economic Forum. 2015. *Strategic Infrastructure and Mitigation of Political and Regulatory Risk in Infrastructure Projects*. Geneva: World Economic Forum.

– 2020a. *Accelerating Digital Inclusion in the New Normal*. Playbook. July.

– 2020b. *How COVID-19 Will Change the Way We Design Our Homes*. Chris Martin. 17 August. https://www.weforum.org/agenda/2020/08/how-covid-19-will-change-what-we-call-home-ddfe95b686.

Wrobel, Leo A., and Sharon M. Wrobel. 2009. *Disaster Recovery Planning for Communications and Critical Infrastructure*. Boston, MA: Artech House.

Wudrick, A. 2017. "Canadian Taxpayers Federation news release." 22 March. https://www.taxpayer.com/news-room-archive/taxpayers-federation--morneau-s--feelings--budget-kicks-the-deficit-can-down-the-road?id=1041.

Wyatt, Edward. 2014a. "F.C.C. Backs Opening Net Neutrality Rules for Debate." *New York Times*, 15 May. https://www.nytimes.com/2014/05/16/technology/fcc-road-map-to-net-neutrality.html.

– 2014b. "F.C.C., in a Shift, Backs Fast Lanes for Web Traffic." *New York Times*, 23 April. https://www.nytimes.com/2014/04/24/technology/fcc-new-net-neutrality-rules.html.

Yglesias, Matthew. 2017. "Trump's $1 Trillion Infrastructure Plan Is Vaporware That's Never Going to Happen." *Vox*, 6 April. https://www.vox.com/policy-and-politics/2017/4/6/15205032/trump-infrastructure-plan.

Young, B. 2003. "Provincial Involvement in Municipal-Federal Relations."
    Paper delivered at the Conference on Municipal-Federal-Provincial
    Relations, Queen's University, Kingston, 9–10 May.

Yuan, X.X., and J. Zhang. 2016. *Understanding the Effect of Public-
    Private Partnerships on Innovation in Canadian Infrastructure Projects.*
    Toronto: Ryerson Institute for Infrastructure Innovation, Ryerson
    University. https://www.pppcouncil.ca/web/P3_Knowledge_Centre/
    Research/Understanding_the_Effect_of_Public-Private_Partnerships_
    on_Innovation_in_Canadian_Infrastructure_Pro.aspx.

Yukon, Northwest Territories, and Nunavut. 2008. *Northern Connections:
    A Multi-Modal Transportation Blueprint for the North.* February.
    Yukon, Northwest Territories, and Nunavut. http://gov.nu.ca/sites/
    default/files/files/Northern_connections.pdf.

Zochodne, Geoff, and Sean Craig. 2019. "Early Facebook Backer Urges
    Toronto to Abandon Sidewalk Labs Project, Saying Google Will
    Exploit the Data." *Ottawa Citizen*, 10 June. https://ottawacitizen.com/
    technology/early-facebook-backer-urges-toronto-to-abandon-smart-city-
    project-with-googles-sidewalk-labs/wcm/odbcd256-5291-471c-af2f-
    b9197944d7ee.

Zuboff, Shosana. 2015. "Big Other: Surveillance Capitalism and the
    Prospects of an Information Civilization." *Journal of Information
    Technology* 30: 75–89.

Index